Situational Method Engineering

Brian Henderson-Sellers • Jolita Ralyté •
Pär J. Ågerfalk • Matti Rossi

Situational Method Engineering

Springer

Brian Henderson-Sellers
School of Software
University of Technology, Sydney
Broadway
New South Wales
Australia

Jolita Ralyté
CUI, Battelle - bâtiment A
University of Geneva
Carouge
Switzerland

Pär J. Ågerfalk
Dept. of Informatics and Media
Uppsala University
Uppsala
Sweden

Matti Rossi
Aalto University
Aalto
Finland

ISBN 978-3-662-52263-9 ISBN 978-3-642-41467-1 (eBook)
DOI 10.1007/978-3-642-41467-1
Springer Heidelberg New York Dordrecht London

Printed on acid-free paper

Springer is part of Springer Science+Business Media (www.springer.com)

Foreword

Despite the vast amount of research undertaken over the years to find a single 'one-size-fits-all' methodological approach to software development projects, it is increasingly accepted that there will never be such a 'holy grail'.

Therefore, several research groups worldwide have adopted an alternative approach to software development. Under the generic banner of 'situational method engineering' or SME, software is developed specifically to fit the requirements of a single industry or a specific project.

SME encompasses all aspects of creating, using and adapting a software development method based on local requirements. Put simply, SME involves engineering a software development method for a particular situation—as opposed to buying an 'off-the-shelf' methodology and using it unchanged.

While each research group has adopted a different approach to SME, their leaders have come together in this book to provide a coherent synthesis.

The authors clearly and compellingly outline the components needed for an industry to put the SME approach to software development into practice. They assess the advantages and disadvantages of using method fragments, chunks or components, and discuss the social context in which method engineering best operates.

The first part of the book concludes with a more formal analysis of SME, using metamodelling techniques, which introduces all the necessary elements.

The second part of the book makes suggestions about the more practical aspects of SME and concludes with several case studies, emphasising how research can become best practice.

This is the first book to provide its readers all the tools they need to fully understand SME. It highlights future research and includes an extensive literature list, which provides an excellent starting point for potential research students undertaking their doctoral or postdoctoral work.

Practitioners will also find value, especially in the second part of the book.

The authors, Brian Henderson-Sellers, Jolity Ralyté, Pär J. Ågerfalk and Matti Rossi, are all well-respected and esteemed researchers in their chosen fields. They have not only undertaken the formal and theoretical research but put their ideas into practice within their local industries.

I commend Henderson-Sellers, Ralyté, Ågerfalk and Rossi on the hugely beneficial research they have undertaken in the area of SME. I am confident that this text will prove an invaluable resource for those interested in improving the standard of software development and the resulting software applications.

Mary O'Kane
NSW Chief Scientist & Engineer

Foreword

Turning research into practical, industry applicable knowledge, especially in information technology, is always a challenge. This book bridges the gap between research and industry applicability in the area of Situational Method Engineering (SME).

SME originated in the mid-1990s; although much of the early work did not label itself as such. In the early days of my own software development company, Object Consulting, we used these early SME ideas to create a toolset, Process Mentor, that has been extensively used in local industry. There are many challenges with introducing such ideas into organisations including competing against the 'not invented here' syndrome, dealing with entrenched 'standards teams' who often slavishly drove off-the-shelf packages or dealing with simple organisational apathy around process. Despite great advances in software development, software process remains a relatively immature area in most organisations.

With an SME approach as described in this book (and encapsulated in products like Process Mentor) the aim is to provide a robust yet flexible mechanism for constructing software development methods, resulting in high quality methods for each situation.

Industry best practice relies on proven techniques and approaches, some of which are formal and some more informal in the form of heuristics. This book provides an excellent and comprehensive review of the research in the SME field in Part 1, and then in Part 2 provides a detailed framework for reviewing and developing an SME approach together with a range of heuristics to construct development methods. As such the book is useful for both researchers as a summary of the latest thinking in the field, as well as the practitioner looking to understand the breadth and depth of material available to them when looking at developing an SME approach. This book deftly balances the advantages of such an approach in terms of practical application, underpinned by the solid theory from worldwide research.

It is an excellent and comprehensive SME book with no rival—and I heartily recommend it for both researchers and practitioners.

Julian Edwards
Chief Operating Officer, Object Consulting

Preface

Most people we know don't read a book's Preface. So, we'll keep it brief.

Why read this book? Why did we write it? The answer to both these questions is straightforward. We, the four authors of this book, have all, independently and more recently collaboratively, been working with Situational Method Engineering for almost two decades. Yet, all our published efforts are in conferences and journals so that when someone wants to join our several SME teams, there is no single source to which we can refer them in order that they can 'get up to speed'.

Now there is. This is the first book-length summary of everything we know about situational method engineering (SME) at the present time.

In this book, we present an overview and introduction to the topic of SME. SME provides a solution to the problem of the selection, creation or modification of existing methodological information in order to provide the 'most appropriate' methodology for an organisation and/or its projects. By a (software development) methodology, we mean all the bits and pieces that are needed for an organisation to undertake a software development. That means understanding how the process works; what the input and output work products are; who are the people involved; what languages are used to describe requirements, design, code, etc.; and when all this happens in terms of scheduling and other project management issues. It also includes evaluation of quality, productivity and other measures of success (or failure). The problem is that previously available methodologies for software—like those published in the early 1990s in the early days of object technology—claim to be appropriate for every conceivable project. This is clearly an ambit claim that is not supported in practice. Rather, SME acknowledges that all (or most) projects are individualistic such that the most efficacious methodology for that particular project needs individual tuning. This is where method construction (using SME) followed by method tailoring comes into its own.

We have structured the book into three parts. Part I deals with all the basic concepts, terminology and overall ideas underpinning SME. In Part II, we explain how you do SME in practice; how to find method parts and put them together and how to evaluate the resulting method. Part III is much shorter and summarises some of the more recent (and futuristic) ideas being discussed in the SME community.

SME's origins, as we shall explain in detail in Chap. 1, resulted from the frustration of finding (or developing) a single method for all situations. The alternative to the one-size-fits-all methodology of the 1980s and 1990s was our recognition that a constructed method, suitably tailored to a specific context or situation that exists within a specific industry sector and/or project could be more efficacious. Early work originated in the Netherlands and then in Finland, Sweden, France, Switzerland and Australia. The authors of this book reflect these trail-blazing centres of SME.

There are several kinds of method parts used in SME. These have arisen from our different projects and are called method fragments, method chunks and method components; there are also 'larger' parts such as patterns that we discuss in Chap. 2. Following this detailed comparison of these method parts, we then introduce the overall social context, in particular the notion of method rationale which, in turn, leads to method-user-centred method engineering (Chap. 3).

These basic ideas, technical and sociological, are then combined in the subsequent chapters. Chapter 4 introduces some of the underlying theory and formal representations for SME, in particular metamodels for method construction and the current ISO standard relevant (ISO/IEC 24744). This chapter also introduces some basic ideas from ontology engineering relevant to our discourse.

In Chaps. 5–9 we examine SME in practice. Chapters 5 and 6 analyse *how* a method can be constructed from method parts—how to identify and locate the parts, approaches for method construction and the importance of reuse. Method configuration and method tailoring are the focus of Chap. 7, including a discussion on supporting tools for construction and customisation.

In Chap. 8, we focus on the more difficult issue of quality assessment—the quality of the method parts, the method base and the constructed method (both on paper and in action). In Chap. 9, we present examples in several domains/contexts of SME-constructed methods.

Chapters 10 and 11 form Part III and address more futuristic ideas within SME. In particular, we look at how recent ideas in services can be usefully addressed from an SME perspective and how large metamodels can themselves be tailored to create project-specific metamodels.

We have thus gathered together these originally disparate strands of SME into a coherent whole so that the 'SME novice' has a single point of entry into this fascinating and highly industry-relevant research topic. Although most SME published work has been in the research area, industry today is moving towards its adoption—as seen in the case studies in Chap. 9—sometimes under a name other than method engineering.

We need to include in this Preface some appreciation of copyright holders and other support. In particular, we note that a number of paragraphs in this book have been included from our previously published research papers.

In particular, we draw heavily on a publication by the first two authors (BH-S and JR) in the *Journal of Universal Computer Science*, 16(3), 424–478 ('Situational Method Engineering: state-of-the-art review').

We also acknowledge the original publications for some text as follows:

Chapter 2 contains some text taken from Henderson-Sellers, B., Gonzalez-Perez, C. and Ralyté, J., 2008, Comparison of method chunks and method fragments for situational method engineering, *Proceedings 19th Australian Software Engineering Conference. ASWEC2008*, IEEE Computer Society, Los Alamitos, CA, USA,

479–488. It also contains some material from Karlsson F and Ågerfalk P J (2009) Towards Structured Flexibility in Information Systems Development: Devising a Method for Method Configuration, *Journal of Database Management*, 20(3), pp. 51–75.

Part of Chap. 3 is based on previous publications by Ågerfalk and Fitzgerald: Ågerfalk P J (2006) Towards Better Understanding of Agile Values in Global Software Development. Proceedings of Eleventh International Workshop on Exploring Modeling Methods in Systems Analysis and Design (EMMSAD'06), Luxembourg, 5–6 June 2006; Ågerfalk P J and Fitzgerald B (2006) Exploring the Concept of Method Rationale: A Conceptual Tool for Method Tailoring, In Advanced Topics in Database Research, Vol. 5, pp. 63–78, (Ed, Siau K) Hershey, PA: Idea Group.

Chapter 4 contains some text taken from Henderson-Sellers, B., 2007, On the challenges of correctly using metamodels in method engineering, keynote paper in *New Trends in Software Methodologies, Tools and Techniques. Proceedings of the sixth SoMeT_07* (eds. H. Fujita and D. Pisanelli), IOS Press, Frontiers in Artificial Intelligence and Applications, vol. 161, 3–35. Some ideas and parts of text of Sect. 7.3.1 are from Kelly, S., Rossi, M., & Tolvanen, J.-P, (2005), What is Needed in a MetaCASE Environment? Journal of Enterprise Modelling and Information Systems Architectures, 1(1), pp. 1–11.

Chapter 6 contains some text taken from Gonzalez-Perez, C., Giorgini, P. and Henderson-Sellers, B., 2009, Method construction by goal analysis, in *Information Systems Development. Challenges in Practice, Theory, and Education* (eds. C. Barry, K. Conboy, M. Lang, G. Wojtkowski and W. Wojtkowski), Springer-Verlag, New York, USA, 79–92. It also contains some material from Karlsson F and Ågerfalk P J (2009) Towards Structured Flexibility in Information Systems Development: Devising a Method for Method Configuration, *Journal of Database Management*, 20(3), pp. 51–75.

Chapter 7 uses a paragraph from Hug, C., Front, A., Rieu, D. and Henderson-Sellers, B., 2009, A method to build information systems engineering process metamodels, *J. Systems Software*, 82(10), 1730–1742.

It also contains ideas and examples originally published by Karlsson and Ågerfalk, MC Sandbox: Devising a Tool for Method-User-Centred Method Configuration, *Information and Software Technology*, 54(5), pp. 501–516.

Chapter 8 uses text originally published in Henderson-Sellers, B., 2011a, Random thoughts on multi-level conceptual modelling, chapter in *The Evolution of Conceptual Modeling* (eds. L. Delcambre and R. Kaschek), LNCS 6520, Springer-Verlag, Berlin, 93–116.

and from two papers presented at the ME 2011 conference in Paris:

Henderson-Sellers, B. and Gonzalez-Perez, C., 2011, Towards the use of granularity theory for determining the size of atomic method fragments for use in situational method engineering, *Engineering Methods in the Service-Oriented Context. 4th IFIP WG8.1 Working Conference on Method Engineering, ME 2011, Paris France, April 2011, Proceedings*, (eds. J. Ralyté, I. Mirbel and R. Deneckère), Springer, Heidelberg, 49–63.

McBride, T. and Henderson-Sellers, B., 2011, A method assessment framework, *Engineering Methods in the Service-Oriented Context. 4th IFIP WG8.1 Working Conference on Method Engineering, ME 2011, Paris France, April 2011, Proceedings*, (eds. J. Ralyté, I. Mirbel and R. Deneckère), Springer, Heidelberg, 64–76.

Section 9.1 utilises the examples from Henderson-Sellers, B., Serour, M., McBride, T., Gonzalez-Perez, C. and Dagher, L. 2004b. Process construction and customization. *Journal of Universal Computer Science*. 10(4), 326–358.

Section 9.4 is based on Rossi, M. and Tuunanen, T., 2010, A method and tool for rapid consumer application development, *International Journal of Organisational Design and Engineering*, 1(1/2), 109–125.

Having said our thanks to publishers of our original research, we also wish to make some personal thanks—to those of our colleagues and students who read our earlier drafts of these chapters, in particular Marko Bajec, Rebecca Deneckère, Sergio Espana, Mahdi Fahmideh Gholami, Akhtar Ali Jalbani, Fredrik Karlsson, Elena Kornyshova, Graham Low, Ben Rogers, Colette Rolland, Motoshi Saeki, Juha-Pekka Tolvanen and Kai Wistrand.

Finally, BH-S acknowledges the continuing support of Ann; JR Colette, Isabelle, Michel; PJA Kajsa, Amanda, Algot, MR Tuuli, Saana, Sippo and Samu.

Glossary of Acronyms

AD	Activity Diagram
ATL	ATLAS Transformation Language
BPM	Business Process Modelling
BPMN	Business Process Modeling Notation
BWW	Bunge-Wand-Weber
B2C	Business to Consumer
CAME	Computer-Aided Method Engineering
CASE	Computer-Aided Software Engineering
CMM	Capability Maturity Model
CMMI	Capability Maturity Model Integration
COBIT	Control Objectives for Information and Related Technology
COMMA	Common Object Methodology Metamodel Architecture
COTS	Commercial Off-The-Shelf
CRC	Class Responsibility Collaborator (cards)
DSDM	Dynamic Systems Development Method
ER	Entity Relationship
ERP	Enterprise Resource Planning
FDT	Formal Description Technique
FIPA	Federation for Intelligent Physical Agents
GOPPRR	Graph-Object-Ports-Property-Relationship-Role
GOPRR	Graph-Object-Property-Relationship-Role
GQM	Goal Question Metric
GUI	Graphical User Interface
IAG	Intention Achievement Guideline
IBIS	Issue-Based Information Systems
IEC	International Electrotechnical Commission
IEEE	Institute of Electrical and Electronics Engineers
IFIP	The International Federation for Information Processing
ISD	Information Systems Development
ISDM	Information Systems Development Method
ISE	Information Systems Engineering
ISG	Intention Selection Guideline
ISO	International Organization for Standardization

IT	Information Technology
JTC1	Joint Technical Committee 1 (between ISO and IEC)
LOC	Lines of Code
MaaS	Method as a Service
MC	Method Configuration
MDA	Model-Driven Architecture
MDD	Model-Driven Development
MDE	Method-Driven Engineering
ME	Method Engineering
MEL	Method Engineering Language
MIS	Management Information Systems
MMC	Method for Method Configuration
MOA	Method-Oriented Architecture
MOBMAS	Methodology for Ontology-Based Multi-agent Systems
MOF	Meta-Object Facility
MOSES	Methodology for Object-oriented Software Engineering of Systems
NIAM	Nijssen's Information Analysis Methodology (later renamed Natural language Information Analysis Method)
OLMS	Object Library Management System
OMG	Object Management Group
OMT	Object Modeling Technique
OO	Object-Oriented or Object Orientation
OOSE	Object-Oriented Software Engineering
OOSPICE	Object-oriented Software Process Improvement and Capability dEtermination
OPEN	Object-oriented Process, Environment and Notation
OPF	OPEN Process Framework
OPM3	Organisational Project Management Maturity Model
OPRR	Object-Property-Relationship-Role
PDD	Process-Data Diagram (later renamed Process Deliverable Diagram)
PMUC	Process Metamodel Under Construction
REMAP	REpresentation and MAintenance of Process knowledge
RUP	Rational Unified Process
SC7	Subcommittee 7 (a committee of ISO/JTC1 dealing with software engineering standards)
SEI	Software Engineering Institute (at Carnegie Mellon University)
SEM	Systems Engineering Method
SEMDM	Software Engineering Metamodel for Development Methodologies
SEP	Software Engineering Process
SIMM	Service Integration Maturity Model
SME	Situational Method Engineering
SMME	Situational Metamodel Engineering
SMSDM	Standard Metamodel for Software Development Methodologies
SOA	Service-Oriented Architecture
SOMA	Semantic Object Modeling Approach

SPC	Software Process Control
SPEM	(version 1) Software Process Engineering Metamodel (version 2) Software & Systems Process Engineering Metamodel
SPI	Software Process Improvement
SPICE	Software Process Improvement and Capability dEtermination
SPLE	Software Product Line Engineering
SPM	Software Product Management
SSG	Strategy Selection Guideline
SUS	System Under Study
TAME	Tailoring A Measurement Environment
UML	Unified Modeling Language
VIBA	Versatile Information and Business Analysis
XP	eXtreme Programming

Contents

Part I

SME Basics

Introduction

1

Summary of What We Will Learn in Chapter 1

- Why a one-size-fits-all methodology is inappropriate for contemporary software development
- The basic components of situational method engineering (SME)
- Why there is ambiguity in terms such as method, methodology and process
- An appreciation of technical ideas regarding models, metamodels and ontologies
- Two possible multilayer architectures useful for SME

1.1 Introduction

What is situational method engineering (SME) and why is it of current interest?

In a nutshell, SME is an alternative approach to software development that includes all aspects of creating, using and adapting a software development method based on local conditions—as opposed to buying (or obtaining as freeware) a methodology[1] 'off-the-shelf' and using it unchanged; in other words, engineering a method for a particular situation. Here, engineering means either creating such a method ab initio and/or modifying an existing method, i.e., the starting point could be either a set of method parts (see Chap. 2) from which a method is constructed (Chap. 6) or it could be an existing base method. That existing method could either be an 'off-the-shelf' method obtained from some supplier (vendor or book-writing methodologist) or could be one constructed from the aforementioned method parts.

[1] We will use method and methodology as synonyms—see Sect. 1.3 for our rationale for this decision.

B. Henderson-Sellers et al., *Situational Method Engineering*,
DOI 10.1007/978-3-642-41467-1_1, © Springer-Verlag Berlin Heidelberg 2014

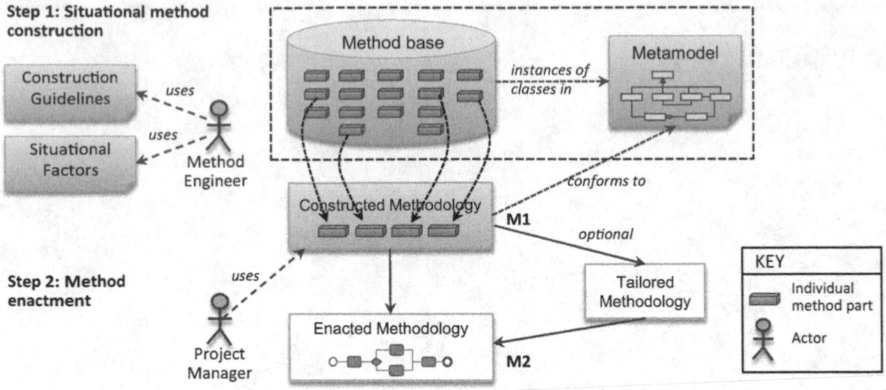

Fig. 1.1 Situational method engineering allows the method engineer to select method parts from the method base (which are all conformant to an element in the metamodel) and construct an organisationally specific methodology using provided construction guidelines and situational factors. This methodology may be tailored prior to enactment for a particular project under the auspices of the project manager (modified from Henderson-Sellers and Ralyte 2010)

If we make modifications to that method, then we are said to be 'tailoring' the method—for a specific situation. Hence method tailoring is also within the remit of SME (Chap. 7). In addition, SME focusses on formalising the use of methods for systems development.

The overall SME context is shown in Fig. 1.1. Method parts are stored in the method base. These are essentially instances of classes in a standardised metamodel. Using predetermined heuristic help in the form of construction guidelines, together with his/her knowledge of the situational factors, the method engineer identifies appropriate method parts in the method base in order to create the in-house or base methodology (labelled M1 in Fig. 1.1). This step (labelled Step 1 and often called method construction) ideally involves local members of the organisation as well as the method engineer (who may or may not be a member of the organisation—often an external consultant). The second step (labelled Step 2) is the customisation of that methodology to the constraints of a specific endeavour, typically a project (methodology M2 in Fig. 1.1). This step is generally referred to as method enactment. Finally, the enacted methodology, created for the organisational endeavour (Fig. 1.1) may need further tailoring by taking into account the project's specific situational context (see more detailed discussion on situational factors later in the book: Chap. 7). This is called 'on-the-fly' method construction by Järvi et al. (2007).

SME arose because of the realisation that one-size-fits-all methodologies can never be totally successful because the software development context and culture in each organisation is different—as are the projects being developed.

In this book, we present an overview and introduction to the topic of SME. We have already seen that SME provides a solution to the problem of the selection, creation or modification of existing methodological information in order to provide the 'most appropriate' methodology for an organisation and/or its projects.

Authors have repeatedly noted that contemporary methodologies are not well suited to practice (e.g., Lyytinen 1987; Glass 2003), while Avison (1996) notes a backlash against formal software development methodologies. Others see process adoption as a 'waste of time' (Baddoo and Hall 2003), although, from a practical viewpoint, Cockburn (2000) argues that it is both appropriate and necessary for an organisation to have available to it a suite of methodologies, rather than insisting on a single methodology for all their projects. Avison and Fitzgerald (2003) suggest that such disillusionment with the application of methodologies, which typically have historically failed to address important social, political and organisational factors (see also Mohan and Ahlemann 2011a), might lead to a 'post-methodology' era in which there are no controls, standards or training. Siau and Rossi (2007) argue that many methodologies lack theoretical underpinnings or empirical evidence of their value. They recommend a three classification-based comparative evaluation. On the other hand, Mirbel (2007) argues that much of the knowledge used by developers is tacit knowledge; indeed, this may be one reason for the poor use of methods in general (as noted by Ralyté 2001). She recommends turning this into explicit or organisational knowledge.

The need for SME can be underlined in terms of flexibility running from

1. Use of a rigid methodology
2. Selection from rigid methodologies
3. Selection of paths within a methodology
4. Selection and tuning of a method outline
5. Modular method construction (Odell 1996, based on Harmsen et al. 1994).

Since the one-size-fits-all methodology is now generally regarded as unattainable (e.g., Brooks 1987; Avison and Wood-Harper 1991; Welke and Kumar 1991; Kumar and Welke 1992; van Slooten and Brinkkemper 1993; Vessey and Glass 1994; van Slooten and Hodes 1996; Fayad et al. 1996; Ter Hofstede and Verhoef 1997; Glass 2000, 2004; Fitzgerald et al. 2003; Wistrand and Karlsson 2004; Börner 2011) and untenable, alternatives have to be sought, particularly ones that take into account the human and organisational elements (Constantine and Lockwood 1994). SME, including method construction and method tailoring (the latter sometimes referred to as method customisation), is the current most optimistic route and forms the topic of this book.

SME is sometimes called, simply, method engineering or ME. Strictly, SME is a subset of ME although in some books and journal papers you will see the acronym ME used to mean *situational* ME. The broader term, method engineering, is defined as the engineering discipline to design, construct and adapt methods, techniques and tools for systems development, a definition analogous to the IEEE[2] definition of software engineering (Brinkkemper 2006). As noted above, a major subtype of ME is SME, which encompasses all aspects of creating a development method for a specific situation (and excludes topics such as comparing methods and method knowledge infrastructures).

[2] Institute of Electrical and Electronics Engineers.

Method Engineering (ME) was introduced by Bergstra et al. (1985) and then, more recently, by Kumar and Welke (1992) who named it methodology engineering; but van Slooten and Brinkkemper (1993) and Brinkkemper (1996) strongly recommend changing this to method engineering, a term that has been generally accepted since Brinkkemper's (1996) definition of method engineering, referred to earlier: "Method engineering is the engineering discipline to design, construct and adapt methods, techniques and tools for the development of information systems". In some research papers, it is called *situated* method engineering (Aydin and Harmsen 2002). Interestingly, Glass (2000) equates the SME approach to an ad hoc approach in that the correct meaning of ad hoc is 'suited to purpose' or 'tailored to the problem at hand'. (This is different to the use of ad hoc in some of the strategies described later, especially those in Chap. 6.)

In this chapter, we give first a very brief overview of SME fundamentals to set the scene to the more detailed chapters that follow. In Chap. 2 we discuss the various kinds of method parts (fragments, chunks, components, etc.). In Chap. 3, we analyse the human side of SME in terms of decision-making and method rationale: whether to include specific method parts in the to-be-constructed method. We then introduce metamodels, process models and other formalisms for SME (Chap. 4). Chapter 5 focusses on the method part scale and reviews the approaches to chunk/fragment identification and construction followed, in Chap. 6, by approaches to method construction from these method parts. Method tailoring is the topic of Chap. 7 as being applicable to either preformed methods or recently constructed methods (i.e., created using the approaches in Chap. 6); including a discussion on tools support. Chapter 8 discusses the all-important question of method quality—how do we know the method we have engineered is the 'best' for that particular situation. In Chap. 9, we give three case studies to illustrate the practicalities of the SME approach. Chapter 10 describes two very new contributions to SME: SMME and SOA, before concluding briefly (Chap. 11) with some overall directions for future research. Throughout the book, we focus on the construction, tailoring and assessment aspects of SME.

1.2 A Brief Overview of SME Fundamentals

In this section, we summarise each of the elements of SME as depicted in Fig. 1.1.

1.2.1 Method Parts

The main focus of SME is the method part, i.e., a small portion of a methodology, either a methodology that already exists or a methodology-to-be. Existing method parts are stored in the method base; but the question is 'What is their origin?' Several sources are used. One main source is existing methodologies from which these parts have been 'carved' out. However, it is important that the format of these carved-out method parts is standardised; otherwise, the chance that they will interoperate is restricted. One common way of ensuring compatibility between method parts is to ensure that each part conforms to a higher level definition given in a metamodel. This also introduces a second source for method parts—creation by instantiation from a standardised metamodel element. Different kinds of method parts are discussed in detail in Chap. 2, where detailed examples are given (e.g., Fig. 2.2).

1.2.2 Metamodels

The method parts each describe, in detail, a specific task, technique, work product, producer, etc.; for example, a description of 'How to draw a use case diagram'. In any constructed methodology, there are likely to be a large number of these method parts. All technique-focussed method parts will be similar in structure—they each adhere to a template; similarly for method parts relating to producers; and to work products and so on. The suite of templates and a representation of how the different kinds of method parts are related to each other comprise the metamodel in which these templates are typically represented by classes.

1.2.3 Method bases

The repository of method parts, often called a 'method base' (Saeki et al. 1993; Harmsen et al. 1994; Brinkkemper 1996; Harmsen 1997; Rolland et al. 1998; Ralyté 1999; Ralyté and Rolland 2001a, b), typically contains atomic-sized fragments but could also contain fragment combinations such as chunks or components (as noted above and discussed in Chap. 2). What it does mean is that the method parts are, in every case, smaller (i.e., fine granular—see Sect. 2.6) than a complete methodology. An immediate advantage (over an off-the-shelf methodology) is that, since method knowledge is now fragmentised and highly structured, it is straightforward to add more fragments to the method base. These additional fragments may occur as a result of specific tailoring to a single organisation, or may need to be added as a consequence of changes in available technology—for example, the recent emergence of web services, e.g., van de Weerd et al. (2005) and support for SOA (see later discussion) are easily added to the method base.

Although in this book our prime application area is that of software development, a method base could in fact contain method parts with a very different orientation; for example, Rupprecht et al. (2000) discuss engineering processes and Buckl et al. (2011) construct a method base for enterprise architecture management, an Application domain also discussed by Winter (2011). Gericke et al. (2009) apply SME in the context of governance, risk and compliance. Other software focussed specialised areas include the application of SME to aspect-oriented computing (Henderson-Sellers et al. 2007c), to teamwork (Tran et al. 2007), to agents (Henderson-Sellers 2005, 2009; Cossentino et al. 2006b; Puviani et al. 2009;

Garciá-Magariño 2013) and to dynamic evolution (e.g., Fung 2011); while Qumer and Henderson-Sellers (2007), Tran et al. (2008a, b) and Espinosa and Garbajosa (2011) used SME for the creation of agile methods.

1.2.4 The Situational Context

Rolland and Prakash (1996) stress the need to include knowledge about the *context of use* of the method parts in a formal way within the method base. Context is here defined as the pair <*situation*, *decision*>. This means that the knowledge stored along with each part describes the situation in which it is relevant and the associated decision that can be made in such a situation. With a similar aim, the notion of *method rationale* (Chap. 3) has been proposed (Oinas-Kukkonen 1996; Ågerfalk and Åhlgren 1999; Ågerfalk and Wistrand 2003; Rossi et al. 2004; Ågerfalk and Fitzgerald 2006). Method rationale concerns the reasons, opinions and arguments behind method prescriptions and why method users (e.g., systems developers) choose to follow or adapt a method in a particular way (Ågerfalk and Fitzgerald 2006). Colloquially, we can think of method rationale as the reasons for choosing a particular design for the to-be-constructed methodology (e.g., MacLean et al. 1991). In other words, method rationale captures the process aspect of the situational engineering of the methodology.

Situational characteristics, often project-focussed, are integrated with the method parts extracted from the method base. Hoppenbrouwers et al. (2011) note that these situational factors may be at the level of the organisation, the process or the individual project. Bekkers et al.'s (2008) examination of the applicability of SME to Software Product Management identified a total of 27 such situational factors. They divided their list into five categories:

- Business units
- Customers
- Markets
- Products
- Stakeholder involvement.

These 27 situational factors (listed in Table 1.1) were used in the construction of agile service-oriented methods by Hoppenbrouwers et al. (2011).

Situational factors, mainly at the organisational level, were also investigated by Nguyen and Henderson-Sellers (2003a). They devised a template questionnaire in order to elicit information about the situational characteristics of any organisation. Bucher et al. (2007), on the other hand, argue that 'situation' has been poorly defined to date. They propose a differentiation between 'context' and 'project type'. A similar concern is echoed by Kornyshova et al. (2010) who propose a four state typology of organisational, human, Application domain and development strategy. As shown in Fig. 1.2, the context is modeled as being composed of these facets, each of which in turn is linked to a number of characteristics, as expanded in Fig. 1.3. (See also discussion of the application of these ideas to method construction in Chap. 6.)

Table 1.1 Situational factors identified by Bekkers et al. (2008)

Development philosophy	Variability of feature requests
Size of business unit team	Application age
Size of development team	Defects per year: total
Customer loyalty	Defects per year: serious
Customer satisfaction	Development platform maturity
Customer variability	New requirements rate
Number of customers	Number of products
Number of end users*	Product lifetime*
Type of customers	Product size
Hosting demands	Product tolerance
Localisation demand	Software platform*
Market growth	Company policy
Market size	Customer involvement
Release frequency	Legislation
Sector	Partner involvement
Standard dominance*	

Those starred were eliminated based on a zero score in their empirical selection study

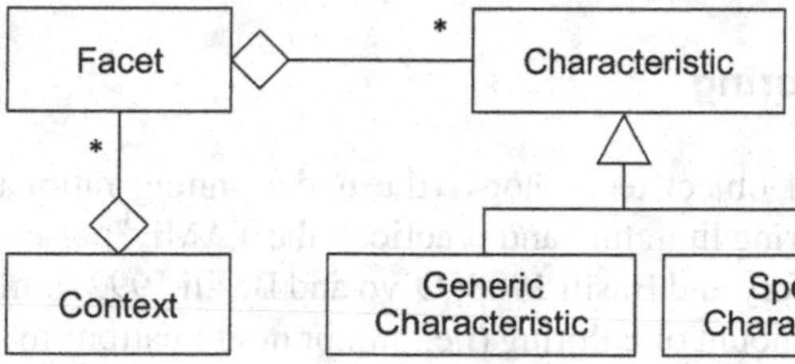

Fig. 1.2 Context model (after Kornyshova et al. 2010) ©IEEE reproduced with permission

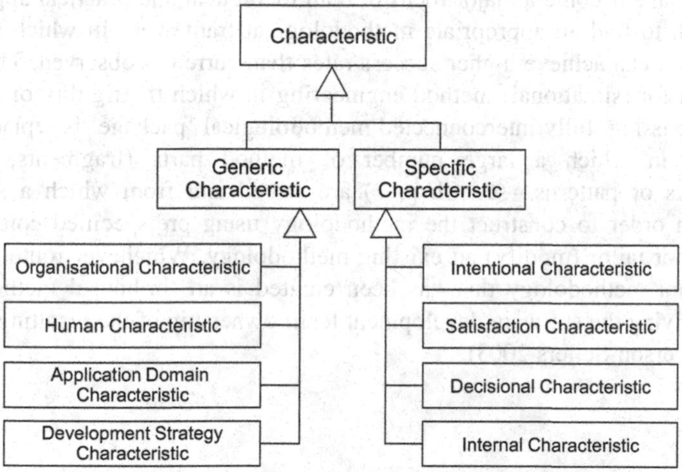

Fig. 1.3 Characteristics typology (after Kornyshova et al. 2010) ©IEEE reproduced with permission

Table 1.2 The notion of 'situation' from three kinds of empirical studies (after Aydin, table 1, 2007)

Representative study	Associated disciplines	Essential features of the very notion of situation
Theory of situation	Linguistics	Partial reality, realism, relations
Situational awareness	Cognitive psychology	Employment of cognitive mechanisms and relevant factors for human knowing
Situated actions	Sociology	Interactions, partial plans and other resources subsumed and produced

With kind permission of Springer Science + Business Media

The notion of 'situation' is also analysed, from a theoretical perspective, by Aydin (2007) (Table 1.2) and contrasted with the notion of 'context' that refers to a collection of relevant conditions and surrounding influences that make a project situation unique and comprehensible (Hasher and Zacks 1984). Together with the notions of agency and method fragment, Aydin summarises these key notions, as shown in Table 1.3.

1.2.5 Method Tailoring

Prior to the adoption of object technology (the underpinning rationale for all of today's method engineering literature and practice), the TAME[3] project (e.g., Basili and Rombach 1987; Jeffery and Basili 1988; Oivo and Basili 1992) aimed to deliver a tool to support some amount of tailoring (i.e., minor modifications to support local conditions) of a pre-existing process or methodology (terminology is discussed with more precision in Sect. 1.3). More recently, construction and customisation/tailoring issues have become a major focus of both theoretical and practical approaches to the push to find an appropriate methodological framework in which software development can achieve higher success rates than currently observed. This is the motivation for (situational) method engineering in which the rigidity of a single, all-encompassing, fully interconnected methodological 'package' is replaced by a repository in which a large number of method parts (fragments, chunks, components or patterns—see Chap. 2) are stored and from which a subset is selected in order to construct the methodology using pre-specified construction guidelines or tailor (modify) an existing methodology. Whichever route is taken, the resultant methodology that has been created is an 'in-house' methodology, i.e., thus giving the software development team ownership of the resulting method (e.g., Henderson-Sellers 2003).

[3] Tailoring A Measurement Environment.

Table 1.3 The four essential notions for SME, according to Aydin (table 2, 2007)

Four essential notions	Basic views (simplistic)	Extension
Situation	Characterised by a number of factors that influence or are being influenced by a method fragment	The limited parts of reality that the agency perceive, reason about and live in
Context	Described in terms of aspects of collectives in the process	Dynamic interplays among collectives of work practice as situated and characterised by the agency
Agency	Adheres to enactment of proposed fragment in the work practice	Interlays among fragments with a certain intention in and for the context
Method fragment	Description of a methodical artefact or any coherent part thereof	Comes into play with the agency in the context when structuring one's thinking and actions

With kind permission of Springer Science + Business Media

1.2.6 Putting the Pieces of SME Together

We can thus summarise the overall SME context, as shown in Fig. 1.1, as follows. Method parts are created and stored in a method base. When an organisation wishes to create an in-house methodology, they extract a set of appropriate method parts, their appropriateness being judged based on local knowledge of the situational or contextual factors. This constructed methodology may be used for all the projects in the organisation unaltered or may require tailoring for specific projects. The application of the methodology to an endeavour (typically a project) is method enactment, which consists of putting individualistic values to the various as-yet-unrequired attributes together with other possible tailoring. This approach is, of course, presaged upon the assumption that the goals of the method to be constructed are known, i.e., it requires knowledge of the purpose of the method-to-be, labelled, by Prakash and Goyal (2007) as "requirements engineering for SME", with an intention matching focus (Table 1.4). Finally, the tailored methodology created for the organisation is performed, i.e., in calendar time.

Situational methods may be created at the organisational level or the project level. Often an organisational level method is created from method parts in the method base (Fig. 1.4) and then further tailoring is done for each of the several projects enacted by that organisation (or often organisational department). This tailoring could be viewed as a modification to an existing method (the organisational method)—equivalent to starting with a readily available methodology—such that the 'extant methodology' is then modified with the addition or modification of method parts (from the method base) to create the new, project-specific situational methodology (Fig. 1.5).

Much of the work done in SME ends here—with an engineered and tailored methodology appropriate for a specific project. This is sometimes called 'method in

Table 1.4 The method development life cycle of Prakash and Goyal (2007)

Stage	Process	Input	Output
Requirements engineering	Intention matching	Intention of the method-to-be obtained from interviews, etc.	Intentionally similar methods to the method-to-be
Design engineering	Architecture matching	Architecture of intentionally similar methods	Architecturally similar methods
Construction engineering	Organisation matching	Organisations of architecturally similar methods	Method-to-be

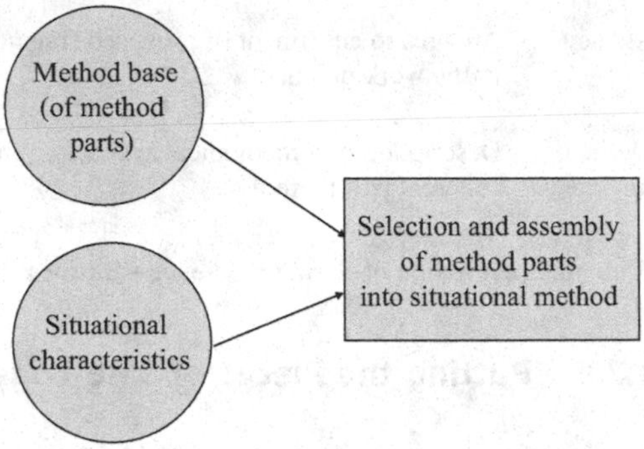

Fig. 1.4 Engineering a situational method at the organisational level

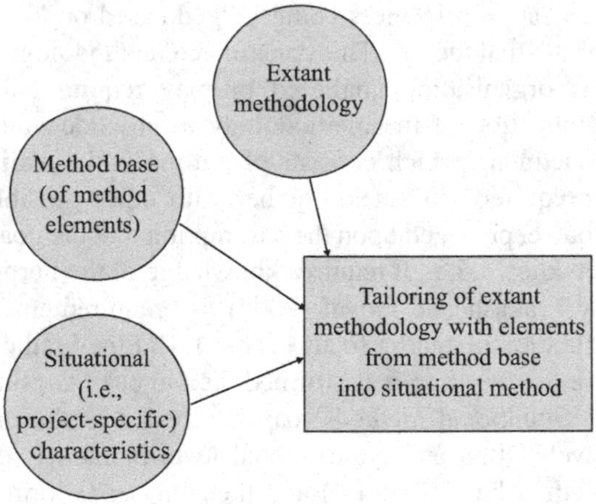

Fig. 1.5 Engineering a situational method at the project level

concept' or 'method as documented' (e.g., Ågerfalk and Fitzgerald 2006). However, there is one further and very important element of software development methodologies; that is, the use of the methodology during the duration of the project. This is often referred to as 'performance' or 'method-in-action' (Fig. 1.6) or method 'in use' (Ågerfalk and Fitzgerald 2006)—see also Chaps. 4 and 8. This is when the software developers execute the situational method on their particular

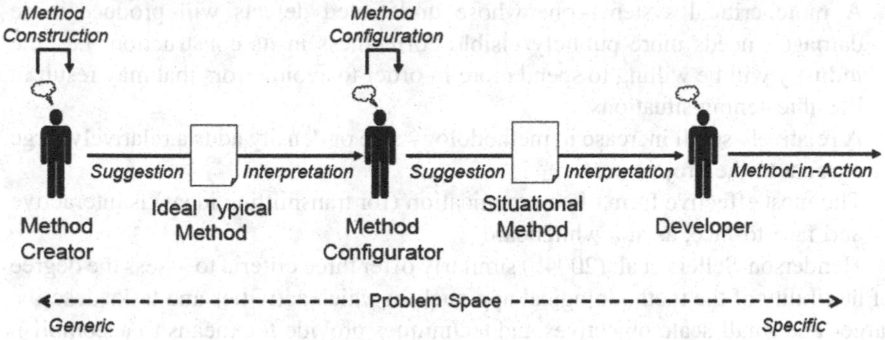

Fig. 1.6 Idealised method, situational method and method-in-action (after Ågerfalk and Fitzgerald 2006). Reprinted by permission of the publisher

project in real time. This method performance is also quite likely to identify further method parts that need modification or alteration. Thus method tailoring (in-action) may also occur during this execution process; this is also part of the remit of SME.

Bajec (2011b) adds a new phase to SME: that of Method Improvement (see also Sect. 7.2). He focusses on the creation of a base method (Method Construction) that is then tailored to an organisation (method configuration) prior to Method Use. At the Method Construction stage, he imposes rules:

- Process flow rule
- Structure rules
- Completeness rules
- Consistency rules
- Facts (Bajec et al. 2007a).

In his more recent work (Bajec 2011a), the focus has been method improvement, with a long-term aim of automatically creating methods and providing these to industry in order to create a 'silent learning cycle' (Bajec 2011b).

1.2.7 Practical Advice

Since, in reality, the method performance reflects the needs of an individual project and situation, any process model (a.k.a. situational method) should specify 'what *can* be done' as well as the more traditional 'what *must* be done' (Rolland et al. 1999). This means that alternatives must be at the root of any process model. Two ways to support such flexibility are the process map (Sect. 4.3) and the deontic matrix (Chap. 6).

Cockburn (2000) suggests a set of principles that might be appropriate for method engineering:

- A larger group (e.g., larger scope, more people, longer timescale) needs a larger methodology (e.g., more roles, more reviews, more work products).

- A more critical system—one whose undetected defects will produce more damage—needs more publicly visible correctness in its construction, i.e., the industry will be willing to spend more in order to avoid errors that may result in life-threatening situations.
- A relatively small increase in methodology size or density adds a relatively large amount to the project cost.
- The most effective form of communication (for transmitting ideas) is interactive and face-to-face, as at a whiteboard.

Henderson-Sellers et al. (2004b) similarly offer three criteria to assess the degree of flexibility of the methodological approach in which activities and tasks describe large- and small-scale objectives and techniques provide the means to accomplish these objectives:

Criterion A: Does the process allow for technique selection for each prescribed task?

Criterion B: Does the process allow for the selection of what activities, tasks and techniques are to be used in a per-project basis, depending on the specific characteristics of the project?

Criterion C: Does the process allow for the customisation of what activities and tasks are performed, and what work products are constructed, depending on the capability level of the organisation and/or development team? (This topic is the focus of the discussion in Henderson-Sellers et al. (2004b) and not discussed further here).

Henderson-Sellers et al. (2004b) further suggest that process selection criteria should include consideration of, *inter alia*:

- Alignment with the organisation's strategy since this is considered by many as a Critical Success Factor for software development (Yourdon 1999).
- Project size since large projects usually require a more sophisticated and formal process whereas small projects generally need a lightweight and fast process such as an agile process.
- Project time frame and other constraints that developers have to satisfy.
- Development type since web and online development requires a different process than that needed for business or distributed applications.
- Safety requirements since critical systems such as life support and airline navigation systems mostly emphasise safety issues.

Other process selection criteria include scalability, complexity, architecture, reliability, maintainability, support, cost and lifespan development.

Many authors are quick to extol the benefits of adopting an SME approach. Unfortunately, it is very difficult to assess these quantitatively; perhaps the best to date are data relating qualitatively to the process improvements gained following adoption of an SME approach (e.g., Serour et al. 2002, 2004) and the action-research studies of Tolvanen (1998) in incremental method engineering. In contrast to the general assumption that SME is efficacious, Ter Hofstede and Verhoef (1997) examine whether SME is even feasible. The problems encountered include:

Determining all situation factors. This can be a problem because there are often too many factors (in excess of 150), they are not always known in advance, they can change during the project and there exist complex dependencies.

Process tools have not been a commercial success. They were found to be too cumbersome to work with, organisations were slow to adopt, they were often inflexible in process definition and they often had poor interfaces to other tools such as those for project management.

The concept of metaCASE is still struggling. Situational tooling is often regarded as feasible only for large organisations while interoperability with other standard tools remains problematical.

Practical advice is offered in terms of process construction using a pattern-based approach. Explicit discussion of patterns is found in, for instance, D'Souza and Wills (1998), Ambler (1998, 1999), Hruby (2000), Fiorini et al. (2001), Gnatz et al. (2001) and Tran et al. (2005) and implicitly in Graham et al. (1997) (see also Chap. 2).

An increasing number of case studies have been published to describe specific example applications (e.g., Firesmith et al. 1998) and domains of applications. For example, Rolland (2002) addressed the Lyee methodology; Aydin and Harmsen (2002) addressed DSDM (dynamic systems development method: Stapleton (1997)) while Zowghi et al. (2005) derive an RE-focussed process based on the Open Process Framework (OPF: Firesmith and Henderson-Sellers 2002). The domain of web content management was analysed by van de Weerd et al. (2005) while a series of papers (e.g., Serour et al. 2002, 2004; Serour and Henderson-Sellers 2004b) describe how SME was used in several industries in Sydney, particularly a legal publisher and an e-government IT support group. Similar studies, performed with industries in Slovenia, are reported in Bajec et al. (2007b) and with health care specialists in Australia by Waller et al. (2006). Enterprise architecture management is addressed by Winter (2011) and Buckl et al. (2011).

While most of the literature focusses on the technological aspects of method acceptance and adoption, Mohan and Ahlemann (2011b, c) stress the need to consider the human aspect. They suggest that it is critical that individual team members are enthusiastic to adopt any approach advocated by management; without this, the methodology adoption will almost surely fail (Mohan and Ahlemann 2011a). Their study of user acceptance is based on a psychological determinism-based study in which they conclude (Mohan and Ahlemann 2011b) that the major determinants in the successful adoption and use of a methodology (pre-constructed or SME-created) are: (1) the value of a methodology, (2) the influence of the team environment, (3) personal beliefs and biases, (4) the characteristics and culture of the team's organisation and (5) their previous habits and experience. Personal characteristics form the basis of the studies of Belbin (1981, 1993) in his identification of factors influencing team success in broad terms. In addition, the individual's perceptions of methodology attributes are analysed by Mohan and Ahlemann (2011c), these attributes being (a) relative advantage (the perception that the new methodology is better than the old), (b) complexity (the degree of understandability of the methodology), (c) compatibility (with existing social cultural values), (d) result demonstrability (how easy it is to see when improvement happens), (e) visibility (of the team member's work to more senior people), (f) triability (the extent to which the methodology can be tested prior to full-scale adoption) and (g) reinventibility (the degree to which the methodology can be tailored). Clearly it is this last attribute that has most direct relevance to SME. Personality testing in the IT context was also discussed by Martínez et al. (2011). They compared five such testing approaches and concluded that a combination of personality tests gave more valuable information for decision making than any single test from the three for which they had collected data: Jung, Big Five and the Tree Test.

1.2.8 Tool Support

Many authors also discuss potential automation of the SME process (e.g., Smolander et al. 1990; Saeki 2003b). Following Harmsen et al. (1994), Odell (1995) suggests that any CAME (computer-aided method engineering) tool should support the following seven features:

- Definition and evaluation of contingency rules and factors
- Storage of method fragments
- Retrieval and composition of method fragments
- Validation and verification of the generated methodology
- Adaptation of the generated methodology
- Integration with a metaCASE tool
- Interface with a method base.

CAME tool creation, validation and utilisation, while necessary in an industry usage context, is deemed outside the scope of this book. Useful references can be found in Tolvanen (1998) based on the MetaPHOR project (Lyytinen et al. 1994; Niknafs and Ramsin 2008). We include a brief discussion of a small number of selected tools in Sect. 7.3.

1.2.9 Concluding Remarks

It should be noted that process modeling languages themselves (e.g., Chou 2002) are also outside the scope of this book. The process modeling literature tends to focus either on ways to use modeling to support flexibility in the Endeavour domain (e.g., Cunin et al. 2001) or on the description or visualisation of processes (e.g., Scheer 2000; Stőrrle 2001; Scott et al. 2001; Becker et al. 2003). In contrast to such *descriptive* approaches, SME attempts to formulate a *prescriptive* model (Rolland et al. 1995). These correspond to the backward-looking and forward-looking models described in Gonzalez-Perez and Henderson-Sellers (2007).

The lack of empirical data is noted by, for instance, Tolvanen et al. (1996), Fitzgerald et al. (2006) and Mohan and Ahlemann (2011a). They urge the collection

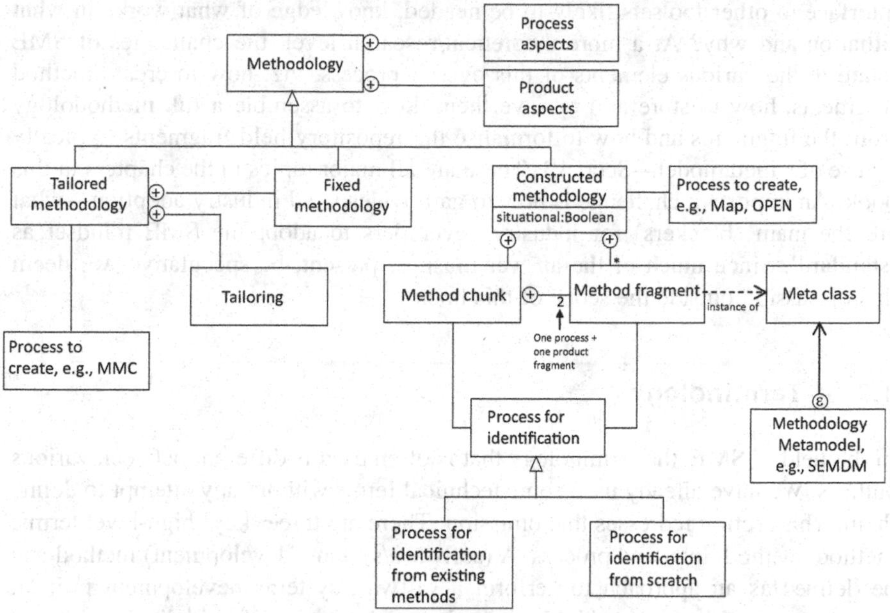

Fig. 1.7 An overall high-level model of the SME approach used to structure this presentation. It is not intended to be a complete metamodel. Note that the 'plus in circle' and 'epsilon in circle' symbols are the OML (Firesmith et al. 1997) icons for a configurational and non-configurational whole-part relationship, respectively, used since these are not supported by UML (Barbier et al. 2003) (after Henderson-Sellers and Ralyte 2010)

of data through longitudinal studies augmented by user satisfaction surveys, as well as the efficacy of action research (see also Tolvanen 1998; Serour 2003).

1.2.10 Summary of SME Basics

The overall approach to SME is synopsised in Fig. 1.7, this time as an object-oriented class model, which also serves as an architecture for the chapters in this book. Methodologies have both process and product aspects. They may be constructed, tailored or fixed. Here, we focus on the first two. Constructed methodologies are the main focus of the book including processes by which such construction occurs and the 'parts' (chunks, fragments, components) from which the methodologies are constructed, typically defined in terms of a metamodel. Also covered here are the processes by which chunk creation, identification and storage support the overall aims of SME. Tailored methodologies similarly require information on processes for the actual tailoring activity.

Some of the challenges for SME include the creation of commercial strength method bases, tools to support method construction, theory and tools to support quality evaluation of the constructed method, the availability of SME tools and their interface to other toolsets likely to be needed, knowledge of what works in what situation and why? At a more theoretical/research level, the challenges of SME relate to the various elements of this overall process, viz. how to create method fragments, how to store and retrieve them, how to assemble a full methodology from the fragments and how to formalise the repository-held fragments (typically by use of a metamodel—Sect. 4.1. These are all major topics in the chapters in this book. An important challenge is how to gain widespread industry adoption—what are the main 'blockers' for industry developers to adopt the SME mindset as 'standard'. Since much of the answer must, at present, be speculative, we deem this discussion outside the scope of this book.

1.3 Terminology

In the field of SME, the terminology that is often used is different between various authors. We have already used some technical terms without any attempt to define them. This section redresses that omission. There are three 'key' high-level terms: method, methodology and process. A (software/systems development) method can be defined as an approach to perform a software/systems development project, based on a specific way of thinking, consisting, *inter alia*, of guidelines, rules and heuristics, structured systematically in terms of development activities, with corresponding development work products and developer roles (played by humans or automated tools) (adapted from Brinkkemper (2006)—see also Henderson-Sellers (1995)). While the etymology of 'methodology' gives its definition as the study of methods, its widespread and common usage to mean 'method' (Jayaratna 1994; Berki et al. 2004) gives it credence in this second meaning (a meaning also given in many modern dictionaries, e.g., the American Merriam-Webster Dictionary: Cockburn (2000)). Indeed, a web search on these terms will reveal the extensive, and often acrimonious and certainly inconclusive, debate on the validity of using what some perceive as an Americanism (methodology) instead of the shorter form (method). For the purposes of our discussion of SME, we will indeed take the words method and methodology as synonyms, since we will not need the term methodology in its etymological sense. It is also the case that some terms work better with 'method'—for example, method construction, method fragment—and others with 'methodology'—for example, as in the phrase 'post-methodology era' (cited above) and 'one-size-fits-all methodology' and its common usage in standards such as ISO/IEC 24744 (ISO/IEC 2007).

The difference in meaning between the words 'process' and 'method/methodology' is harder to pin down. In general terms, a process is a way of acting, of doing something. Thus the way you relocate yourself from home to the work environment follows some (usually predefined—or least practised and often repeated) set of steps, i.e., a description of the process a.k.a. 'process model'. To complement this process model, which is sometimes, somewhat inaccurately, called a 'process', there are other things that a software developer must be cognizant of: in particular, the work products produced and consumed and the people and tools involved in that

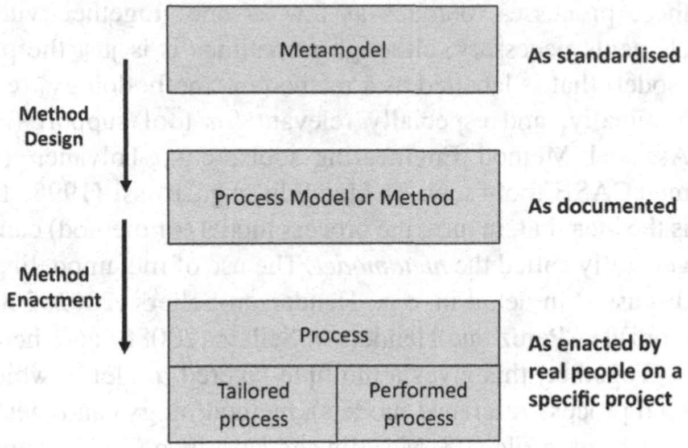

Fig. 1.8 Three 'layers' of process and method terminology (after McBride and Henderson-Sellers, figure 2, 2011) (With kind permission of Springer Science + Business Media)

production and consumption. Time sequencing is also of significant interest and concern. The word we will use here for this overall combination will be methodology[4] (Fig. 1.8). In other words, a methodology (or sometimes just 'method') encompasses absolutely everything needed for software development—Cockburn (2000) calls this a 'Big-M methodology', Glass (2000) the 'capital-M Methodology'. Many authors use the description of an overall methodology as having two (often intertwined—or at least interdependent) aspects: product and process (e.g., Rolland et al. 1999), to which should be added a third: the people focus.

Another viewpoint is that the process describes what is actually done in real time with a real team on a real project. This is particularly the case in the capability assessment field where the focus of a capability assessment is *the process as it is performed* (e.g., Paulk et al. 1993; Dorling 1993; ISO/IEC 1998)—although often, for example, in ISO 12207 (ISO/IEC 1995), processes are described as being at a smaller granularity and defined solely in terms of purpose and outcomes (elements of the describing process model). With this viewpoint, each process focusses on what is input to that process and what is output, i.e., it is seen as a 'transformation engine'. It should be noted that there are both a static and dynamic aspect to such a notion of process, i.e., the process (static enactment) whereby real developer's names, deadlines and deliverables replace the generic placeholders in the process model and the dynamics of the process as it is actually enacted (Conradi 2001). Greenwood et al. (2001) call the static enactment a 'process model instance' and the dynamic enactment 'process performance'.

Others talk of process models (e.g., Finkelstein et al. 1994; Gnatz et al. 2001; http://www.opfro.org) and process reference models (ISO/IEC 1995, 1998), in contrast to the process as enacted on an individual endeavour, e.g., project. It is the description of the process model or process reference model that is typically documented in books, in reports or on a website (although it is often labelled 'process' rather than 'process model'). A methodology is then a collection of

[4] Strictly speaking we should say 'software development methodology' since clearly the word 'methodology' can be applied in a wide range of human endeavours.

these processes (perhaps as few as one) together with the product and people elements necessary, although sometimes it is just the process collection (process model) that is labelled as a method or 'methodology' (e.g., Berki et al. 2004).

Finally, and especially relevant for tool support (e.g., CAME or Computer Assisted Method Engineering tools, e.g., Tolvanen (1998); Saeki (2003b) or metaCASE tools such as MetaEdit, e.g., Rossi (1995, 1998); Kelly et al. (1996)) is the idea that, in turn, the process model (or method) can itself be modelled. This is generally called the *metamodel*. The use of metamodeling in method engineering is discussed in detail in, e.g., Henderson-Sellers (2002, 2006a), Greiffenberg (2003), Gonzalez-Perez and Henderson-Sellers (2008b) and, here, in Sect. 1.4.

Together, this gives a multiple-layered model in which process, process model (and process reference models), method(ology) and metamodel can be depicted as suggested in Fig. 1.8. Marttiin and Koskinen (1998) point out that this can lead to a differentiation between method engineering (ME) and process engineering (PE). They note that in the two environments, the word 'meta' has a slightly different significance: in ME, the model of a method is the metamodel whereas in PE the model of a process is a process model defined by a process modeling language. Such a differentiation has also led to a literature focussed on PE, process families (e.g., Simidchieva et al. 2007) and software process improvement (SPI) (e.g., Conradi et al. 1993; Cunin et al. 2001)—and see also Chaps. 7 and 8, respectively. In this book, however, we subsume process engineering as a part of SME.

Figure 1.8 also underlines the three areas of interest in SME viewed as a process: method design, method tailoring (a.k.a. configuration) and method performance (a.k.a. implementation)—as discussed by, e.g., Cervera et al. (2011) and above with respect to Fig. 1.6 (albeit with slightly different terminology) (see also Chap. 8).

Finally in our terminological discussion, we note that we have used various terms to describe the small pieces of method. We have suggested 'method fragment' or simply 'fragment' as the atomic description of a method part. Larger complexes include 'chunks' (e.g., Ralyté 2004), 'components' (e.g., Karlsson and Wistrand 2006) and 'conglomerate' (ISO/IEC 2007). We defer a detailed analysis of this crucial element of SME to Chap. 2. In the meantime, we propose using the word 'part' as a generic supertype to these four terms.

1.4 Overview of Modeling, Metamodeling and Ontologies

In this section, we give a brief introduction to models, abstraction, domain ontologies and metamodels. We defer a detailed discussion of these topics, including how they are interrelated, to Chap. 4.

1.4.1 Modeling

A model can be said to be a simplified representation of (part of) the real world, called generically the System Under Study or SUS. Simplification is generally undertaken by the application of abstraction, which, as Henderson-Sellers (2011a) notes, is crucial for modeling (and metamodeling—see Sect. 1.4.3). Abstraction can be defined informally by

1) abstraction maps a representation of the problem to a new, more "abstract" representation. (This is the essence of modeling.)
2) by preserving relevant, desirable properties, the abstraction process allows one to solve the original problem
3) by throwing away details, the result of the abstraction process provides a simpler problem to be solved than the original (Giunchiglia and Walsh 1992)

An abstraction mapping used to create a model thus removes (unnecessary) detail (Ghidini and Giunchiglia 2004; Keet 2007).

Abstraction is used in modeling in many ways. Two such application approaches are relevant to SME: the use of abstraction to create token and type models (e.g., Kühne 2006). The former are one-to-one mappings between two models of different levels of detail (different granularity); while the latter have one-to-many relationships between a single type and all the instances that conform to that type. Type models are of the greater interest and application for SME and use the so-called granularity abstraction (for further details, see Sect. 8.3.1). One characteristic of type modeling is that the representation language used for the types and that used for the instances is different (see also discussion in Henderson-Sellers 2012).

1.4.2 Domain Ontologies

A domain ontology is a special kind of model (Fig. 1.9) in that it uses the open world assumption and is typically a description of what exists, i.e., it is a backward-looking model (in comparison to a system model which may be backward or forward looking and typically uses a closed world assumption). It describes things that exist in one specific domain and how these things are related. For example, Fig. 1.10 shows a domain ontology for the Wine industry domain. It can be seen that each box describes a different sort of wine and that each is modeled as a subtype, recursively to the 'ancestral' Wine class. In other words, it describes the current knowledge base in this particular domain, while remaining extensible as new knowledge is generated.

In addition to models and metamodels, there has been much recent interest in the incorporation of ontological thinking into SME, software engineering in general and conceptual modeling (e.g., Guarino 1998; Wyssusek and Klaus 2005; Green and Rosemann 2005; Calero et al. 2006; Hesse 2008a, b; Henderson-Sellers et al. 2013). Ontological thinking and the relationships between ontologies and models and metamodels are all discussed in Sect. 4.2 in more detail.

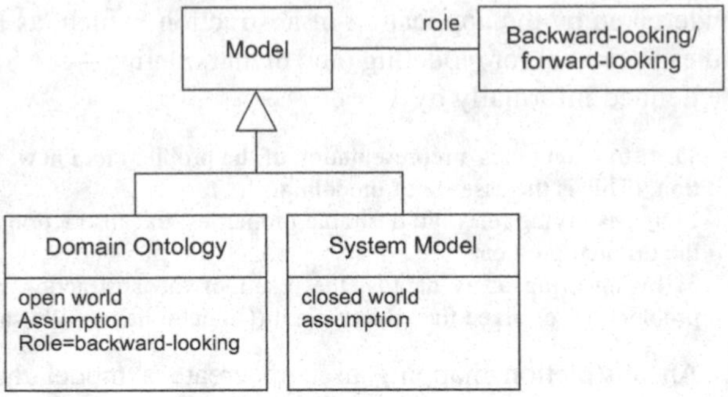

Fig. 1.9 There are various kinds of models. Two of interests are the system model (e.g., a UML design model) and a domain ontology

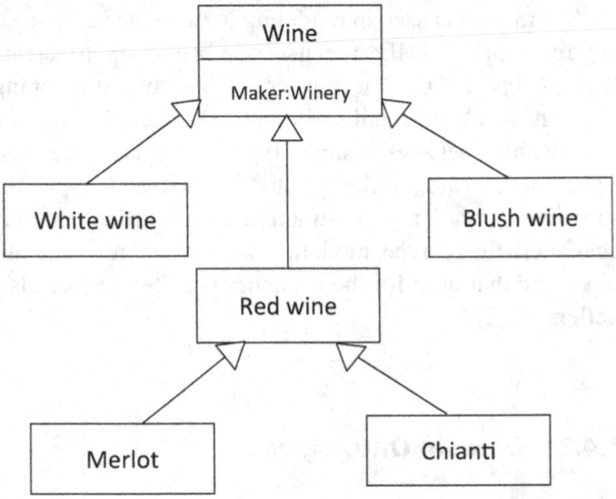

Fig. 1.10 Part of a domain ontology for the wine industry (after Henderson-Sellers, figure 5.4, 2012) (With kind permission of Springer Science + Business Media)

1.4.3 Metamodels in SME

The use of metamodeling in software engineering has been increasingly gaining credence and visibility since it was first proposed as a vehicle for facilitating convergence of OO modeling languages (Monarchi et al. 1994). A metamodel is best defined as 'a model of models' (Flatscher 2002; OMG 2003; Favre 2004) and is itself a model (e.g., Henderson-Sellers 2011b). "That is, a metamodel makes statements about what can be expressed in the valid models of a certain modeling language". (Seidewitz 2003).

In contemporary software engineering and modeling, one of the first attempts to formalise the structure of Fig. 1.8 and create a multilevel architecture to support metamodels as well as models resulted in the creation of a four-level hierarchy under the auspices of the Object Management Group (OMG) in the late 1990s. Models in each 'layer' are type models for those in the layer immediately below. This gave rise to the statement that this linkage should be represented as an 'instanceOf' relationship and the overall approach became known as strict metamodeling (e.g., Atkinson 1997, 1999). Figure 1.11 depicts this OMG architecture in which the layers have a label of the form Mx ($x = 0$–3). Although it is commonly said that the four levels in Fig. 1.11 are 'layers of abstraction' or

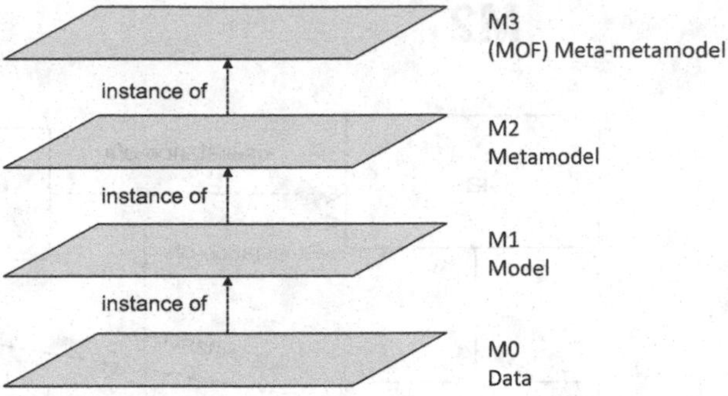

Fig. 1.11 The four layer hierarchy of the OMG, itself based on ANSI (1989) (after Henderson-Sellers and Unhelkar 2000) ©Pearson Education Limited

'abstraction levels', e.g., Jørgensen (2004); OMG (2007), it should be remembered that, as noted above (Sect. 1.4.1), abstraction primarily focusses on the removal of detail and it is perfectly possible to have abstraction relationships (between two sets or classes) that are not the type–instance (classification) relationship that is required for the construction of Fig. 1.11.

The architecture of Fig. 1.11 supports the definition of the Unified Modeling Language (an OMG standard). UML is in fact a metamodel (or M2 model) that is depicted as a comprehensive suite of class diagrams that provide rules for any classes and relationships that one would wish to utilise in a (M1) model, i.e., a user-defined model in a specific domain of interest.

For example, while a UML model of the Banking domain represents entities within a bank (the language is that specified by the domain ontology elements), the UML metamodel, on the other hand, represents concepts such as *class* or *association* (elements of the modeling language not the domain ontology) that are totally independent of the Banking (or indeed any other) domain (Fig. 1.12) and instead represent *types* of entities in the SUS.

However, when we move to processes and methodologies, as we need to do in SME, a problem arises as a consequence of the use of the type–instance semantics of Fig. 1.11. Specifically, it should be noted that an attribute that is specified on a type must be given a value (sometimes called a slot value) in the instance (Fig. 1.13). For methods, we need slot values at M0 but definitions at M2. This is not possible with the architecture of Fig. 1.11 and has led several researchers to seek alternative architectures and solutions that are also useful for SME. One specific architecture, highly suitable for SME, is that developed for and utilised in ISO/IEC 24744 International Standard (ISO/IEC 2007) a.k.a. SEMDM (software engineering metamodel for development methodologies). In this architecture, shown in Fig. 1.14, the layers (now called 'domains') are defined in terms of an industrial software development environment: an Endeavour domain where people work, using tools, methods and heuristics documented and available in the so-called Method domain and a Definitional domain labelled here as the 'Metamodel domain'. Coupled with the use of powertypes (see Sect. 4.1, especially Fig. 4.8), this architecture resolves the problem of defining attributes of classes in the metamodel but not allocating slot values until the Endeavour domain (see Chap. 4) for a full explanation of how this works).

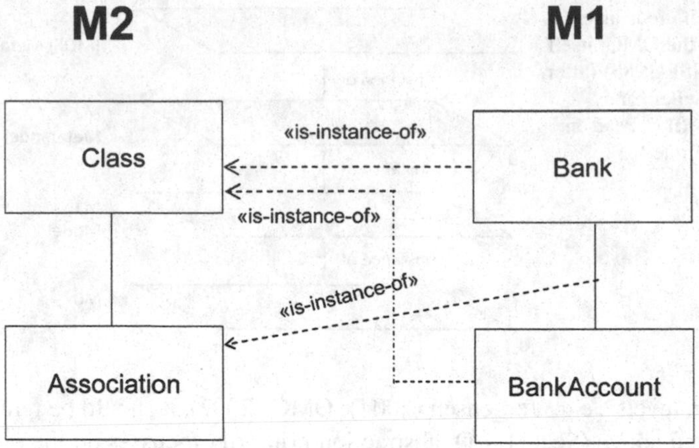

Fig. 1.12 Elements in the Banking domain (OMG level M1) and their metamodel counterparts (OMG level M2) (reprinted from Henderson-Sellers 2007, with permission from IOS Press)

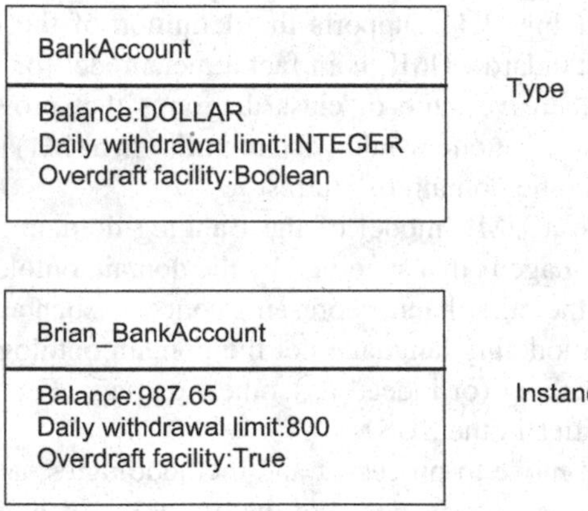

Fig. 1.13 Example illustrating the type–instance relationship showing how an attribute on the type is given a value at the instance

While early SME literature did not explicitly discuss metamodeling, it is now much more generally accepted that the ideas of metamodeling, especially those from the object-oriented and software engineering communities (as summarised, for instance, in Gonzalez-Perez and Henderson-Sellers 2008b), are highly applicable to the SME context (e.g., Madhavji (1991), Rolland et al. (1995), Ralyté et al. (2003) refer to it as the "core technique in SME". Rolland and Prakash (1996), Tolvanen et al. (1996), Jarke et al. (1998)). In fact, one of the main SME approaches, that of the OPEN[5] Process Framework (e.g., Henderson-Sellers and Graham 1996; Graham

[5] OPEN is an acronym for Object-oriented Process, Environment and Notation (Graham et al. 1997).

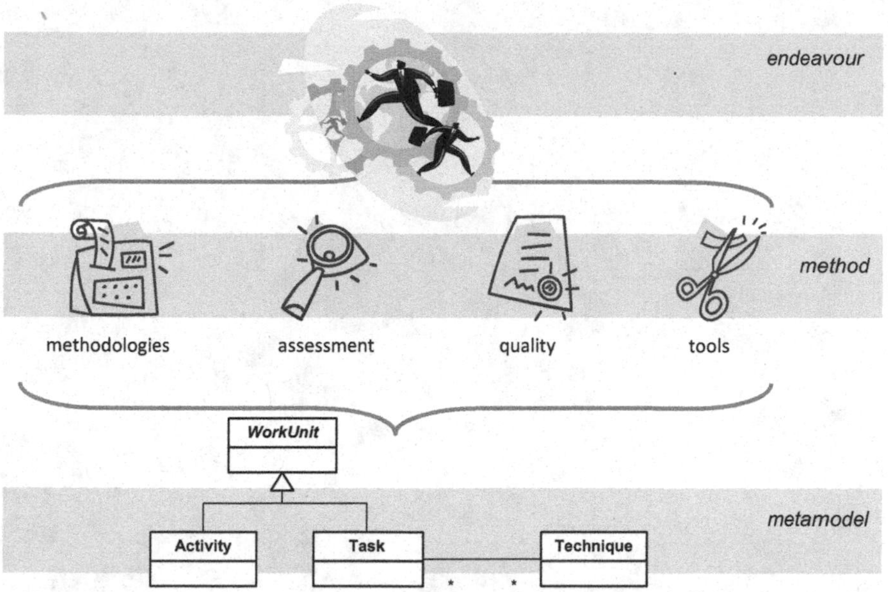

Fig. 1.14 The three domains of AS4651 and ISO/IEC 24744 (This is inverted with respect to the OMG architecture shown in Fig. 1.11 in order to stress the important of people in the Endeavour domain) and the fact that the metamodel provides the foundational level (after Henderson-Sellers 2006a)

et al. 1997; Henderson-Sellers et al. 1998; Firesmith and Henderson-Sellers 2002), was created from the beginning with a metamodel at its core.

1.5 Summary

In this introductory chapter, we have set the scene for our discussion of SME. We first explained why there is a problem of the 'one-size-fits-all' approach to methodology adoption/usage, arguing that an SME approach can offer substantial benefit in that context. The basic ideas were summarised in Figs. 1.1 and 1.4 and various 'phases' in the life cycle addressed in Figs. 1.6 and 1.8. We therefore subsequently outlined, in Sect. 1.2, the main elements in Fig. 1.1; namely, method parts, method bases, the situational context, method tailoring and, finally in that section, some practical advice.

Our discussion of terminology in Sect. 1.3 highlights the significant disparity in usage in both the literature and practice of terms such as method, methodology and process. We then introduced in Sect. 1.4 some of the technical aspects of SME, particularly with respect to modeling, domain ontologies and metamodels. This led to the introduction of the influential four layer architecture of the OMG in Fig. 1.11 as well as a more recent architecture more closely aligned with reality (Fig. 1.14) and used in ISO/IEC 24744 (a.k.a. SEMDM). This basic grounding in SME will be built on in subsequent chapters.

Summary

Method Chunks, Method Fragments and Method Components

2

Summary of What We Will Learn in Chapter 2

- What is a method fragment, a method chunk and a method component and how they compare
- A basic appreciation of viewpoints and granularity
- How guidelines and descriptors are helpful in retrieving method parts from a method base

In Chap. 1, we used the name 'method part' to refer generically to some piece of a methodology smaller than the whole methodology. In the research literature, many names have been used, sometimes with the same semantics, sometimes the same name with different semantics. However, the bulk of the literature talks of (1) method fragments, (2) method chunks or (3) method components.[1] These three different concepts are then utilised in SME approaches based on their focal utilisation. In each case, the overall definition must depend upon an appropriate metamodel. In this chapter, only fleeting reference will be made to these underpinning metamodels, which will themselves be a major focus of Chap. 4.

2.1 Method Fragments

The term *method fragment* was coined by Harmsen et al. (1994) and popularised by Brinkkemper (1996) by analogy with a software component: ". . . a description of an IS[2] engineering method, or any coherent part thereof" (Harmsen 1997).

[1] This term is used in much of the SME literature and should not be confused with the term 'component' as used in, for instance, component-based software engineering (e.g., Heineman and Councill 2001).

[2] Information Systems.

B. Henderson-Sellers et al., *Situational Method Engineering*,
DOI 10.1007/978-3-642-41467-1_2, © Springer-Verlag Berlin Heidelberg 2014

Ter Hofstede and Verhoef (1997) define a fragment as "a coherent part of a metamodel, which may cover any of the modelling dimensions at any level of granularity". This suggests that these authors see a 'fragment' as a small piece of the metamodel in contrast to the majority of authors in SME who prefer to use 'method fragment' to denote an element of method-to-be-constructed, i.e., an element *conformant to* or perhaps *generated* from the metamodel. In passing, we note that Eberle et al. (2009) reinvented the term and (erroneously) claimed it to be 'new'.

Although method fragments can reside on any layer of granularity and hence even constitute a complete method, they are in practice usually thought of as the smallest building blocks of a method. That is, at the concept layer of granularity (Brinkkemper et al. 1999), see later discussion in Sects. 2.5 and 2.6.

Method fragments are preferred by those who aim for maximum flexibility and reusability at the slight expense of an additional effort for method construction (cf. using method chunks or components as described later in this chapter).

Typically, then, the type of a method part (in this section, we discuss method fragments) is defined in terms of an element in a metamodel (see Chap. 4). This means that the basic kinds of method parts are dictated by whatever elements are in the metamodel that is used. There is general agreement that there are at least three basic kinds of atomic fragments (Fig. 2.1)—some metamodels support more kinds and all metamodels support subtypes of these three basic kinds: Producer, WorkUnit and WorkProduct (although the names may differ between sources). This triad is seen, for example, in OMG's SPEM (Software & Systems Process Engineering Meta-Model: OMG 2008), the OPEN Process Framework (OPF: Firesmith and Henderson-Sellers 2002) and the International Standard of ISO/IEC 24744 (ISO/IEC 2007). We can think of the fragments that conform to a single element (a class) in the metamodel (Fig. 2.1) as being in some sense 'atomic' in that they are not composed of other fragments. This is in contrast to method chunks (as we shall see in the next section), which are composites of two or more atomic method fragments (typically a process fragment plus a product fragment).

In much of the SME literature, two of the three kinds of method parts are discussed in detail: the work units and the work products. These are typically referred to as 'process parts' and 'product parts', respectively. The third, a 'producer part' is well supported in, for example, the OPF repository (Firesmith and Henderson-Sellers 2002) but is absent from many other fragment repositories.

Product parts may be linked to modelling languages such as the notations used in OMT (Object Modelling Technique: Rumbaugh et al. 1991), OOSE (Object-Oriented Software Engineering: Jacobson et al. 1992) or UML (Unified Modeling Language: OMG 1997, 2001) (as noted in Ralyté 2004) or in proposals such as that of Hruby (2000). More typical are approaches with fragments that are product-focussed and fragments that are process-focussed. Examples here are the atomic method fragments stored in the repository associated with two research projects: the OPEN Process Framework (Graham et al. 1997; Henderson-Sellers et al. 1998; Firesmith and Henderson-Sellers 2002) and the JECKO framework (Mirbel and de Rivieres 2002). However, it should be noted that sometimes these atomic process-

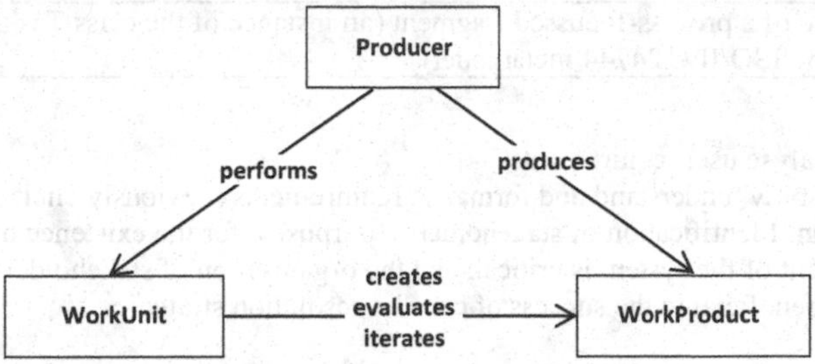

Fig. 2.1 The triangle of Producer, WorkUnit and WorkProduct that underpins SPEM, OPF and ISO/IEC 24744 standards for software engineering process modelling (after Henderson-Sellers and Gonzalez-Perez, figure 3, 2010) (with kind permission of Springer Science + Business Media.)

focussed method fragments are called by other names, e.g., 'process component' in the industrialised version of the OPF (http://www.opfro.org).

An example of a process fragment is shown in Fig. 2.2. As we shall see later, the specific fields in this example refer to attribute fields specified in the underpinning metamodel—here, ISO/IEC 24744 (ISO/IEC 2007) is used to effectively provide a template that is then completed individualistically for each method fragment conformant to that particular metamodel.

It should, nevertheless, be noted that, although method fragments are individually defined, there are often relationships between them. All fragment-based approaches utilise some type of association between those process-oriented fragments, the product-oriented fragments and the producer-oriented fragments (where available). For instance, in fragments conformant to the International Standard ISO/IEC 24744 (a.k.a. SEMDM or the software engineering metamodel for development methodologies), fragments can be linked by actions, where the form of the action is defined by an element in the SEMDM, this element representing a single usage event whereby a process fragment is executed on a product fragment. This International Standard defines a 'type' for each action that can specify whether the action uses, creates or modifies the work product that is the target of the action. For example, a methodology might contain a requirements validation task that takes a draft requirements work product (a document) as its input. The responsibility of the task (which is a process-oriented method fragment—a subtype of Work Unit in Fig. 2.1) is to modify this document through a pre-specified validation process with two outputs: a modified requirements document and a requirements defect list. This example in fact utilises two actions—one to map the task to the requirements document with the type 'modify' and one to link the task to the output work product of the requirements defect list with the type of 'create'. Thus, the connections between process fragments and product fragments are clearly specified—although we should note that these actions (in SEMDM) are considered as lightweight entities in the constructed methodology since they provide simply a mapping between what we might call the heavyweight process and product fragments. In other words, an action is not a container element; in contrast to the notion of 'method chunk', which we describe in the next section.

a) Example of a process-focussed fragment (an instance of the class TaskKind found in the ISO/IEC 24744 metamodel)

Attributes

Name: Analyse user requirements
Purpose: Study, understand and formalise requirements previously elicited.
Description: Identification of stakeholders' 'purposes' for the existence or the development of the system is critical; and the organisation of stakeholders into groups is beneficial to the success of conflict resolution strategies.

This Task aims to take the user requirements and understand their full depth. Analysis of user requirements is thus the interface between the identification of the user requirements and the first steps in creating the business model for those requirements (and the subsequent object model). One interesting way of doing this is by building a rich picture in which the complexity of the situation, as well as the wishes, concerns, agenda, aspirations and conflicts between various stakeholders is depicted as a drawing (annotated cartoons are often used) in order to highlight the issues, to open a forum for debate and discussion and to help arrive at a better understanding of the needs and wants of the stakeholders, as well as facilitating a consensus view. A rich picture is therefore a medium of communication, understanding and conflict resolution. Rich pictures are drawn and used in group situations where various stakeholders are present.
Another group technique that has proven useful is using CRC cards in which cards are created each representing various objects and types recognised as being, or likely to be a part of the system. Individuals in the group then use these cards to simulate various possible iterations through the system and play out likely and/or important scenarios. Doing this has proven effective in highlighting missed opportunities, bottlenecks, overlooked functionality and a myriad other issues potentially detracting from a good understanding of the system and the requirements.

Minimum capability level: 1

Relationships

Causes (Action kinds):
- Modifies Requirements Specification Document, mandatory.

Results in (Outcomes):
- Requirements have been analysed and understood.

Includes (Task kinds):
- (none)

Is involved in (Task-technique mapping kinds):
- Context modelling
- CRC cards
- Domain analysis
- Rich pictures
- Scripting
- Simulation

Is involved in (Work performance kinds):
- Business Analyst, mandatory.
- Customer, recommended.

Fig. 2.2 (continued)

b) Example of product-focussed fragment (an instance of the class WorkProductKind found in the ISO/IEC 24744 metamodel)

Attributes

Name: Software Requirements Specification Document

Description: The *Software Requirements Specification* is a document that specifies all requirements of the software components of a system application. It is useful for communicating the software's operational and quality requirements to their stakeholders as well as communicating the software's design constraints. It has the following contents:

- Four introductory sections: Document objectives; Intended audience; References; Organisation of Document
- Software Components.
- Operational Requirements – The functional requirements of the system, in the form of a use case model:
  - External Type W (Hardware, Software, Role)
    - External X – A specification of a specific external including all of its use cases
      - Use Case Y – A specification of a specific use case of the external including all of its paths
        - Use Case Path Z – A specification of a specific path through the use case.
- Quality Requirements – The specification of all required system-level quality factors.
- Design Constraints – The specification of all software-focussed design constraints.

The Software Requirements Specification is developed and maintained by the software requirements team with significant inputs from the domain experts team. It can be started as soon as the software-specific parts of the system requirements specification and system architecture specification are relatively stable. It is maintained during the life of the application to remain relevant as new requirements are added and existing requirements are changed.

The following usage guidelines are relevant to the Software Requirements Specification:

- Consider removing the quality requirements from this document if a system requirements specification is developed because most quality requirements are really at the system level rather than at the software level.
- Consider including the contents of the external interface specification here instead of producing a separate external interface specification document if there is no system requirements specification, the size of the Software Requirements Specification is small enough and there are few external interfaces.
- Modify the existing Software Requirements Specification and associated template and inspection checklist to meet the specific needs of the application.

Instantiate the Software Requirements Specification by using the software requirements specification workflow documented in the requirements procedure.

Relationships

Is acted upon by (Action kinds):

- Created by Elicit requirements, mandatory.
- Modified by Analyse requirements, mandatory.
- Modified by Document requirements, mandatory.
- Read by Develop class models, mandatory.

Fig. 2.2 Two example fragments, the details of each following the standard template as specified by the ISO/IEC 24744 metamodel (for details of the metamodel, see Chap. 4)

2.2 Method Chunks

Rather than using atomic method fragments, several authors prefer a coarser granular concept for SME, which they call a *method chunk* (Rolland and Prakash 1996; Plihon et al. 1998; Rolland et al. 1998; Ralyté 1999, 2004; Ralyté and Rolland 2001a, b; Mirbel and Ralyté 2006). The notion of a chunk as compared to a fragment has both advantages and disadvantages (discussed in detail in Sect. 2.4); one primary difference being that the effort of method construction (Chap. 6) is less than when using method fragments. A method chunk is defined as *the combination of a process part* (*also called a guideline*) *plus a product part* (Ralyté and Rolland 2001b) (the third of the basic fragment types shown in Fig. 2.1 (Producer) not being utilised). Informally, a method chunk is described as 'an autonomous and coherent part of a method . . . supporting the realisation of some specific ISD (Information Systems Development) activity'. The process part is said to 'refer to' the product part and subsumes all the kinds of linkages (construction, modification, etc.) that are possible between the separate parts of the chunk. This coupling of a single process part and a single product part uses the definitions of Ralyté (1999), which in turn expands the process-only focus of the definition of chunk in Rolland et al. (1995) and (Rolland 1998). It should, however, be noted that sometimes other names for a chunk are used—for instance, in Cossentino et al. (2007) and the FIPA[3] proposal for an agent-oriented method fragment, the appellation of fragment is given to the concept that is defined here as a method chunk (see also later discussion of Fig. 4.14 in Chap. 4).

The method chunk links a process-oriented fragment to a product-oriented fragment in a single package in order to decrease the number of entities needed to construct a full methodology. However, it should be noted that for a chunk consisting of one process part, call it ProcA, together with the product-oriented part, ProdB, created for one particular methodological situational context, it is perfectly possible that in another situation, ProcA will be linked not to ProdB but to ProdC or vice versa—ProdB might be linked to a different procedural part, say ProcD. This kind of flexibility led the authors to use a many-to-many cardinality between the process part and the product part in the underpinning metamodel description (Chap. 4) to indicate this possibility of temporal changes in the bonding within the chunk. Henderson-Sellers and Ralyte (2010) note that, over the last few years, this definition of a chunk has matured, being revised to take into account that, for a particular method chunk, a single process part outputs one or more product parts and also allows multiple product part inputs (e.g., Ralyté 2004). Thus, a multiplicity of one (process part) to many (product parts) should be appropriately used to replace the (inappropriate) many-to-many relationship in their original metamodel (see later discussion in Chap. 4).

[3] Foundation for Intelligent Physical Agents, now an IEEE Computer Society standards organisation.

We have seen that the body of the chunk is essentially the combination of a process part and a product part. However, an additional element is included in this SME approach. Each chunk is also given an interface that describes the situation when the chunk can be usefully applied together with a statement of the objective of the chunk (called the 'intention'). These elements can be viewed as preconditions and postconditions for the effective utilisation of each chunk. The underlying mindset is probably that of traditional process flow/workflow and is strongly influenced by the original work on Guidelines (Sect. 2.7) and Maps (detailed in Sect. 4.3) of Rolland et al. (1999) in which the chunk can be viewed as a 'black box' that acts as a transformation engine to change an input work product into an output work product, much as is done in the ISO/IEC International Standard 12207 (ISO/IEC 1995, 2008).

As well as having an interface, each chunk can be linked to a descriptor, which focusses on reuse capabilities. This not only defines the context in which the chunk can be reused by capturing criteria as proposed by Mirbel and Ralyté (2006) but also identifies the *Origin* of the method chunk. Mirbel and Ralyté (2006) suggest that the reuse intention, which describes the objective or intention of the chunk, can be formally stated as verb + target + parameters (Prat 1997). For example, the informal method chunk intention 'Construct a use case model following the OOSE approach' can be reformatted as $\text{Construct}_{\text{verb}}$ $(\text{a use case model})_{\text{target}}$ $(\text{following the OOSE approach})_{\text{parameter=manner}}$. In this example, the reuse intention of this method chunk would be formalised as $\text{Specify}_{\text{verb}}$ $(\text{functional system requirements})_{\text{target}}$ $(\text{following use case modelling strategy})_{\text{parameter=manner}}$.

Descriptors can also be connected to other elements such as *Experience Reports*, which detail experience gained from previous usages of that particular chunk. In addition, information on any other chunks that might be either (a) incompatible or (b) alternatives to the current chunk could be included here (Mirbel and Ralyté 2006). The formal definition of Descriptors is deferred until Sect. 2.7.

The rationale for using an interface/body description for a chunk has been discussed (Henderson-Sellers et al. 2008). On the face of it, because of the overlap of terminology, a situational method engineer might imagine that the notion of interface here is identical to that used in OO programming—based on Parnas' (1972) original ideas of information hiding. In OO programming, it is important to hide the implementation of the class (the 'body') from its interface (the services offered by the class). Henderson-Sellers et al. (2008) propose three possible reasons for this:

(a) To isolate the variability of the implementation from the interface, so that the implementation could change without affecting the interface
(b) To actually hide non-disclosable data from users
(c) To contain any run-time errors and avoid their propagation to other components (Meyer 1997)

In contrast to this information hiding rationale that is viewed as critical for OO programming, for the SME chunk approach, there is no information that needs to be hidden—both body and interface need to be visible to the method engineer. Consequently, in our discussion here, we need to note that the terms body and

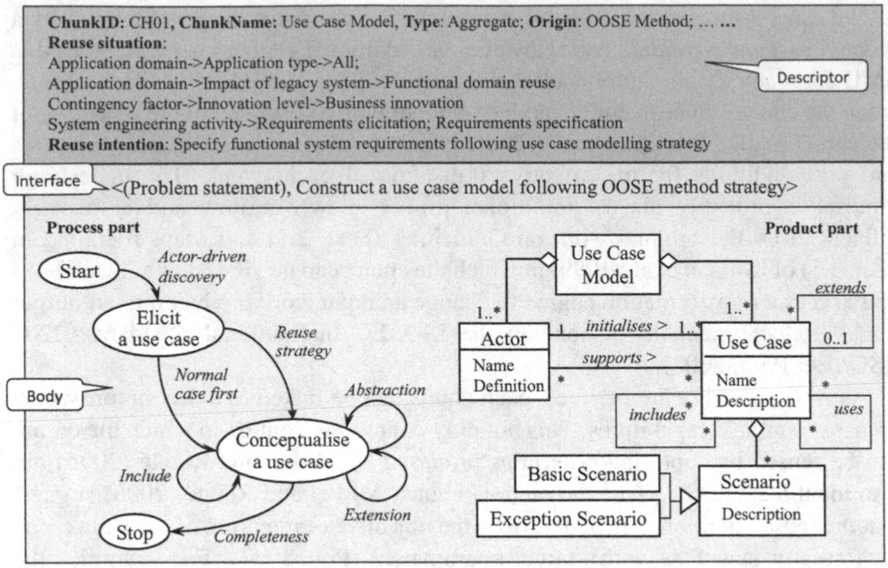

Fig. 2.3 An example of a method chunk, consisting of a single process part and a single product part. A chunk has a body plus an interface as well as an affiliated descriptor. Details of the origin, reuse situation, reuse intention and experience report have been only partially presented in order to retain clarity (after Henderson-Sellers et al. 2008) ©IEEE reproduced with permission

interface have a different interpretation. The chunk body refers to the detailed information that is to be actually incorporated into the methodology whereas the descriptor merely details the situation/intention contextual information about the chunk. This is undoubtedly useful from a conceptual modelling viewpoint since it supports the notion of a chunk as a black box or transformation engine, as discussed earlier.

An example of a method chunk is shown in Fig. 2.3. The left hand side illustrates the process part of the chunk expressed as a 'map' (Rolland et al. 1999 and see full discussion in Sect. 4.3). The right hand side shows the linked product part of the chunk, here expressed as a UML class model describing the underpinning metamodel. Other elements of the chunk are shown in the top part of the diagram. The situation, intention and descriptor are all shown here. Thus, this part captures the 'guidelines' associated with the holistic nature of the chunk (e.g., Ralyté and Rolland 2001b; Ralyté 2004).

Finally, we note that chunks can be at one of a range of granularities (Rolland and Prakash 1996)—indeed, Ralyté (2004) argues that even the fully constructed methodology may be regarded as a chunk. This approach is mirrored in the relationships in SPEM Version 1 (OMG 2002) in which a *Process* is a subtype of *ProcessComponent*—see later discussion in Chap. 4. This contention does raise some issues that are not yet resolved since there would appear to be no obvious way of modelling such a full methodology in terms of the chunk definition of one

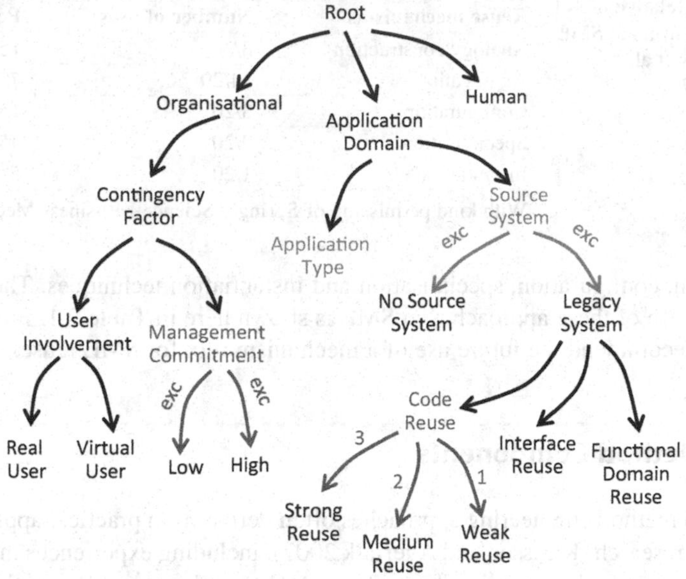

Fig. 2.4 Example of a Reuse Frame (after Mirbel 2006)

process part plus one product part; certainly not in the Endeavour domain of a project performance (Henderson-Sellers et al. 2008).

In an interesting paper, Mirbel (2006) moves between chunks and fragments in her quest for a way to federate method parts. She argues that if chunks (and by implication components—see Sect. 2.3) are broken down into their constituent parts (i.e., method fragments), then these atomic method parts can be federated in order to share knowledge across methodologies and projects. These shared atomic elements are the set from which the organisation's 'best practices' can be extracted. Clearly, this also enhances the possibilities for large-scale reuse (of method parts). In this context, Mirbel (2006) proposes a 'Reuse Frame' (Mirbel and Ralyté 2006), which she sees as an ontology for ISD. The meaningfulness is determined using similarity metrics (discussed further in Chap. 8). The Reuse Frame is depicted as a tree structure (Fig. 2.4) 'in which nodes are linked through three different kinds of refinement relationships: refinement into node to specify more specific aspects, more specific and classified aspects, more specific and exclusive aspects'. The root node is said to be mandatory, as are the three nodes that specify the main aspects: Human, Organisational and Application domain. Precision is increased as one travels down the tree. Any such route—from node to leaf—is called an 'aspect'. These are used to derive the complementary 'Reuse Context', in turn used in the metrics calculation (see Chap. 8).

Reuse mechanisms for SME are also investigated by Becker et al. (2007) who itemise opportunities in terms of patterns, components, modules and reference models. These basic entities can then be reused by the application using

Table 2.1 Relative use of reuse mechanisms in SME (after Becker et al., table 3, 2007)

Reuse mechanisms	Number of uses	Percentage
Analogy construction	3/20	15
Aggregation	14/20	70
Configuration	3/20	15
Specialisation	9/20	45
Instantiation	1/20	5

aggregation, configuration, specialisation and instantiation techniques. Their analysis of the use of these approaches in SME is shown here in Table 2.1. From these data they recommend the future use of a mechanism mix for SME reuse.

2.3 Method Components

Situational method engineering approaches often derive from practical applications and action research (Karlsson and Ågerfalk 2007), including experiences in method tailoring, as we shall discuss in Chaps. 7 and 9. One such approach uses the notion of a 'method component'. As with method chunks, method construction effort is less than with method fragments, set in the additional context of method rationale (see details in Chap. 3). Röstlinger and Goldkuhl (1994) introduced the method component concept and its utilisation in a component-based approach to promote a view of methods as constituted by exchangeable and reusable components. Each component consists of descriptions for ways of working (a process), notations and concepts (see also Goldkuhl et al. 1998). A process describes rules and recommendations for systems development and informs the method component user what actions to perform and in what order. Notation refers to semantic, syntactic and diagrammatic rules for documentation. Concepts form the basic categories of the process and the notation. A method component can be used separately and independently from other components or be used in combination with other method components. Importantly, each method component addresses a certain aspect of the problem at hand. The concept was further developed by Ågerfalk (1999, 2003) who defines it as 'the smallest meaningful assembly of method fragments to address a certain aspect of a problem [... It] consists of product fragments (notation), process fragments (process) and concept fragments (concepts) used in the other two types of fragments'. In this view, a method component, per se, is a method part at some intermediate layer of granularity (see Sects. 2.6 and 8.3.1).

Exploring further on the notion of 'smallest meaningful assembly' in relation to the practical usefulness of method components in actual method engineering projects, Wistrand and Karlsson (2004) and Karlsson and Wistrand (2006) conclude that a method component is a 'self-contained part of a system engineering method expressing the process of transforming one or several artefacts into a defined target artefact and the rationale for such a transformation'. An important part of this definition, emphasised by Karlsson and Ågerfalk (2009a, b) and Wistrand (2009), is the 'method rationale' captured by a method component. As we shall see in more detail in Chap. 3, this concept intends to capture the reasons why a particular method component is useful in a particular context and why it is designed the way it is. Generally, a method component is said to consist of two parts: its content and its rationale. Indeed, the prime focus of this approach is this notion of method rationale (Ågerfalk and Fitzgerald 2006), an idea that resonates with but goes beyond the notion of 'intention' found in the Descriptor of the method chunk approach and the Guideline of the SEMDM (see also Ågerfalk et al. 2007). As we shall see in Chap. 3, the method rationale part of the method component consists of goals and values, which represent the reasons behind method parts. A goal is a verifiable state of the world towards which effort is directed. Each goal is anchored in the method creator's values (Goldkuhl et al. 1998; Ågerfalk and Fitzgerald 2006). Goals and values are important parts of the perspective (Goldkuhl et al. 1998) or philosophy (Fitzgerald et al. 2002) of a method or method component. Karlsson and Ågerfalk (2009b) even argue that method rationale is more important than the work products as such. Method rationale is what makes it possible to address the goals that are essential to reach specific project objectives. Prescribed actions and artefacts are only the means to achieve something, and method rationale can therefore prevent developers from losing sight of that ultimate result and can help them find alternative ways forward (Ågerfalk and Fitzgerald 2006). Method rationale is also critical to ensure that, when combining method components, chunks or fragments, one understands whether or not 'apples' are being mixed with 'oranges' in terms of philosophies underlying the components (Ågerfalk and Åhlgren 1999)—indeed something that is sometimes desired in order to bring multiple perspectives to the table.

Similarly to method chunks, method components subscribe to the idea of information hiding, inspired by the traditional use of the component concept in software engineering (McIlroy 1968; Stevens and Pooley 2006). According to Karlsson and Ågerfalk (2009b), in practical method engineering it is often desirable to hide unnecessary details during method configuration, providing a kind of encapsulation. Exactly how a task is executed is not interesting from an external point of view of the component. Rather, a user of a component (i.e., a method engineer or systems developer) is primarily interested in what can be achieved by using a component and its required input. This reduction of complexity is achieved via the 'method component interface', which refers to a selection of method elements and rationale relevant to the present task. The interface creates an external view of method components, and its content depends on the present task (Karlsson and Wistrand 2006).

Clearly, the definition of 'method component' offers some flexibility, which has proven useful in practical method engineering situations (Karlsson 2005; Karlsson and Ågerfalk 2009a, b). It does have some similarity with the definition in ISO 12207 (ISO/IEC 1995) of a 'process', although it is positioned as a more specific lower-level concept as it excludes the (potentially common) case of multiple outputs from a process element (it would thus require several method components to achieve such a process).

A method component is said to consist of method elements, which can be thought of as method fragments at lower layers of granularity than the component itself. The method component has an artefact focus in that it contains zero or more input 'artefacts' (called work products elsewhere in this book) and an output artefact (or deliverable) together with the transformation engine, for example, a task (Karlsson and Wistrand 2006; Karlsson and Ågerfalk 2009b). This focus on work products resonates with the work product pool approach of Gonzalez-Perez and Henderson-Sellers (2008a), which identifies work product fragments before work unit fragments. Karlsson and Wistrand (2006) go on to define the method component as 'a self-contained module for producing the deliverable'. How this relates to the method chunk and the method fragment is further discussed in Sect. 2.4.

A similar approach is also seen in that of Rupprecht et al. (2000) who use 'process building blocks'—although their context is not software engineering but manufacturing. Indeed, as noted earlier, Mirbel (2006) identifies the need for industries to share best practices and introduces the notion of a federation of method chunks (Sect. 2.2)—similar in both motive and construction to the SEMDM's Conglomerate.

2.4 Fragments, Chunks and Components: A Comparison

We have now introduced the three kinds of SME method elements that are most visible in the research literature:

- The method fragment, which refers to a single concept in the metamodel and may have a process, a product or a producer focus—Fig. 2.1. An example of an actual method fragment is shown in Fig. 2.2.
- The method chunk, which is a combination of a process-focussed fragment and a product-focussed fragment and is also seen as an important contribution to the utilisation of a 'map' for facilitating method construction (see Sect. 4.3). An example of a method chunk is shown in Fig. 2.3.
- The method component, which consists of input and output work products and the 'process' used to transform the one into the other—together with a highly visible method rationale. An example of a method component is depicted in Fig. 2.5.

Several authors have sought to contrast and/or unify these various definitions (e.g., Mirbel and Ralyté 2006; Cossentino et al. 2006a; Ågerfalk et al. 2007; Sunyaev et al. 2008; Henderson-Sellers et al. 2008). For example, Fig. 2.6 from Mirbel and Ralyté (2006) shows four kinds of method 'component' (although this use of the name component clashes with our use of it in this book). They show that a method chunk consists of process fragment(s) and a product fragment (two subtypes of Method Fragment). They also introduce two other kinds of method element: pattern and road-map. Patterns may be generic conceptual patterns

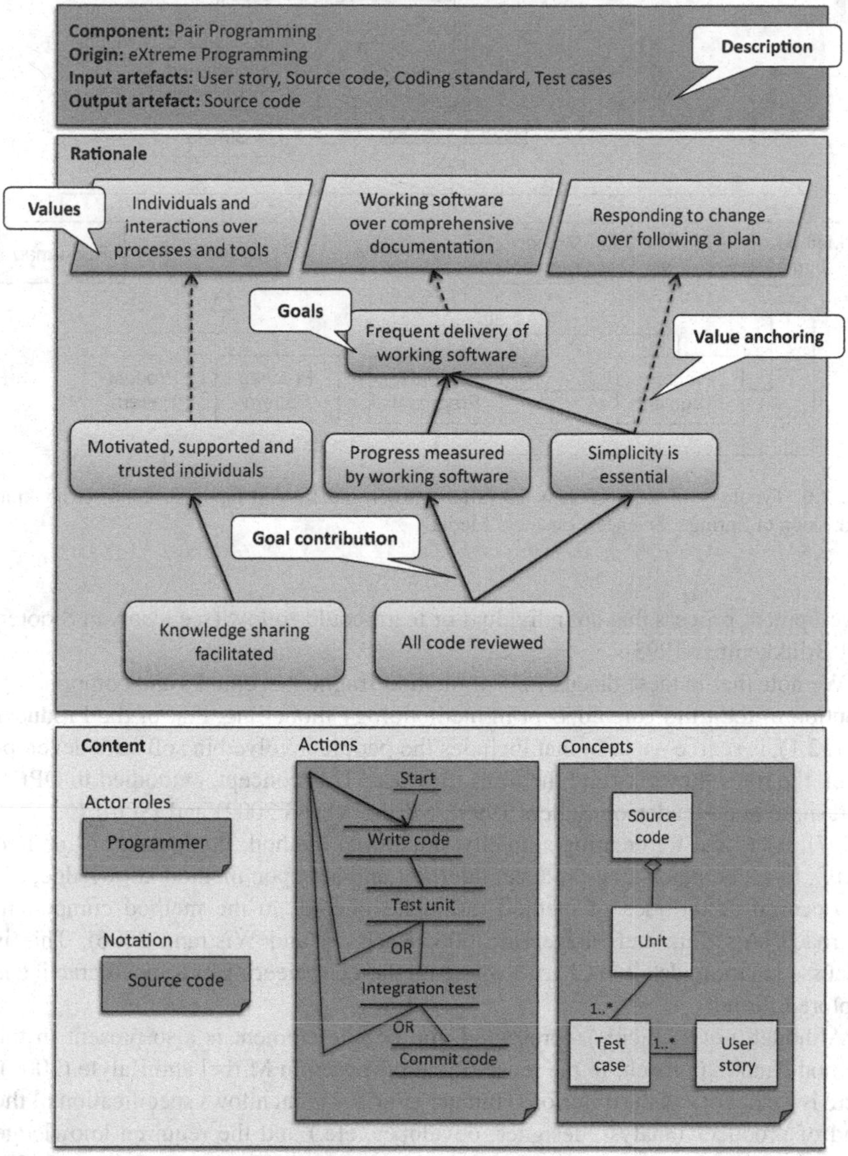

Fig. 2.5 Example of a method component

(Rolland and Plihon 1996; Rolland and Prakash 1996), decision-making patterns for enterprise modelling (Rolland et al. 2000) or domain-specific patterns, as discussed by Deneckère and Souveyet (1998). These patterns are the methodological equivalent of design patterns as documented by Gamma et al. (1994) or Buschmann et al. (1996). On the other hand, a road-map is described by Mirbel and Ralyté (2006) as specifying one particular, chosen route through the

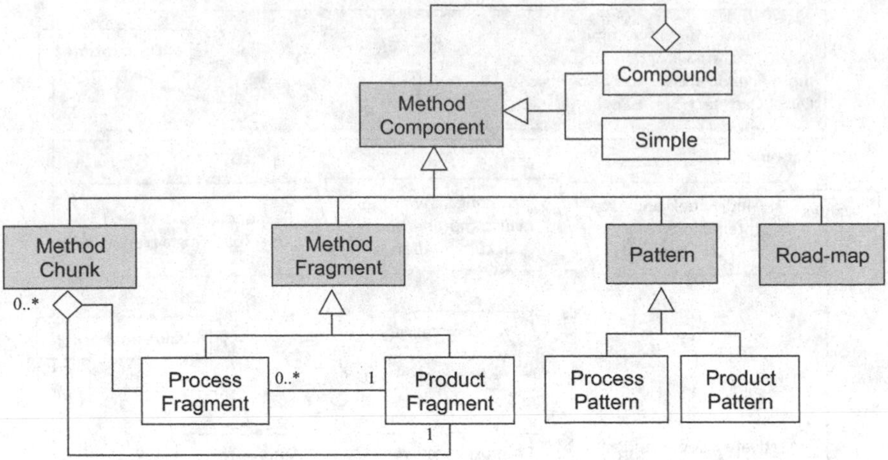

Fig. 2.6 Typology of method elements (after Mirbel and Ralyté, figure 2, 2006) (with kind permission of Springer Science + Business Media)

development process that an individual or team could follow (see also van Slooten and Brinkkemper 1993).

We note that in these discussions of method fragments, chunks and components, mention of the third core concept in methodology modelling, that of the Producer (Fig. 2.1), is scarce—a term that includes the people involved in software development, the roles they play and the tools they use. This concept, embodied in OPEN (Firesmith and Henderson-Sellers 1999), SPEM (OMG 2002) and ISO/IEC 24744 (2007), is critical for creating a quality situational method. Producers, or 'method users', as social actors that produce, interpret and act upon method knowledge, are also central to the idea of method rationale inherent in the method component approach (Ågerfalk and Fitzgerald 2006; Karlsson and Wistrand 2006). This is discussed in more detail in Chap. 3 where method engineering as a social practice is explored further.

Although not explicitly represented, the people element is also present in the method chunk approach. In the reuse frame proposed in Mirbel and Ralyté (2006), there is a category of the criterion 'Human' (Fig. 2.4) that allows specification of the kind of producer (analyst, designer, developer, etc.) and the required knowledge level (beginner, medium, expert). With this in mind, Henderson-Sellers (2007) proposed adding this third kind of core method element (Producer Fragment as a subtype of Method Fragment) to the representation of Fig. 2.6 (renaming the ambiguous Method Component of Mirbel and Ralyté 2006 as Method Part and including SEMDM's Conglomerate)—as shown in Fig. 2.7.

Henderson-Sellers et al. (2008) report on the debate surrounding the efficacy of method chunks in comparison to method fragments. The advantage of using a method chunk (which is one process fragment coupled fairly tightly to a product fragment) is clearly the speed of chunk selection since for any particular

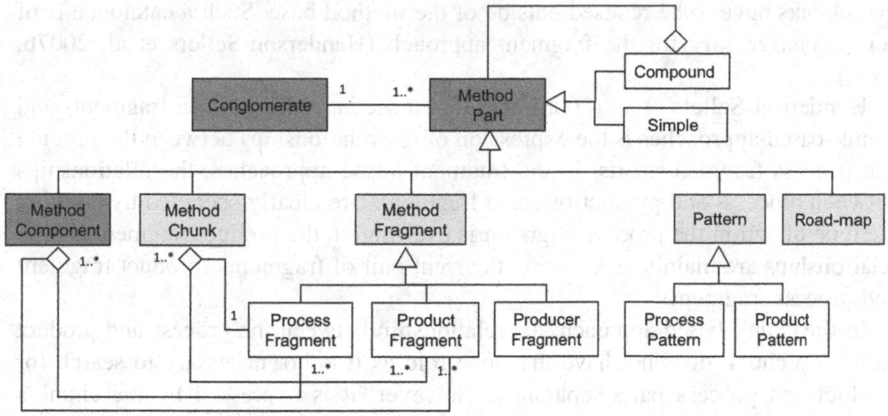

Fig. 2.7 Model to link together various kinds of method part

methodology construction fewer chunks are needed than method fragments to construct the same method. However, this relies on the specific relevant configurations already having been stored in the method base. Furthermore, there is likely to be duplication in that, for instance, a specific product part or a specific process part may reside in more than one chunk. In real-life, it is unlikely that such one-to-one linkages will be universal. Indeed, as these authors remark, if all such linkages *were* one-to-one, then the flexibility of method construction offered by SME would be totally redundant since everything would be 'hard-wired'.

In reality, some techniques and work products can be used with more than one task such that several method chunks may contain the same product part but a different process part (Ralyté 2004); some tasks have multiple output products (one to many); some tasks modify existing products or have multiple inputs—and there are other examples in industry situations where a one-to-one linkage is not viable. Furthermore, assuming a one-to-one connection between process and product part of a chunk, when such many-to-one situations occur, a separate one-to-one chunk for *each* specific configuration needs to be created such that, for instance, there is one chunk for one process fragment plus one product fragment; a second chunk for the same process fragment but with two different output product fragments, a third one for three outputs and so on (Henderson-Sellers and Ralyte 2010). In addition, even if this were legitimised[4] in some way within the chunk approach, a catalogue would be needed for the method base (i.e., the knowledge base that a method engineer would use in searching for appropriate chunks—Sect. 1.2.3), which could rapidly fill up with partially duplicated, overlapping chunk descriptions—even though in the method base itself these would be stored as individual non-overlapping fragments. The disadvantage of this single copy method base is

[4] For instance, a pair of overlapping chunks (with a fragment in common) might appear to be a solution but introduces significant and difficult new problems from a conceptual viewpoint.

that chunks have to be realised outside of the method base. Such a catalogue is of course unnecessary for the fragment approach (Henderson-Sellers et al. 2007b, 2008).

Henderson-Sellers et al. (2008) note that a second difference in fragment- and chunk-based approaches is the expression of the relationships between the product and process fragments/parts. In the fragment-based approaches, the relationships between process- and product-oriented fragments are clearly specified by defining the type of action the process fragment is exerting on the product fragment. These relationships are mainly used to find the right pair of fragments (product fragment and process fragment).

In the chunk-based approach, the relationship between the process and product parts of a chunk does not have the same role as it is not necessary to search for product and process parts separately. However, it is expressed by the chunk's *Intention*. For example, the intention of a chunk: 'Create a Use Case model' states that the process part provides guidelines 'to create' the product: 'a use case model'. The intention is one of the parameters used to select the appropriate method chunks in a given situation.

In a similar vein, Cervera et al. (2011) note the advantage of an atomic fragment in that it makes possible the linkage of one process fragment with several product fragments as well as the reuse of one product fragment in conjunction with different process fragments. They also note that the fragment, as opposed to the chunk, conceptualisation aligns with the metamodel in standards such as SPEM (OMG 2005a, 2008) as well as ISO/IEC 24744 (ISO/IEC 2007, 2010a).

Despite these differences, fragment-based, chunk-based and component-based approaches share a number of commonalities. To start with, all acknowledge the need to capture information about the situation where use of any particular method support may make sense. In fact, this is a crucial aspect of *situational* method engineering, and hence its name. Chunk approaches implement this via the chunk interface plus descriptor, which centralise situational information in a single place. In ISO/IEC 24744, as an example of a fragment-based approach, information has been modularised using different criteria, and situational information is distributed across different classes. First of all, the *Guideline* class is designed to capture information about where and how a method fragment (or collection thereof) can be used. Secondly, the *MinCapabilityLevel* attribute of the *WorkUnitKind* class captures the minimum capability or maturity level at which a particular process-oriented fragment is meant to be used, thus contributing to the establishment of a methodological situation.

Information about the intention of using a particular component is also captured by both approaches but, again, in different ways. The chunk approach uses an explicit intention description within the chunk interface. ISO/IEC 24744, on the other hand, captures intention in a more heterogeneous (and, possibly, richer) way. Two types of intention are distinguished: the intention of selecting a particular method fragment, and the intention of performing a particular process-oriented fragment (a work unit) or creating a particular product-oriented fragment (a work product). The first kind of intention (why a fragment has been selected) is expressed by the dependencies that exist between process-oriented and product-oriented fragments and are implemented by the *ActionKind* class, as described in Sect. 2.1; the products being created or modified by the enactment of the process fragment *are* the intention of selecting it. The intention of a product fragment, similarly, is given by the process fragments that modify, destroy or read the product fragment. With regard to the second kind of intention (why a certain process-oriented fragment must be enacted), the *Purpose* attribute of the *WorkUnitKind* class in ISO/IEC 24744 captures this information.

Another similarity between the fragment-based and chunk-based approaches is related to capturing information that may complement the specification of a method component, such as bibliographic references. The chunk approach manages this through chunk descriptors, while ISO/IEC 24744 implements it through classes such as *Reference* and *Source*.

Similar to method chunks, the method component is a higher-level construct than the method fragment. As described above, Ågerfalk (1999) suggested that a method component should be thought of as the smallest meaningful assembly of method fragments to address a certain aspect of a problem. Specifically, method components always reside on the 'artefact layer of granularity' (in terms of method fragments) and represent a non-hierarchical concept. The latter means that method components cannot consist of other method components. This is to reflect the notion that method components are the smallest coherent parts of a method that are practically useful. This design choice is based on two empirical observations (Karlsson 2005). The first, and most important, is that empirical experience has shown that systems developers tend to focus on the work products when configuring situational methods, and these are typically viewed as non-hierarchical patterns. Secondly, it has proven difficult to justify the complexity of hierarchical concepts in situational method engineering.

As stated above, the method component construct draws significantly on the idea of method rationale—the systematic treatment of the arguments and reasons behind a particular method (see Chap. 3). While the intention of a method chunk is typically expressed in terms of the action that immediately satisfies the intention, method rationale aims to direct method engineers' attention to the underlying assumptions of those actions and promote a critical attitude towards the different parts of a method. As shown by Ågerfalk and Fitzgerald (2006), this can be used, for example, to identify or engineer additional method components that suit a particular situation when a suggested method component cannot be used; for example, finding other ways to involve users (higher-level goal) if an 'onsite customer' (direct intention) is infeasible, such as in a global software development project.

A specific design feature of method components that sets the construct apart from fragments and chunks is that it is defined in terms of the output work product that it produces. This means that a method component always has one, and only one, output work product (or artefact), but may take zero or more as input.

Table 2.2 Summary comparison

	Method fragments	Method chunks	Method components
Support for process	Yes	Yes	Yes
Support for work products	Yes	Yes	Yes
Support for producers	Yes	No	Inherent in method rationale
Attributes of element	Dependent upon type	Always the sum of process part plus product part Use of descriptor important	A combination of input work product, output work product and work unit
Connection between process and product parts	Ad hoc based on situation	Hard-wired	Loose connection between components
Situational information	Guideline, reference and source	Interface and descriptor	Component interface with representation of method rationale
Capability assessment	MinCapabilityLevel	No	No
Multiple inputs and outputs to a process element	Yes	Yes	Zero or more inputs, always one output

Interestingly, the ontological analysis of Iacovelli and Souveyet (2011) identifies a differentiator between the method chunk and the method component, as described above, as being that a method component is potentially larger than a chunk as a consequence of its incorporation of a temporal element that is not present in the method chunk (Iacovelli 2011). This may not always be the case and depends on the granularity of the work products to be handled by a particular SME approach.

These comparisons are summarised in Table 2.2. It can be seen that all options support process and product but chunks do not offer any support for producers. Chunks, however, have a strong link between process and product parts whereas this connectivity is more 'manual' with the other options. As might be expected, situational context is incorporated in all approaches but using different structures and keywords. Only fragments reflect support for capability assessment (as discussed here in Chap. 8). Finally, both fragments and chunks support multiple inputs and outputs whereas in the method component-based approach only one output is permitted.

Finally, as noted in Fig. 2.7, another kind of method part of current interest is the pattern. Buckl et al. (2007, 2011) suggest there are three different sorts of patterns useful for SME for Enterprise Architecture Management (a subdiscipline that focusses on processes for controlling and improving IT support in an organisation, thus addressing not just IT issues but also business process, business goals and strategic direction setting):

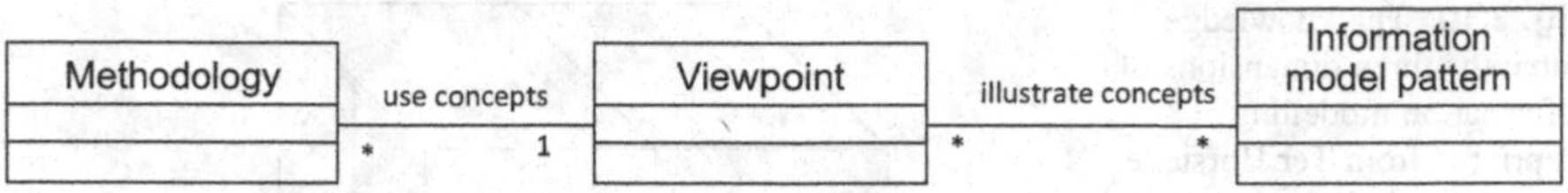

Fig. 2.8 Interrelationships between methodology, viewpoint and information model patterns (after Buckl et al. 2007)

Overview Section	
Id	A unique alphanumerical identifier
Name	A short and expressive name for the pattern
Alias	Names this pattern is also known as (optional)
Summary	A short summary of the pattern of about 100 words
Solution Section	
Information Model	An information model fragment in a certain language, together with additional documentation
Consequence Section	
Appliance	Guidance on how to use the information model pattern
Consequence	Consequences resulting from the usage of the pattern

Fig. 2.9 Template for information model patterns (after Buckl et al. 2007)

- Method patterns, which focus on the ordering of steps needed to address a given problem.
- Viewpoint patterns, which define the notations to be used.
- Information model patterns, which structure the information needed by a method that is visualised with one of the viewpoints.

These are interrelated, as shown in Fig. 2.8. The description of each pattern follows the layout of a prescribed template—the template for information model patterns is shown in Fig. 2.9.

Patterns have also been applied in the agile context by Tasharofi and Ramsin (2007). These authors propose an agile life cycle of three consecutive phases as a generic description of all agile methodologies. They then recast this in terms of a number of phase process patterns: Initiation, Development Iterations and Release. Each phase is then said to be composed of a number of constituent-interrelated stages (note that this is terminology that is different from that of ISO/IEC 24744). Their application to an agile environment is accomplished via a metamodel based on the OPF metamodel (Firesmith and Henderson-Sellers 2002).

2.5 Dimensions and Viewpoints

In the context of situational method engineering, Ter Hofstede and Verhoef (1997) suggest that method fragments fall into categories defined on three orthogonal axes:

- Method/application/operational—called the levels of abstraction, leading to notion of instance-of between levels.
- Process/product—a dynamic versus static discrimination.
- Conceptual/representational knowledge (clear distinction between concepts and notation).

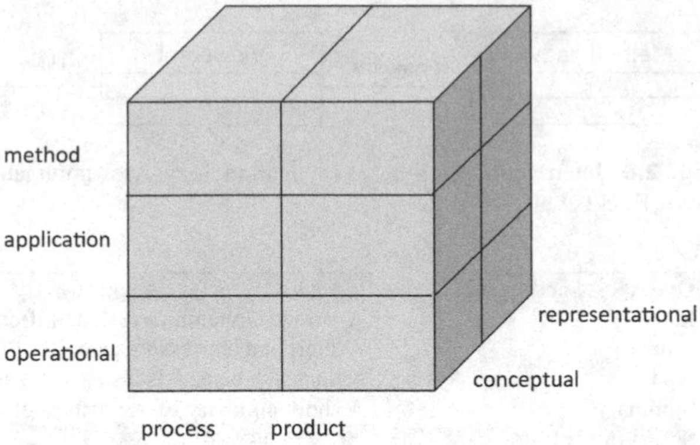

Fig. 2.10 The knowledge cube: the three dimensions of information modelling (reprinted from Ter Hofstede and Verhoef 1997 with permission from Elsevier)

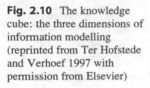

They capture these ideas as a three dimensional-cube (Fig. 2.10). The vertical dimension represents the abstraction level. Although at first sight this would appear to be a similar set of levels to those of the often-quoted metamodel hierarchy developed by the Object Management Group (OMG depicted in Fig. 1.11), the names associated with these layers (method,[5] application, operational) are much more closely aligned with those derived, ab initio, in the AS4651 metamodelling standard (Standards Australia 2004—see also Henderson-Sellers and Gonzalez-Perez 2005a) and utilised in the ISO/IEC (2007) 24744 standard (see also Henderson-Sellers and Gonzalez-Perez 2005b; Gonzalez-Perez and Henderson-Sellers 2006b, 2008b). In other words, the terms used in this cube (Fig. 2.10) are more closely aligned with the 'real world' of software development (as in Fig. 1.14) than with the artificiality of a set of abstraction layers defined only in terms of one particular representational relationship (instance-of) (Fig. 1.11).

The second dimension of product versus process compares the answers to the questions 'What should be produced?' versus 'How should it be produced?'—a sentiment echoed by many authors (see below for further discussion)—although these authors' claim that such a strict dichotomy is not well justified.

The third dimension differentiates between the conceptual or semantic character and its representation (e.g., diagrams, text) purely used as a communication tool. In language theory terms, this is the difference between the abstract syntax and the concrete syntax. Although this axis is noted to be orthogonal to the other two, we will not discuss it in any detail here, deeming it out of scope for our purposes.

Four, rather than three, dimensions have been applied to SME by Nehan and Deneckère (2007) in order to underpin the views notion, based on the original ideas of Jarke and Pohl (1992). These views are subject (dealing with the nature of the situational method), system (with its representation), usage (method rationale and

[5] Although the name method here more closely aligns with the Metamodel domain rather than Method domain in ISO/IEC 24744.

Table 2.3 Examples of method knowledge (after Tolvanen 1998)

Type of method knowledge	Examples of method knowledge
Conceptual structure	Each process may have sub-processes
Notation	Representing sub-diagrams for processes, balancing the data flows between decomposed process and its sub-diagram
Process	Top-down modelling of processes
Participation and roles	Division of labour based on sub-processes
Development objectives and decisions	Design choices are made by partitioning the system into sub-processes
Assumptions and values	An information system can be effectively designed by partitioning its processes

needs of users) and development (method construction). Views have facets. For example, in the usage view, reuse of components leads to the identification by these authors of two facets: construction technique and knowledge representation. The former links to the various styles of process construction such as assembly-based and extension-based (see full discussion in Chaps. 6 and 7, respectively) while the latter links to the kind of method part being used (fragment, chunk, component, pattern, etc.).

In another representation of the various kinds of knowledge, Tolvanen (1998) uses a shell model, with six embedded shells exemplified in Table 2.3 (listed from the inside out).

In Brinkkemper et al. (1998), the three dimensions are perspective (product or process), abstraction level (conceptual or technical) and layer of granularity (method, stage, model, diagram or concept)—dimensions not dissimilar from those of Ter Hofstede and Verhoef (1997) shown in Fig. 2.10. A similar approach is described by Rolland and Prakash (1996) but their three abstraction levels are component, method construction pattern and framework. In fact, Rolland and Prakash (1996) propose two orthogonal classifications: (1) component or framework or pattern and (2) forest (which may be of trees) or a tree or a context (of which there are three kinds: executable, choice and plan). In Rolland and Prakash (1996), granularity levels are said to be contexts, trees and forests of trees. These permit coarse granular chunks such as the whole of OMT to be regarded as a single component. Some are reusable as is and some need instantiating first (see later formalisation in Gonzalez-Perez and Henderson-Sellers (2005)).

Methods to support software engineering (SE) processes must be contextual. A tree is then composed of contexts plus links (refinement or composition). The method itself is the forest created from these trees of contexts. Contexts, trees and forests are the three kinds of chunks stored in the method base. This notion of method chunk strongly couples the process part to the product part.

The three kinds of context, seen as highly important by Rolland and Prakash (1996), are executable context, choice context and plan context. These relate to:

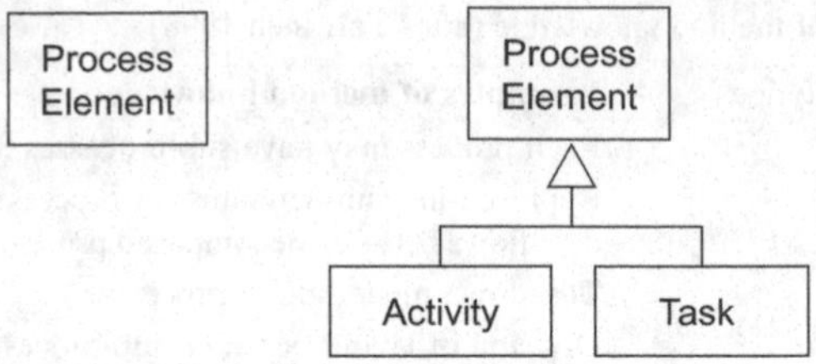

Fig. 2.11 Alternative representations for Process Element—fine granular (left hand side) or coarse granular (right hand side) (after Henderson-Sellers and Gonzalez-Perez, figure 5, 2010) (with kind permission of Springer Science + Business Media)

- Executable—decision is directly applicable inducing a transformation in the product under development.
- Choice—selecting a context to represent a particular strategy in order to resolve the issue raised by the context.
- Plan—an aggregation of sub-issues, each of which corresponds to a sub-decision associated with the component situation of the macro issue (the aggregate of the sub-issues).

2.6 Granularity

Granularity describes whether a system or fragment shows many details (fine granular a.k.a. fine-grained) or is at a much higher level of abstraction (coarse granular or coarse-grained). A simple example of a coarse and finer granular representation of relating to process elements is shown in Fig. 2.11. We can thus talk about a model that consists of a small number of entities as having coarse granularity or of a large number of entities as possessing fine granularity (Unhelkar and Henderson-Sellers 1995).

Using conclusions from an earlier study of the granularity of metamodels (Henderson-Sellers and Gonzalez-Perez 2010), in the context of SME there are two major areas needing to be addressed:

1. The impact on method fragments of the scale and granularity of the metamodel, e.g., definitions of method fragment types such as Activity, Task and Step as compared to simply ProcessElement (Fig. 2.11) (similarly Phase, Life cycle, etc.), i.e., the granularity of the metamodel (see Sect. 8.2 and Henderson-Sellers and Gonzalez-Perez 2010).
2. The size of method fragments generated (usually by instantiation) from such method element definitions (made at the meta level). Henderson-Sellers and Gonzalez-Perez (2011) explain how granularity affects method fragments by focussing on a single example—that of fragment generation from the Task subtype of the WorkUnit meta class (Fig. 2.1).

These and other quality issues are discussed in more detail in Chap. 8.

2.7 Guidelines and Descriptors

Guidelines and descriptors were mentioned briefly in Sect. 2.2. Here, we examine these important concepts in more detail.

Guidelines originate from the application of a 'map' to describe method construction (see Sect. 4.4). They refer to the process part of the chunk and how it is applied in an actual methodology. Indeed, Ralyté and Rolland (2001b) state that a method chunk can be described as 'process driven' since the chunk is based on the 'decomposition of the method process model into reusable *guidelines*'[6] i.e., the guideline is the name for the process part of the chunk (Ralyté 2004). With this addition of a guideline, a chunk can represent both method knowledge and a (sub) process aspect, as well as supporting the combination of a process-focussed part and a product-focussed part.

As well as a guideline, the chunk has an associated descriptor (as we noted earlier). This descriptor is said to extend the contextual view captured in the signature or interface, in order to define the context in which the chunk can be reused (see also Fig. 2.3). Formally, we can say

$$\text{descriptor} = < \textit{reuse situation}, \textit{reuse intention} > \qquad (2.1)$$

The descriptor also captures additional information such as the origin of the chunk, its type (simple or complex) and a textual description of its objective—see Rolland et al. (1998), Ralyté (1999, 2001), Ralyté and Rolland (2001b) and Mirbel and Ralyté (2006) for more information on this topic. As we noted earlier, the role of the descriptor is to ease chunk retrieval. Rolland and Prakash (1996) advocate describing semantics of stored chunks in such a way as to ease this retrieval, an idea suggested also by Freeman and Henderson-Sellers (1991) who proposed the use of a Full text storage, free text retrieval package for management of libraries of OO classes. In other approaches, a *descriptor* "plays for a method chunk the same role as a meta-class does for a class"[7] (De Antonellis et al. 1991). Furthermore, grouping of chunks can be used to permit hierarchical searching (Rolland and Prakash 1996) and hence more effective retrieval, an idea not unlike the faceted classification approach of Prieto-Diaz and Freeman (1987).

In summary, the incorporation of a descriptor into the method chunk definition provides information that could be useful for method engineers in chunk selection for the construction of a method to suit a particular situational context (the prime focus of SME). It should be stressed, however, that the sole purpose of the Descriptor is to assist in chunk selection. Once the chunk has been identified,

[6] Guidelines are discussed in more detail in Chap. 4 and, together with other process construction advice, in Chap. 6.

[7] This is hard to comprehend since the meta class to class relationship is that of Type–Instance whereas a descriptor is on the same meta level as a class and linked to it via a regular association.

ready for inclusion into the embryonic methodology, the descriptor becomes redundant; after that, only the chunk body has value. Further evaluation is then undertaken regarding the suitability of the chunk for the method-to-be-constructed. Such an evaluation could, for instance, be based on the similarity measures proposed by Ralyté and Rolland (2001a) or using some of the quality metrics discussed in Chap. 8.

The method component concept, and its associated method for method configuration (MMC), takes the idea of the descriptor even further by including in the interface of a component (the external description used in method configuration and SME) not just reuse intention but essentially a goal hierarchy that provides a more elaborate understanding of the rationale underlying a certain component. The inner workings of method components, such as its process, concepts and notation (essentially its 'guidelines'), are encapsulated and typically 'hidden' from method engineers and other method users. This is to reduce complexity, working on the assumption that the various people involved are familiar with the base method from which the components are drawn. However, if the situation so requires, the required content can certainly be revealed.

2.8 Summary

The chunk approach offers simplicity of archival and selection that therefore matches well simple situational method engineering challenges. If the requirements for the method construction only need one-to-one linked process+product fragments and the personnel and tools involved are minimalist (and matching them into the chunks can be done by hand), then the chunk approach could work well—although to the best of our knowledge there are no industry case studies using the chunk approach.

Fragments, on the other hand, require a slightly deeper understanding of the architecture of the repository and the way that fragments can be linked, e.g., using ActionKind of the ISO/IEC 24744 International Standard. However, the linkages achieved are more flexible and support a wider range of conceptual amalgamation, permitting create, read and write access depending upon the specific situation. This approach also permits ad hoc many-to-many relationships, while retaining individuality of fragments stored in the method base (repository). A fragment-based approach to SME has been successfully used in a number of industry projects, e.g., Henderson-Sellers and Serour 2005; Coulin et al. 2006; Bajec et al. 2007b; Henderson-Sellers and Qumer 2007.

Thus, in both engineering methodologies and using them on software engineering development projects, the process revolves around identification of the fragments/chunks and their linking together as appropriate. At the same time, it must be ensured that the resulting methodology has both quality as a static methodology model, is internally consistent and, most importantly, when applied to a real endeavour (e.g., a software application development) adds value to the software engineering organisation. Current successful applications of SME have in fact undertaken these construction and quality assessment steps manually. However, repository tools to provide both higher quality construction and semi-automated assistance in method construction as well as overall management of the chunks/fragments contained in the repository are sorely needed. One such example, still in prototype form, is MethodMate (see discussion in Gonzalez-Perez 2005). This tool supports the population of the repository with fragments and their retrieval to construct a method, together with initial support for project enactment. Third party commercial companies are also likely to make announcements of commercial tools supporting such a 24744-based approach.[8]

In the context of SME, we have evaluated two issues regarding the definition and descriptions of the method parts that are stored in a method fragment repository or method base. Firstly, we have contrasted the models for a method fragment, which depicts either a solely process-focussed concept, a product-focussed concept or a producer-focussed concept with that for a method chunk, which is a combination of a single process-focussed fragment with a single product-focussed fragment, and with a method component, which encompasses method rationale, i.e., a user/producer perspective.

From a conceptual modelling point of view, insisting on a one-to-one relationship between process fragment and product fragment in a method chunk often creates an artificial model that does not relate simply to real-life requirements; consequently we have recommended a modification to allow for multiple product parts (Fig. 2.7). From a software engineering point of view, there is a possibility that this chunk approach loses the flexibility that is at the core of SME and may introduce potential maintenance problems.

In terms of capturing situational information, we found that the chunk and fragment approaches do this equally well but with different mechanisms. Situational information is captured in the chunk approach in the chunk's interface whereas the fragment approach, as embodied for instance in ISO/IEC 24744, uses dependency relationships and an *ActionKind* class in its metamodel. Bibliographic information is also captured differently in the two approaches: chunk descriptors or implemented (in the 24744 approach) by *Reference* and *Source* classes in the metamodel.

Our analysis of the use of body and interface as terms in describing chunks identifies a different meaning from what a programmer might infer: information hiding. Rather, the use of these terms in the chunk approach identifies, at the conceptual level, knowledge of the chunk and knowledge of the situation/intention of the chunk.

Throughout this analysis, we have used the ISO software engineering metamodel for development methodologies (ISO/IEC 2007) as a means of

[8] The details are commercially confidential at the time of writing, made available to the authors under a non-disclosure agreement.

providing a theoretical underpinning for our identification of similarities between the chunk and fragment approaches and for the mappings between them.

Finally in this chapter, we have introduced the basic ideas of viewpoints and granularity as well as describing how guidelines and descriptors help in the task of retrieving of method parts from a method base.

Method Engineering as a Social Practice 3

Summary of What We Will Learn in Chapter 3

- The importance of social practices in SME
- The concept of method rationale
- How social practices are incorporated into evolutionary method engineering and method-user-centred method engineering

Formalised systems development methods are used in systems development as a means to express and communicate knowledge about the systems/software development process (Ågerfalk and Fitzgerald 2006). Since methods are social constructs, they embed various assumptions about people and systems development as a social practice (Introna and Whitley 1997; Russo and Stolterman 2000). Essentially, methods encapsulate knowledge of good design practice so that developers can be more effective, efficient and confident in their work. Nonetheless, it is a well-known fact that many software organisations do not use methods (Iivari and Maansaari 1998; Nandhakumar and Avison 1999) and, when methods are used, they are not used straight out of the box but are tailored to suit the particular development situation (Fitzgerald et al. 2003). This tension between the method 'as documented' and the method 'in use' has been described as a 'method usage tension' between 'method-in-concept' and 'method-in-action' (Lings and Lundell 2004).

If a method is to be accepted and used, method users must perceive it as useful in their development practice (Riemenschneider et al. 2002). In general, for someone to regard a piece of knowledge as valid and useful, it must be possible to rationalise that knowledge, i.e., it must make sense to developers and be possible to incorporate into their view of the world.[1] This is particularly true in the case of method

[1] Ethnomethodologists refer to this property of human behaviour as 'accountability' (Garfinkel 1967; Dourish 2001; Eriksén 2002); people require an account of the truth or usefulness of

B. Henderson-Sellers et al., *Situational Method Engineering*,
DOI 10.1007/978-3-642-41467-1_3, © Springer-Verlag Berlin Heidelberg 2014

prescriptions since method users are supposed to use these as a basis for future actions, and thus use the method description as a partial account of their own actions. Hence, the type of knowledge that is codified as method descriptions can best be understood as a form of 'action knowledge' (Goldkuhl 1999; Ågerfalk et al. 2006).

In order to understand better the rationalisation of system development methods, several different approaches have been investigated. Each examines the pros and cons of different alternatives and the impact of making specific choices. One approach is that of eliciting the requirements for the methodology using typical strategies from the requirements engineering literature (as discussed further in Sect. 6.2), perhaps using a goal-based approach (see the overview of several such goal-oriented requirements engineering (GORE) approaches by Lapouchnian 2005, and also one particular example in Sect. 6.4.2).

In this chapter, however, we focus on the concept of method rationale as developed in the literature (Oinas-Kukkonen 1996; Ågerfalk and Åhlgren 1999; Ågerfalk and Wistrand 2003; Rossi et al. 2004; Ågerfalk and Fitzgerald 2006). Method rationale concerns the reasons and arguments behind method prescriptions, and why method users (e.g., systems developers) choose to follow or adapt a method in a particular way. This argumentative dimension is an important but often neglected aspect of systems development methods (Ågerfalk and Åhlgren 1999; Ågerfalk and Wistrand 2003; Rossi et al. 2004). One way of approaching method rationale is to think of it as an instance of 'design rationale' (MacLean et al. 1991) that concerns the design of methods, rather than the design of computer systems (Rossi et al. 2004). This aspect of method rationale captures how a method may evolve and what options are considered during the design process, together with the argumentation leading to the final design (Rossi et al. 2004), thus providing insights into the process dimension of method development. A complementary view on method rationale is based on the notion of purposeful-rational action. This aspect of method rationale focusses on the underlying goals and values that make people choose options rationally (Ågerfalk and Åhlgren 1999; Ågerfalk and Wistrand 2003). It also provides an understanding of the overarching conceptual structure of a method's underlying philosophy.

3.1 Methods as Action Knowledge

A method description is a linguistic entity and an instance of what can be referred to as action knowledge (Goldkuhl 1999; Ågerfalk 2004). The term 'action knowledge' refers to theories, strategies and methods that govern people's action in social

something in order to accept it as valid. According to ethnomethodologist Harold Garfinkel (1967), actions that are accountable are 'visibly-rational-and-reportable-for-all-practical-purposes'.

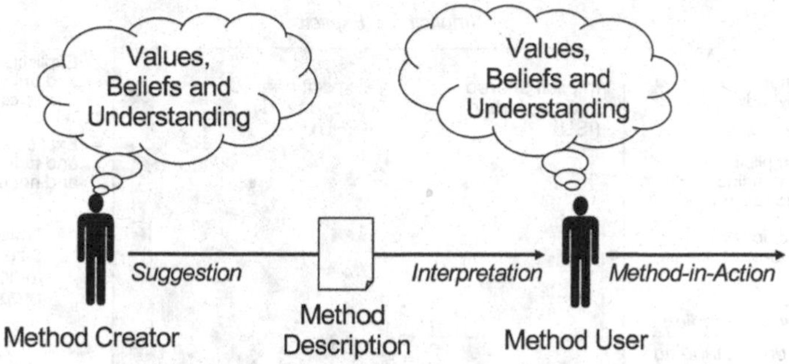

Fig. 3.1 Method descriptions in a communication context (after Ågerfalk and Fitzgerald 2006). Reprinted with permission of the publisher

practices (Goldkuhl 1999). The method description is a result of a social action[2] performed by the method creator directed towards intended users of the method. A method description should thus be understood as a suggestion by the method creator regarding how to perform a particular development task. This 'message' is received and interpreted by the method user, and acted upon by following or not following this suggestion (see Fig. 3.1), i.e., by transforming the method description (or 'formalised method') (Fitzgerald et al. 2002) or 'method-in-concept' (Lings and Lundell 2004) into a method-in-action. The 'method as message' is formulated based on the method creator's understanding of the development domain and on his or her fundamental values and beliefs. In such a team-based environment, shared understanding is critical—this may be implicit or explicit, some of which may be true and some false (Fig. 3.2). Similarly, the interpretation of a method by a method user is based on his or her understanding, beliefs and values.

It is possible to distinguish between five different aspects of action knowledge: a *subjective*, an *intersubjective*, a *linguistic*, an *action* and a *consequence* (Goldkuhl 1999; Ågerfalk 2004). Subjective knowledge is part of a human's 'subjective world' and is related to the notion of 'tacit knowledge' (Polanyi 1958). Subjective knowledge is shown as two 'clouds' in Fig. 3.1. This would be the type of knowledge that someone possesses after having interpreted and understood a method. Intersubjective knowledge is 'shared' by several people in the sense that they attach the same meaning to it and are able to meaningfully communicate (parts of) it among themselves. This could imply that the communicator (method creator) and interpreter (method user) agree on some of the elements of the 'clouds' in Fig. 3.1, and that they thus attach the same meaning to, at least parts of, a particular method. Linguistic knowledge is expressed as communicative signs, for example, as the written method description in Fig. 3.1. As the name suggests, action knowledge is expressed, or manifested, in action. This is the action aspect of knowledge

[2] According to sociologist Max Weber, social action is that human behaviour to which the actor attaches meaning and which takes into account the behaviour of others, and thereby is oriented in its course (Weber 1978).

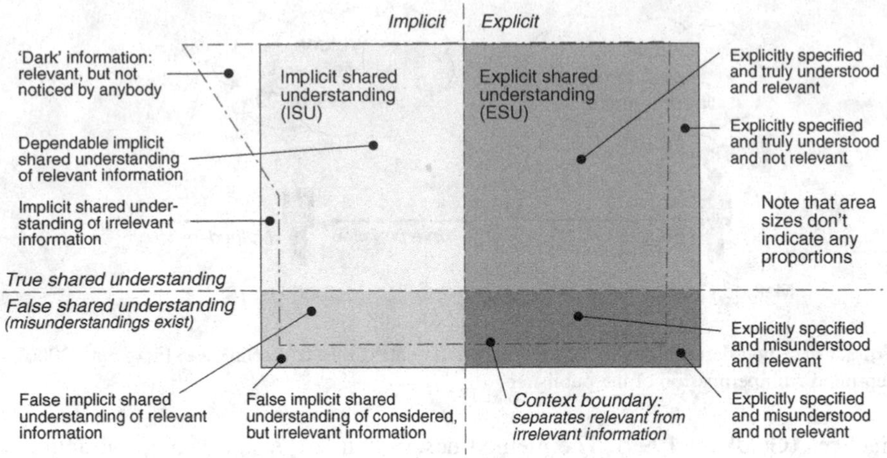

Fig. 3.2 Forms and categories of shared understanding: implicit versus explicit and true versus false. In addition, this diagram identifies the possibility of 'dark' information, i.e., information that no stakeholders are aware of (after Glinz and Fricker 2013)

or 'method-in-action'. Finally, traces of the action knowledge might be found in materialised artefacts, which constitute a consequence aspect of the knowledge. This would correspond to, for example, models and documentation produced as well as the actual software developed.

3.2 Method Stakeholders

When we think of software and systems development methods, what usually spring to mind are descriptions of ideal typical[3] software processes. Developers use such descriptions in practical situations to form what can be referred to as methods-in-action (Fitzgerald et al. 2002). Method engineering acknowledges that a method used in an actual project typically deviates significantly from the idealised process described in method handbooks and manuals (Iivari and Maansaari 1998; Nandhakumar and Avison 1999; Fitzgerald et al. 2003). Such adaptations of methods can be made more or less explicit and be based on more or less well-grounded decisions.

Methods need to be tailored to suit particular development situations (see also Chap. 7) since a method, as described in a method handbook, is a general

[3] Max Weber introduced the notion of an 'ideal type' as an analytic abstraction. Ideal types do not exist as such in real life, but are created so as to facilitate discussion. We use the term here to emphasise that a formalised method, expressed in a method description, never exists as such as a method-in-action. Rather, the method-in-action is an appropriation of an ideal typical formalised method to a particular context. At the same time, a formalised method is usually an ideal type created as an abstraction of existing 'good practice' (Ågerfalk and Åhlgren 1999).

description of an ideal process. Such an ideal type needs to be aligned with a number of situation-specific characteristics or ‘contingency factors’ (van Slooten and Hodes 1996; Karlsson and Ågerfalk 2004).

When a situational method has been devised, or ‘engineered’, and is used by developers in a practical situation, it is likely that different developers disagree with the method description and adapt the method further to suit their particular hands-on situational needs. As a consequence, the method-in-action will deviate not only from the ideal typical method but also from the situational method.

Altogether, this gives us three ‘abstraction levels’ of method: (a) the ideal typical method that abstracts details and addresses a generic problem space, (b) the situational method that takes project specifics into account and thus addresses a more concrete problem space and (c) the method-in-action, which is the manifestation of developers’ actual behaviour ‘following’ the method in a concrete situation. It follows from this that both the ideal typical method (a) and the situational method (b) exist as linguistic expressions of knowledge about the software development process (middle ‘level’ of Fig. 1.8). At the same time, the method-in-action represents an action aspect of that knowledge, which may of course be reconstructed and documented post facto (in addition to the way it is manifested in different developed artefacts along the way) (lower ‘level’ of Fig. 1.8).

Figure 3.3 offers an alternative visualisation of these three abstraction levels of method and corresponding actions and communication between the actors involved. In Fig. 3.3, the Method User of Fig. 3.1 has been specialised into the Method Configurator and the Developer (method creators and method configurators are collectively referred to as method engineers). Method configurators use the externalised knowledge expressed by the method creator in the ideal typical method as one basis for method configuration and subsequently communicate a situational method to developers. What is not shown in Fig. 3.3 is that method construction, method configuration and method-in-action rely on the actors’ interpretation of and assumptions about the development context. The developer ‘lives’ within this context and thus focusses his or her tailoring efforts on a specific problem space. The method creator, on the other hand, has to rely on an abstraction of an assumed development context and thus focusses on a generic problem space. Finally, the method configurator supposedly has some interaction with the actual development context, which provides a more concrete basis for configuring a situational method.

In both method construction and method configuration, the method communicated is a result of social action aimed towards other actors as a basis for their subsequent actions. This means that method adaptation, in construction, configuration and in-action, relies on the values, beliefs and understanding of the different actors involved—and this is where method rationale comes into play.

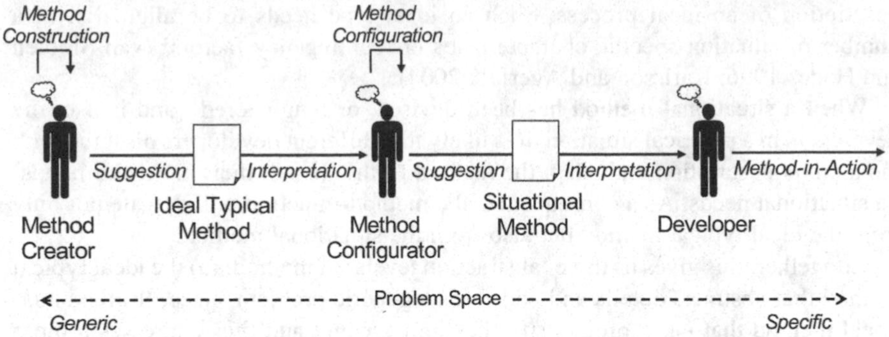

Fig. 3.3 Levels of method abstraction in methods as action knowledge (after Ågerfalk and Fitzgerald 2006). Reprinted with permission of the publisher

3.3 Method Rationale

Since methods represent knowledge, they also represent rationale. Therefore, a method user 'inherits' both the knowledge expressed by the method and the rationale of the method constructor (Ågerfalk and Åhlgren 1999). It can be argued that, regardless of the grounds, method tailoring (both during configuration and in-action) is rational from the point-of-view of the method user (Parnas and Clements 1986) who must decide whether to follow, adapt or omit a certain method or part thereof. Such adaptations are driven by the possibility of reaching 'rationality resonance' between the method and the method users (Stolterman and Russo 1997). That is, they are based on method users' efforts to understand and ultimately internalise the rationale expressed by a method description.

From a process perspective, method rationale can be thought of as having to do with the choices one makes in a process of design (Rossi et al. 2004). Thus, we can capture this kind of method rationale by paying attention to the questions or problematic situations that arise during method construction. For each question, we may find one or more options, i.e., 'solutions' to that question.

As an example, consider the construction of a method for analysing business processes. In order to graphically represent flows of activities in business processes, we may consider the option of modelling flows as links between activities, as in UML Activity Diagrams (OMG 2010). Another option would be to use a modelling language that allows for explicitly showing communicative and material results of each action and how those results are used as a basis for subsequent actions, as in VIBA[4] Action Diagrams (Ågerfalk and Goldkuhl 2001; Ågerfalk 2004). To help explore the pros and cons of each option, we may specify a number of criteria as guiding principles. Then, for each of the options, we can assess whether it

[4] Versatile Information and Business Analysis.

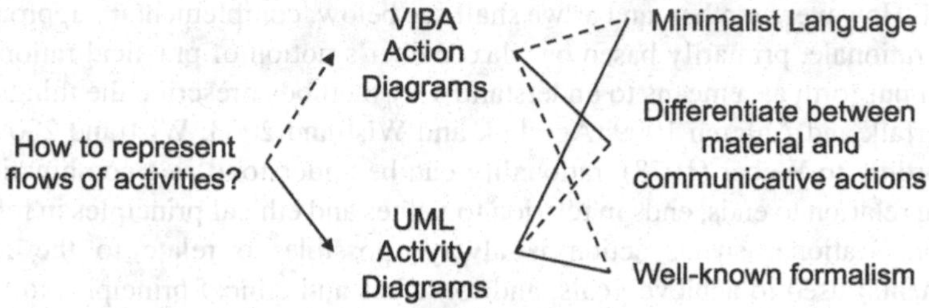

Fig. 3.4 Method rationale as choosing between options VIBA Action Diagrams and UML Activity Diagrams for modelling activity flows (based on the Question, Option, Criteria Model of Design Space Analysis (MacLean et al. 1991)). The solid arrow between 'situation' and 'option' indicates the preferred choice; a solid line between an option and a criterion indicates a positive impact, while a dashed line indicates a negative impact (after Ågerfalk and Fitzgerald 2006). Reprinted with permission of the publisher

contributes positively or negatively with respect to each criterion. Let us, for example, assume that one criterion (a) is that we want to create a visual modelling language (notation) with as few elements as possible in order to simplify models (a minimalist language). Another criterion (b) might be that we want a process model that is explicit regarding the difference between material actions and communicative actions[5] in order to focus developers' attention on social/communicative aspects and material/instrumental aspects, respectively (thus a more expressive language). Finally, a third criterion (c) might be that we would favour a well-known modelling formalism. The UML Activity Diagram option would have a positive impact on criteria a and c, and a negative impact on criterion b, while the VIBA Activity Diagram option would have a positive impact on criterion b, and a negative impact on criteria a and c. If we do not regard any of the criteria as being more important than any other, we would likely choose UML Activity Diagrams.

Figure 3.4 depicts this notion of method rationale as based on explicating the choices made throughout method construction. The specific example shown is the choice between VIBA Action Diagram versus UML Activity Diagram.

This model of method rationale is explicitly based on the Question, Option, Criteria Model of Design Space Analysis (MacLean et al. 1991). Other approaches to capture method rationale in terms of design decisions are, for example, IBIS/gIBIS[6] (Conklin and Begeman 1988; Conklin and Yakemovic 1991; Nguyen and Swatman 2000; Conklin et al. 2003; Rooksby et al. 2006) and REMAP[7] (Ramesh and Dhar 1992). The process-oriented view of method rationale captured by these approaches is important, especially when acknowledging method engineering as a continuous evolutionary process (Rossi et al. 2004) as will be discussed below in

[5] Material actions are actions that produce material results, such as painting a wall, while communicative actions result in social obligations, such as a promise to paint a wall in the future. The latter thus corresponds to what Searle (1969) termed 'speech act'.

[6] Issue Based Information Systems.

[7] REpresentation and MAintenance of Process knowledge.

Sect. 3.4. However, another, and as we shall see below, complementary approach to method rationale, primarily based on Max Weber's notion of practical rationality, has been put forth as a means to understand why methods prescribe the things they do (Ågerfalk and Åhlgren 1999; Ågerfalk and Wistrand 2003; Wistrand 2009).

According to Weber (1978), rationality can be understood as a combination of means in relation to ends, ends in relation to values and ethical principles in relation to action. Rational social action is always possible to relate to the means (instruments) used to achieve goals, and to values and ethical principles to which an action conforms. Thus, we cannot judge whether or not means and ends are rational without considering the value base upon which we consider the possibilities.

In this view of method rationale, all fragments or components of a method are related to one or more goals (see also Sect. 6.4 on goal-based method construction techniques). If a fragment is proposed as part of a method, it should have at least one reason to be there. We refer to this as the goal rationale of a method. Each goal is, in turn, related to one or more values. If a goal is proposed as the argument for a method fragment, it too should have at least one reason to be included. We refer to this as the value rationale of a method. Figure 3.5 depicts this notion of method rationale, which also includes the idea that goals and values are related to other goals and values in networks of achievements and contradictions. The diagram also includes the actor who subscribes to a particular rationale. Using the terminology introduced above, an actor could be a method creator, a method configurator or a method user.

Each goal is anchored in the method creator's values (Goldkuhl et al. 1998; Ågerfalk 2006; Ågerfalk and Fitzgerald 2006) and goals and values form the essence of the perspective (Goldkuhl et al. 1998) or philosophy (Fitzgerald et al. 2002) of an Information Systems Development Methods (ISDM). Method rationale makes it possible to address the goals that are essential to reaching specific project objectives. Prescribed actions and artefacts, on the other hand, are the means to achieving something (such as the goals). Method rationale can therefore prevent developers from losing sight of that ultimate result and can help them find alternative ways forward. This was clearly evident in Karlsson and Ågerfalk's (2009a) study of method configuration in an agile context and Karlsson's (2013) longitudinal study of the use of method rationale in method configuration.

However, when defining method components in practical SME, Karlsson and Ågerfalk (2009b) suggest restricting the modelling of method rationale to goals only. This suggestion is purely pragmatic and based on the empirical finding that method engineers and developers tend to reason about the purpose of certain method components and often omit discussion of values. It is also important to note that for practical reasons we are not searching for objective goal statements but rather for pragmatic and situated statements that describe the use and effects of method components.

To illustrate how the concepts of method rationale fit together, we will return to the example introduced above. Assume we have a model following Fig. 3.5 populated as follows (assuming that the classes in the model can be represented

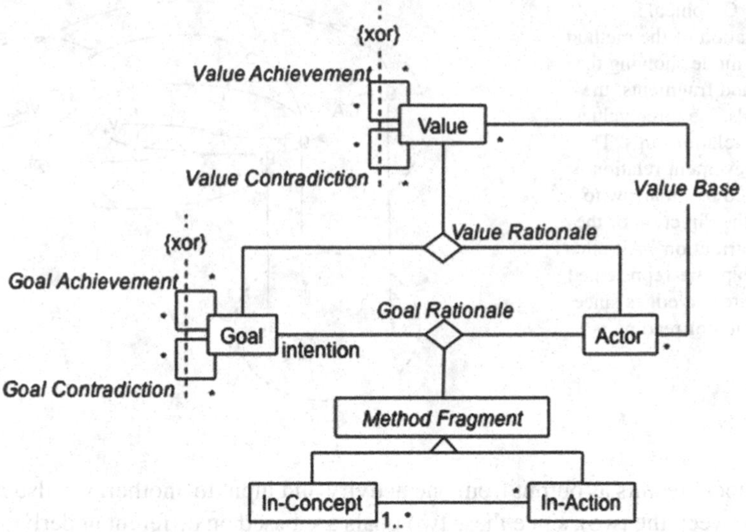

Fig. 3.5 Method rationale as consisting of interrelated goals and values as arguments for method fragments (after Ågerfalk 2006)

as sets and associations as relations between sets, i.e., as sets of pairs with elements from the two related sets). Note that we assume that the actors involved are the creators of the respective fragments, so these are not included in the analysis. This could easily be done and can be used as an additional analytic tool to verify consistency within and across methods with respect to underlying values and how these are reflected in particular method fragments.

A set of method fragments F = {f_1: Representation of the class concept; f_2: Representation of the activity link concept; f_3: Representation of the action result concept}; A set of goals G = {g_1: Classes are represented in the model; g_2: Activity links are represented in the model; g_3: Activity results are represented in the model}; A set of values V = {v_1: Model only information aspects; v_2: Minimalist design of modelling language; v_3: Focus on instrumental v. communicative; v_4: Use well-known formalisms}; Goal rationale $R_G = \{(f_1, g_1), (f_2, g_2), (f_3, g_3)\}$; Value rationale $R_V = \{(g_1, v_2), (g_1, v_3), (g_1, v_4), (g_2, v_1), (g_2, v_2), (g_2, v_4), (g_3, v_3)\}$; Goal achievement $GA = \{(g_3, g_2)\}$; Value contradiction $VC = \{(v_1, v_3)\}$; $VA = GC = \emptyset$.

A perhaps more illustrative graphical representation of the model is shown in Fig. 3.6. If we view each method fragment in the model as possible options to consider, then the goals and values can be compared with the criteria in a structured way. Given that we know that what we want to describe in our notation is a flow of activities (or more precisely the links between activities), we can disregard f_1 outright, since its only goal is not related to what we are trying to achieve. When considering f_2 and f_3, we notice that each is related to a separate goal. However, since there is a goal achievement link from g_3 to g_2, we understand that both f_2 and f_3 would help satisfy the goal of representing visually a link between two activities

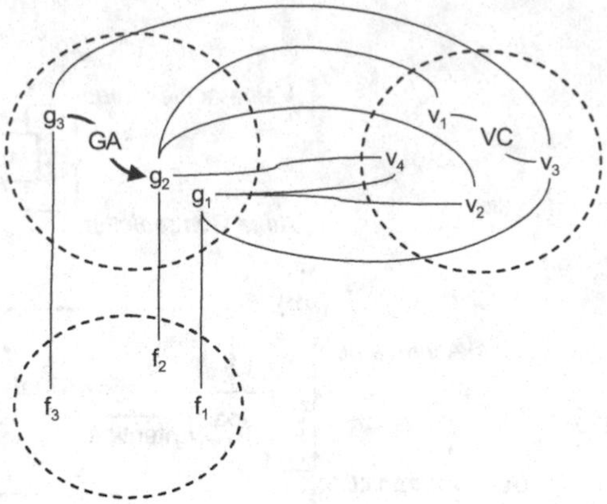

Fig. 3.6 Graphical representation of the method rationale mode showing the tree method fragments, the three goals, the three values and their relationships. The goal achievement relation is represented by an arrow to indicate the direction of the 'goal contribution'. All other relationships are represented by non-directed edges since the direction of reading is arbitrary

(if we model results as output from one activity and input to another, we also model a link between the two), since these two goals are based on different underlying and contradictory values. Since g_2 is related to v_1, and g_3 to v_3, we must choose the goal that best matches our own value base. This could and should be expressed by the criteria we use. If, for example, we believe that it is important to direct attention to instrumental versus communicative aspects (v_3), then we should choose g_3 and consequently f_3. If, on the other hand, we are only concerned with modelling information flows, then g_2 and consequently f_2 would be the option to choose.

Empirical observations show that the method component's overall goals and artefacts are important during method configuration (Karlsson and Ågerfalk 2004) and hence they are part of the interface. An artefact, as discussed above, is designated as an input and/or a deliverable (output). This is necessary in order to deal with the three fundamental actions that can be performed on an artefact: create, update or delete. In cases where an artefact is only created by a method component it is classified as a deliverable. If the artefact can be updated by the same method component, it is also classified as an input. Furthermore, a component can have one or more input artefacts, but has only one deliverable (which thus defines the 'layer of granularity' of the component).

The concept of method rationale described above applies to both construction of methods and refinement of methods-in-action (Rossi et al. 2004). Since method descriptions are means of communicating knowledge between method creators and method users, it could be used as a bridge between the two and thus as an important tool in achieving rationality resonance, as discussed above.

From the earlier example in this section, we can see that method rationale is related to both the choices we make during method construction and to the goals and values that underpin the method constructs we choose among. The example used above was at a very detailed level, focussing on rationale in relation to method fragments at the concept layer of granularity. The same kind of analysis could be performed at any layer of granularity and may consider both process and product fragments (i.e., both activities and deliverables). As an example, let us consider the use of agile methods for globally distributed software development. This may seem counter-intuitive in many ways. One example is that agile methods usually assume that the development team is co-located with an on-site customer present at all time (Beck 2000). By analysing the reasons behind this method prescription (i.e., the suggestion by the method creator), we may find that we can operationalise the intended goals of co-location (such as increased informal communication) into other method prescriptions, say utilising more advanced communication technologies. In this way, we could make sure that the method rationale of this particular aspect of an agile method is transferred into the rationale of a method tailored for globally distributed development. Thus, we may be able to adhere to agile values even if the final method does look quite different from the original method. That is to say, the principles espoused by the method creators may be logically achieved to the extent that they are relevant in the particular context of the final situational method.

It is important to see that method rationale is present at all three levels of method abstraction (Fig. 3.3): ideal typical, situational and in-action. At the ideal typical level, method rationale can be used to express the method creator's intentions, goals, values and choices. This serves as a basis for method configurators (i.e., those who tailor a situational method) and developers in understanding the method and how to tailor it to best advantage. In the communication between configurator and developer, method rationale would also express why certain adaptations were made when configuring the situational method. If we understand different developers' personal rationale, we might be able to better configure or assemble situational methods.

Combining the two aspects of method rationale gives us a structured approach to using method rationale both as a tool to express and document a method's rationale, and as a tool to analyse method rationale as basis for method construction, assembly, configuration and use.

3.4 Evolutionary Method Engineering

Method engineering involves a learning process in which the current level of expertise and the situation influence the outcomes (Hughes and Reviron 1996). Thus, any organisation that develops systems not only delivers them but also learns how to perform system development and to mobilise associated knowledge (methods), but also improves their development capabilities (learning by doing). The development organisation builds its knowledge about how its methods work in certain development situations. These experiences complement the codified method knowledge and should lead into better applications of the method in the future. Checkland (1981) was an early advocate of a learning-based approach to method development through cyclical action research. In this view, evolutionary method engineering is seen as a continuous refining process. However, as Lyytinen and Robey point out (1999) large parts of this experience are lost since the experiences are seldom collected and interpreted—thus emphasising the importance of retrospectives (Kerth 2001).

Methods can never gather all previous knowledge and anticipate all future development situations. Therefore, it is fruitful to view methods from an organisational learning perspective. This perspective analyses system development situations and the role of methods through 'reflection-in-action' (Schön 1983). In Schön's view, a large part of a designer's knowledge of ISD is a result of his or her reflections of the situation, rather than being determined by the methods. In real life, the method-in-action is adapted and interpreted by designers based on their understanding of the events and contingencies. At the same time the current version of the method is a result of those reflections so that designers' tacit understandings are made explicit so that they can be made understandable to others (Nonaka 1994).

Rossi et al. (2004) claimed that reflection-in-action and technical-rationality are complementary in systems development and both explicit and tacit knowledge are needed to develop systems. Thus, a good method should adapt to a situation and provide cognitive frames and norms that designers can use, but also challenges the use of their experiential knowledge (Argyris and Schön 1978). Such a learning view has been called evolutionary method engineering (Tolvanen 1998). Because evolutionary SME aims to continually improve ISD methods it can be regarded as a learning process in which individuals (Schön 1983), communities and organisations (Nonaka 1994) create, memorise and share knowledge about system development through codifying it to methods. This double loop learning leads to continuous modification and augmentation of an organisation's methods. In evolutionary ME, method evolution is seen to be necessary since organisations have to deal with different method versions for different implementation targets and development contexts (as for example with UML (OMG 2010)).

Two different types of method evolution have been identified (Rossi et al. 2004): changes to methods reflecting general requirements of changed technical and business needs, and those relevant to the ISD situation at hand. The former relates to the general genealogy of methodical knowledge within the method developer and user community, and the latter with how these general evolutions are adapted into local situations and affect development practices. We can anticipate that user-centred method engineering calls for extensive local modifications and possibilities for evolutionary variants of methods.

3.5 Method-User-Centred Method Engineering[8]

A problem in situational method engineering, similar to software and systems engineering, is that requirements, here method requirements, need to be specified and managed. Evolutionary method engineering addresses the management problem by allowing method requirements to evolve over time. The initial specification

[8] We acknowledge contributions of Dr. Fredrik Karlsson to this section.

of method requirements calls for specific techniques. One such technique, as partly explored in relation to the MC Sandbox tool, has been borrowed from user-centred design and termed method-user-centred method engineering (Karlsson and Ågerfalk 2012). These authors provide extensive discussion about method-user-centred method engineering along with a case study on the use of these ideas as implemented in MC Sandbox (see also Sect. 7.3.2).

3.5.1 Method Requirements

Methods exist for the purpose of supporting project members during development projects. These people are users of the method in the same sense that end-users are users of software. Hence, method users impose requirements on methods in much the same way that end-users have requirements on information systems. The actual content of requirements engineering processes varies, although often the core activities include elicitation of problems and solutions, negotiation of problems to solve and solutions to adopt as well as commitment to implement the selected solutions. The requirements are developed during these activities and a number of challenges are evident.

Firstly, method requirements are not always clear, neither to the method engineer nor to the method user—partly because the systems development task is not always well understood, partly because the project members' method varies. The first problem indicates dependencies between systems development and method engineering, which is why we discuss situational methods in the first place. These dependencies are not always possible to identify completely initially. Rather they become visible incrementally, which is also acknowledged in incremental method engineering as discussed in Chap. 7. The second problem illustrates the necessity to improve the communication about what is possible to achieve and reasonable to expect from the method at hand. Method users will learn about the possibilities offered by the method and discover new requirements as a project progresses.

Secondly, there is not just one set of requirements, since requirements are by nature emergent and constantly negotiated and renegotiated (Chakraborty et al. 2010; Holmström and Sawyer 2011). Different stakeholders with different interests typically bring their own set of requirements to the table. Klein and Hirschheim (2001) emphasise the importance that these different interests are 'understood and debated'. Depending on the selection of method users, the method requirements are therefore likely to be different. Developing a shared understanding is therefore of prime importance (see earlier discussion of Fig. 3.2).

It is also true that not all stakeholders have the same power and possibility to influence the requirements process (Coughlan et al. 2003). In any case, these different sets of requirements can of course be (at least partly) conflicting. In some cases, apparent conflicts are based on misunderstandings that can be solved through clarification. Conflicts can also arise due to differences in perspectives and what is perceived as important during the project. Stakeholders may not share the same value base, as discussed in Sect. 3.3 above.

Finally, project resources may not allow for all requirements to be considered. A situational method will thus only solve stakeholders' needs and problems to a certain degree. Thus, the method requirements process must include ways to handle method requirements conflicts and requirements viewed as negotiated commitments to be fulfilled during the project.

3.5.2 Why Method-User-Centred?

In software and systems engineering, end-users have to conceptualise, explicate and negotiate their requirements; creativity has to be stimulated in that process (Maiden et al. 2004). Malcolm (2001) suggests that user-centred approaches are especially appropriate when addressing tacit, semi-tacit and future systems knowledge. Arguably, mental models and tacit knowledge are as crucial to successful method engineering as to systems design. Stolterman (1992) addressed the importance of understanding the method creators' mental model of their created method. Stolterman and Russo (1997) use the terms public and private rationality for this purpose. Public rationality is the intersubjective understanding of prescribed actions and results, and about why a specific part of a method is prescribed. This is therefore what we refer to as method rationale in this book. Private rationality is expressed 'in the skills and in the professional ethical and aesthetic judgments' of a person (Stolterman and Russo 1997). The method creator has to influence not only public rationality but also the private rationality of the method user. Otherwise, method users may not be able to use the method to its fullest potential. Consequently, it is important to involve method users early when crafting a situational method. Just as when involving end-users early in systems development, this involvement should focus on method-user-centred aspects.

3.5.3 Bringing User-Centred Ideas to Situational Method Engineering

Gould and Lewis (1985) proposed three principles that are included in what we today call user-centred design: (1) early focus on users and tasks, (2) empirical measurement and (3) iterative design. According to Cato (2001), it is possible to conceptually view user-centred design as a triad: the user, the use and the information. This triad focusses on who is using the technology, how technology is used and what is required to support that use. Translated into situational method engineering, we should thus focus on who the method users are as a team and these users' needs during a project (i.e., what kinds of challenges are found in the project), and how methods are used in the organisation. Furthermore, designing a situational method is an iterative process where the method is continuously evaluated and, if necessary, changed. Although a user-centred approach shifts the emphasis in software development from technology to people, Constantine and Lockwood (1999) stress that it should be more than this—that we should focus on *usage* rather than user. In their usage-centred design (UCD) approach (Constantine 1996), they advocate five key elements:

- Pragmatic design guidelines
- Model-driven design process
- Organised development activities
- Iterative improvement
- Measures of quality.

Storyboarding (Higgins 1995) and prototyping (Boar 1984) are techniques frequently used in user-centred approaches to create a feel for a proposed solution (e.g., Carroll 1994; Hall 2001) and to visualise commitments made. The idea is to make the design more tangible by letting use-scenarios and visualisations drive the design process. Visualisation often starts with low-fi prototypes, which make it possible to identify potential problems early and at a low cost (Rettig 1994). A paper-based storyboard typically captures the structure, possible navigation through the information system, information provided by the system and by the user and the result of users' actions (Cato 2001).

Nickols (1993) emphasises that a prototype is a working model that is subject to negotiation. It therefore does not have to be complete in terms of functionality. Low-fi and high-fi prototypes differ in the sophistication of their technical implementation and the cost of change. Low-fi prototypes implement less technical complexity and are hence less expensive to change. They also implement less functionality. High-fi prototypes, on the other hand, typically implement more complex functionality and are therefore more accurate but also more costly to change.

Transferring these basic ideas to situational method engineering shows that visualising the method design and its parts is essential to SME. Prototyping also involves a continuous evolution of the prototype and its design. Naumann and Jenkins (1982) present prototyping as consisting of four activities: identify basic requirements, develop a working prototype, implement and use and revise and enhance. The two latter activities are performed iteratively, somewhat similar to evolutionary method engineering (Sect. 3.4) and scenario-based approaches (Rolland et al. 1999). It is not surprising, then, that the implementation of evolutionary method engineering in a tool like MetaEdit+ (Sect. 7.3.1) shares several characteristics with high-fi prototyping. Consequently, evolutionary method engineering could be complemented with an approach where the method users are involved more directly in the initial tailoring of the method. However, this may be difficult to achieve since method engineering tends to be a detailed process, especially if high-fi prototypes, such as runtime CASE-tool implementations of methods, are brought into the equation.

As a complement, it may therefore be fruitful to use also low-fi prototypes and storyboarding in situational method engineering as suggested by Karlsson and Ågerfalk (2012) and implemented using MC Sandbox as described in Sect. 7.3.2. This approach combines the idea of visualising the situational method as a storyboard by reducing the amount of detail. Clearly, that approach shares similarities with the map construction approach presented by Rolland et al. (1999)—see

Chap. 4. The focus of method-user-centred method configuration is on what method parts add value to the development project and its members as a team. Hence, it moves away from the use of complex meta languages when working closely with method users, similarly to the way prototypes are used in discussions with end-users instead of complex diagrams and source codes. The underlying idea is facilitate method users to formulate their requirements, debate them as a team and explicate their commitments. Essentially, the use of prototyping and storyboarding facilitates the negotiation of several mental models and makes implications tangible. The prototyping tool can at the same time act as a documentation tool during elicitation and negotiation of method requirements.

Altogether, these ideas affect the concepts, the models and the meta methods that we use in situational method engineering. Even more importantly, they affect the tools that we use in the process. Essentially, tools have to support the simplification of method modules to emulate a low-fi prototype. Still, they must provide the information needed for discussing and negotiating method support and potential results of different choices. MC Sandbox, as described in Sect. 7.3, is explicitly designed to deal with these constraints but certainly other tools can be used to achieve similar effects.

3.6 Summary

This chapter has highlighted that situational method engineering is a social process that needs to pay attention to human factors such as values, attitudes and knowledge. Method rationale has been presented as a way to understand how methods encapsulate rationality and how different stakeholders may perceive a method differently. Evolutionary method engineering and method-user-centred method engineering were introduced as two current approaches that aim to take human and social aspects of SME into account by acknowledging that method requirements are constantly renegotiated and evolving. The two approaches have been shown to be complementary and could be used together in order to properly address the social aspects of SME in practice.

Formal Descriptions 4

Summary of What We Will Learn in Chapter 4

- A mathematical description of metamodels
- The value of metamodels in SME
- Metamodel-based standards, especially ISO/IEC 24744, to support SME
- The value of ontologies and the difference between domain ontologies and foundational ontologies
- Process models for method construction, especially the MAP formalism

In this chapter, we look at formal ways of addressing situational method engineering, method parts (fragments, chunks, components, etc.) and method construction. In Sect. 4.1 we discuss various metamodelling approaches at a variety of scales, from full method to single fragment descriptions. Section 4.2 is a brief discussion on ontologies and the use proposed for these in SME. In Sect. 4.3, in contrast to the static models of Sect. 4.1, we outline several formal descriptions of ways of constructing methods, while in Sect. 4.4 we comment on a few other formal approaches.

4.1 Metamodels for SME

Since, as we have noted, a metamodel is a 'model of models' (Sect. 1.4.3), in our SME context, those models are in fact methodologies or methods (we use the terms synonymously). They are in fact prescriptive or forward-looking models that represent any possible methodology that can be created. We will adopt here the definition of methodology that was proposed and justified by Gonzalez-Perez and Henderson-Sellers (2006a): a methodology is *a specification of the process to follow and the work products to be generated, plus consideration of the people and tools involved, during a software development effort*. Gonzalez-Perez and

B. Henderson-Sellers et al., *Situational Method Engineering*,
DOI 10.1007/978-3-642-41467-1_4,

Henderson-Sellers (2007) note that "since a methodology needs to consider both process and product aspects, and a methodology metamodel must be able to represent any possible relevant methodology, then process and product aspects must be integrated within the metamodel (Atkinson and Kühne 2001b; Rolland 2005)".

For SME, we take this grammatical analogy and use it to state that "a software development process defines the actions to be performed when developing software, but these actions are meaningless without a detailed definition of the producers that execute the actions and the products that are involved" (Gonzalez-Perez and Henderson-Sellers 2007). In other words, a methodology that solely describes work products is inadequate unless some process for creation and utilisation is also included. [This is, by the way, why UML is not a methodology but only a notation.] However, as we shall see later, it is certainly possible to focus on the work products as the main element in a software development process such that the method engineer, in creating a methodology, starts with the last work product and chains backwards asking, successively and iteratively "What task is needed to create this work product?" and "What work product(s) need to exist before I can execute this task?" (Gonzalez-Perez and Henderson-Sellers 2008a).

4.1.1 Background and History

Here, we build on the basic ideas of metamodels and ontologies in Sect. 1.4 by evaluating their application to a number of specific metamodels in the literature, bearing in mind the type of method element (Sects. 2.1–2.4), the motivations and viewpoints of the authors (Sect. 2.5) and the granularity (Sects. 2.6 and 8.3).

These ideas are summarised in Fig. 4.1, which shows such a stacking (over only three levels) in the horizontal direction: from metamodel to process model and then to process model instance. The second dimension in this figure is said to be that of 'individualisation' (vertical): from domain-specificity to organisational scale to specific projects. [We also note but without discussion here that the former architecture (Fig. 1.11) has been subject to much criticism recently especially in the context of what is called ontological versus linguistic metamodelling (e.g., Bézivin and Lemesle 1998; Bézivin and Gerbé 2001; Atkinson and Kühne 2001b; Seidewitz 2003; Gonzalez-Perez and Henderson-Sellers 2006a, 2007, 2008b; Gašević et al. 2007; Laarman and Kurtev 2010; Atkinson et al. 2010; Eriksson et al. 2013).]

Metamodels thus provide a set of rules for defining models. They are the modelling language (for a design model or for a methodology), linked closely to ideas of ontology (e.g., Henderson-Sellers 2011b). The activity of creating that metamodel is called metamodelling (Fig. 4.2). As a process, metamodelling has much in common with modelling, since both represent some SUS (system under study). Thus, the heuristics of modelling are equally applicable to metamodelling (e.g., Hoppenbrouwers et al. 2005).

The history of the utilisation of metamodels and metamodelling in SME was first outlined by Tolvanen (1998). He reported on the use of models using

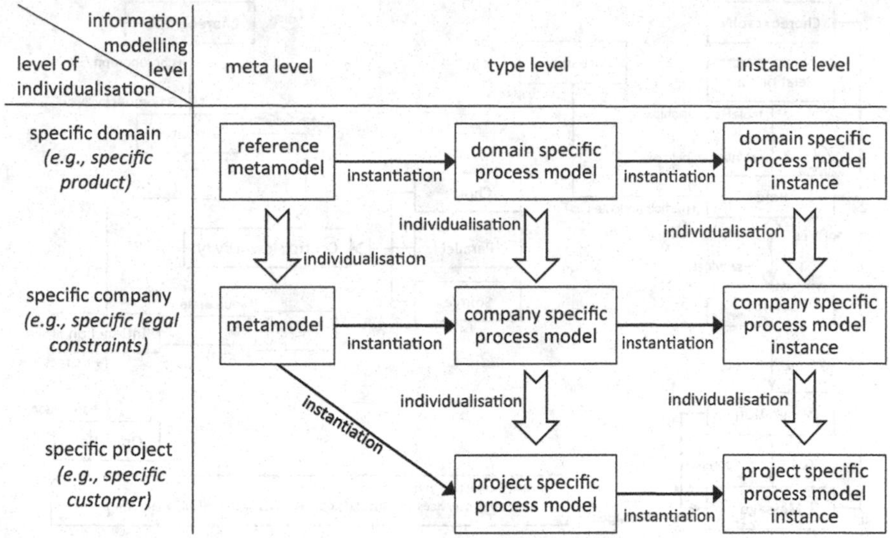

Fig. 4.1 Levels of modelling (Rupprecht et al., figure 1, 2000) (With kind permission of Springer Science + Business Media)

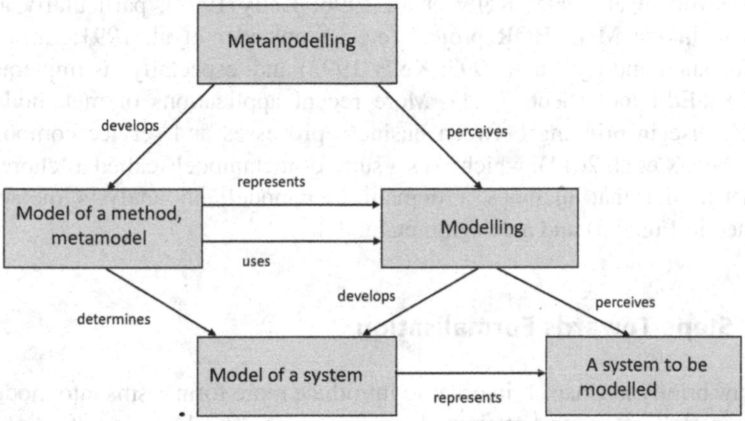

Fig. 4.2 Relationship between modelling and metamodelling (after Brinkkemper 1990)

Entity-Relationship (ER) and NIAM[1] notations by, for instance, Smolander (1990) and ter Hofstede et al. (1993). Extending the ER model by the addition of the role concept (Welke 1988; Smolander 1992) resulted in the Object-Property-Relationship-Role (OPRR) model. A further extension to GOPRR (the 'G' standing for graph) has been used extensively (e.g., Tolvanen et al. 1993; Araujo and Rossi

[1] Nijssen's Information Analysis Methodology (later renamed Natural language Information Analysis Method).

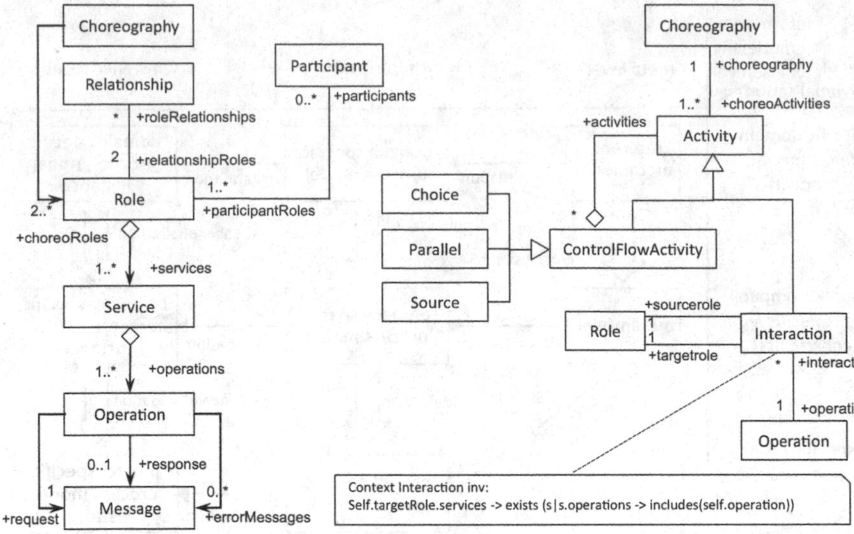

Fig. 4.3 The analysis metamodel of Cortez Cornax et al. (figure 5, 2011) (With kind permission of Springer Science + Business Media)

1993; Marttiin et al. 1995; Kelly et al. 1996; Kelly 1997), particularly as the metamodel in the MetaPHOR project (e.g., Smolander et al. 1991; Smolander 1992; Tolvanen and Lyytinen 1993; Kelly 1993) and, especially, as implemented in the MetaEdit tool (Sect. 7.3.1). More recent applications of metamodelling include its use in bridging between business processes and service composition (Cortes Cornax et al. 2011), which uses a suite of metamodels called a 'choreography' metamodel that includes a domain metamodel, an analysis metamodel (illustrated in Fig. 4.3) and a design metamodel.

4.1.2 Steps Towards Formalisation

As we saw briefly in Chap. 1, in order to introduce more formalisms into modelling and metamodelling, several attempts have been made to add rules to the informal multilayering shown in Fig. 1.8. One description, briefly introduced in Chap. 1 and widely adopted, is that of four-level (MOF[2]) architecture shown in Fig. 1.11. The levels are defined in terms of the so-called strict metamodelling (Atkinson 1997, 1999) in which the only relationship permitted between layers is that of 'instance-of' and, at the same time, there can be no 'instance-of' relationships *within* any single layer. In OMG parlance, the layers are known as Mx layers. In strict metamodelling, then, we can say that an entity (e.g., class) in the lower layer (Mx) is an instance of some entity (class) in the Mx+1 layer such that the

[2] Meta object facility.

relationship is, ideally, a type–instance relationship exemplified in the 'classification' relationship. Consequently, one could argue (e.g., Flatscher 2002) that the higher level entity defines the intension and the lower level entity the extension. This is also borne out by the recent analysis, using speech act theory, of Eriksson et al. (2013).

This four-level structure of Fig. 1.11 has many benefits and works well for modelling languages like the UML (for which it was after all initially developed) but has also created many problems, especially (1) when process modelling and particularly enactment is introduced—as we discuss below and/or (2) when it is realised that this structure, so well aimed at creating modelling languages—and hence often called 'linguistic metamodelling'—is also used for modelling with a more ontological focus. While this 'debate' of ontological versus linguistic metamodelling is well outside the scope of this book (we refer you to the discussions in Gonzalez-Perez and Henderson-Sellers 2008b and in Henderson-Sellers et al. 2013 and Eriksson et al. 2013; as well as the introduction of mathematical representations in Henderson-Sellers 2012), its resolution will have some impact on SME purely as a consequence of the need for all elements of SME to have a metamodelling underpinning in order to ensure its formal specification (see also discussion in Sect. 4.1.3). Part of that formalisation debate involves the use of mathematical set theory and/or category theory (e.g., Whitmire 1997) to represent in a formal manner aspects of metamodelling and hence of SME.

The current ideas underpinning metamodelling are an extension of type–instance modelling. Thus, in modelling we typically model a set of instances by the class to which the instances belong. This class defines the type. An example is that of the BankAccount type/class with instances of Brian'sAccount; Jolita'sAccount and Pär'sAccount. If we now consider the plethora of classes, like BankAccount within the class model, then we can say, by analogy, that these are all instances belonging to some set, which becomes a type when we add the intensional definition for the concept (Kühne 2006; Eriksson et al. 2013). That type is the Class with instances such as BankAccount class, the Bank class and the Customer class. In other words, we have created another type–instance relationship (Fig. 4.4). If we align this idea with the architecture of Fig. 1.11, then we can say that the Class class belongs to the M2 level, the BankAccount class to M1 and Brian'sAccount to M0. Alternatively, if we use the architecture of Fig. 1.14, then we can similarly state that the Class class belongs to the Metamodel domain, the BankAccount class to the Method domain and Brian'sAccount to the Endeavour domain. When we use these types of architectures in SME, the M0/Endeavour domain becomes more important than in creating design models—as we might do using UML. In that case, we need to use the version of the OMG architecture shown in Fig. 4.5 or the ISO architecture of Fig. 1.14.

While the type–instance relationship is useful across two layers, when extended to three layers there is a problem since we need to have all the attributes standardised in the meta-level declaration of the class to which they belong but only need to allocate values to some of them at the M1/Method domain leaving others to have individual values allocated in the method enactment—in the

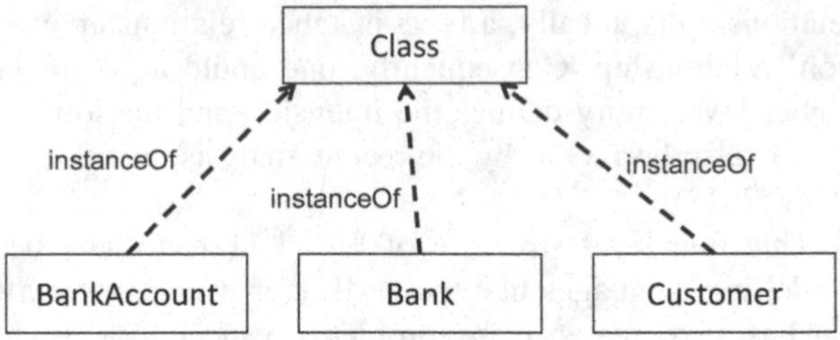

Fig. 4.4 Example of a type and some of its instances

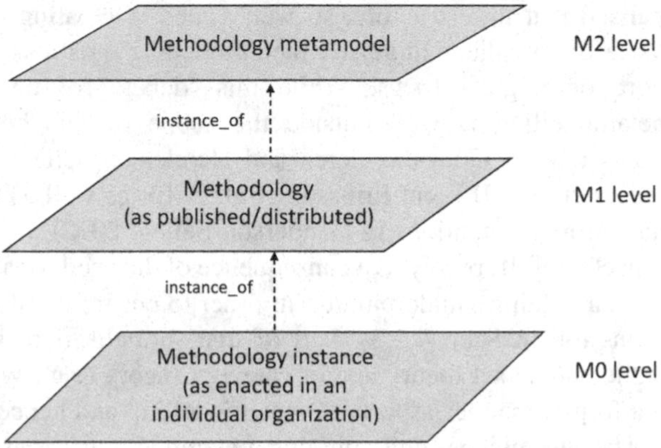

Fig. 4.5 OMG's multi-level hierarchy—the bottom three layers adopted for process and method(ology) (after Henderson-Sellers and Ralyte 2010)

Endeavour domain. This is problematic for SME because an instance of a type cannot be further instantiated (Gonzalez-Perez and Henderson-Sellers 2007) because instantiation is not transitive and, secondly, because an instance must, by definition, refer to an individual. Since instantiation needs a collection of some sort (e.g., set) from which to select an individual, an individual and a set cannot be used interchangeably (Fig. 4.6). This is especially important for methodology modelling—see Fig. 4.5 in which the Mx levels have been relabelled accordingly. The problem occurs here because methodologies are enacted on real projects and hence the 'M0' level becomes of prime importance. This M0 level represents the 'personalisation' or 'customisation' of a process model (or methodology) to a specific project and the performance of that project in real time (Fig. 1.8). There are many attributes of process elements that need to be stated in the metamodel (M2) but not given values until M0. This is not possible in the architecture of Fig. 4.5 since anything defined at level Mx MUST be given a value at the level below, i.e., Mx−1. The inability of the OMG architecture to support enactment is the biggest obstacle to its wider adoption in the process-focussed communities of software developers and, in particular, to situational method engineers.

Recognising that for SME the four-layer architecture of Fig. 1.11 as modified for processes (Fig. 4.5) is unhelpful (as discussed above), we turn instead to the more recent architecture shown in Fig. 1.14 and developed originally as part of the Australian Standard AS4651 (2004) and then used in the ISO/IEC Software Engineering Metamodel for Development Methodologies, SEMDM (ISO/IEC 2007, 2010a).

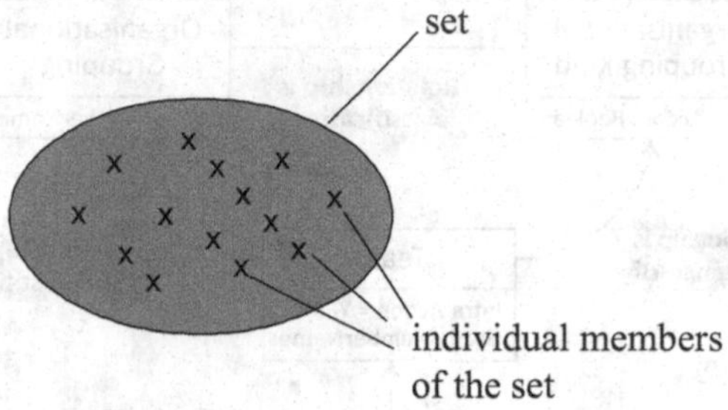

Fig. 4.6 A set is a collection of individual elements (called members). A set S is defined by $S = \{s_i\}$, $i = 1$ to n (after Henderson-Sellers, figure 6, 2011a) (With kind permission of Springer Science + Business Media)

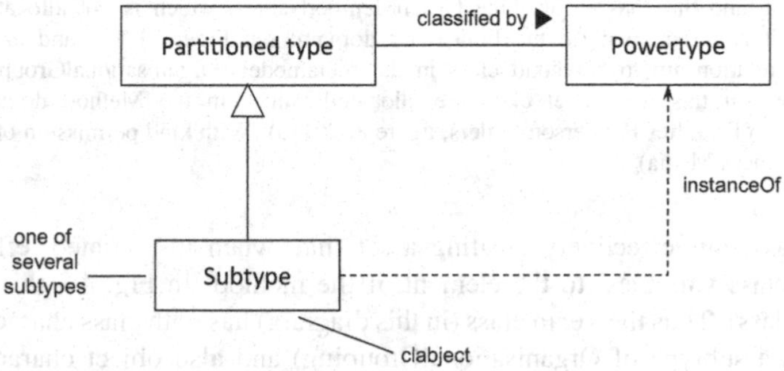

Fig. 4.7 Powertypes (after Henderson-Sellers, figure 2.12, 2012) (With kind permission of Springer Science + Business Media)

As we saw in Chap. 1, rather than insisting on the use of strict metamodelling to define the layers of interest, this approach focusses on what actually happens in an industrial software development environment, i.e., people work on projects (the Endeavour domain in Fig. 1.14), those projects utilise standards, tools, methods, etc. and these are described in the Method domain and, finally, those Method domain entities must be defined—this is done in the Metamodel domain. The transmission of attributes from the standardisation in the Metamodel domain through to the Endeavour domain where they are given values is accomplished by the use of powertypes (Odell 1994) following the original proposals of Gonzalez-Perez and Henderson-Sellers (2006a). A powertype is a type whose instances are subtypes of a second type—the partitioned type (Fig. 4.7).

Powertypes in the metamodel are implemented as a powertype pattern (Henderson-Sellers and Gonzalez-Perez 2005c) that consists of a class which will be the supertype for a specialisation relationship creating a Method domain class that is then instantiated to the Endeavour domain (thus supporting directly the enactment of the method) together with a class that represents the 'kind' of thing being formalised. This 'Kind' class provides a partitioning rule for the Metamodel

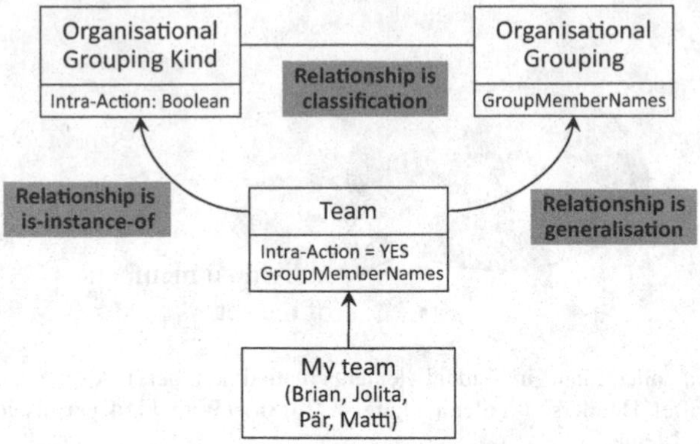

Fig. 4.8 A powertype representation for Team. This method fragment inherits from OrganisationalGrouping and thus has an attribute GroupMemberNames, which is not allocated actual values until it is instantiated (in the Endeavour domain: see Figure 1.14), and also has an instantiation relationship to a second class in the metamodel (OrganisationalGroupingKind). The attributes on this meta-level class are allocated values in the Method domain—here Intra-Action = YES (after Henderson-Sellers, figure 8, 2011a) (With kind permission of Springer Science + Business Media)

domain class thus effectively creating a set that, when instantiated, effectively allocates 'class variables' to the element of the method (in Fig. 4.8 this class is the Team class). Thus the Team class (in this diagram) has both class characteristics (since it is a subtype of OrganisationalGrouping) and also object characteristics (since it is an instance of OrganisationalGroupingKind). This duality led Atkinson (1997) to invent the name 'clabject' = class + object. Clabjects are an important contribution to ensuring that the methods we construct using SME have value both in the Method domain (to help the team create an organisational method) and in the Endeavour domain (to help the team tailor their constructed method to a particular set of situational characteristics). These forms of construction and tailoring are discussed in Chaps. 6 and 7, respectively.

4.1.3 Standardising the Methodology Metamodel

Many of the early object-oriented methodologies did not use a formalisation such as a metamodel, relying instead on textual definitions. Many of these were identified and ambiguities located (and fixed) as part of the COMMA[3] project (Henderson-Sellers and Bulthuis 1996, 1998). Emerging from these deliberations were two modelling languages: the OPEN Modeling Language (Firesmith et al. 1997) and the embryonic Unified Modeling Language (OMG 1997). As well as further developing this usage of metamodels to underpin the UML, the Object

[3] Common Object Methodology Metamodel Architecture.

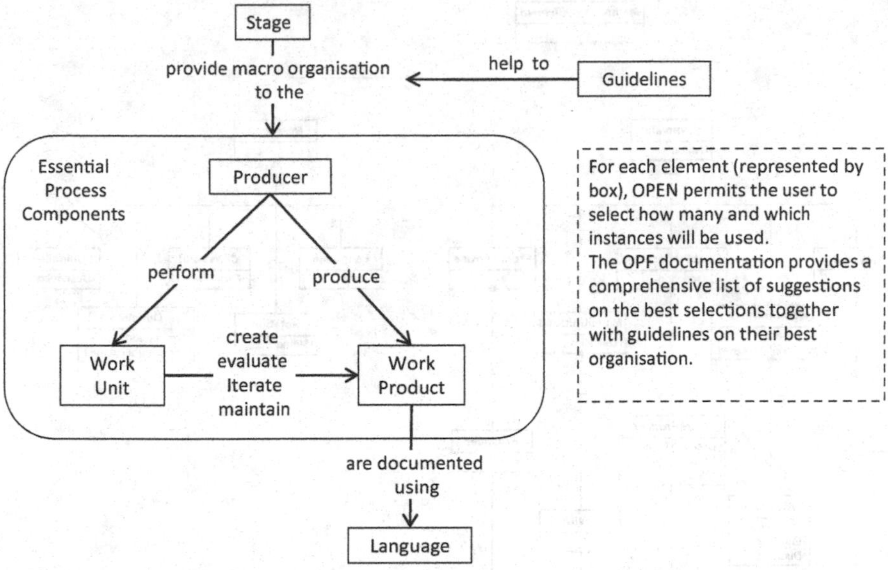

Fig. 4.9 The 3 + 2 core classes of the OPF process-focussed metamodel (after Firesmith and Henderson-Sellers 2002) © Pearson Education Limited

Management Group then went on to use metamodels for the MOF (meta object facility), SPEM (software process engineering metamodel) standards as well as the MDA (Model-Driven Architecture) initiative to use models in a particular way (from a computationally independent model or CIM to a platform-independent model or PIM; then the platform-specific model or PSM and finally to code). As noted earlier, method-focussed (rather than modelling language-focussed) metamodels were also developed into the Australian Standard 4651 (Standards Australia 2004) and the ISO/IEC 24744 International Standard (ISO/IEC 2007), and it is these method-focussed metamodels that have the most relevance to SME.

For modelling methodologies and hence many aspects of SME, it is generally agreed that there are at least three core classes in the metamodel (as shown in Fig. 2.1). Several method-focussed metamodels, however, include other core classes. Figure 4.9 illustrates the core structure of the OPEN Process Framework's metamodel (Firesmith and Henderson-Sellers 2002) in which the three core classes of Fig. 2.1 are augmented by two additional classes: Stage and Language. Stages describe calendar time and provide 'containers' for the work units once they have been sequenced (in one or more timelines). Language provides an additional resource that is effectively independent of the other core classes (and hence shown in Fig. 4.9 as a support class.)

Guidelines (in Fig. 4.9) refer to the heuristics given in Firesmith and Henderson-Sellers (2002). Advice on method constructed is further discussed in Chap. 6 of this book where other contributions to this topic are also highlighted.

In a later standard (SEMDM: ISO/IEC 2007), the process-focussed elements of the OPF and SPEM were augmented by a concordant support for modelling

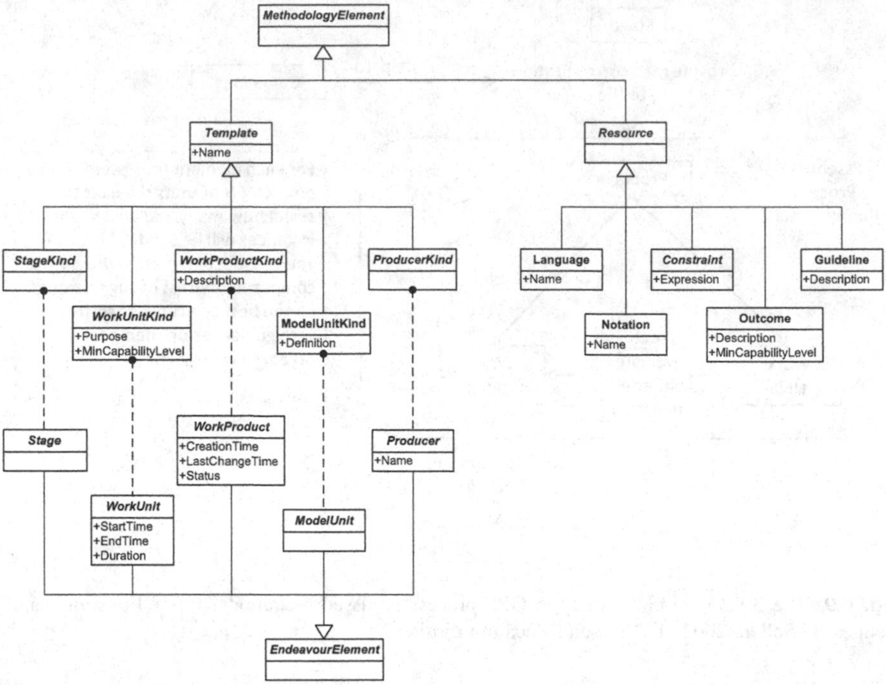

Fig. 4.10 The core of ISO/IEC 24744. Most classes occur as pairings within powertype patterns (depicted by dashed lines) but some do not. Most elements in a constructed methodology are thus clabjects (Atkinson 1999), having both a class facet and an object facet. In this way, class facet attributes occur in the Method domain as specifications for slot values in the Endeavour domain. Reproduced with permission from SAI Global Ltd. under Licence 1308-c138. All ISO standards are obtainable from http://www.iso.org and from http://www.saiglobal.com

languages by the introduction of the ModelUnit/ModelUnitKind classes in the standardised metamodel (Fig. 4.10). Indeed, ISO/IEC 24744 is highly amenable to supporting method fragments, method chunks, etc. in SME with a 'top' element called simply 'MethodologyElement', similar to the notion of method fragment as utilised here. As can be seen from Fig. 4.10, the standard includes classes that allow the method engineer to define various kinds of activities, tasks, techniques, producers and phases—these are the elements of the Method domain's process model or methodology. (This part of the SME process can be undertaken using other process metamodels such as OMG's SPEM (OMG 2005a).) ISO/IEC 24744 also includes classes that can be used in SME to define model kinds, languages and model unit kinds; as well as associations between process-related classes and product-related classes. This means that, unlike SPEM, which has no guaranteed integrative capability with the product aspects of a method, SEMDM provides solid linkages between process and product elements in the methodology. For example, a methodologist could define a task kind named 'Write class code', which specifies what to do in order to write the source code for any given class. This task

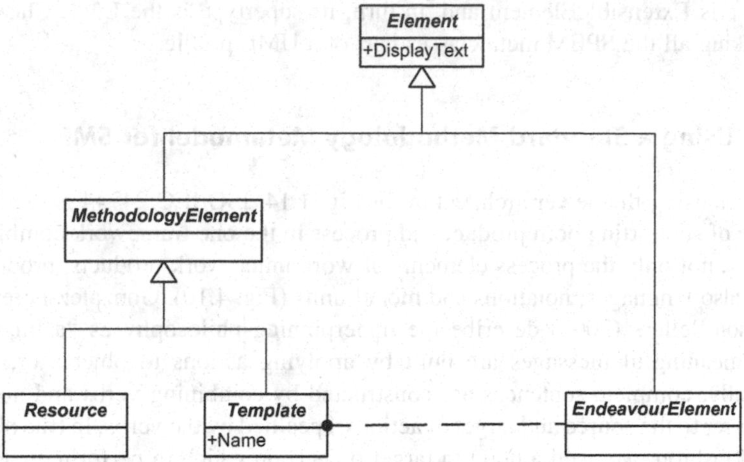

Fig. 4.11 Top level classes in the ISO/IEC 24744 metamodel (after ISO/IEC 2007) (reproduced with permission from SAI Global Ltd. under Licence 1308-c138). All ISO standards are obtainable from http://www.iso.org and from http://www.saiglobal.com

specification, however, is meaningless unless there is a clear understanding of what a class is. Although SPEM would allow the method engineer similar support for the definition of such a task, since it does not integrate product modelling aspects, no meaningful link is necessarily established between this task and the concept of a class. This means that it is possible for the method engineering to (accidentally) include a Class definition that is totally incompatible, ambiguous or unintelligible to other users. SEMDM avoids this problem because the method engineering can define a model unit kind named 'Class' with an appropriate definition and then link the 'Write class code' task kind to the 'Class' model unit kind to reflect the fact that the said task refers to the said model unit kind.

This newer methodology metamodel also introduced four other supporting 'Resource' classes: Notation, Constraint, Outcome and Guideline. Furthermore, this metamodel is highly supportive of method engineering in its description within the standard's documentation. Although SEMDM does not have a class *explicitly* called 'method fragment', the class in the 24744 metamodel that has this responsibility is the 'MethodologyElement' class (Fig. 4.11), to which all elements in the designed methodology (the 'ideal typical method' of Fig. 1.6) are conformant. In addition SEMDM supports an EndeavourElement (Fig. 4.11), which supports all the situationally specific method elements needed in enactment (the 'situational method' of Fig. 1.6).

In contrast, the OMG's SPEM metamodel is both process-focussed—rather than methodology-focussed in that it does not integrate modelling languages for work products—and also negligent of an explicit class to represent method fragment or method chunk: again called simply 'Element' (OMG 2002). In SPEM Version 2 (OMG 2008), the likely analogue is Process Element although we note that its supertype is ExtensibleElement and, in turn, its supertype is the UML Classifier; thus making all the SPEM meta classes part of a UML profile.

4.1.4 Using a Standard Methodology Metamodel for SME

As well as using the newer architecture of Fig. 1.14, ISO/IEC 24744 is the prime example of supporting both product and process in the one framework combining, as it does, not only the process elements of work units, work products, producers, etc. but also languages, notations and model units (Fig. 4.10). Gonzalez-Perez and Henderson-Sellers (2007) describe the underpinning philosophy as "a linguistic simile: meaningful messages are built by applying actions to objects or, more specifically, complete sentences are constructed by combining verbs and nouns". Nouns refer to the source and target of actions, specified by the verbs. In true object-oriented fashion, we need a noun (a target object) on which to perform an action, i.e., verbs alone and nouns alone are meaningless.

When using these process-focussed and method-focussed metamodels, it is generally said that the method fragment is instantiated from one of the metamodel elements. More precisely, the method fragment is created such that it is conformant to a metamodel element/class (Bézivin and Gerbé 2001). Whichever phraseology is used, we can picture each method fragment as containing fields of information, each field being defined in the metamodel (Fig. 4.12). In addition, when using ISO/IEC 24744, it must be remembered that all these fragments have both a class facet and an object facet and are thus clabjects (Atkinson 1997). As noted earlier, this approach supports not only method fragments in the Method domain (Fig. 1.14) but also the enactment of these fragments both in a situational method and in its performance (Fig. 1.8). This results from the use of the powertype pattern in the metamodel—seen in Fig. 4.13 as the Document/DocumentKind pair. The method fragment in this example, Requirements Specification Document, derives its object facet by being an instance of DocumentKind (and thus attributes such as Name and MustBeApproved on DocumentKind are given values in the method fragment) as well as a class-like nature, because the fragment is a subtype of Document. This class-like nature permits attributes defined on the meta class (here, Title and Version) to still be declarations and not value attributions in the method fragment (in the Method domain); these attributes then being given values in the enactment—here to 'MySystem' Requirements Specification. The former set of values is applicable to all (instances of) requirements documents, whereas the latter set of values are project-specific. In other words, the powertype-based structure of ISO/IEC 24744 provides a facility for a method fragment to have some attributes given a value in the Method domain while other value allocations are deferred until the Endeavour domain (Gonzalez-Perez and Henderson-Sellers 2006c)—a solution that is not possible when using the strict metamodelling approach exemplified in the OMG architecture of Fig. 1.11—and hence also in SPEM. In addition, this powertype-based approach provides semantic integrity between the process and product aspects of a methodology such that both aspects use the same ontological

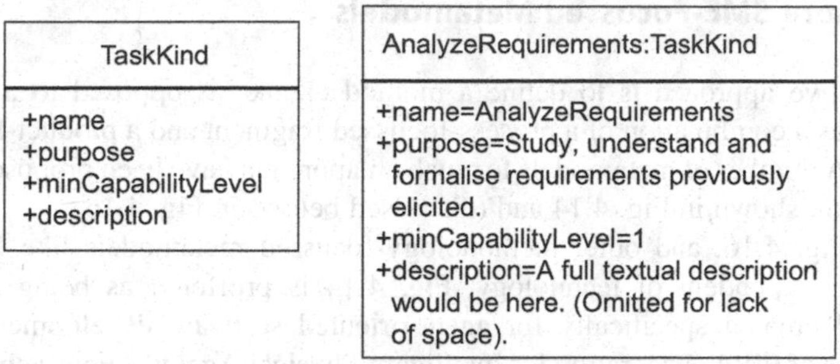

Fig. 4.12 A metamodel class (TaskKind) from ISO/IEC 24744 with all its attribute fields and, alongside, a method fragment conformant to this metamodel class (cf. Fig. 2.2)

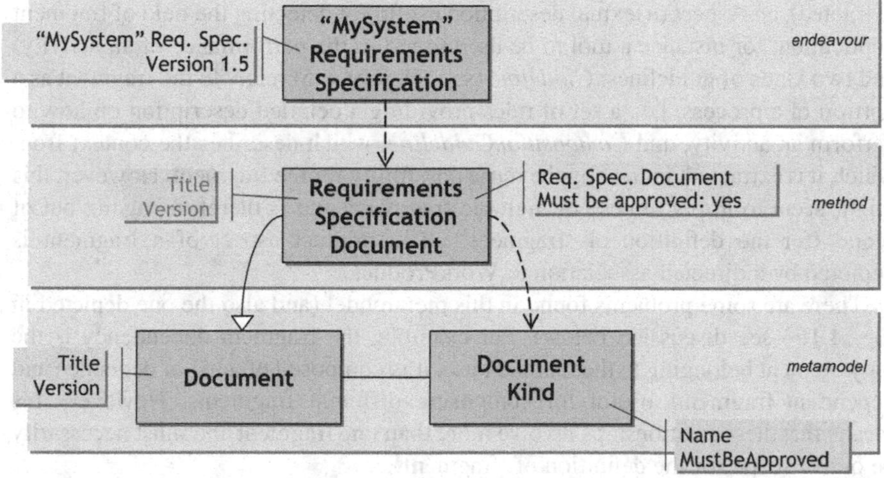

Fig. 4.13 The use of powertype instantiation (e.g., in ISO/IEC 24744) to transmit attribute values to either the Model domain or the Endeavour domain (after Henderson-Sellers 2006a)

commitment—again not guaranteed when linking SPEM or OPF to a modelling language like UML (see, e.g., discussion in Gonzalez-Perez and Henderson-Sellers 2008b).

Finally, we should remember that granularity is highly relevant to both the metamodel and the method fragment aspects of SME (as discussed in Sect. 8.3). Although discussed recently in the SME literature (Henderson-Sellers and Gonzalez-Perez 2011), it should be noted that there are, as yet, no absolutes, nor any substantial metrics, for this characteristic (see also Hobbs 1985).

4.1.5 More SME-Focussed Metamodels

An alternative approach is to define a method chunk (as opposed to a method fragment) as a combination of a process-focussed fragment and a product-focussed fragment. A number of metamodels for such an approach have been proposed—two examples are shown in Fig. 4.14 and (discussed below) in Fig. 4.16.

While Fig. 4.16, and other methodology-focussed metamodels like ISO/IEC 24744, is independent of technology, Fig. 4.14 is proffered as being a chunk metamodel created specifically for agent-oriented software development under the auspices of FIPA (Federation for Intelligent Physical Agents—now a committee within the IEEE Standards responsibility). The metamodel in Fig. 4.14 describes a chunk (inappropriately labelled 'Fragment') as a combination of a ProcessDescription, a Glossary (a list of terms that facilitate the understanding of fragment concepts when applied to a context different from the one from which it was extracted), an Aspect (a textual description useful for detecting the field of fragment application, for instance a tool to be used to aid in the performance of an activity) and two kinds of guidelines: *Guideline* (see also Chap. 6) refers to the fragment as a portion of a process, i.e., a set of rules providing a detailed description on how to perform an activity; and *CompositionGuideline*, which describes the context from which it is extracted, indicating the reuse possibility for the fragment. However, this might seem to imply the use of multiple fragments and is therefore, again, out of scope (for the definition of 'fragment'). The product aspect of a fragment is depicted by a directed association to WorkProduct.

There are some problems found in this metamodel (and also the one depicted in Fig. 4.16—see discussion below). For example, the fragment dependency is the only element belonging to the method base; it is composed of a list of dependee and dependant fragments useful for composing different fragments. However, this means that these relationships involve more than one fragment and must necessarily be out of scope for the definition of 'fragment'.

It is also possibly worth showing the pre- and postconditions for a fragment although these should probably not be an intrinsic part of the *definition* of a method fragment.

Henderson-Sellers (2007) argues that the other classes in Fig. 4.14 can all be challenged as being out of scope. A fragment only has a process description if it is a process-focussed method fragment! However, it turns out (Cossentino 2006) that the metamodel in Fig. 4.14 is for a *chunk* (with a process part and a product part) not for a generic fragment. This means that the aggregation relationship (white diamond) to ProcessDescription should be balanced by a similar relationship to WorkProduct. Furthermore, the generalisation relationships to WorkProduct are clearly out of scope and should be omitted as should the coarse granular classes in Fig. 4.14 of GuardCondition and Constraint. The link to MetaModelElement Type is arcane and, in any case, its subtypes are unnecessarily technology-specific (to agent technology), whereas metamodels for a methodology or for a process should be independent of the technology that is to be used to implement the methodology/process. In Fig. 4.14, ProcessDescription is shown as an aggregation

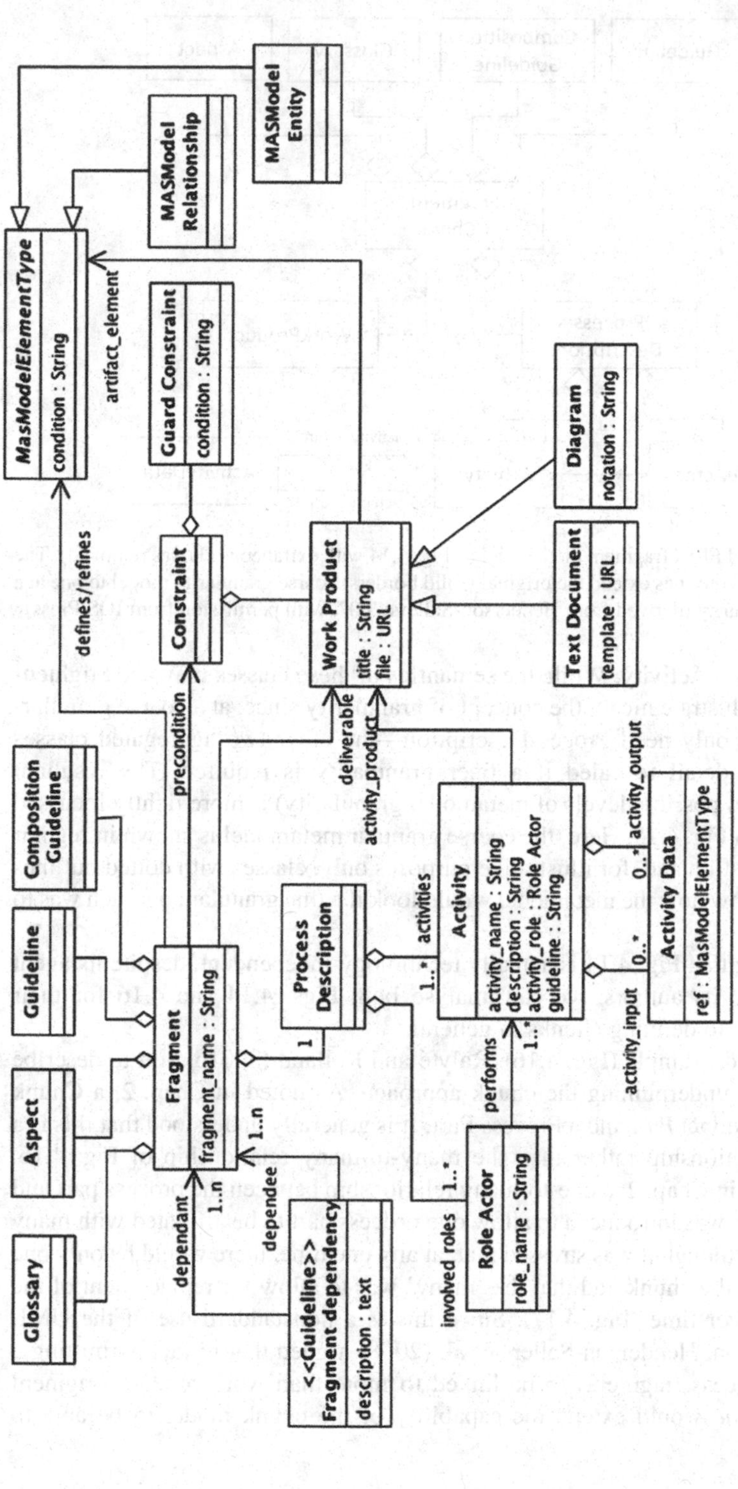

Fig. 4.14 The metamodel of the FIPA the so-called method fragment (actually a method chunk) (after Cossentino et al. 2007) and reprinted with permission of the publisher © Inderscience

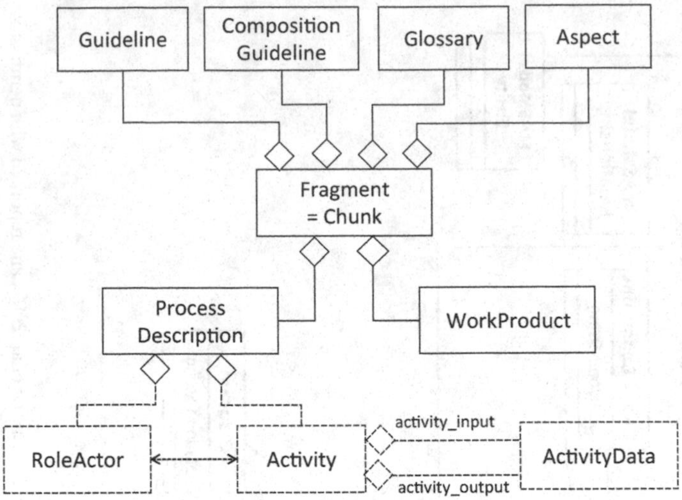

Fig. 4.15 Revised FIPA fragment metamodel (=Fig. 4.14 with extraneous classes removed). The classes with dotted outlines extend the original (solid borders) coarse granularity model to one at a much finer granularity (derived from Henderson-Sellers 2007, with permission from IOS Press)

of RoleActor and Activity. While the semantics of these classes may need tightening, this does illustrate nicely the concept of granularity since, at a coarse granularity, one would only need ProcessDescription—the other two aggregated classes showing more detail revealed if a finer granularity is required. The resultant metamodel (two possible levels of metamodel granularity) is more tightly focussed and is shown in Fig. 4.15. Here, the coarse granular metamodel is shown in regular UML class notation and, for illustrative purposes only, classes with dotted outlines are added to show how the metamodel would look if a fine granular approach was to be adopted.

Recognising that Fig. 4.14 is actually technology-independent, despite its agent focus given by its authors, we can analyse both Figs. 4.14 and 4.16 for their appropriateness to defining chunks in general.

In the second example (Fig. 4.16), Ralyté and Rolland (2001b) aim to describe the metamodel underpinning the chunk approach. As noted in Chap. 2, a Chunk consists of a Product Part and a Process Part. It is generally understood that this is a one-to-one relationship rather than the many-to-many relationship of Fig. 4.16. Later, as noted in Chap. 2, a one-to-many relationship between the process part and the product part was introduced to allow one process part to be affiliated with many product parts although it was stressed that, at any one time, there would be only one product part in the chunk and that the 'many' was to allow for replacement of the product part over time (Fig. 4.17). Since this is a nonstandard use of the UML standard notation, Henderson-Sellers et al. (2008) argued that in fact permitting a work unit (process fragment) to be linked to more than work product fragment *at the same time* would extend the capability of the chunk model to be able to

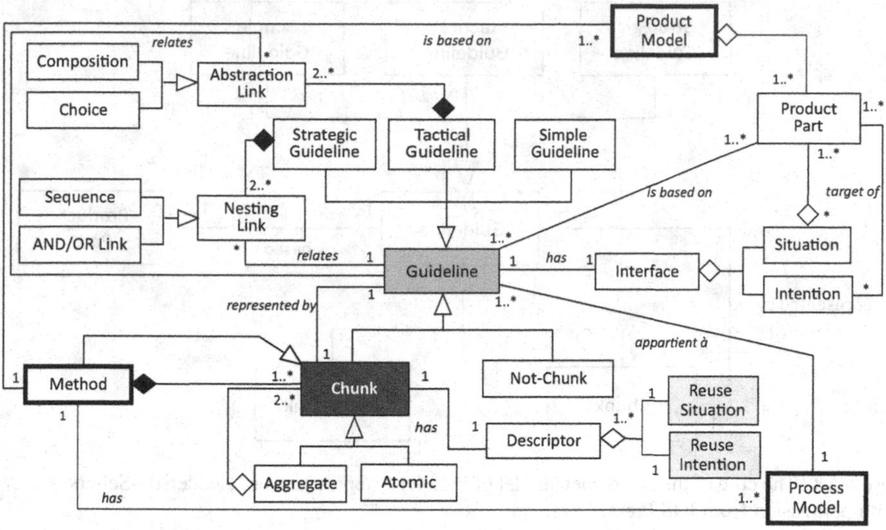

Fig. 4.16 The method metamodel of Ralyté and Rolland (figure 3, 2001b) (With kind permission of Springer Science + Business Media)

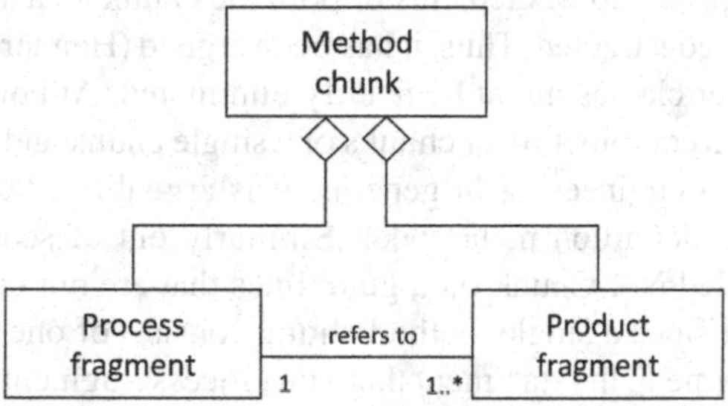

Fig. 4.17 Revision of Method Chunk to be one process fragment plus one or more product fragments

represent a work unit with two outputs (e.g., modifying a document and producing a list of changes to that document) but it would also permit the use of a descriptive figure like Fig. 4.17 to be interpreted in a more traditional way.

Furthermore, as can be seen in Fig. 4.16, while there is a meta class called Product Part there is no complementary Process Part. This is because the Process Part appears under its synonym of Guideline and, as consequence, the Chunk class, through its specialisation relationship to Guideline, is a kind of Process Part. Thus, if Chunk is a kind of Guideline (i.e., a kind of Process Part) then it would appear that a Chunk is *only* a Process Part. The relationship of Guideline (Process Part) to Product Part is named 'is based on', which appears not to supply the 'aggregation' name of a chunk as consisting of a process part and a product part.

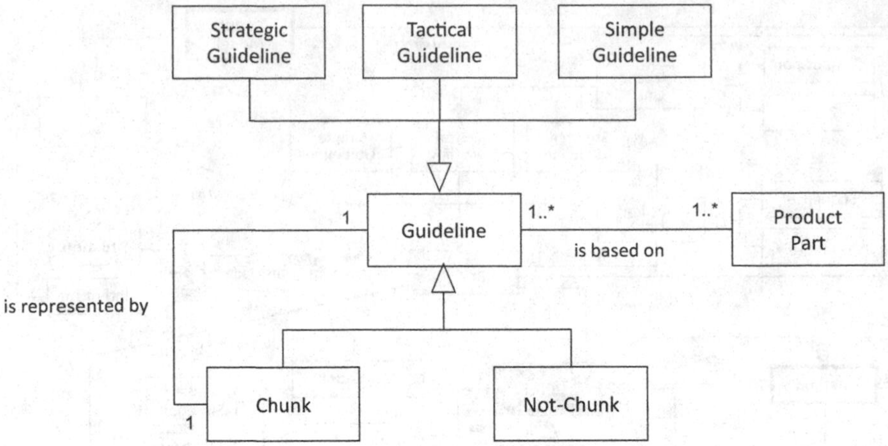

Fig. 4.18 The core of the chunk metamodel of Fig. 4.16 (reprinted from Henderson-Sellers 2007, with permission from IOS Press)

As discussed in our first example, the scope of these metamodels is unclear. In this second example, which is intended to focus on a chunk in the context of method engineering, there appears to be elements of both the chunk idea and the process by which chunks can be constructed. Thus, it has been argued (Henderson-Sellers 2007) that some of the other classes might be readily eliminated. Although a method can clearly be viewed as a combination of chunks or a single chunk and is highly relevant to situational method engineering in general, it is arguable whether it should be included in a chunk definition metamodel. Similarly out of scope for defining a Chunk is a class called Not-Chunk (i.e., guidelines that are not chunks). Finally, it should be noted that since a single method chunk consists of one process fragment plus one product fragment, the statement that one process fragment can be associated with several product fragments provides an internal inconsistency, i.e., a contradiction within the tenets of chunk modelling.

In order to seek further clarity, Fig. 4.18 depicts the essence of Fig. 4.16 in which a second problem is clear. There is overlapping subsetting (without a discriminator) between Guideline subtyped as Chunk or Not-Chunk and Guideline subtyped as either StrategicGuideline, TacticalGuideline or SimpleGuideline. The latter subtyping relates to the *process* of creating a 'map' whereas the former aims to represent the entities that may appear in that map. Henderson-Sellers (2007) therefore respectfully suggested that Fig. 4.18 is an inappropriate metamodel to describe the clear intentions of chunk modelling as represented textually or in diagrams like Fig. 2.3 in Chap. 2. It is speculation that perhaps the method *construction* idea encapsulated in earlier publications as a 'map' (Rolland et al. 1999), which relies on Strategic, Tactical and Simple Guidelines, has been concatenated with the static architectural demands of a chunk metamodel. At the very best, this is multiple partitioning (with no discriminator) (cf. McGregor and Korson 1993).

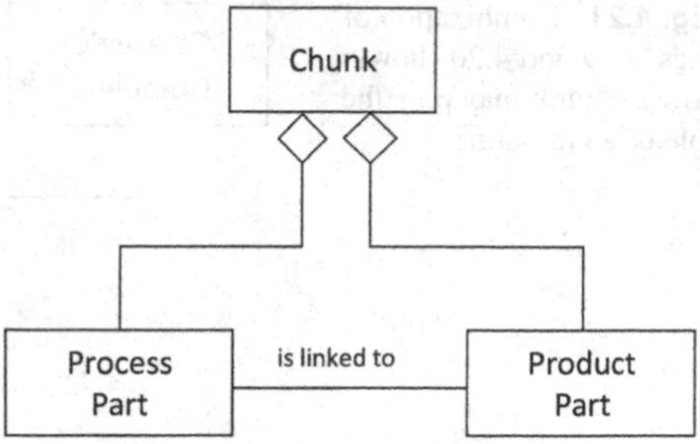

Fig. 4.19 Reformulation of Chunk with a process part and a product part

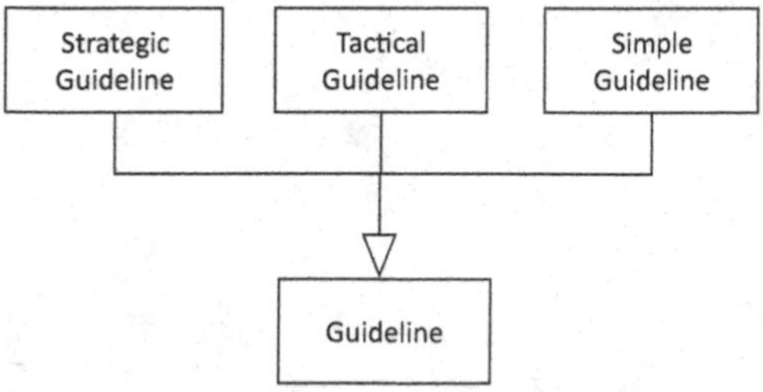

Fig. 4.20 Reformation of the Guideline part of the metamodel of Fig. 4.18

To rectify this, it is proposed that a new metamodel discriminates clearly between the chunk definition classes (Fig. 4.19) and those relating to Guidelines (Fig. 4.20). However, we should also retain the spirit of Fig. 4.16 in maintaining a linkage between Chunk and Guideline—but rather than a specialisation relationship, the association relationship of Fig. 4.21 would seem to be more appropriate—at least from a model quality viewpoint, Fig. 4.21 is an improvement on Fig. 4.18.

4.1.6 Incorporating Method Rationale[4]

Method rationale, interfaces, goals and descriptors were discussed qualitatively in Sects. 2.2 and 2.3 and Chap. 3. Here, we introduce a more formal means of expressing these ideas.

As noted in Chap. 2, a method component consists of zero or more input and exactly one output work product together with the 'process' used to transform the one into the other—together with a highly visible method rationale. From a metamodelling viewpoint, the method component has two views (Wistrand and Karlsson 2004; Karlsson and Wistrand 2006). These are shown in Fig. 4.22 (the internal view) and Fig. 4.23 (the external view), showing how these method components can be combined to form an ISDM. Figure 4.22 illustrates the method

[4] We acknowledge contributions of Dr. Fredrik Karlsson to this section.

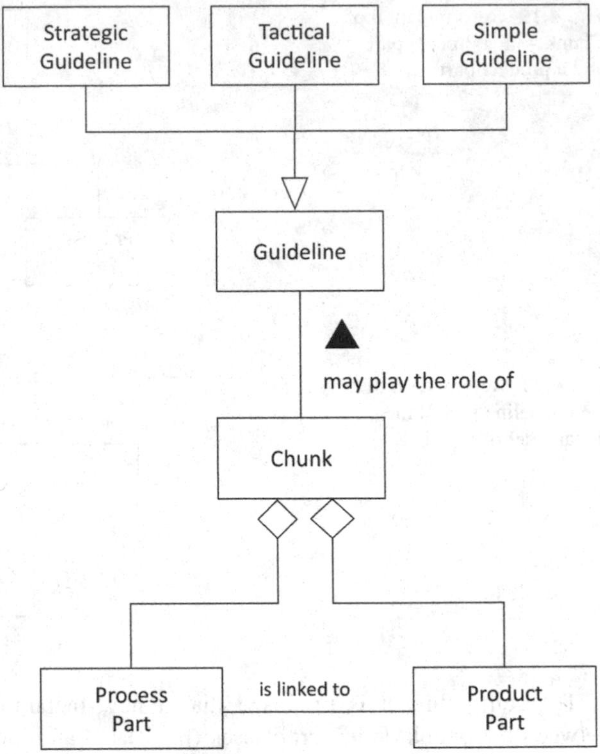

Fig. 4.21 Combination of Figs. 4.19 and 4.20 showing how a Chunk may play the role of a Guideline

component as consisting of 'method elements' (essentially method fragments at a lower layer of granularity than the component as such) and their associated goals. A method element is of one of five subtypes.

Firstly, there are three interrelated parts often mentioned in the literature: prescribed action, concept and notation. *Prescribed actions*, structured into a process, guide the performance of development activities and tell method users what to do in specific situations. Prescribed actions are formulated in terms of *concepts* that direct method users' attention towards specific phenomena in the Problem domain. Concepts thus form the language by which developers' understanding of the Problem domain, and of the method, is expressed and communicated. Results of prescribed actions are typically documented using a specified notation, which gives concepts a concrete representation (for example, as diagrams).

Based on lessons learned from empirical observations (Karlsson and Ågerfalk 2004, 2009b), the *artefact* and the *actor role* complement these three core categories as the two remaining types of method element. In these studies, project members tended to focus on the work products during method configuration and software development projects. This is also supported by previous research that emphasised the importance of "keeping the focus on what is being produced" (Cameron 2002, p. 72). Artefacts are deliverables from, as well as inputs to, the

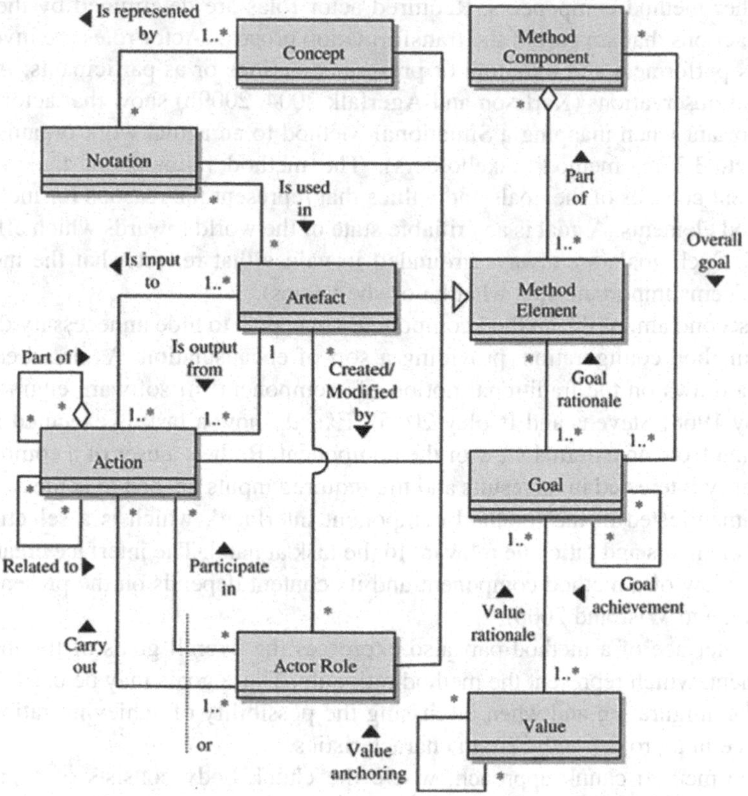

Fig. 4.22 The method component construct (internal view) (after Wistrand and Karlsson, figure 1, 2004) (With kind permission of Springer Science + Business Media)

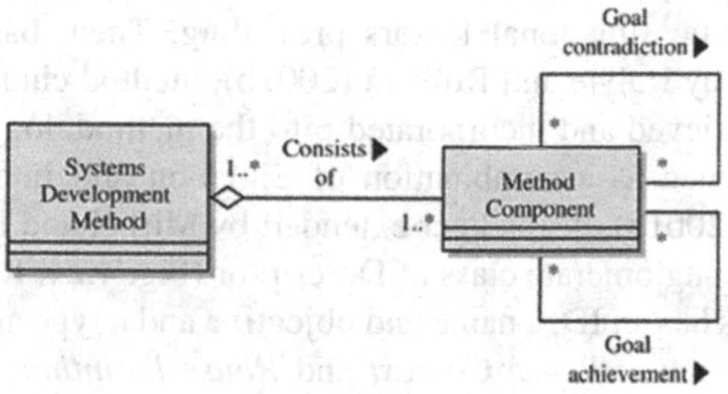

Fig. 4.23 Method component construct (external view) (after Wistrand and Karlsson, figure 2, 2004) (With kind permission of Springer Science + Business Media)

transformation process. In this context, the term 'input' should be understood in a loose sense. Information Systems Development Methods are viewed as heuristic guidelines and *specified* inputs are only *recommended*, not strictly enforced. However, most method components have at least one input. The obvious exception is method components that initiate new activities later to be integrated with the results from other method components. Required actor roles are determined by the prescribed actions that are part of the transformation process. Actor roles are involved either as performers and initiators of prescribed actions or as participants. Again, empirical observations (Karlsson and Ågerfalk 2004, 2009b) show that actor roles are important when mapping a Situational Method to an actual work organisation (see Sect. 3.2 on method stakeholders). The method rationale of the method component consists of the goals and values that represent the reasons for inclusion of method elements. A goal is a verifiable state of the world towards which effort is directed. Such goals are always grounded in values that reflect what the method creator deems important (i.e., what he or she values).

The second aim of the method component concept is to hide unnecessary details during method configuration, providing a sort of encapsulation. As noted earlier, this idea draws on the traditional notion of 'component' in software engineering (McIlroy 1968; Stevens and Pooley 2006). Exactly how a task is executed is not interesting from an external view of the component. Rather, a user of a component is primarily interested in its results and the required inputs needed to achieve them. This is manifested in the 'method component interface', which is a selection of method elements and rationale relevant to the task at hand. The interface creates an external view of a method component and its content depends on the present task (Karlsson and Wistrand 2006).

The interface of a method part also expresses the overall goals of the method component, which represent the method rationale. These goals may be used during method configuration and when discussing the possibility of achieving rationality resonance in a project with certain characteristics.

In the method chunk approach, where the chunk body consists of a process fragment plus a product fragment, a chunk also has an interface. This interface is the vehicle for describing the methodological situation in which chunk can be applied together with a prescription of the objective or 'intention' of the chunk. As outlined in Chap. 2, the interface is used primarily for chunk selection in the context of the specific situational factors prevailing. Then, based on similarity measures described by Ralyté and Rolland (2001b), method chunk body—process plus product—is retrieved and incorporated into the methodology under construction. Originally defined as a combination of Situation and Intention (Fig. 4.16: Ralyté and Rolland 2001b), it was later extended by Mirbel and Ralyté (2006) and Mirbel (2006) to a conglomerate class of Descriptor (Fig. 4.24: Ralyté et al. 2006). The Descriptor class has an ID, a name and objective and a type and consists of two classes focussed on reuse: *Reuse Context* and *Reuse Intention*, only hinted at in earlier work (Ralyté 2004; Mirbel and Ralyté 2006). Each method chunk has a descriptor and there is also an associated *Experience Report*, which is used to document, post facto, how the method chunk has been used. Also documented is the *Origin* of the chunk. In Fig. 4.24, then, the Descriptor has a strong focus on reuse, in comparison with the *Interface* class, which supports formal inclusion of information on both the *Situation* and the *Intention* (as discussed in Chap. 2).

In the fragment approach, as exemplified in SEMDM, these ideas of method rationale are supported in the metamodel classes called Guideline, Constraint and

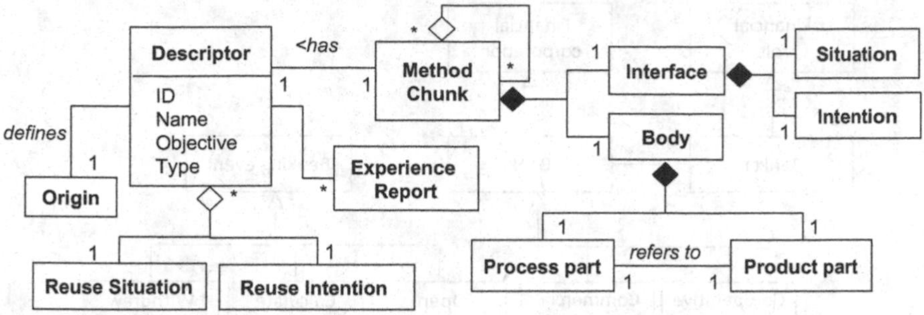

Fig. 4.24 Revised metamodel for method chunk (after Henderson-Sellers et al. 2008). ©IEEE reproduced with permission

Outcome. Constraints are subtyped into Precondition and Postcondition; Guidelines give advice on how to use the method fragment during method enactment and Outcome is defined as 'observable result of the successful performance of any work unit of a given kind', used to assess the performance of work units.

The main difference between the fragment approach and the method rationale approach of Ågerfalk and colleagues (Ågerfalk and Wistrand 2003; Karlsson and Ågerfalk 2004, 2009a, b; Ågerfalk 2006; Ågerfalk and Fitzgerald 2006) is that, while intentions refer to the immediate goal to be achieved by a method following action, the latter approach emphasises that these goals are structured into goal hierarchies and are grounded in values. This facilitates analyses of why an intention is an intention in a particular model and on what grounds, provided a certain value foundation; the intention may be replaced with another intention (and thus method component) more suitable to the situation at hand. An example, used earlier in Chap. 3, is the intention of having an onsite customer as suggested by the eXtreme Programming method (Beck 2000). This may not be feasible in, for example, a globally distributed project. Then, by analysing what higher level goals and values the onsite customer practice is supposed to support, it may be possible to find other ways to achieve those same goals (or goal structures) while adhering to the same values; for example, by using a product marketing group as a customer proxy that prioritise features based on potential revenue, as was the case in the study by Ågerfalk and Fitzgerald (2006). More generally, as pointed out by Ågerfalk and Åhlgren (1999), it can be used in method reconstruction (i.e., in defining a formalised method based on successful development practices in actual projects), verification of proposed achievements (i.e., analysing to what extent a method actually operationalises the claims made by its constructor), consistency checking of aggregated activities (i.e., analysing to what extent all prescribed actions in an aggregated activity are related to goals that are related to the activity as a whole or to sub-goals of the activity) and in method assembly to validate that all suggested components contributes towards the same goals and that these match the particular development context in the development organisation at hand (i.e., analysing rationality resonance).

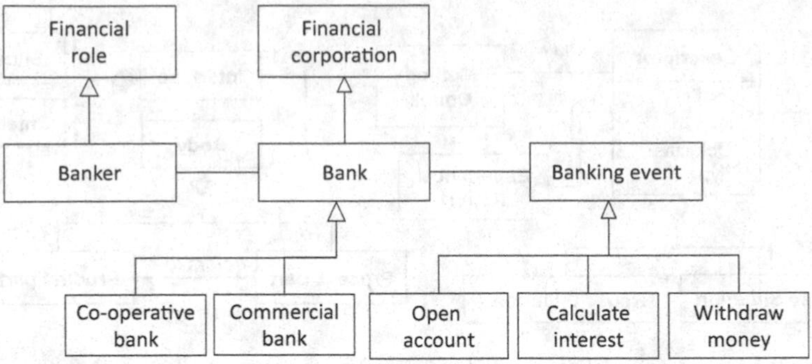

Fig. 4.25 Part of an ontology pertinent to the Banking domain (reprinted from Henderson-Sellers 2011b with permission from Elsevier)

4.2 The Value of Ontologies

To supplement these metamodels, several authors explore the possibilities of also using ontologies to help formalise SME. In philosophy, the terms ontology and epistemology are well defined as the study of (a) existence and (b) of (human-created) knowledge, respectively. However, in software engineering, most authors equate 'ontology' with (b) or, more commonly, as a noun describing the output of that aforementioned study (e.g., Guizzardi 2005, 2007); for example, the hierarchical or network representation of a domain of knowledge for the banking industry is essentially a documentation of knowledge in a particular domain of interest; in other words, it is a formal construction capturing knowledge that is agreed upon by many domain experts (Gruber 1993) and therefore is eminently reusable (Fig. 4.25). This is called a 'domain ontology'. In the SME context, an ontology can be understood both by humans and by machines and can therefore be used to facilitate communication within an IT system—either between people themselves or between people and the IT system. Examples of domain ontologies abound, e.g., *Swoogle* (http://swoogle.umbc.edu/) *and Ontolingua* (http://www.ksl.stanford.edu/software/ontolingua/).

The use of ontologies in information systems and software engineering has been growing rapidly over the last 2 decades (e.g., Guarino 1998; Wyssusek and Klaus 2005). Ontologies have featured in several agent-oriented methodologies, such as MOBMAS (Tran et al. 2006; Tran and Low 2008), which Beydoun et al. (2005, 2006) argue can provide an integrative platform across other methodologies as well as improving the quality of both product and process. Other ontology-focussed methods are summarised in Corcho et al. (2006).

A domain ontology is a kind of model (Fig. 1.9); however, the term 'ontology' is also often applied to a second kind of model, the foundational ontology. A specific kind of ontology called a foundational ontology or, alternatively, a high-level ontology provides 'meta-level' concepts for the domain ontologies (e.g., Guizzardi and Wagner 2005a, b) that document real-world descriptors of business entities (e.g., Saeki and Kaiya 2007; Henderson-Sellers 2011b). In other words, a

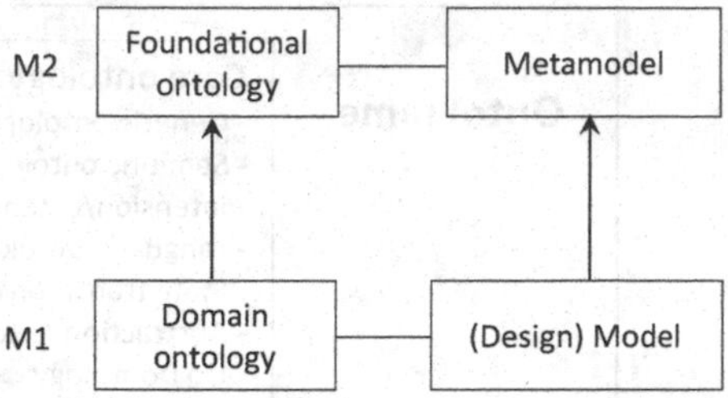

Fig. 4.26 Aligning meta levels for models and ontologies

foundational ontology may be used at the same abstraction level as a metamodel and a domain ontology at the same abstraction level as a (design) model, with each pair linked via an appropriate semantic mapping (Fig. 4.26). Linkages between models and ontologies have been investigated by a number of authors (e.g., Kaschek 2005; Atkinson et al. 2006) and linkages between metamodels and ontologies by, for example, Devedzic (2002) and Aßmann et al. (2006). Ruiz and Hilera (2006, p. 64) note the confusion between the terms metamodel and ontology, suggesting that this may be because they are often depicted with the same language and/or because their target is different: method and model derivation for metamodels but knowledge representation for ontologies.

Much of the work in integrating ontological thinking into software engineering uses a definition of ontology based on the treatise of Bunge (1977, 1979), often as elaborated by Wand and Weber (1988, 1990, 1993, 1995) into what is commonly referred to as the BWW (or Bunge-Wand-Weber) ontological framework—although this has been criticised strongly by Wyssusek and Klaus (2005) and Wyssusek (2006) who argue that the Bunge approach to ontology is not representative of contemporary discussions in the philosophical ontology research arena, despite its widespread adoption in information systems and software engineering research. Nevertheless, the BWW model is widely cited although only the first of its three models (representation, state-tracking, decomposition) (Wand 1996) is generally used for information systems/software engineering ontological assessments (Recker et al. 2007). Example applications of the BWW framework include studies of the ontological completeness (or otherwise) of object-oriented (OO) modelling languages including the UML (Opdahl and Henderson-Sellers 2000, 2002) and of the whole-part relationship in OO modelling languages (Opdahl et al. 2001).

Henderson-Sellers (2011b) thus concluded that the term 'ontology' could be applied at several 'meta levels', as can the term 'model'. Of specific interest to software engineering and SME are domain ontologies (that parallel analysis and design models) and foundational ontologies (a.k.a. meta ontologies) that have similar characteristics to modelling languages and metamodels.

Leppänen (2007) introduces a comprehensive ontological framework, OntoFrame, for use in SME. It has four main elements (Fig. 4.27): a core ontology, contextual ontologies, layer-specific ontologies and method ontologies. This framework also incorporates earlier work of the author. For instance, the ISD ontology is described in Leppänen (2006). It comprises a number of domains (purpose, actor,

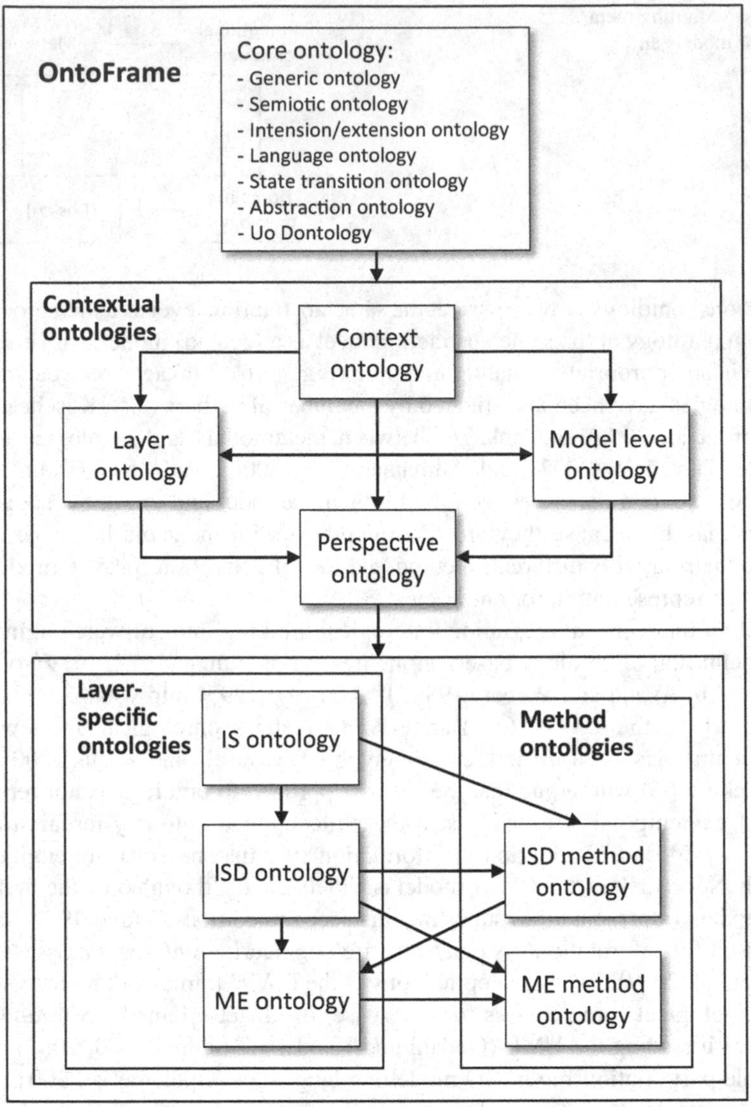

Fig. 4.27 Structure of OntoFrame (after Leppänen 2007)

time, object, facility, location and actions (Fig. 4.28)), each of which is described by a metamodel (an exemplar is given in Fig. 4.29—for the Purpose domain).

Niknafs et al. (2007) introduce ontology into method engineering as a proposed extension of the assembly-based approach to method construction (see Chap. 6). Other authors who integrate ontology-based thinking into software engineering do not do so in terms of SME (e.g., Hesse 2008a, b), although Gonzalez-Perez and Henderson-Sellers (2006b) make the suggestion that a metamodel such as ISO/IEC

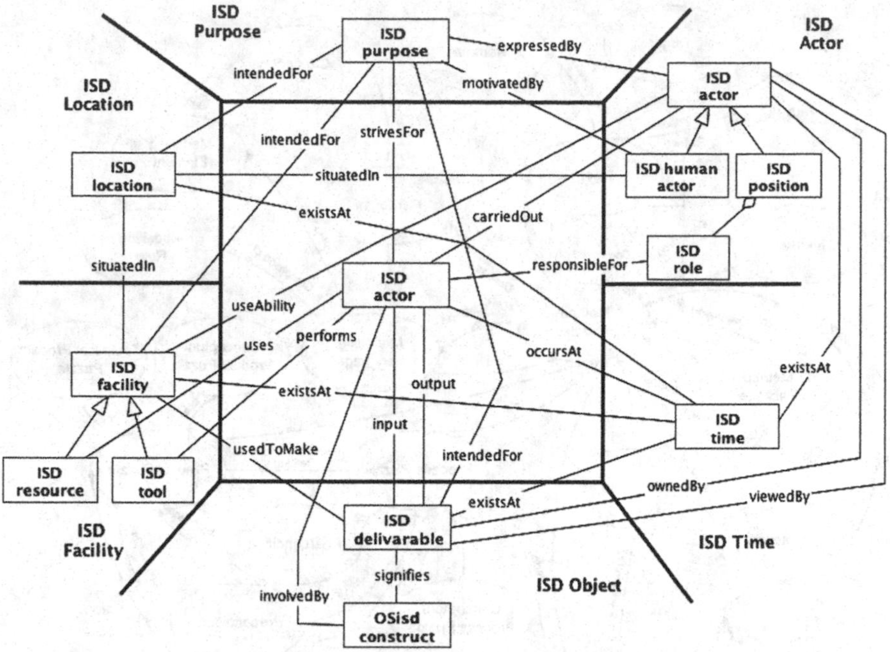

Fig. 4.28 Relationships between the seven domains of the OntoFrame (after Leppänen 2006)

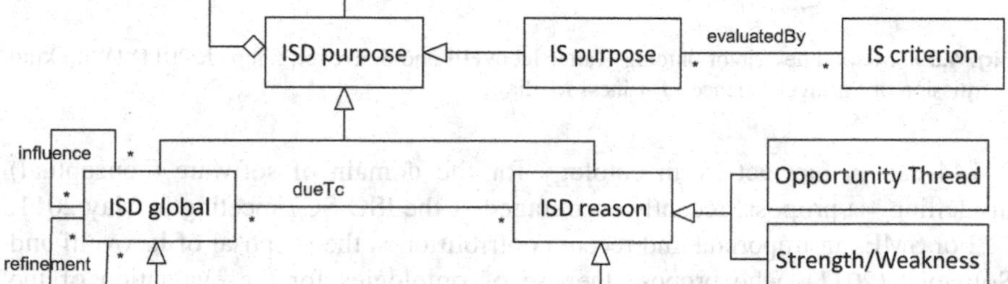

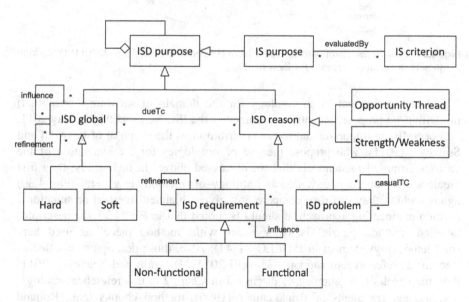

Fig. 4.29 Metamodel for the Purpose domain (after Leppänen 2006)

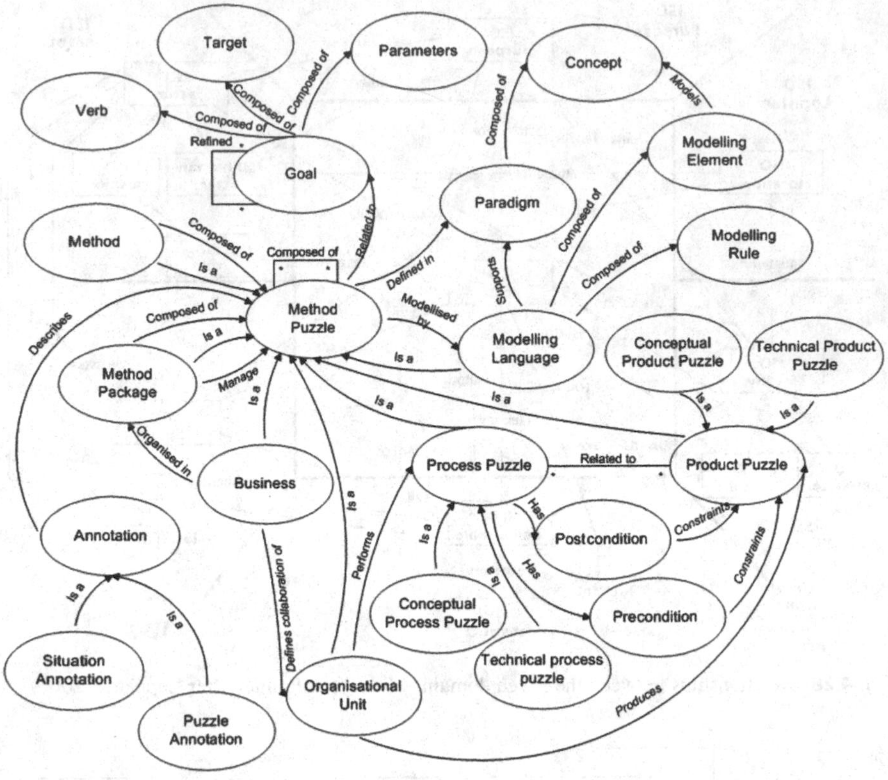

Fig. 4.30 Method descriptor ontology (after Iacovelli and Souveyet, figure 1, 2011) (With kind permission of Springer Science + Business Media)

24744 can in fact act as an ontology for the domain of software (conceptual) modelling—a proposal recently encouraged at the ISO SC7 meeting in May 2011.

For SME, an important and recent contribution is the proposal of Iacovelli and Souveyet (2011), who propose the use of ontologies for the evaluation of the various proposed metamodels that we discussed above. In their study, they first create a reference ontology, i.e., an ontology of 'method' in general (Fig. 4.30) against which they can then compare any given 'branded' method or situational method engineering approach. It should be noted that in Fig. 4.30, the descriptor labelled 'method puzzle' is synonymous with 'method piece' as used here (or MethodologyElement in ISO/IEC 24744). Also, those descriptors labelled as 'technical' refer to tool support (Iacovelli 2011). Iacovelli and Souveyet (2011) then map each of the approaches discussed in Chap. 2 to this reference ontology, i.e., method fragments of Brinkkemper (1996), method chunks (e.g., Rolland et al. 1998), method components (Wistrand and Karlsson 2004; Karlsson and Ågerfalk 2004), OPF method components (actually fragments in this book's nomenclature) (e.g., Henderson-Sellers 2002; http://www.opfro.org) and, in a

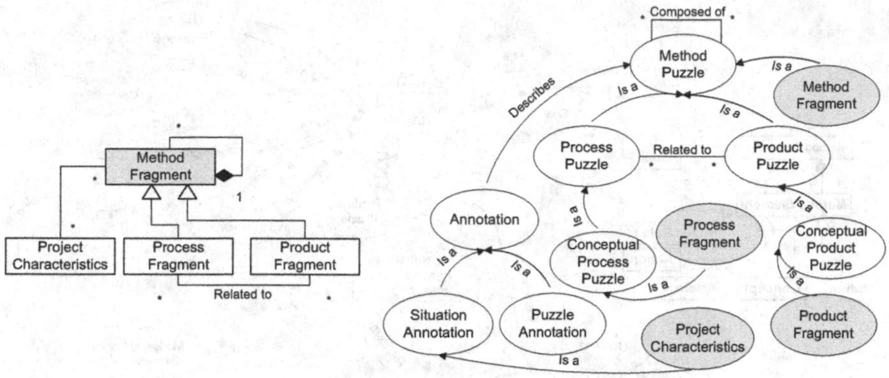

Fig. 4.31 Metamodel and ontology mapping for Brinkkemper's method fragment (after Iacovelli and Souveyet, figure 2, 2011) (With kind permission of Springer Science + Business Media)

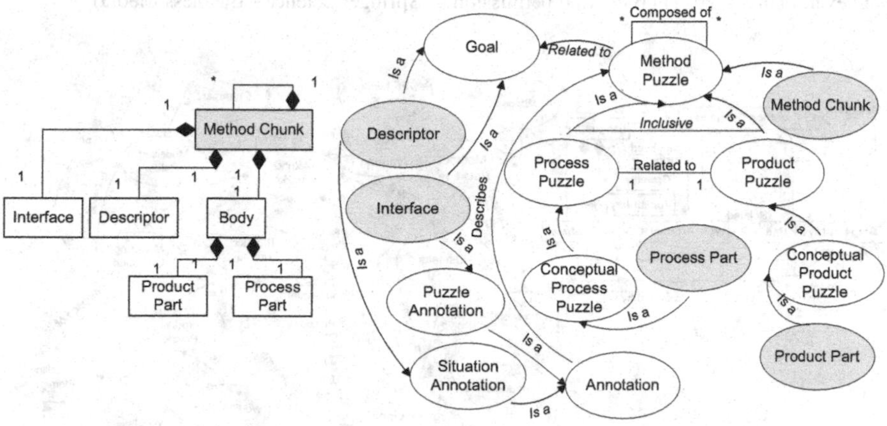

Fig. 4.32 Metamodel and ontology mapping for method chunks (after Iacovelli and Souveyet, figure 3, 2011) (With kind permission of Springer Science + Business Media)

slightly different vein but commensurate with new directions in SME, SOA-oriented method parts (Guzélian and Cauvet 2007) (see also Sect. 10.1). These diagrams (reproduced here as Figs. 4.31, 4.32, 4.33, 4.34 and 4.35) open up new research directions for SME and a formal underpinning for future analyses that will bring the various SME approaches even closer together (cf. also Ågerfalk et al. 2007)—an aim also of this book.

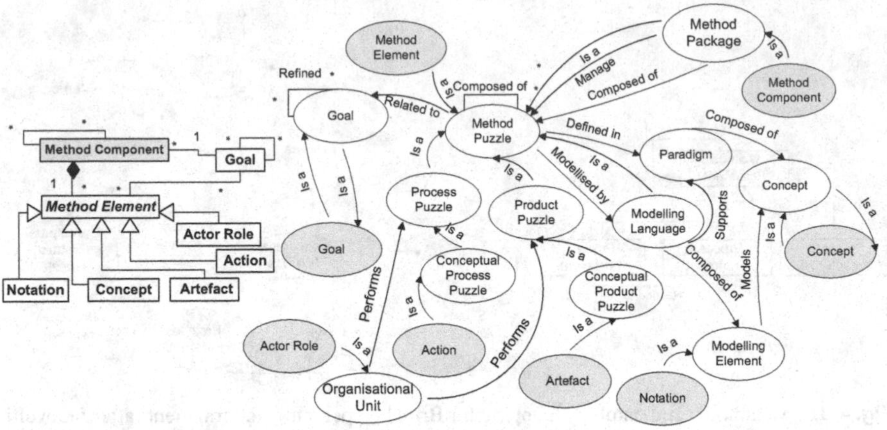

Fig. 4.33 Metamodel and ontology mapping for method components (after Iacovelli and Souveyet, figure 4, 2011) (With kind permission of Springer Science + Business Media)

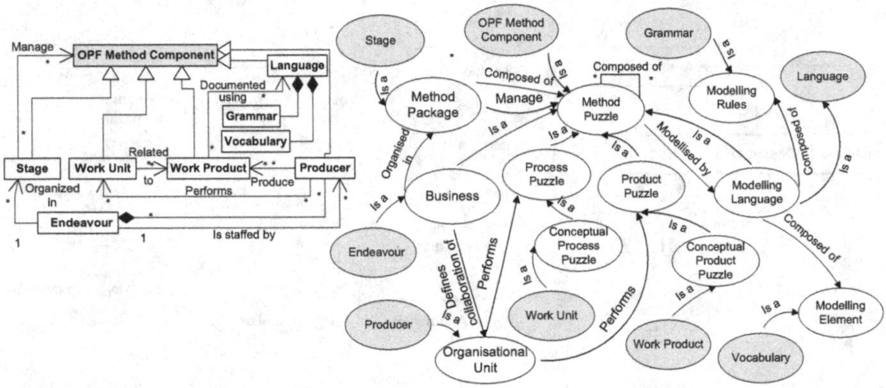

Fig. 4.34 Metamodel and ontology mapping for OPF method components (after Iacovelli and Souveyet, figure 5, 2011) (With kind permission of Springer Science + Business Media)

4.3 Process Models for SME

Several authors classify process metamodels[5] (e.g., Rolland 1998; Hug et al. 2009). Activity-oriented process metamodels focus on building process models by concentrating on the activities and tasks performed in producing a product together with their ordering (Rolland 1998). They typically comprise Work Units that have Work Products as inputs and outputs and that are performed by Producers playing a

[5] According to our discussion in Sect. 1.3 these should really be called process models. Here we keep the nomenclature adopted by these specific authors in order to link back to the source articles.

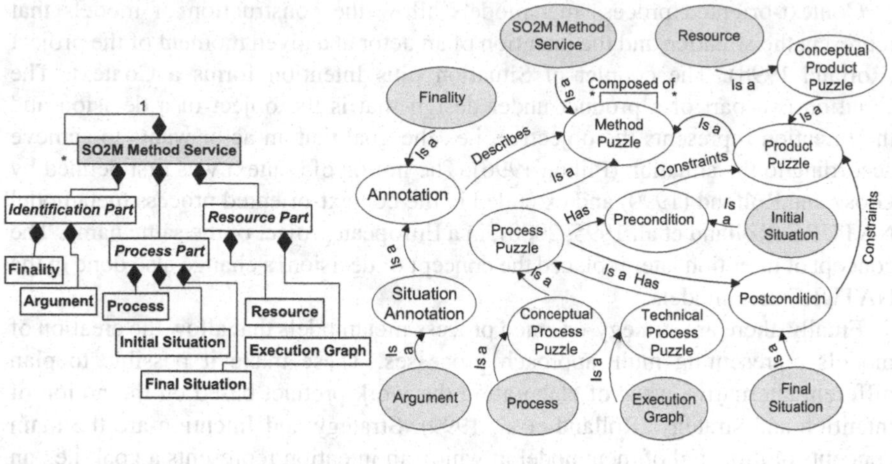

Fig. 4.35 Metamodel and ontology mapping for SO2M method services (after Iacovelli and Souveyet, figure 6, 2011) (With kind permission of Springer Science + Business Media)

specific Role. Examples of activity-oriented process models include SPEM (OMG 2005a), the Open Process Framework (OPF 2005), OOSPICE (OOSPICE 2002), SMSDM (Standards Australia 2004) and SEMDM (ISO/IEC 2007, 2010a) although some of these, such as SPEM and ISO 24744, include other viewpoints such as product in varying degrees of detail. The process models of methods such as RUP (Kruchten 1999), XP (Beck 2000) and SCRUM (Schwaber and Beedle 2001) are also instances of activity-oriented process metamodels and thus are activity-oriented process models.

The second identified category is that of product-oriented process metamodels. These permit the instantiation of models that couple work products to the activities that generate them (Rolland 1998). They utilise a definition in which work products have an associated State together with appropriate interstate transitions. This work product state represents the situation of a product at a precise moment of the process, the transitions being defined between these states in order to represent the order in which the states can change. The transitions relate a source state to a target state and are triggered by an event. Examples here are the metamodel for statecharts (Harel 1987) and State Machines (OMG 2007), as well as the metamodel of the Entity Process Model (EPM) (Humphrey and Kellner 1989) and the State-Transition template (Finkelstein et al. 1990).

Thirdly, decision-oriented process metamodels are used to create methods that focus on the successive transformations of a product due to decision-making processes (Rolland 1998). They count the concepts of Issues that need answers defined as Alternatives; an Alternative can be supported or refuted by Arguments and an Issue is a problem met during method construction. IBIS (Kunz and Rittel 1970) was probably the first such approach to use a decision-oriented process—later improved by Potts and Bruns (1988), Potts (1989) and in the DAIDA project (Jarke et al. 1992).

Context-oriented process metamodels allow the construction of models that represent the situation and the intention of an actor at a given moment of the project (Rolland 1998). The couplet of Situation plus Intention forms a Context. The situation is a part of a product under design that is the object of a decision and the intention represents the objective, i.e., the goal that an actor wants to achieve according to the situation (Plihon 1996). The notion of context was first defined by Grosz and Rolland (1990) and extended in the context-oriented process metamodel NATURE (Rolland et al. 1995, 2000), in a European project of the same name. The concept of intention later replaced the concept of decision, a change also done in the NATURE metamodel.

Finally, there are strategy-oriented process metamodels that allow the creation of models representing multi-approach processes. These make it possible to plan different alternative ways of elaborating the work product based on the notion of intention and strategy (Rolland et al. 1999). Strategy and Intention are the main concepts of this kind of metamodel in which an intention represents a goal, i.e., an objective to be achieved. A strategy is a manner by which to achieve that intention (Zoukar 2005). [As far as we know, MAP (Rolland et al. 1999) is the only strategy-oriented process metamodel published to date, although a goal-focussed SME approach for process model construction is described in Gonzalez-Perez et al. (2009) and the work product pool approach of Gonzalez-Perez and Henderson-Sellers (2008a) is also loosely related in that context.] The process model of the requirement engineering method 'CREW-l'Ecritoire' (Rolland et al. 1999) has also been formalised using MAP. MAP has also been used to represent an engineering method for matching ERP[6] functionalities and organisational requirements (Zoukar and Salinesi 2004). Situation and Intention feature strongly in the method chunk approach to SME, as described in this book (see also Brinkkemper 1996).

As noted above, many of the processes involved in situational method engineering can be described by one of the process models outlined above and notated using the concept of a *map* (Rolland et al. 1999). A map is described as a directed labelled graph consisting of nodes representing *intentions* and edges to represent *strategies*. An intention captures the notion of a task to be accomplished whereas the strategy suggests the way in which this goal can be achieved. Ralyté and Rolland (2001a) note that the core concept in a map is the *section* (Fig. 4.36). This is defined as a triplet given by

section = <*source intention*, *target intention*, *strategy*> or $<I_i, I_j, S_{ij}>$

A map is then a composition of a number of sections, expressed by the authors as

map = ∑*section* = ∑<*source intention*, *target intention*, *strategy*> *plus a Start and a Stop intention* (Rolland et al. 1999).

Figure 4.37 depicts, stylistically, the elements of a map. Let us assume that there are three intentions (represented here by the nodes I1, I2 and I3) forming a fragment of a map in which intention I1 has already been achieved. The question is what

[6] Enterprise Resource Planning.

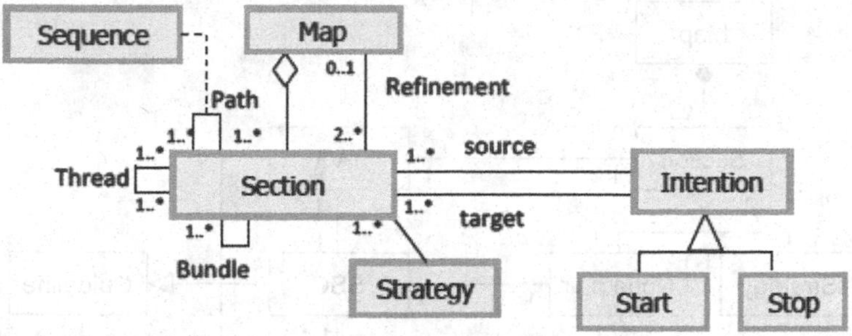

Fig. 4.36 Metamodel formalism of the 'map' process representation (after Deneckère et al. 2009) ©IEEE reproduced with permission

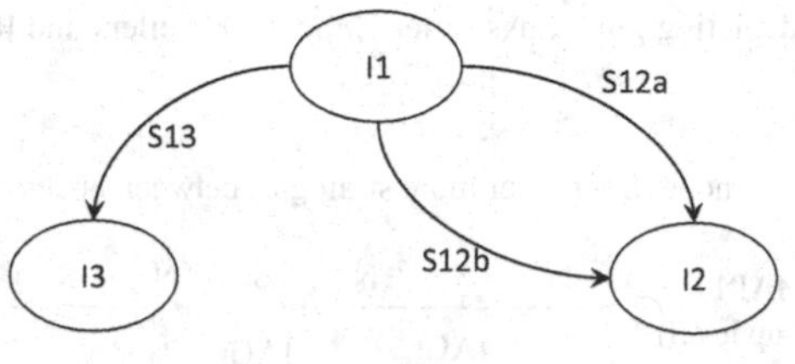

Fig. 4.37 Stylised representation of a map fragment showing associated Intention Achievement Guidelines (IAGs) (after Henderson-Sellers and Ralyte 2010)

intention is the next and by what strategy is it achieved. From the viewpoint of I1, the first problem is whether to select intention I2 or intention I3. Advice on this selection is needed. Let us say I2 is selected. We note that this can be achieved by one of two strategies, S12a and S12b—but which should be selected? Advice on this selection is needed. Once a strategy has been selected (say S12a), then advice is needed on how to enact the selected strategy.

These three pieces of required advice (said to embody *method knowledge*) are represented as *guidelines* (Rolland et al. 1999). These are, respectively, an Intention Selection Guideline (ISG), associated with the source intention; a Strategy Selection Guideline (SSG), associated with a pair of intentions $<I_i, I_j>$, and an Intention Achievement Guideline (IAG), associated with a section (node pair plus strategy) (Fig. 4.38). In the example of Fig. 4.37, when the decision is being made regarding moving from node I1 to either I2 or I3, the advice is given as an ISG. Having made a selection (in the above example I2), the means to make the transition—a choice of several strategies—is given by an SSG. The actual enactment of the selected strategy (here S12a) also requires advice—from the IAG.

Both the ISG and SSG are navigational guidelines. It is the IAG that embodies potential sub-processes and can therefore itself be represented as an (embedded) map. Since an IAG shows how to realise the target intention from the source intention using the selected strategy (Ralyté and Rolland 2001b), it is said to depict 'tactics'. Indeed, Ralyté and Rolland (2001a) suggest that it is the merging of the

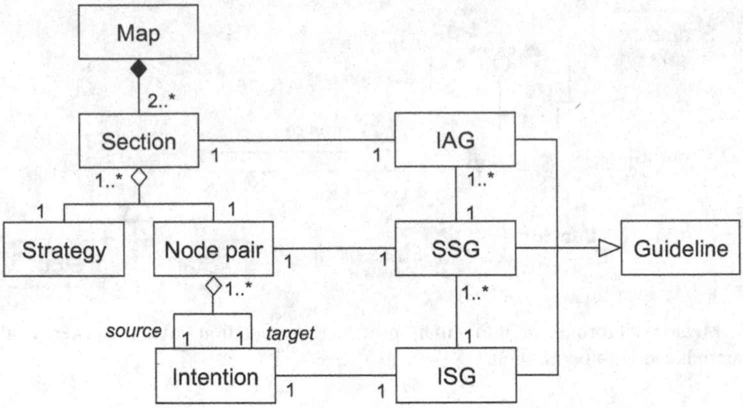

Fig. 4.38 Metamodel depicting guidelines (after Henderson-Sellers and Ralyte 2010)

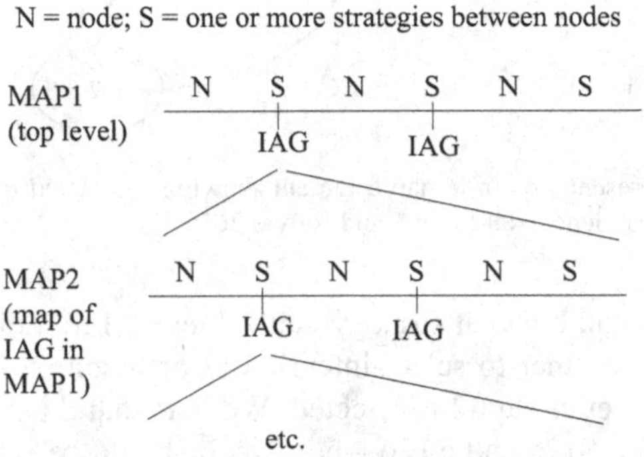

Fig. 4.39 The notion of levelling within a map (after Henderson-Sellers and Ralyte 2010)

tactical aspects of guidelines with the strategic aspects of the map that provides most value to SME.

Finally, it should be noted that there is a recursive possibility of a section being refined as an entire map at a lower level of granularity (Ralyté and Rolland 2001a; Ralyté 2004)—somewhat akin to the levelling notion of data flow diagrams (Fig. 4.39). Thus the strategy (S) linking two nodes is explicated by an IAG. This IAG, which represents a mini-process, can therefore itself be represented as a map. Thus at a lower level, the IAG itself is depicted as a set of nodes and edges (strategies). Then recursively each strategy in this lower level map can be elaborated upon with an IAG, which in turn could be represented as a map. And so on.

Guidelines embody method knowledge and are described in terms of a body that encapsulates this knowledge, together with a signature (Rolland et al. 1999). The signature of a guideline (later renamed interface by this research group) is a combination of a situation and a relevant intention.

signature = <*situation*, *intention*>

Type of guideline	Map reference	Guideline signature
IAG_i	$< I_i, I_j, S_{ij} >$	(sit(I_i), I_j)
ISG_i	$< I_i >$	(sit(I_i), *Progress from* I_i)
SSG_i	$< I_i, I_j >$	(sit(I_i), *Progress to* I_j)

Note: Sit(I_i) refers to the product situation after I_i has been achieved.
Progress refers to a class of intentions in order to progress in the process.
In contrast I_j, I_i are achievement intentions.

Fig. 4.40 Correspondence between the kind of guideline and the guideline signature (after Rolland et al., figure 7, 1999) (With kind permission of Springer Science + Business Media)

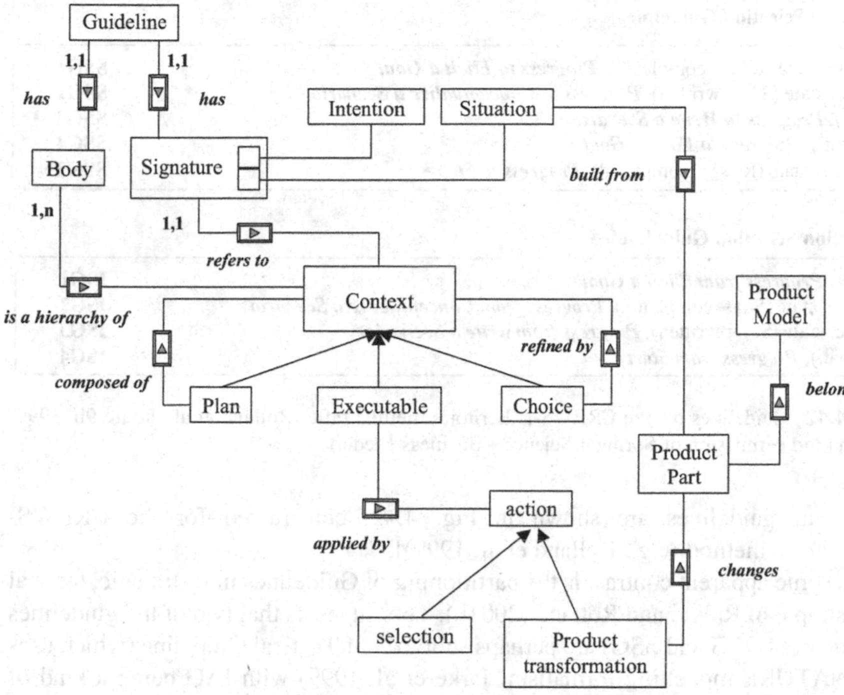

Fig. 4.41 The guideline metamodel (after Rolland et al., figure 8, 1999) (With kind permission of Springer Science + Business Media)

For the navigational guidelines (i.e., ISG and SSG), the relevant intentions represent the progress to or from the intention rather than the intention itself (Fig. 4.40). The situational part refers to the product part(s) resulting from the achievement of the source intention, i.e., it plays the role of a precondition. The body of a guideline can be Executable, Plan or Choice with two different contextual relationships: composition or refinement (Fig. 4.41). It describes how the chunk should be applied in order that the intention is achieved (Ralyté 2004). [Some

Intention Achievement Guidelines (IAG)

<(G), ***Elicit a Goal with case based discovery strategy***>	**IAG1**
<(RC: state (RC) = completed), ***Elicit a Goal with composition strategy***>	**IAG2**
<(RC: state (RC) = completed), ***Elicit a Goal with alternative strategy*** >	**IAG3**
<(RC: state (RC) = completed), ***Elicit a Goal with refinement strategy*** >	**IAG4**
<(Stat.), ***Elicit a Goal with linguistic strategy*** >	**IAG5**
<(Stat.), ***Elicit a Goal with template driven strategy***>	**IAG6**
<(G), ***Write a Scenario with template driven strategy*** >	**IAG7**
<(G), ***Write a Scenario in free prose***>	**IAG8**
<(Sc: state (Sc) = written), ***Conceptualize a Scenario with computer support strategy***>	**IAG9**
<(Sc), ***Conceptualize a Scenario manually***>	**IAG10**
<(RCs: state (RCs) = completed), ***Stop with completeness strategy***>	**IAG11**

Strategy Selection Guideline

<(RC: state (RC) = completed), ***Progress to Elicit a Goal***>	**SSG1**
<(Sc: state (Sc) = written), ***Progress to Conceptualize a Scenario***>	**SSG2**
<(G), ***Progress to Write a Scenario***>	**SSG3**
<(Stat.), ***Progress to Elicit a Goal***>	**SSG4**
<(RCs: state (RCs) = completed), ***Progress to Stop***>	**SSG5**

Intention Selection Guideline

<(G), ***Progress from Elicit a Goal***>	**ISG1**
<(RC: state (Sc) = completed), ***Progress from Conceptualize a Scenario***>	**ISG2**
<(Sc: state (Sc) = written), ***Progress from write a Scenario***>	**ISG3**
<(Stat.), ***Progress from Start***>	**ISG4**

Fig. 4.42 Guidelines for the CREWS-L'Ecritoire method (after Rolland et al., figure 9b, 1999) (With kind permission of Springer Science + Business Media)

exemplar guidelines are shown in Fig. 4.42, constructed for the CREWS-L'Ecritoire method (e.g., Rolland et al. 1999)].

In some apparent contrast is the partitioning of Guidelines into strategic, tactical and simple of Ralyté and Rolland (2001b). This suggests that two of the guidelines of Fig. 4.38 (ISG and SSG) are perhaps subtypes of Tactical Guideline (which uses the NATURE modelling formalism: Jarke et al. 1999) with IAG being a kind of Strategic Guideline, which itself is closely associated with the Map concept, as suggested by Ralyté and Rolland (2001b).

The map approach has been shown to be equivalent to a regular graph, i.e., any set of data that can be visualised in terms of a vertex set and an edge set (Deneckère et al. 2009)—for which a metamodel is shown in Fig. 4.43. In order to create an equivalence, these authors identify the need to augment the map metamodel (of Fig. 4.36) by a weight criterion associated with each section (called Indicator in Table 4.1 and Fig. 4.44). This weight may be either static (those known in advance) or dynamic (those evaluated 'on-the-fly')—see Table 4.1. Deneckère et al. (2009) then show how easy it is to map between the map approach and the graph approach (Fig. 4.44).

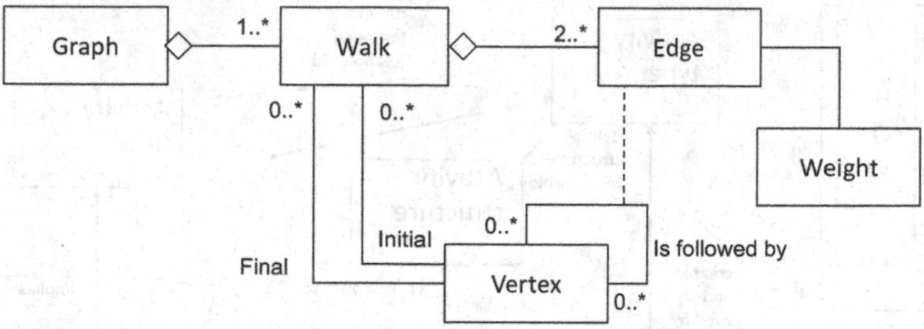

Fig. 4.43 Metamodel for the graph approach (after Deneckère et al. 2009) ©IEEE reproduced with permission

Table 4.1 Indicator values (after Deneckère et al. 2009) ©IEEE reproduced with permission

Static indicators		
Cost	Scale from 0 to 10	Indicates the potential cost that the section realisation will involve
Time	Scale from 0 to 10	Shows the time that the engineer will have to spend to realise the section
…	…	
Dynamic indicators		
Goal state	Scale from 0 to 10	Gives an evaluation about the completeness of the intention realisation
Guideline realisation	Scale from 0 to 10	Indicates the percentage of realisation of the guideline corresponding to the section

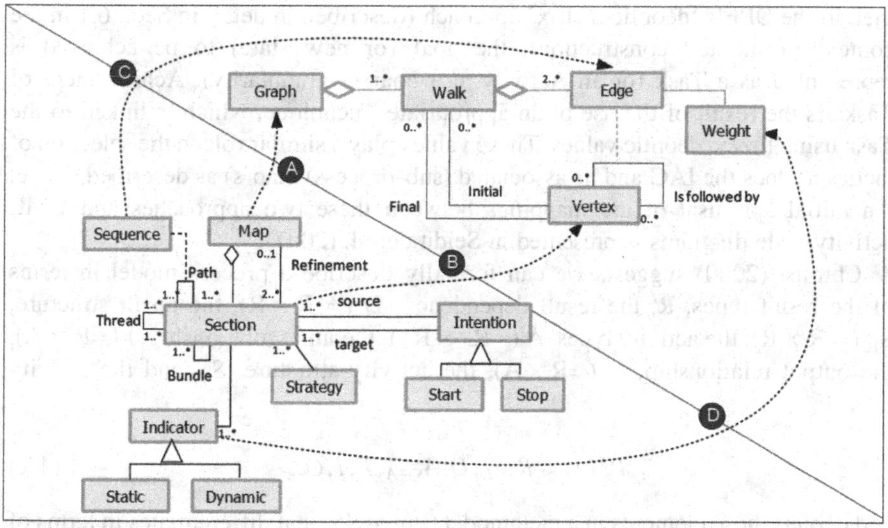

Fig. 4.44 Correspondence between map and graph (after Deneckère et al. 2009) ©IEEE reproduced with permission

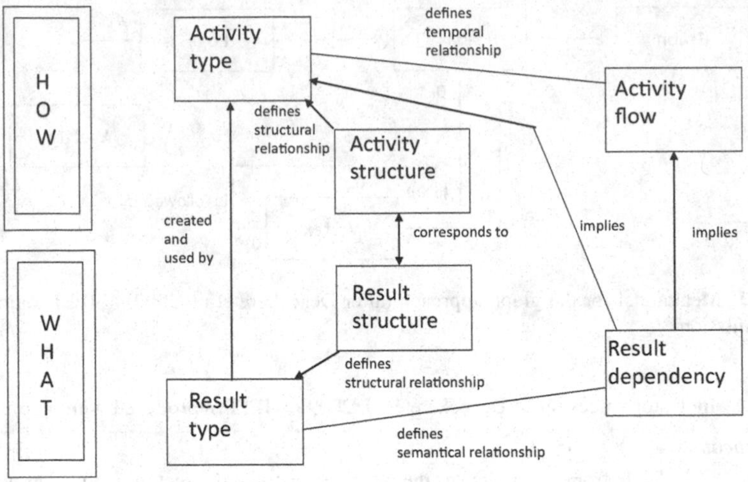

Fig. 4.45 Cascade model: a process metamodel (after Chroust, figure 2, 2000) (With kind permission of Springer Science+Business Media)

In summary, the map approach to visualising and enacting a process model explicitly recognises the role of *strategies* in realising goals (a.k.a. intentions), and provides a multi-thread and multi-flow, non-deterministic approach to process (and hence method) engineering in which dynamic SME is the rule rather than the exception (Rolland et al. 1999). Indeed, it is entirely feasible to add new nodes and/or arcs (strategies) dynamically as the process map is enacted.

Whereas, in the 'map' approach, the node represents a goal or an objective to be met, in the OPF's 'deontic matrix' approach (described in detail in Sect. 6.1 in the context of method construction), the goal (or new state) to be achieved is represented as a Task (or an Activity at a coarser granularity). Achievement of Tasks is the result of the use of an appropriate Technique, which is linked to the Task using fuzzy, deontic values. These values play a similar role in the selection of tactics as does the IAG and its associated (sub-process) map(s) as described above. An initial appraisal of the mappings between these two approaches and UML activity-style diagrams is presented in Seidita et al. (2007).

Chroust (2000) suggests we can formally describe a process model in terms of the result types, R, the result dependency, D (= R × R), the result structure, S_R (= R × R), the activity types, A (=R* × R*), the input relationship, I (=R × A), the output relationship, O (=R × A), the activity structure, S_A, and the activity flow, F.

$$PM = < R, S_R, D, A, S_A, F, I, O > \quad (4.1)$$

and depicts these elements in a metamodel (Fig. 4.45) that differentiates in terms of the 'how' (various activity meta classes) and the 'what' (various result meta classes).

One potential problem with *all* overly simplistic process models that adopt an input–output model (such as that described above) is that there is no opportunity to clarify the nature of the relationship between the work product and the process element. Naming XX as an output from process PP confounds several possibilities: for example, whether PP has created XX or whether it has updated it (from a previous incarnation). A similar ambiguity exists for the relationship between an input work kind and the process into which it is input—will PP change the input or merely read it for information? To solve this, ISO/IEC 24744, for example, includes a concept called ActionKind, which specifies clearly the specific roles played by related work products. This is done with the Type attribute, which can signal a Create, ReadOnly, Modify or Delete event. Furthermore, input/output-based approaches are useless from an enactment perspective, because a tool cannot 'reason' about the dependencies and life cycles of the work products if the only information it has refers to inputs and outputs. By using the ActionKind approach, a tool can derive work product life cycles, determine dependencies and 'reason' about the methodology as enacted.

A slightly different approach to method visualisation that attempts to combine process and product elements was proposed by van de Weerd et al. (2006)—similar in intent to the earlier proposal of Saeki (2003a). Called a 'process-data diagram' (later renamed as Process Deliverable Diagram) or PDD, this diagrammatic approach combines a UML Activity Diagram and a UML class diagram (see also Vlaanderen et al. 2011). It was originally described as follows: "The process-data diagram we use consists of two integrated meta-models". However, Henderson-Sellers (2007) raises the concern that this means that these are not two metamodels in the OMG sense since the left hand side is an (M1 level) UML Activity Diagram. The second concern raised is that the right hand side contains concepts that appear to be at the M2 level (e.g., OPENCONCEPT) yet this appears several times and therefore violates several tenets of metamodelling.

Although linking process and product diagrams is clearly advantageous, there are many problems—for instance, as identified by Atkinson and Kühne (2001b). In the PDD of Fig. 4.46, for example, there is an introduced relationship between process and product elements (the dashed arrow in the diagram) that requires definition (in a metamodel)—a suggested such metamodel diagram is given in Fig. 4.47 (Henderson-Sellers 2007).

There have been attempts to formalise the PDD (van de Weerd et al. 2007; Jeusfeld 2011). Figure 4.48 shows the metamodel proposed by van de Weerd et al. (2007), which is clearly a UML M2-level class diagram style—despite its (inaccurate) label as a 'meta-metamodel'. Contrasting this with Fig. 4.47, we note that Fig. 4.48 does not explicitly support the difference between open and closed concepts and appears to rename Process as Method. It also introduces a differentiation between ProcessFragment and DeliverableFragment, which is in line with many authors' interpretation of situational method engineering (Brinkkemper 1996).

More recently, Jeusfeld (2011) has analysed the most recent PDD version (supplied to him via a seminar at his university in 2010). An example is shown in

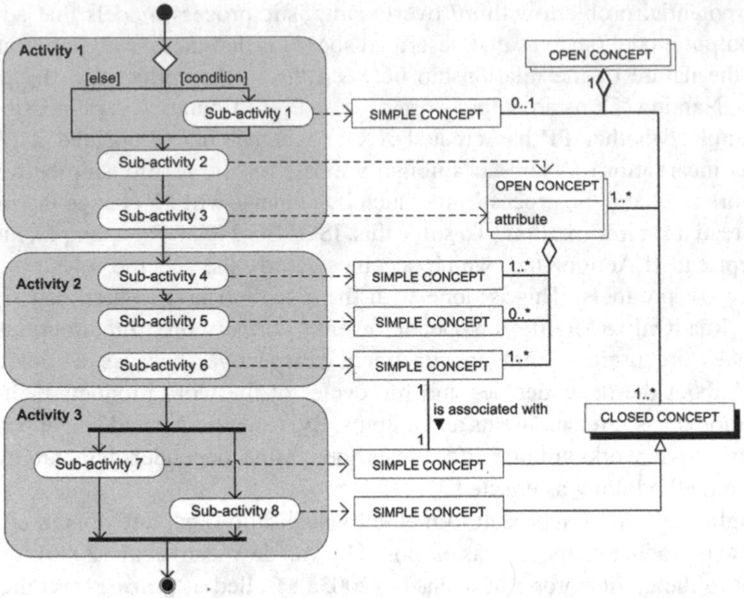

Fig. 4.46 Example process-data diagram (after van de Weerd et al. 2006) © John Wiley and Sons Limited. Reproduced with permission

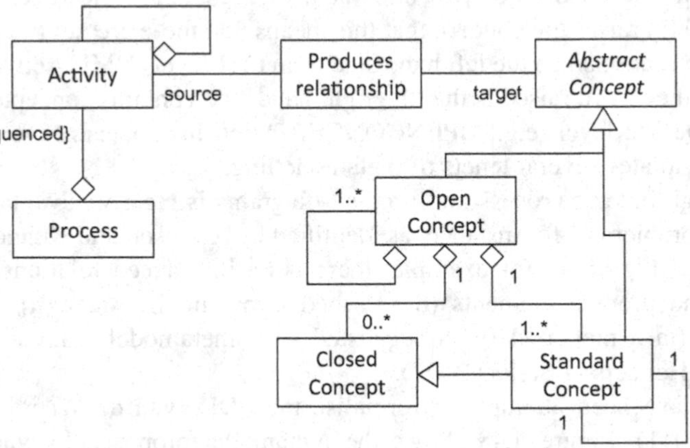

Fig. 4.47 Metamodel diagram proposed for the PDD (reprinted from Henderson-Sellers 2007, with permission from IOS Press)

Fig. 4.49. His aim is to ensure that the PDD provides for the checking of fragment composition and traceability as well as raising some database-oriented concerns. Jeusfeld (2011) suggests that the PDD is in fact a workflow model that includes the work products *within* the confines of the workflow. He identifies the potential cross-layer connections as identified by Atkinson and Kühne (2001b) wherein the work

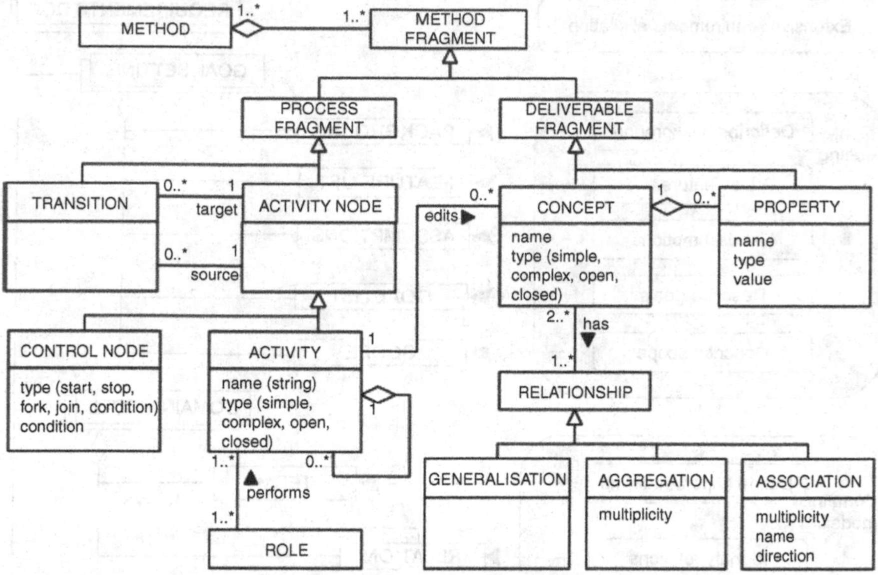

Fig. 4.48 Metamodel of process-data diagram (after van de Weerd et al., figure 3, 2007) (With kind permission of Springer Science + Business Media)

product and the action of making that work product are at different OMG meta levels. He argues that the PDD is able to depict such cross-level situations, used to link a product part with a process part.

4.4 Other Formalisations

Although it is generally acknowledged that all fragments should adhere to a metamodel definition (Sect. 4.1), formal semantics are still needed, and not just for the structural and representational aspects. It is the *meaning* that must be correctly captured (Ter Hofstede and Verhoef 1997). This could be done by using clear and concise natural language, a process algebra, temporal logic or Petri nets, e.g., Ter Hofstede and Verhoef (1997), Sunyaev et al. (2008). An approach of increasing interest is the use of ontologies, both for underpinning models and metamodels (Sect. 4.2). An interesting study by Iacovelli and Souveyet (2011) maps several SME styles onto a reference ontology (Fig. 4.30). More technical approaches to formalisation need, in the future, also to embrace previously ignored people issues, as addressed, for example, by the 'ways of working' of Rolland et al. (1995).

One theoretical proposal is the ER-based language MEL (Method Engineering Language) (Brinkkemper 1996; Brinkkemper et al. 2001), which anchors method descriptions in an ontology, especially useful for SME. MEL has representation for both the product and the process aspects of method fragments and chunks at varying levels of granularity and is founded on first order predicate logic (Harmsen and

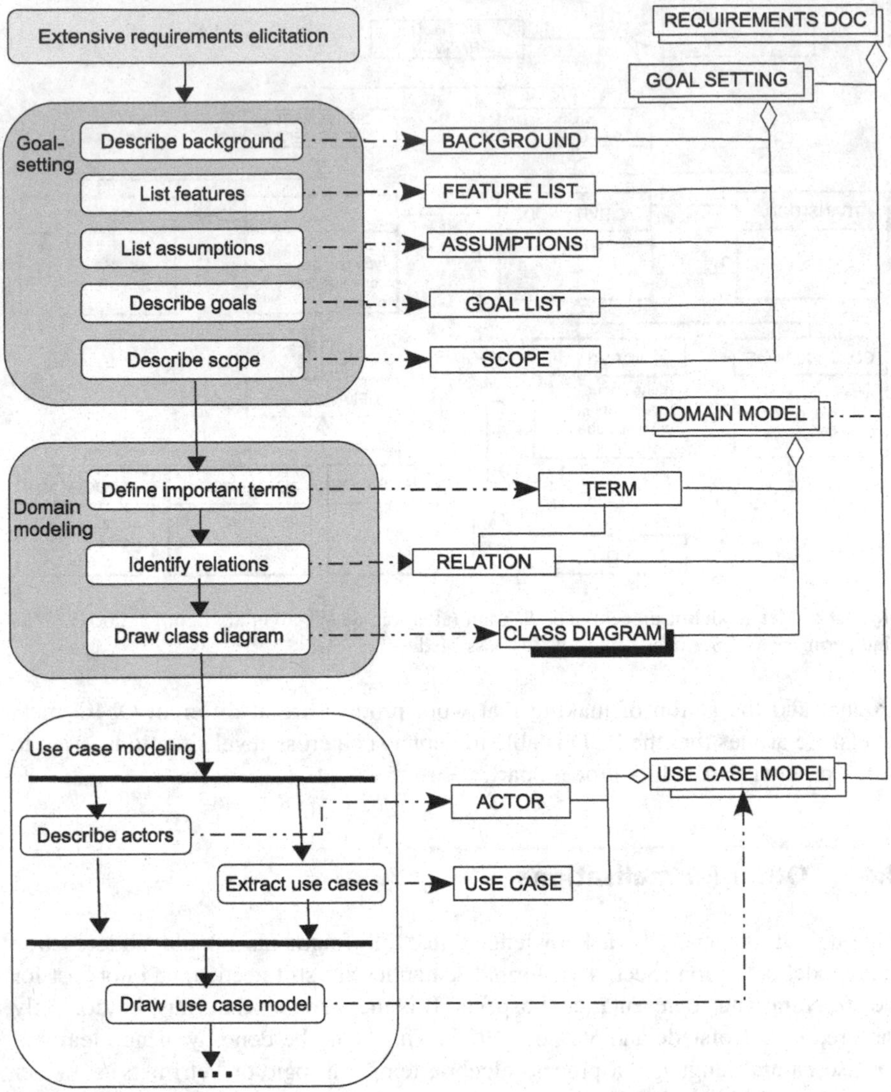

Fig. 4.49 Example PDD—excerpted from a web engineering method (after Jeusfeld, figure 1, 2011) (With kind permission of Springer Science + Business Media)

Saeki 1996). It has a number of keywords (Table 4.2) as well as an underpinning metamodel (Fig. 4.50). A simplified example for the description of a product fragment is given in Fig. 4.51.

In addition, MEL has basic operations to insert and remove fragments in and out of the method base, to retrieve fragments and to assemble them into a situational method. It also has syntactic constructs to compose a complex process from activities, such as sequencing, conditions, iterations, parallelism and non-determinism.

Table 4.2 Some keywords of MEL and their descriptions

MEL keyword	Description
(a) For product fragments	
PREREQUISITE	Relates product fragments required by a process fragment
ASSOCIATION	Association between fragments including cardinality and roles
PART OF	Aggregation relationship
IS_A	Generalisation relationship
PRECEDE	Ordering
RULE	Specifies a static constraint
(b) For process fragments	
MANIPULATED BY	Insertion and maintenance of fragments in method base
DECISION	Fork in process
ITERATION	Iteration in process
(c) Both process and product fragments	
PROPERTY TYPE	Type allocated to a property
PROPERTY VALUE	Value of a property
METHOD OBJECT	Method fragment, association or symbol

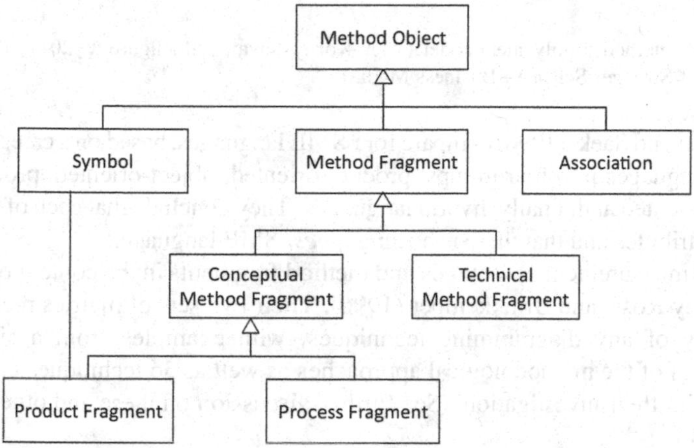

Fig. 4.50 A portion of the metamodel for MEL (derived from Harmsen and Saeki 1996)

```
PRODUCT Object:
    LAYER Concept;
    PART OF Use Case Model;
    SYMBOL Rectangle;
    NAME TEXT;
    ASSOCIATED WITH {(send,),(receive,)}.
```

Fig. 4.51 Exemplar description of a product fragment using MEL derived from the work of Brinkkemper et al. (2001)

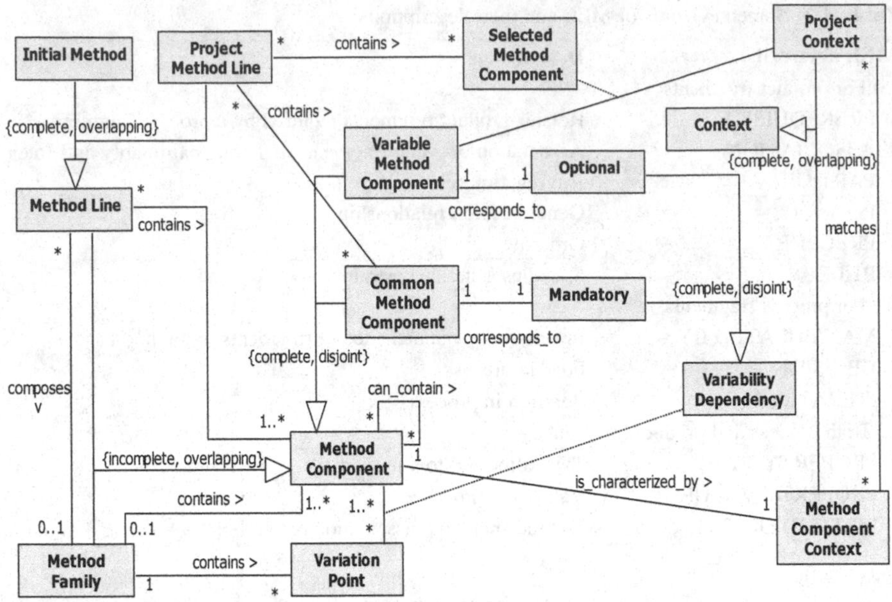

Fig. 4.52 A method family metamodel (after Kornyshova et al., figure 1, 2011) (With kind permission of Springer Science + Business Media)

Harmsen and Saeki (1996) compare four SME languages, based on a categorisation of these languages into four groups: product-oriented, object-oriented, process- and decision-oriented and, finally, hybrid languages. They conclude that each of these has positive attributes and that there is no single *best* SME language.

Formal measurement of methods and method fragments in the context of SME is proposed by Rossi and Brinkkemper (1996). Their two sets of metrics measure the complexity of any diagramming techniques, with examples from a significant number (11) of the methodological approaches as well as 36 techniques contemporaneous with their investigation. (See further discussion on these and other metrics in Chap. 8.)

More recently, some investigations (e.g., Cervera et al. 2011; Zdravkovic et al. 2011) have been made of possible links between SME and Model-Driven Engineering (MDE) (a.k.a. MDD or Model-Driven Development) or its OMG instantiation as MDA (Model-Driven Architecture: OMG 2003; Mellor et al. 2004). Saeki (2002) also investigates the potential value of model transformations in SME. Using graph rewriting rules, he proposes an approach to method construction applicable to any formal description technique (FDT) that can be used to transform either model diagrams or metamodel diagrams.

The idea of process and method families (a.k.a. method lines) is introduced from a formal viewpoint by Kornyshova et al. (2011) in terms of a method family metamodel, as shown in Fig. 4.52. These authors also adapt the MAP approach

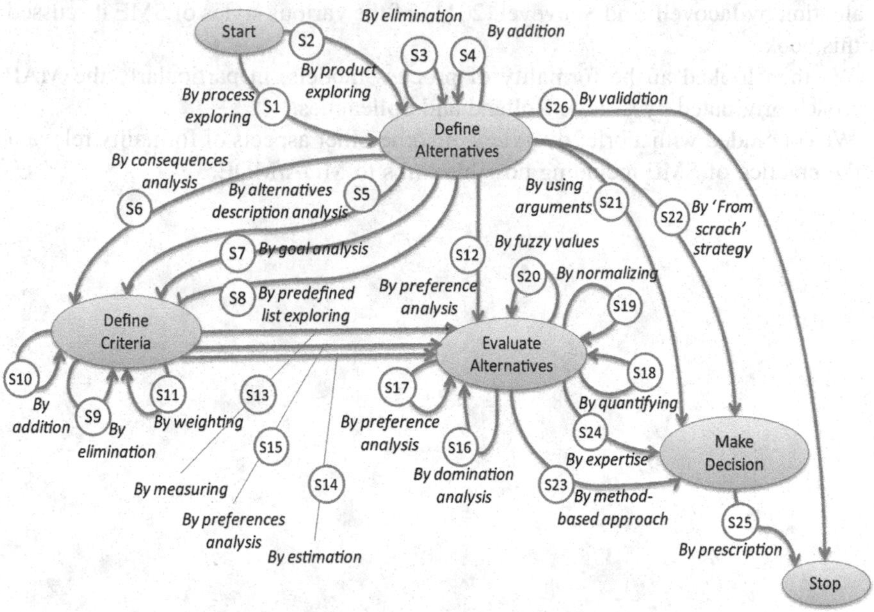

Fig. 4.53 A map representing a method family for decision making (after Kornyshova et al., figure 4, 2011) (With kind permission of Springer Science + Business Media)

described earlier in this chapter to create method families (an example of method family is shown in Fig. 4.53—see also Chap. 7).

4.5 Summary

Formal aspects of SME encompass metamodels, tools and some more mathematical descriptions. In this chapter, we first examined in detail what is meant by a metamodel and how such a model is used in SME. In particular, we have seen how the mathematically based powertype is used to create an architecture in which an SME approach is able to support both the methodology (process model) and the enactment of that methodology on real-life projects and other endeavours. This led into a discussion about standardisation; in particular the ISO/IEC International Standard 24744, which has directly applicability to the specification of method fragments and uses the powertype approach (Fig. 4.10). We also included some other metamodel-based approaches outside of the standards arena and included some suggestions of model improvements, including the incorporation of method rationale, goals and descriptors (as discussed in Chap. 3). In Chap. 7 we will discuss the tool support for method construction and use.

In Sect. 4.2, we evaluated how ontologies, both domain ontologies and foundational ontologies, may offer value to SME, including a detailed ontological evaluation by Iacovelli and Souveyet (2011) of the various styles of SME discussed in this book.

We then looked at the formality of process models, in particularly the MAP approach originated by Colette Rolland and colleagues.

We concluded with a brief overview of some other aspects of formality relevant to the practice of SME including possible links to MDA/MDE.

Part II

Applying SME in Practice

Identification and Construction of Individual Method Chunks/Fragments

5

Summary of What We Will Learn in Chapter 5

- How to construct method parts from (a) modular existing methods, (b) non-modular existing methods and (c) from scratch
- How to create method parts from existing repository contents
- How to identify potentially reusable and useful method parts for storage in a method base

In the first few chapters, we have set the scene by defining, both informally and formally, the ideas behind situational method engineering in terms of method fragments, method chunks, method components and method rationale. We have also briefly discussed issues of granularities and interfaces. However, we have to date neglected to answer the vital question "Where do these method fragments, method chunks, etc. come from?" This is the topic of this chapter.

In the following, we will use the terminology of 'method part' (introduced in Chap. 2) when we wish to refer to all the flavours of method fragments, method chunks, method components, method patterns, etc. although, in some cases, techniques apply only to, say, finding method chunks and are irrelevant for method fragment identification or vice versa. In that case, we will use the specific terminology of chunk, fragment, etc. as appropriate.

We can say that a method part might pre-exist in some published or otherwise available methodology; it might be able to be extracted from some published or otherwise available methodology; or it might need to be constructed ab initio to fulfil some specific (new) need. In the case of method chunks, there is a fourth possibility: that of creating a new chunk from parts of pre-existing chunks (in the repository a.k.a. method base).

Ralyté (2004) notes that several authors (e.g., Harmsen 1997; Brinkkemper et al. 1998; Ralyté and Rolland 2001b) propose extracting method parts from existing methods but offer no advice on how to do this. She therefore fills this

B. Henderson-Sellers et al., *Situational Method Engineering*,
DOI 10.1007/978-3-642-41467-1_5, © Springer-Verlag Berlin Heidelberg 2014

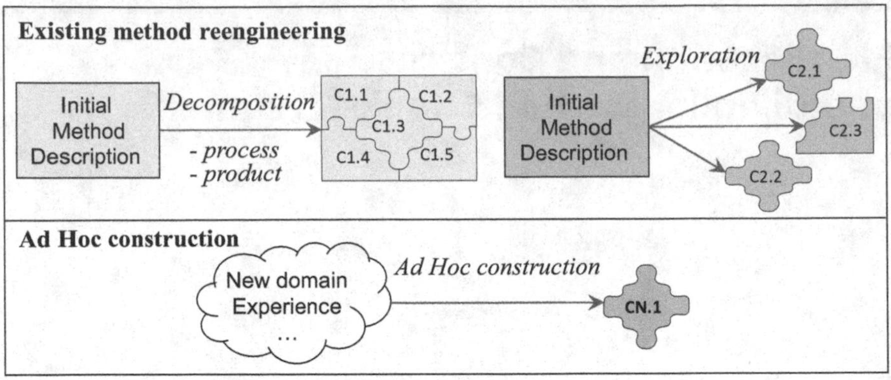

Fig. 5.1 Different approaches for method part construction (after Ralyté 2004)

gap with two possible approaches which she names as: (1) existing method reengineering, which uses the technique of decomposition in order to modularise the whole method or that of exploration, and (2) ad hoc construction (Fig. 5.1). These two approaches are described in detail in Sects. 5.2 and 5.3 below, respectively. Both can be described by the same process (map) model[1]—see later discussion of Fig. 5.4. But first, let us consider the less likely but much easier topic of acquisition of method parts from existing modularised methods (Sect. 5.1).

5.1 Parts from Modular Existing Methods

Probably the easiest way to construct method parts for your method base is to extract these from another modularised and pre-existing methodology. However, few if any of these exist or, rather, are publicly available—although there are some exceptions (e.g., Serour et al. 2002).

If a modular existing method has been identified, then, when extracting parts from its method base, one must be careful to check that the same metamodel is being used. If not, then some revision may be necessary to realign the extracted part to the new metamodel. If the metamodels are similar, this needs little effort (e.g., reformulating OPF method fragments to fragments conformant to the ISO/IEC 24744 metamodel); if the metamodels are dissimilar, then the effort needed may well outweigh the benefits gained from this approach.

Similarly, the granularity of both the metamodel and the method parts should be carefully considered (Henderson-Sellers and Gonzalez-Perez 2010, 2011).

[1] From Sect. 4.2, we note that a map consists of a number of *intentions* (source and target) linked by a number of (possibly only one) *strategies* (see also Rolland et al. 1999).

5.2 Parts from Non-modular Existing Methods

Most of the SME literature focusses on identifying and using method parts from *existing* methodologies in a plug-and-play format. This is called 'existing method reengineering' by Ralyté (2004), who notes that, since most existing software development methods are inherently *non*-modular, extracting appropriate modularised method parts can present difficulties. As noted above, method reengineering decomposes an existing complete method into method parts. This decomposition when applied to method *chunk* construction may be either process-driven or product-driven (see further discussion below).

Although Ralyté and Rolland (2001b) focus specifically on the definition of new method *chunks* by reengineering them from existing methods, much of their work is equally applicable to all the sorts of method parts. The overall process of such 'assembly-based method engineering' is shown in Fig. 5.2a. From an initial, pre-existing method, a set of reengineering guidelines is applied (see below) to recast the existing method in a modular format. These new method parts are then put into the method base from which, in due course, new methods can be created by the application of 'method construction guidelines' to a selection of method parts from the method base (as discussed in detail in Chap. 6). The upper part of Fig. 5.2a is expanded in Fig. 5.2b, which shows that in applying the method reengineering process model the method metamodel (Fig. 4.16 here) is instantiated as the basis for the method parts to be abstracted from the initial method description by the method engineer. Thus, when the method engineering decomposes an existing, interconnected method, he/she needs to be aware of the situational context that will help to determine not only the method part's content but also the metamodel to which the method part's structure needs to be conformant (see also Bézivin and Gerbé 2001). Some possible metamodels were discussed in Chap. 4, one of the major ones being the ISO/IEC International Standard 24744 (ISO/IEC 2007, 2010a)—see also panel discussion reported in Ågerfalk et al. (2007).

From their analysis of the papers of Song (1995), Punter and Lemmen (1996) and Brinkkemper et al. (1998), Ralyté and Rolland (2001a) suggest that previous work was highly focussed on method fragments as independent units. To extend these ideas, Ralyté and Rolland (2001b) introduce the map representation (that we described in Sect. 4.3) for the process of method part identification and definition. To formalise the ideas of Fig. 5.1, first we need to determine the contextual guidelines (i.e., the requirements) for the target method part(s). This is the so-called reengineering process, which allows the ideas represented in the cartoon of Fig. 5.2 to be represented as a map first and then decomposed into method parts. This process model (Fig. 5.3) includes four intentions or 'steps': first a section is defined, a section being <*source intention*, *target intention*, *strategy*>. Next, a guideline is defined that identifies the situation and intention *of the method part*. These first two intentions represent the process for method map construction as proposed in Rolland et al. (1999) and are relevant when the input method is not available in a modularised format, i.e., it has no formalised process model as a map. Thirdly, the method part itself can now be identified based on the specification

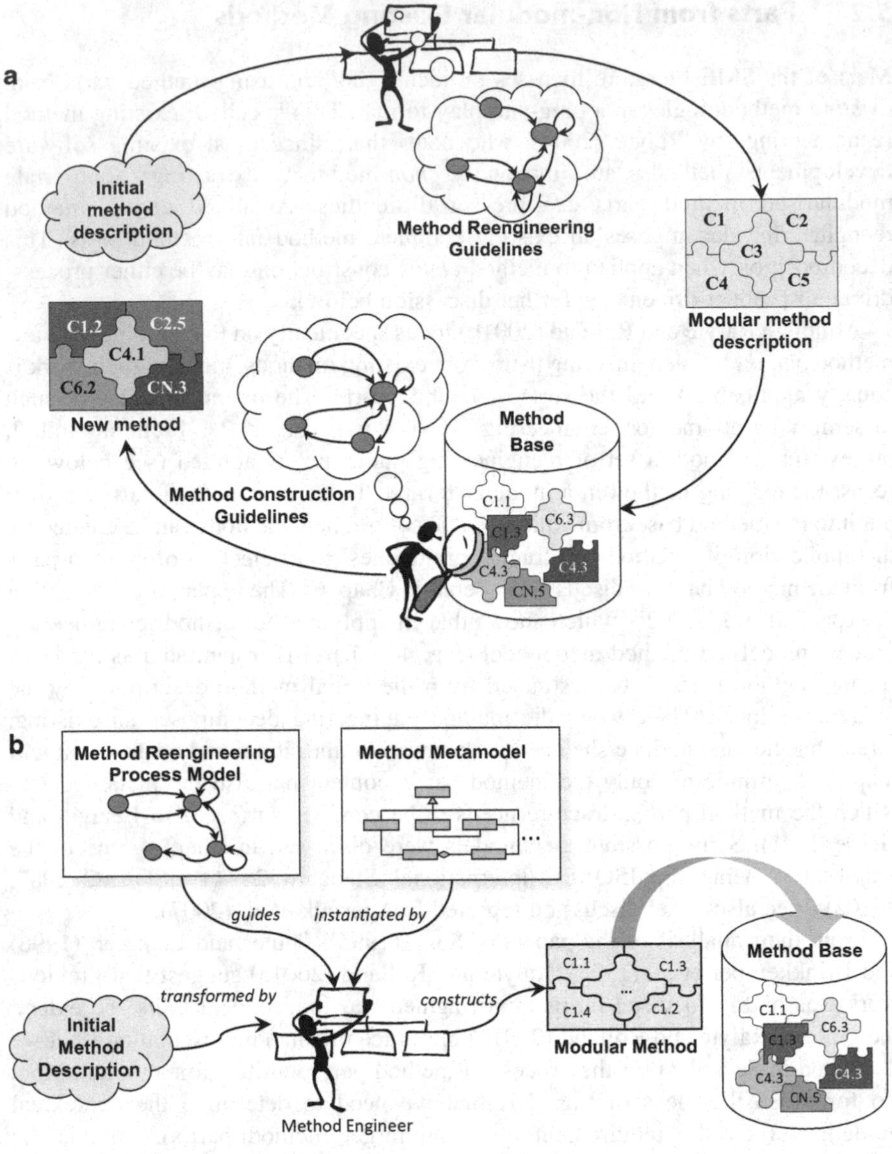

Fig. 5.2 (**a**) Assembly-based method engineering (after Ralyté and Rolland, figure 1, 2001b) (With kind permission of Springer Science + Business Media.). (**b**) An approach to method reengineering (after Ralyté and Rolland, figure 2, 2001b) (With kind permission of Springer Science + Business Media)

stated in the interface (part of the guideline), i.e., we now create/identify a method part that fits the pre-selected guideline/interface specification. Having identified the method part, it is then formally defined, verified and checked for completeness. The latter two intentions focus on ensuring the reusability of the part.

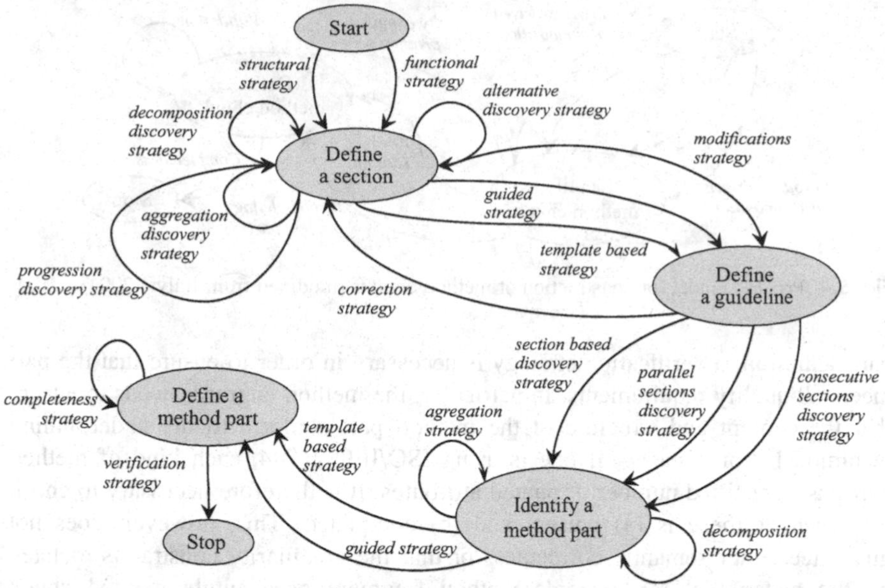

Fig. 5.3 Method reengineering process model. Intentions are shown as oval symbols and the strategies by the arcs linking the oval-shaped nodes (modified from Ralyté and Rolland, figure 4, 2001b) (With kind permission of Springer Science + Business Media)

To satisfy these intentions (of Fig. 5.3), Ralyté and Rolland (2001b) offer a set of strategies. To satisfy the first intention (*Define a section*), there are two strategies: structural and functional. The former is used when there is no pre-existing formal model of the method under consideration, the latter when there is already formal knowledge attached to this method. New sections may then be defined recursively using one of the four strategies, as shown in Fig. 5.3, originally developed in the context of method chunks but in fact more generally applicable. The decomposition and aggregation discovery strategies have obvious meaning: the alternative discovery strategy substitutes a previously existing strategy and the progression discovery strategy helps to create a new section as a progression from an existing one. Strategies associated with the next section (*Define a guideline*) are threefold: template-based, guided and modification; the last of these linking together changes in guidelines and changes in sectioning. For *Identify a method part*, there are three suggested strategies. The first (section-based discovery) assumes that every section of the map may be regarded as a method part with an associated intention achievement guideline (IAG)—actually the IAG associated with this section forms the basis for the method part. The parallel section discovery strategy identifies the IAG associated with parallel sections and aggregates them into a new guideline. Similarly, the consecutive sections discovery strategy assists in identifying the IAG associated with consecutive map sections and in integrating them appropriately to give the guideline for the new aggregate chunk. Finally, *Define a method part* has two strategies, similar in character to those of *Define a guideline*. Following method

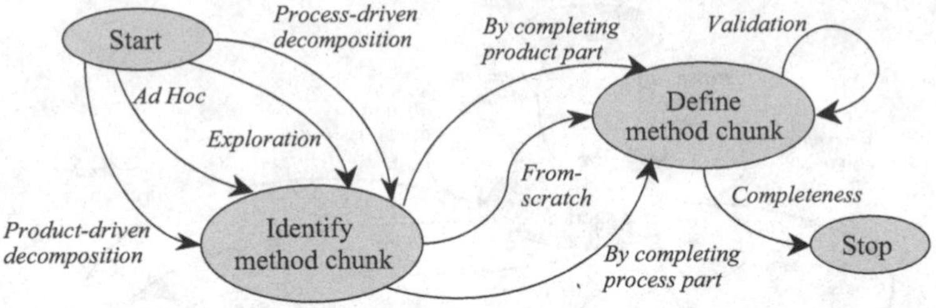

Fig. 5.4 Process model for construction of method chunks (modified from Ralyté 2004)

part definition, a verification strategy is necessary in order to ensure that the part meets all quality requirements. In particular, the method engineer needs to ensure that the content and structure of the method part conform to the underpinning metamodel. For instance, if one is using ISO/IEC 24744, each kind of method part has a specified number of named attributes. It is therefore necessary to check that each of these is (a) present and (b) completed. This, however, does not guarantee either semantic correctness or that the granularity constraints dictated by the metamodel for a single method fragment or a single method chunk (e.g., Fig. 4.24) have been met. Based on mathematical theories of abstraction and granularity, Henderson-Sellers and Gonzalez-Perez (2011) discuss the impact of granularity constraints on method fragment construction, including consideration of its atomicity (or otherwise). However, determining solid and objective heuristics for ensuring that fragments are atomic is an unresolved issue at the time of writing—subjectivity and therefore experience of the method engineer is at present still required.

Figure 5.4 focusses on the two intentions of *Identify a method chunk* and *Define a method chunk*. (This diagram is chunk-specific as it differentiates process- and product-focussed aspects of a chunk.) For the *Identify a method chunk* intention, there are four possible strategies: *Process-driven decomposition*, *Product-driven decomposition*, *Exploration* and *Ad hoc* (thus refining the strategies suggested in Ralyté and Rolland 2001b—Fig. 5.3). Ralyté (2004) argues that process-driven decomposition is more likely and more powerful, thus concentrating on the process-driven decomposition and exploration strategies only. We note that the process-driven decomposition corresponds to the first three intentions (and related strategies) of the earlier method reengineering process model presented in Fig. 5.3.

The second important strategy, according to Ralyté (2004), is the exploration strategy for method chunk identification. This aims to discover multiple purposes for an existing model, often when the process part of the chunk is unspecified, i.e., when the only availability is a product fragment that requires, for a chunk definition, to be linked to an appropriate process-focussed fragment; in other words, this strategy is not applicable to method fragment identification. This leads to the creation of alternatives for the process model as well as accompanying guidelines. The relevant guideline (IAG3 of Table 5.1) states that the *Exploration strategy* considers different possibilities to use a model (or a method). "The chunk

Table 5.1 IAGs provided by the process model for method chunk construction (after Ralyté 2004)

ID	Section	Guideline description
IAG1	<Start, Identify method chunk, Process-driven decomposition>	This guideline proposes to redefine the process model of the method under consideration into a strategic guideline first and next to consider each of its sections and/or different combinations of sections as a reusable and autonomous guideline and a potential basis for a method chunk
IAG2	<Start, Identify method chunk, Product-driven decomposition>	This guideline deals with the method product model decomposition into autonomous and reusable parts. If the method product model is not formalised yet, the guideline helps to construct the corresponding product model by using a metamodelling technique and then to identify parts of this metamodel as potential product parts of method chunks
IAG3	<Start, Identify method chunk, Exploration strategy>	This guideline proposes to consider different possibilities to use a model (or a method). The chunk identification process can be based on the goal and/or situation analysis; the same model can be used to satisfy different engineering goals and can be applied in different engineering situations
IAG4	<Start, Identify method chunk, Ad Hoc strategy>	The Ad Hoc identification focusses on the analysis of some specific Application domain and identification of method requirements supporting engineering of this domain
IAG5	<Identify method chunk, Define method chunk, By completing product part>	This guideline helps to extract the product part used by the chunk process part from the method product model or to formalise it
IAG6	<Identify method chunk, Define method chunk, By completing process part>	This guideline helps to define the process part of the method chunk allowing to satisfy its objective by using the corresponding product part
IAG7	<Identify method chunk, Define method chunk, From scratch>	This guideline helps to define the product and process models satisfying the objective of the method chunk
IAG8	<Define method chunk, Define method chunk, Validation>	This guideline proposes the rules for method chunk quality and coherence validation
IAG9	<Define method chunk, Stop, Completeness verification>	This guideline verifies if all the identified method chunks were defined

identification process can be based on the goal and/or situation analysis; the same model can be used to satisfy different engineering goals and can be applied in different engineering situations". This is depicted as a map in Fig. 5.5, which shows a single intention, achieved through either a situation-driven or goal-driven strategy.

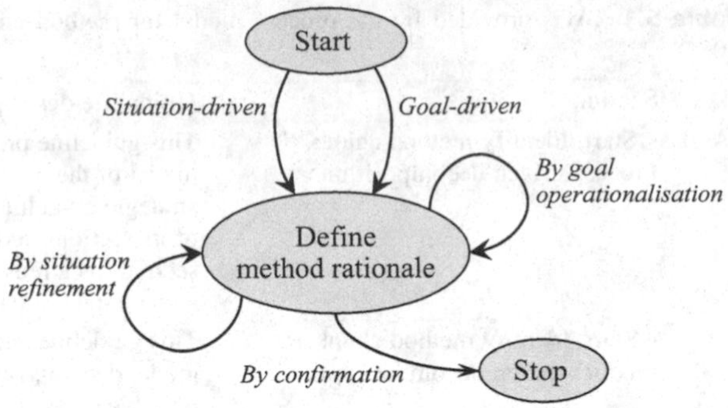

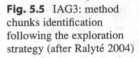

Fig. 5.5 IAG3: method chunks identification following the exploration strategy (after Ralyté 2004)

For the *Define a method chunk* intention (Fig. 5.4), there are three possible strategies identified: *By completing process part*, *By completing product part* and *From scratch*. The selection of one of these strategies depends on how the method chunk was identified previously. If *Process-driven decomposition* was applied, the product part of the chunk has to be formalised next following the *By completing product part* strategy, i.e., the metamodel of the chunk product part has to be created. Conversely, if the *Product-driven decomposition* was used to identify the chunk, its process model has to be formalised next following the *By completing process part* strategy, i.e., by using any process modelling formalism (i.e., Map or activity diagram). Finally, the *From scratch* strategy is needed when both product and process parts of the method chunk have to be formalised following its identification in an *Exploration* or *Ad Hoc* way. Strategies relating to ad hoc approaches are further discussed in Sect. 5.3.

The process model for method chunk construction (Fig. 5.4) is completed with a collection of guidelines. For each map section, there is an IAG. The progress in the map, the selection of the next intention and next strategy to apply is guided by the intention selection and strategy selection guidelines (ISG and SSG). All these guidelines (IAG, ISG and SSG) are summarised in Tables 5.1, 5.2 and 5.3.

The discussion above and the guidelines presented in Tables 5.1, 5.2 and 5.3 demonstrate that the definition of method chunks to form non-modular methods is mainly based on the analysis, decomposition and formalisation of two method perspectives—process and product. The choice of the perspective to start the chunk identification depends on how the original method is specified. Indeed, these two perspectives are not always equally specified in the method description. Most methods prioritise the product perspective by formalising diagrams without well-defined guidelines on how to use them. Other methods offer some informal narrations and recommendations on how to construct different models that they propose. Finally, only a few methods provide a fully formalised process perspective. In any case, the complete definition of a method chunk requires formalising both perspectives.

Of course, this chunk-focussed approach can be adapted for the definition of other types of method parts, i.e., method fragments.

Table 5.2 ISGs provided by the process model for method chunk construction (after Ralyté 2004)

ID	Intention	Guideline description
ISG1	I_0: Start	Progress to the intention I_1: *Identify method chunk* if one of the following preconditions is satisfied
		– There exists a method to reengineer
		– There is a method chunk that could be decomposed
		– There is a model to explore
		– There exists an Application domain to be supported by method chunks
		– There is an engineering goal to be satisfied by a method chunk
		– There is an engineering situation to be supported by a method chunk
ISG2	I_1: Identify method chunk	Progress to the intention I_2: *Define method chunk* if at least one method chunk have been identified
ISG3	I_2: Define method chunk	Progress to the intention I_4: *Stop* if all identified method chunks have been defined
		Progress to the intention I_2: *Define method chunk* if at least one method chunk has been defined

Table 5.3 SSGs provided by the process model for method chunk construction (after Ralyté 2004)

ID	<Source intention, target intention>	Guideline description
SSG1	<Start, Identify method chunk>	Select the IAG1 if there exists a method to reengineer providing a more or less formalised process model, or a method chunk that could be decomposed into the smaller ones
		Select the IAG2 if there exists a method to reengineer providing only its product model
		Select the IAG3 if there is a model to explore
		Select the IAG4 if there exists an Application domain to be supported by method chunks or there is an engineering goal to be satisfied by a method chunk or there is an engineering situation to be supported by a method chunk
SSG2	<Identify method chunk, Define method chunk>	Select the IAG5 if the process part of the chunk has been defined
		Select the IAG6 if the product part of the chunk has been defined
		Select the IAG7 if the product and process parts of the chunk have to be defined from scratch
SSG3	<Define method chunk, Define method chunk>	Select the IAG8 if at least one method chunk has been defined
SSG4	<Define method chunk, Stop>	Select the IAG9 if all identified method chunks have been defined

5.3 Parts from Scratch

The third way of creating method parts, and one that was more evident in the early days of SME, is to create them 'from scratch'. This approach has already been depicted in the map diagrams of Figs. 5.1 and 5.4 above. Ralyté (2004) discusses this construction, which is also particularly useful for supporting the emergence of new technologies, such as web development (e.g., Henderson-Sellers et al. 2002b) or agents (e.g., Henderson-Sellers 2005; Low et al. 2010).

Ad hoc/from scratch construction is aimed at a more subjective process by which new ideas are consolidated into an appropriate method part for inclusion in a full, newly oriented methodology (Chap. 6). The aim is to encapsulate both new theories and, in particular, new experiences. Thus, the inputs to the construction process may well be verbal, informal and experiential. A term that is often used in industry is 'best practice'. From a research viewpoint this has no adequate definition. However, since SME is not only research and theoretically based but also practically focussed for use in industry, the idea of 'best practice' should not be discounted. What is needed are some more objective measures of whether a practice is 'best' other than a statement from an industry 'pundit' (which, unfortunately from a research point of view, is often the case). Nevertheless, when constructing a method part from scratch, an expert's intuition is often needed to blend together industry ideas of what is best practice in the particular focus area and what can be shown to be acceptable from a research and quality viewpoint. Thus, the ideas of method fragment quality and constructed method quality, discussed in Chap. 8, are paramount.

In the early days of SME, most of the industry-strength repositories of method parts (e.g., the early versions of the OPF repository, currently available at http://www.opfro.org) had a significant input of best practice. At that time, the role of metamodels, although appreciated, had not reached the degree of sophistication and standardisation that we discussed in Chap. 4. With the advent of metamodels such as that of the OPEN Process Framework (Firesmith and Henderson-Sellers 2002) and, later, OMG's Software Process Engineering Metamodel (SPEM) (OMG 2005a, 2008) and the international standard ISO/IEC 24744 (ISO/IEC 2007), more objectivism could be added such that now, when new technologies demand a whole new suite of method parts (agents, SOA, etc.), best practice, theory and metamodel conformance all play roles in a synergistic construction of method parts 'from scratch'. [Some of these quality ideas are discussed below (Sect. 5.5) in terms of creating a really reusable and high quality method base or repository of method parts.]

5.4 Creating New Method Parts from Existing Repository Contents

Although identified here as a separate approach to method part identification and construction, this has strong similarities to the first approach (Sect. 5.1) in that method parts already exist—in Sect. 5.1 in a method and here in a method base.

Two possibilities are immediately evident: (1) modification of existing method parts to become new ones and (2) amalgamation of several (probably atomic) method parts to create a larger chunk, component or pattern.

If method parts stored in the repository have all been verified as being atomic, then it is unlikely that they will participate in any further modification by themselves. However, if, as is often the case, the method parts stored in the method base have grown 'organically', then it is quite likely that some of the stored method parts, although supposedly atomic, are not so. (This could also occur if a more fine granular metamodel has replaced a coarser granular one during the lifetime of the method base.) Such a situation, that of organic growth, has been observed to occur during the evolution of the method fragments in the OPF method base. Henderson-Sellers and Gonzalez-Perez (2011) observe that in the original published version of OPEN (Graham et al. 1997), modelling was seen as beginning to subsume and replace the subactivities of object-oriented analysis and object-oriented design. Despite the use of the word 'modelling' within the subactivity called Evolutionary Development, itself embedded within the Build Activity of the OPEN Process Framework, in the formal description, modelling was really captured totally in the Task: Construct the object model. However, the description of this 'task' was extensive in both detail and scope and, indeed, in a later publication (Firesmith and Henderson-Sellers 2002, p. 274), the increasing size of this task was noted, where it is stated: "In this fairly Large-scale Task . . .", i.e., this task could no longer be considered to be atomic. These granularity problems were compounded when the OPF repository of method fragments was extended to support agent-oriented method construction. Consequently, the stored method fragment required some attention before it could be considered reusable. This was accomplished by replacing the single, bloated 'task' with 17 tasks (listed in Table 5.4), spanning both object technology and agent technology (Henderson-Sellers and Gonzalez-Perez 2011).

At the same time, an overall *Construct the model using the selected technology/paradigm* Activity (conformant to the ISO/IEC 24744 Process meta class) was created. Such a 'promotion' is in line with the philosophy underpinning the MDA and model transformations as well as the use of metonymy for creating a granularity abstraction hierarchy. This new activity then consists of a large number of tasks, these tasks being those listed in Table 5.4 where each one meets the notion of abstraction atomicity.

A more likely requirement is to amalgamate two or more method parts from the method base, for instance, in creating a method chunk. This has similarities to the exploration strategy discussed above in Sect. 5.2. It is likely that there are two stored parts: one product-focussed and one process-focussed. If we need to create an appropriate method chunk, then these need to be merged. Of course, first we need to be sure that the best available process and product parts have been retrieved prior to any such amalgamation. This was probably first discussed by Brinkkemper et al. (1998). They use as their example the construction of an object chart, as originally described in Coleman et al. (1992), from a statechart (Fig. 5.6) and a class model (Fig. 5.7). They argue that the amalgamation is relatively easy because there

Table 5.4 List of tasks 'carved out' of the original OPF construct the object model task (details given in Henderson-Sellers and Gonzalez-Perez 2011)

Identify classes and objects
Identify roles to be played by objects
Identify responsibilities of each class
Add stereotypes[a]
Implement responsibilities as class operations/methods and attributes
Identify class–class relationships including possible meronymic (whole-part) representations
Identify inheritance hierarchies
Add constraints such as cardinalities
Specify object behaviour, including its life cycle
Define state transition diagrams for each class, as necessary
Then, from our studies of agent modelling, we can identify tasks such as
Identify each agent in the system-to-be
Specify the tasks associated with each agent
Describe the roles that an agent may play in the system-to-be
Describe the ontology associated with each agent
Define the internals of each agent (agent structure)
Design the behavioural aspects of each agent
Design the interactions between agents

Note: [a]Stereotypes should be used with caution (e.g., Henderson-Sellers and Gonzalez-Perez 2006b), only when necessary and appropriate (and ensuring that each stereotype is correctly defined)

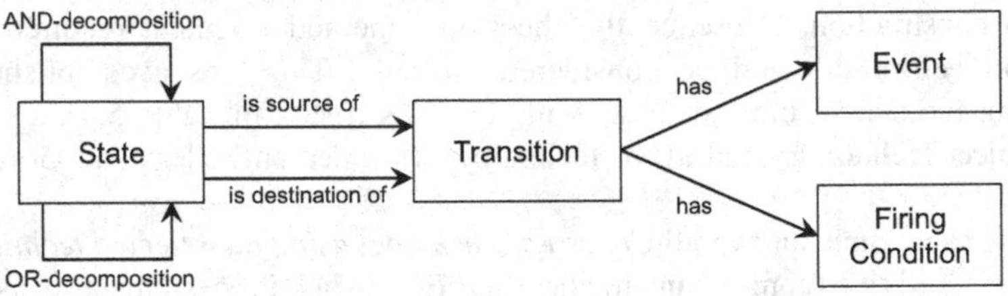

Fig. 5.6 Method part for statechart as presented by Brinkkemper et al. (figure 1, 1998) (With kind permission of Springer Science + Business Media)

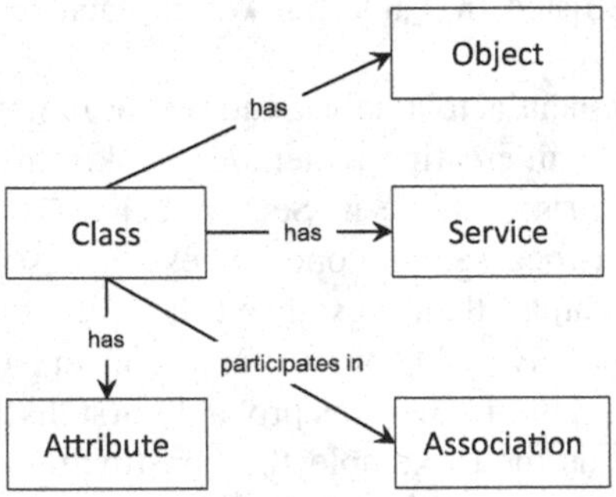

Fig. 5.7 Method part for class diagram as presented by Brinkkemper et al. (figure 2, 1998) (With kind permission of Springer Science + Business Media)

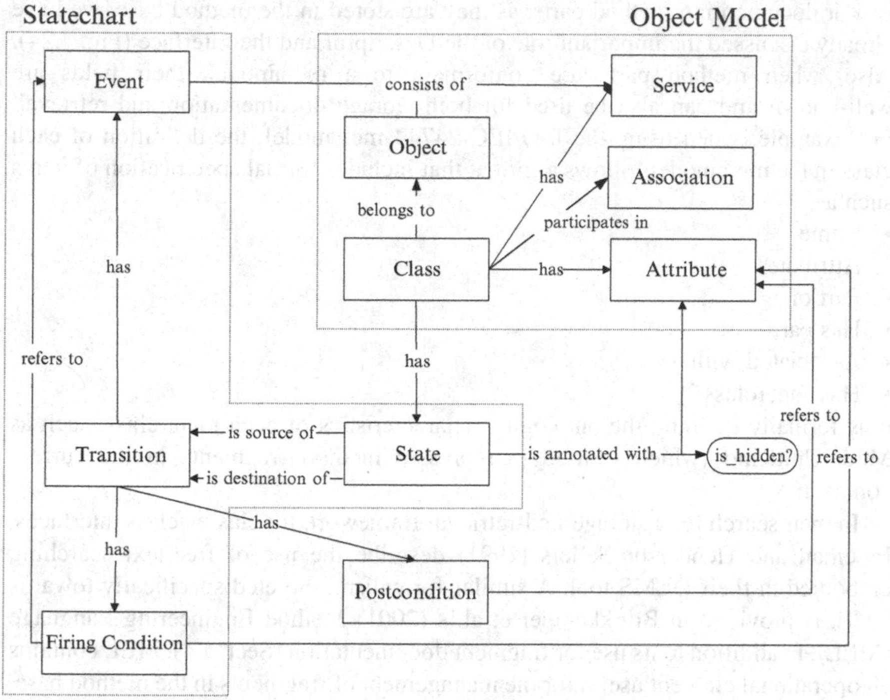

Fig. 5.8 Method part for merger of statechart and class diagram to form Fusion's object chart—as presented by Brinkkemper et al. (figure 3, 1998) (With kind permission of Springer Science + Business Media)

is no overlap but several connection points (e.g., between class and state); furthermore, the granularity and level of abstraction of each of these method parts is the same. Had it not been, then merging of method parts can become difficult if not impossible. In this case, both method parts refer to work products and the resultant; larger method part (Fig. 5.8) is also a work product. Other examples could be the amalgamation of a process part and a product part to form an integrated method chunk—as discussed above.

5.5 Identifying Reusable and Useful Method Parts for Storage in Repository

Although SME can be used to create method parts, and hence a full method, for a specific, one-off purpose, it is more usual to consider that SME will be used to create a comprehensive suite of method parts that can be stored in a method base or a method repository that can be used later multiple times. It is therefore important that these method parts are not only of good quality but are sufficiently well documented that they can be accurately retrieved on future occasions.

For documenting method parts, as they are stored in the method base, we have already discussed the important role of the Descriptor and the Interface (Fig. 4.24). Also, when method parts are conformant to a metamodel, their fields are well-known and can also be used for both storage documentation and retrieval. For example, when using the ISO/IEC 24744 metamodel, the definition of each class in the metamodel follows a format that includes formal specification of items such as:

- Name
- Attributes
- Part of
- Has part
- Associated with
- Has superclass

thus formally defining the ontological characteristics of each meta class, such as ModelUnitKind (which is used to represent method fragments in the current context).

In their search for a storage-and-retrieval framework for classes/class interfaces, Freeman and Henderson-Sellers (1991) describe the use of free-text searching embodied in their OLMS tool. A similar formalism, targeted specifically towards SME, is provided in Brinkkemper et al.'s (2001) Method Engineering Language (MEL). In addition to its use for fragment documentation (Sect. 4.4), MEL contains an operational element useful for the management of fragments in the method base, e.g., for the insertion into the database of fragments by use of its *methods administration function*.

To facilitate later retrieval, the documentation stored in one of the above-mentioned formats should provide adequate information for searching the method base. These metamodels categorise the method parts by the meta class to which they are conformant. Searching may also be needed across the free format descriptions. Furthermore, as noted by Ter Hofstede and Verhoef (1997) (and above), consideration should also be made of the levels of *coherency* and *granularity*. If the fragment is too coarse, it will require further decomposition after retrieval and before use; if too fine, then more construction effort will be required. Tools to undertake such searching are becoming available and are discussed in detail in Sect. 7.3. As an example, MetaEdit+ supports the retrieval of method components through search functionality for method part descriptions.

5.6 Summary

SME requires the creation and storage for later reuse of good quality method parts, be they atomic method fragments, method chunks, method components, method patterns, etc. The reusability of the parts can be enhanced considerably by paying attention to the recording of method rationale. This chapter has discussed the several ways in which these method parts may be created, as well as raising some issues regarding the quality (e.g., granularity, conformance to a metamodel) that is required of all these method parts in order that they may be retrieved from an existing method base and used to construct industry acceptable and useful methodologies. How these pieces are put together to form a full-scale methodology for software development is the topic of the next chapter.

Processes for Creating a Methodology from Method Parts

6

Summary of What We Will Learn in Chapter 6

- Appreciate the several ways in which the map approach of Chap. 4 can be used to create methodologies from method parts
- Compare and contrast map-based construction with deontic matrices and activity diagrams
- Understand the value of good requirements prior to method construction
- Appreciate the value of for reuse and with reuse for method parts
- How to use goals to drive SME's method construction activity
- How method configuration may help create a quality methodology

6.1 Approaches and Strategies

So far, we have discovered how to create method parts and what sort of underpinning formalisms are available; now we address the construction aspects, i.e., how to create a full, industry-strength methodology for software development from these method parts. This may be accomplished in a bottom-up fashion, starting with the identification of method parts and then 'gluing' them together; or commencing with the top-level architecture and recursively refining the detail to identify the method parts.

In this chapter, we first look at several overall strategies for method construction. We then consider establishing the requirements for the method and what that means in terms of locating suitable candidate method parts in the repository before finally discussing the method construction process itself. In later chapters, we will look at fine-tuning this basic method, a technique often known as *method tailoring*.

One major means of process construction is again based on the 'map' presentation model that we introduced in Chap. 4 and that we used extensively in Chap. 5. Figure 6.1 shows how this map approach of Rolland et al. (1998) and Ralyté (1999)

DOI 10.1007/978-3-642-41467-1_6,

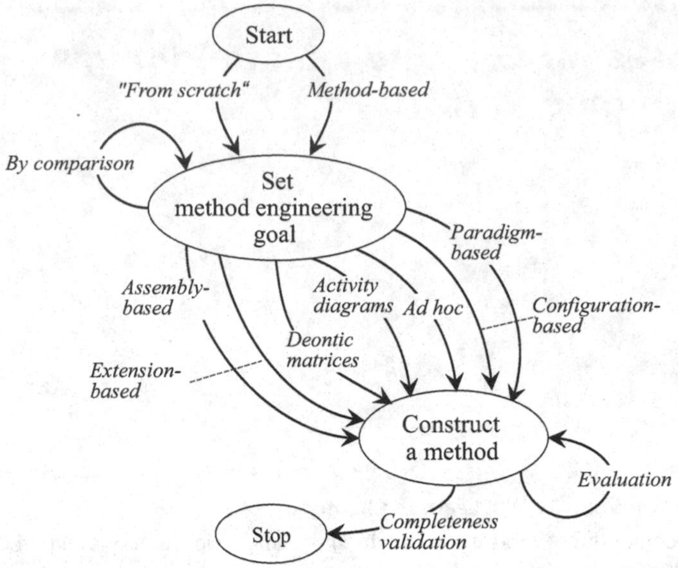

Fig. 6.1 Generic process for SME showing seven alternative strategies

can be used to describe a generic process model, a.k.a. a 'modular method metamodel' (Ralyté and Rolland 2001a). They propose that the use of this map-based model offers the possibility of representing any method by a conglomerate of reusable method chunks where we can consider that

- A method is a kind of chunk (at the highest level)
- A method is composed of several chunks
- A chunk can also be viewed as a kind of guideline (as described in Chap. 2)

This generic process model (Ralyté et al. 2003) describes the process by which a software development method(ology) is created as the output of an SME approach. It includes seven kinds of SME approaches: namely Assembly-based, Extension-based, Paradigm-based, Configuration-based, deontic matrices, activity diagrams and ad hoc (Fig. 6.1) and permits the combination of them in a particular SME process.

Figure 6.1 depicts two core intentions: *Set method engineering goal* and *Construct a method*. The first of these intentions represents two possibilities for the method engineer: either (1) taking an existing methodology as his/her base and making some adaptations and modifications. These adjustments in this so-called *Method-based* strategy may be in terms of (a) enhancement, (b) extension or (c) restriction. Alternatively, (2) if no base methodology seems appropriate, then a *From scratch* strategy is recommended.

The second core intention in Fig. 6.1, *Construct a method*, can be achieved with one of the seven different strategies. Using repository-stored method parts is labelled as an *Assembly-based* strategy (originally described in Ralyté and Rolland (2001a)). The second option, *Paradigm-based*, may be abstraction-based (Rolland 2002;

Ralyté et al. 2005), instantiated from a metamodel or adapted (Tolvanen 1998). The third option, named *Extension-based*, uses patterns applied to existing methods (originally described in Deneckère and Souveyet (1998) and Deneckère (2001)). These three strategies are augmented by a fourth, ad hoc, by Ralyté et al. (2004).

Other authors have proposed alternative approaches, which can be represented here (Fig. 6.1) as additional strategies in the 'map' visualisation. The fifth option uses deontic matrices (Sect. 6.1.3) to construct a method (e.g., Graham et al. 1997) whilst the sixth promotes the use of UML-style Activity Diagrams (Sect. 6.1.4). Finally, a configuration-based strategy is outlined by, e.g., Karlsson and Ågerfalk (2004, 2009b)—discussed in Sect. 6.1.5.

Once constructed, the method is then evaluated (*Evaluation strategy* in Fig. 6.1).

Perhaps of most interest here are the *Assembly-based* (Sect. 6.1.1) and *Paradigm-based* (Sect. 6.1.2) strategies. They are expanded into more detailed maps shown in Fig. 6.2 for the *Assembly-based* strategy and Fig. 6.3 for the *Paradigm-based* strategy. (The third strategy, *Extension-based*, is discussed in Chap. 7, Fig. 7.4.)

6.1.1 The Assembly-Based Approach

For the Assembly-based process model (Fig. 6.2), the intention *Select method parts* is described below in Sect. 6.3 and the intention *Assemble method parts* in Sect. 6.4.3. In turn, the *Requirements-driven* strategy can be expanded (Ralyté 2002) as described in Sect. 6.2.

Additional advice on chunk identification is offered in Kornyshova et al. (2007). As their basis, they take the typology of van Slooten and Hodes (1996), merging it with the ideas in Mirbel and Ralyté (2006), which they then offer as an extension to the assembly-based approach of Fig. 6.2 (as shown in Fig. 6.4). They then apply multi-criteria techniques that allow them to integrate new parameters into the chunk selection. Four new sections are proposed, all of which utilise four dimensions to represent project characteristics: Organisational, Human, Application domain and development strategy. Each dimension then has several characteristic values identified for it. As an example, Table 6.1 shows those for the human dimension.

The four new sections are as follows:

1. Specify Project Characteristics by using the Project characterisation strategy, which allows the method engineer to identify the critical aspects of the project.
2. Specify Project Characteristics by Refinement strategy, which is highly similar to the basic section.
3. Select Method Chunks by Project Characteristics (PC)-driven strategy, in which the multi-criteria techniques come to the fore for the selection of alternative method chunks. The section is expanded into two main intentions of *Define weights* and *Define priorities* (Fig. 6.5). The weighting allows a choice to be made between two intentions.
4. Select Method Chunks by Verification strategy, which aims to verify the efficacy of the multi-criteria technique usage.

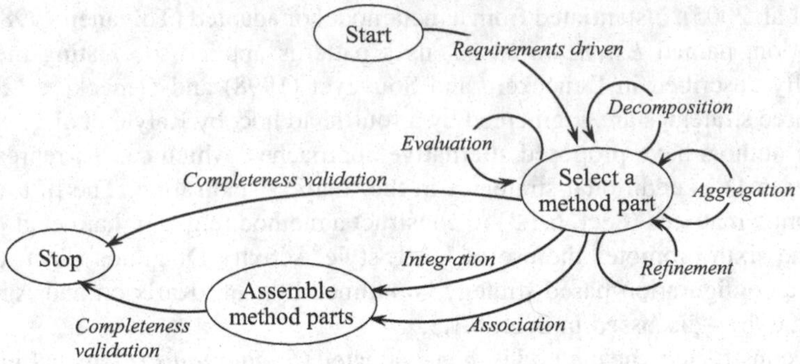

Fig. 6.2 Assembly-based process model for SME (redrawn from Ralyté and Rolland (2001a) and Ralyté et al. (2003), slightly modified from Henderson-Sellers and Ralyte (2010))

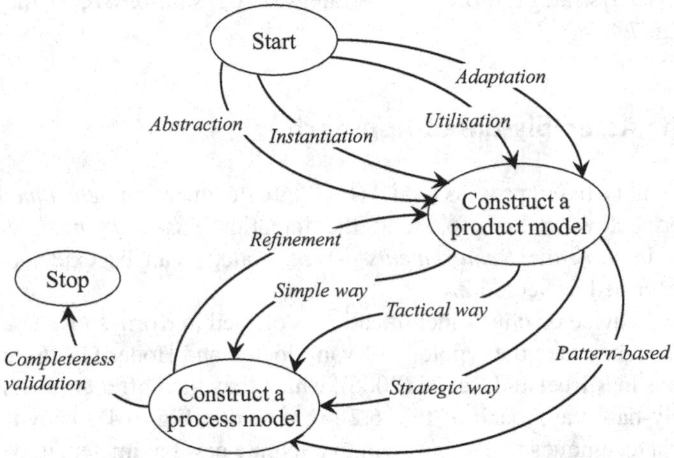

Fig. 6.3 Paradigm-based process model for SME suitable for a chunk-focussed method construction (after Ralyté et al., figure 7, 2003, With kind permission of Springer Science + Business Media)

This overall approach (using the map approach) is not dissimilar from the contingency-based approach of van Slooten and Hodes (1996) that introduces the notion of a 'route map'—a technique used later by Aydin and Harmsen (2002). In this approach, there are two kinds of building blocks for SME: the method fragments themselves (of two kinds: standard and adapted) plus route map fragments. The latter may refer to strategies (as in the map idea above), activities and products as well as project management. They introduce a number of such route map fragments:

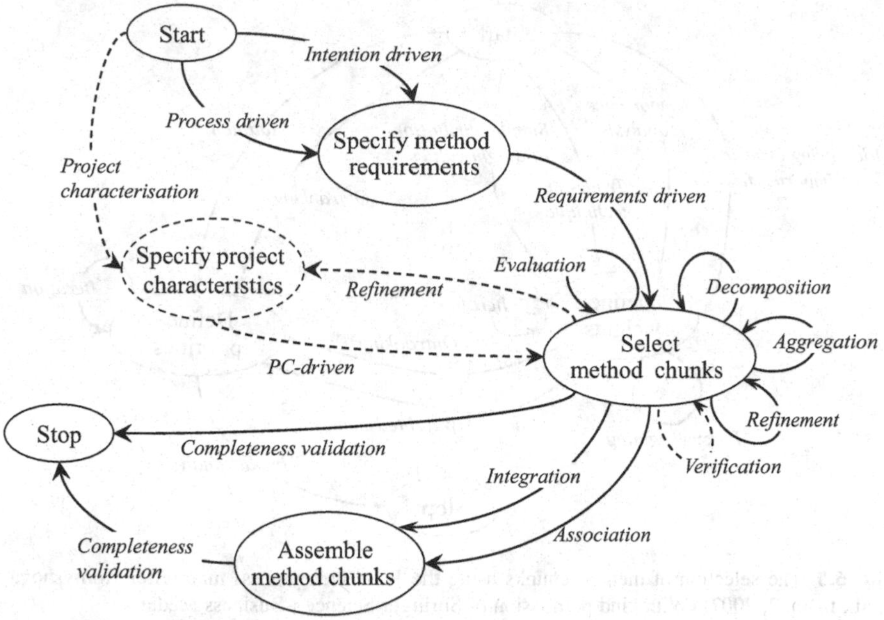

Fig. 6.4 Modified assembly-based approach (with the original approach of Fig. 6.2 in solid lines and the extension in dashed lines) (after Kornyshova et al., figure 1, 2007) (With kind permission of Springer Science + Business Media)

Table 6.1 Example possible values for the human dimension

Characteristic	Values	Source
Resistance and conflict	{low, normal, high}	1, 3
Expertise (knowledge, experience and skills)	{low, normal, high}	1, 2, 3
	{tester, developer, designer, analyst}	2, 3
Clarity and stability	{low, normal, high}	1, 2, 3
User involvement	{real, virtual}	2, 3
Stakeholder number	Num	3

After Kornyshova et al., table 2, 2007 (With kind permission of Springer Science + Business Media)
Note: Source 1 is van Slooten and Hodes (1996); source 2 is Mirbel and Ralyté (2006) and source 3 is Kornyshova et al. (2007)

- Tracing and dividing
- Delivery
- Realisation
- Establishing subprojects
- Project organisation
- Project management products and activities
- Development
- System development products and activities.

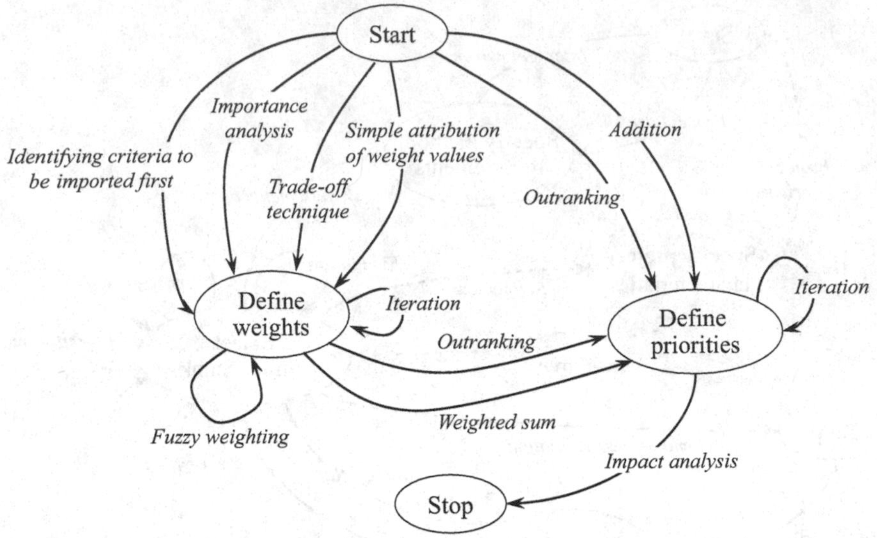

Fig. 6.5 The selection of method chunks using the PC-driven process map (after Kornyshova et al., figure 2, 2007) (With kind permission of Springer Science + Business Media)

Aydin and Harmsen (2002) refer to the route map approach as the S^3 model (Situation, Scenario, Success) and recommend its use via a case-based approach as a way to incorporate past experiences into the decision-making process.

6.1.2 The Paradigm-Based Approach

Ralyté et al. (2003) carefully distinguish between an Assembly-based approach where the fragments are already assumed to exist, probably having been abstracted from existing methodologies, and a Paradigm-based approach, which generates fragments from a metamodel (see also Cervera et al. 2011). Despite their assertion that the key issue to SME is the use of metamodels, this is only rationalised using process maps as one of the three possible approaches. This is in contrast to, for example, the work of the OPEN Consortium (described in brief below), in which the whole approach is presaged upon the use of an underpinning metamodel. There, *all* fragments are created from the metamodel and then stored in the method base (e.g., Firesmith and Henderson-Sellers 2002). As new technologies are introduced, it is likely that the pre-existing fragments in the method base will be insufficient to construct a methodology for the new situation. In such a case, fragments will need to be created ad hoc (the fourth option) in conformance with the metamodel and then either used for only the new situation or, with appropriate quality control, stored in the method base (e.g., Han et al. 2008).

The process map for a Paradigm-based strategy for method construction, shown in Fig. 6.3, has two main intentions: *Construct a process model* and *Construct a*

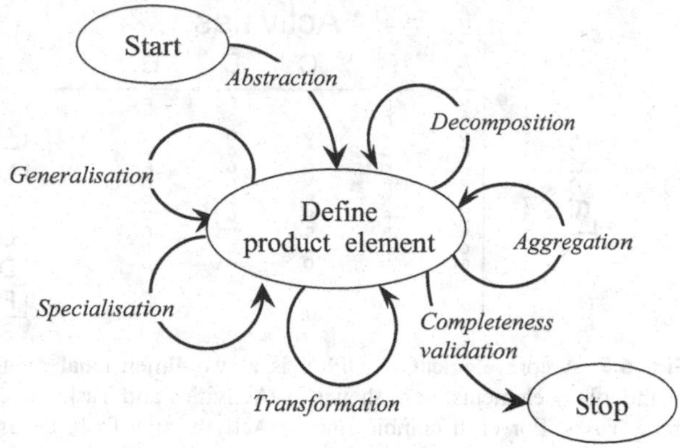

Fig. 6.6 Details of the Abstraction strategy (after Ralyté et al., figure 8, 2003) (With kind permission of Springer Science + Business Media)

product model. In Ralyté et al.'s (2003) (and earlier papers), the elemental units of a process/method are taken to be chunks (as opposed to fragments). Consequently, in Fig. 6.3 we see the necessity (in their approach) to define both the process and product aspects—hence the duality of the intentions. Four strategies are shown to help achieve the intention: *Construct a product model*. These four offer the following support:

- Adaptation of a metamodel to specific circumstances;
- Adaptation of a process or product model;
- Instantiation of a metamodel;
- Abstraction by raising or lowering the abstraction level of a given model.

Details of this last strategy are given as an exemplar in Ralyté et al. (2003)—see Fig. 6.6. The intention *Construct a process model*, on the other hand, has strategies identified as Simple, Context-driven, Strategy-driven and Pattern-driven with a recursive Refinement strategy. The first two strategies are derived from the NATURE project (e.g., Rolland et al. 1995; Jarke et al. 1999), the third from Rolland et al. (1999), where it is called 'map formalism' and the last proposes to define a process model as a collection of situational patterns. It is noted that this intention must follow that of *Construct a product model* since the process must conform to the product model. This adds a specific bias to the construction of a method chunk.

6.1.3 The Deontic Matrix Approach

The fifth approach to method construction listed above is the use of deontic matrices introduced in MOSES (Henderson-Sellers and Edwards 1994) and SOMA (Graham 1995b) and now embodied in the OPEN Process Framework (Graham et al. 1997; Henderson-Sellers et al. 1998; Firesmith and Henderson-Sellers 2002—see also http://www.open.org.au for other OPEN-related resources). This approach is also captured and formalised with the DeonticValue enumerated type in ISO/IEC 24744. A deontic matrix (Fig. 6.7) is a two-dimensional matrix of

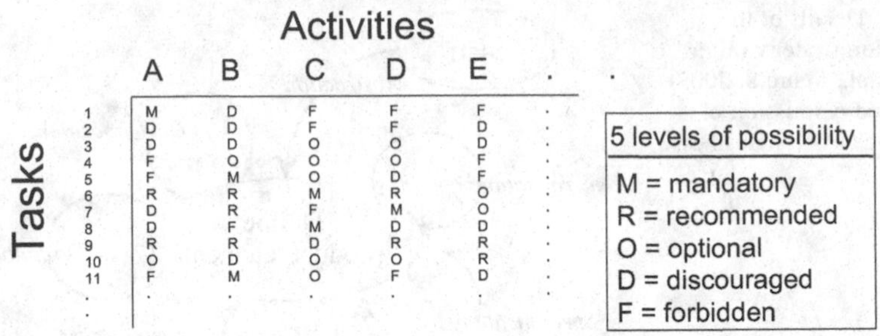

Activities
A B C D E . .
Tasks
1 M D F F F
2 D D F F D
3 D D O O D
4 F O O O F
5 F M O D F
6 R R M R O
7 D R F M O
8 D F M D D
9 R R D R R
10 O D O O R
11 F M O F D
5 levels of possibility
M = mandatory
R = recommended
O = optional
D = discouraged
F = forbidden

Fig. 6.7 A core element of OPEN is a two-dimensional relationship between each pair of methodology elements, here shown for Activities and Tasks. Each Activity may require one or more Tasks. For each combination of Activity and Task, an assessment can be made of the likelihood of the occurrence of that combination using five levels of possibility (labelled M, R, O, D or F) (after Henderson-Sellers and Ralyte 2010)

values, each value representing the possible or likely relationship between a pair of method fragments chosen from the OPF repository. In this approach, one of five values of possibility is allocated to each matrix element. These allocate, in the view of the person(s) completing the matrix (preferably a team including the project manager and the software developers and, optionally, an external method engineer), the recommended linkages. These possibilities range from mandatory, recommended through optional to discouraged and forbidden. They may reflect absolutes, e.g., you never use a Task to create a class diagram in order to produce a use case diagram; or, more likely, reflect the organisational culture—'this is how we do it here' (e.g., Serour et al. 2002). In practice, we have found that some managers like to mandate particular practices in order to retain not just control but homogeneity (often the case for learning teams) whilst, in sophisticated teams, often the work products are agreed upon but different developers prefer different work units (work practices) for the creation of these work products.

Often, the team takes a top-down approach, identifying first the high level goals, perhaps expressed as OPEN Activities (ISO 24744 Processes). Other teams prefer a bottom-up approach in which they first crystallise their lower-level elements, perhaps starting with tasks or with work products (Gonzalez-Perez and Henderson-Sellers 2008a). Whichever approach (top-down or bottom-up) is chosen, a set of deontic matrix values is the end result.

Although offered as a way to construct a full organisationally specific method and, with the introduction of situational characteristics also a project-specific method (i.e., method tailoring and configuration)—and indeed useful for so doing—it has more recently been recognised that there is a closer synergy between the deontic matrix approach and the map approach, as intimated in Chap. 4. Part of the deontic matrix approach relates to allocating possibilities to certain interactions between method fragments. This is therefore data that could be used in decision making (as indeed it is intended), but decision making not in the manual sense of determining whether to select a method fragment pair in a binary sense (Yes/No) but as one input to the decisions made possible through the strategies of the map approach. Thus, it can be suggested that the map approach should be augmented by adding a deontic pair or a deontic guideline to the IAG defined in Fig. 4.40 and illustrated in Fig. 4.42.

The use of deontic matrices when using the OPF approach or when using an approach based on ISO/IEC 24744 enables the method engineer, in conjunction with the on-site software developers, to make recommendations regarding fragment selection and appropriate fragment–fragment configurations, as discussed above. Work units may be, for instance, tasks or techniques. These fragments need to be linked together and to fragments for roles/producers and to the work products (and their supporting languages) needed throughout the software development exercise. Calendar time comes from fragments instantiated from the Stage meta class (Fig. 4.9 in Chap. 4). This 'filling in' of the various deontic matrices can either be done manually by the method engineering team or, in the future, with the help of support tools (e.g., Henderson-Sellers and Nguyen 2004). The resultant matrices are, of course, highly dependent upon the method engineer's decisions, based on the organisational response to questions such as those in Table 6.2. A comparison of two such matrices, one for a small B2C project and one for a large B2C project, derived from two in-depth industry case studies (Haire 2000), is presented by Henderson-Sellers et al. (2002a)—see Table 6.3.

6.1.4 The Use of UML Activity Diagrams

A sixth possibility is the relatively straightforward application of UML Activity Diagrams (ADs) (e.g., Seidita et al. 2007). In these, each process-focussed action is represented by an Activity in the AD. Typical steps for method construction are given as: (1) identifying the needs for the new method by analysing the application context; (2) selecting, from existing methods, those meeting some required aspect; (3) analysing selected methods and storing them in a method base and (4) assembling method fragments into a new method to obtain situational methods. The method thus constructed (or, rather, the process part of it) can also be readily visualised using activities in an AD. However, ADs are most useful for depicting the workflow of the process model once the fragments have been both selected and put together and seem to offer less support in fragment selection and assembly, wherein the method engineer's expertise plays a more important part.

Saeki (2003a) and Van de Weerd et al. (2006) both use a variation on this approach to link such an AD to an architectural style model to depict the associated product part—the so-called PDD (see definition in Chap. 4). However, this is really a largely deterministic and descriptive (rather than prescriptive) approach to process modelling. This approach needs the method engineer to be able to select a set of existing method fragments that could fit the application context on the basis of personal knowledge and expertise, argued by these authors to be quite straightforward.

Table 6.2 Questions and answers for incorporating into a tool for automated generation of deontic matrices

Question	Possible answers
What is the maturity level (by CMM standard), at which your organisation is currently assessed or aims to achieve?	Level 1 (Initial)
	Level 2 (Repeatable)
	Level 3 (Defined)
	Level 4 (Managed)
	Level 5 (Optimising)
Which of the following best describes the domain of the software product being developed?	E-Business
	Embedded system
	MIS
	Process control
	Real time
What is the level of quality that the information system should have?	Low
	Normal
	High
What is the estimated size of the final software product being developed?	Small and not complex (less than 10,000 LOC)
	Medium and moderately complex (between 10,000 LOC and 50,000 LOC)
	Large and very complex (between 50,000 LOC and 1,000,000 LOC)
	Very large and immensely complex (more than 1,000,000 LOC)
What is the estimated size of the project team on this project?	Small (1–3 members)
	Medium (4–9 members)
	Large (more than 9 members)
What is the level of criticality of the software product being developed to a successful mission?	Low; normal; high or very high
What type of user interface is required?	No user interface involved
	Text-based user interface
	Graphical user interface
To what extent does the project depend on activities from other projects within the organisation?	Low
	Normal
	High
To what extent do the members of the project team possess enough knowledge and experience to develop the required software product?	Low
	Normal
	High
To what extent will the goals, needs and desires of the users remain stable over time, thus enabling a stable specification of the functional requirements to be made?	Low
	Normal
	High
To what extent are the goals, needs and desires of the users clear and coherent, thus enabling a sound specification of the functional requirements to be made?	Low
	Normal
	High

(continued)

Table 6.2 (continued)

Question	Possible answers
To what extent is there sufficient time available for the project?	Low
	Normal
	High
To what extent was the applied technology and/or the applied methods, techniques and tools new to the organisation?	Low
	Normal
	High
To what extent is the level of reuse required in the development project?	Low
	Normal
	High
Does the software product being developed involve the use of a database system?	Does not involve the use of a database
	Use an OO database
	Use a non-OO database
Does the software product being developed involve a distributed environment?	Yes
	No

After Nguyen and Henderson-Sellers (2003a)

Table 6.3 Comparison of deontic matrix values for a small as compared to a large B2C project

Small projects see no need to undertake a feasibility study, whereas this is optional for large projects
Getting business approval is seen as optional for small projects, but highly recommended for large projects
In small projects, there seems to be no need to identify the *sources* of the requirements, although, of course, *Task*: *Identify user requirements* is mandatory
Small projects use no tasks focussed on distributed computing
Architectural design is optional for small projects, mandatory for large
All the tasks associated with the *Component Selection Activity* as seen as of low priority (D for discouraged) whereas for larger projects they are recommended or, at worst, optional
Creation of reusable components (for the future) is discouraged in small projects but encouraged in larger ones
Optimisation of the design is seen as mandatory for large projects, optional for small
Choosing toolsets, hardware, project teams, etc. is all but ignored in small projects (D for discouraged) whereas in large projects these tasks are recommended
Interestingly, the OPEN Task: *Specify individual goals* is forbidden in small projects but optional for large
Small projects tend to be standalone whereas large projects tend to be integrated with other, pre-existing systems. This leads to values for OPEN Task: *Establish data take-on strategy* of F and M, respectively—the opposite ends of the possibility spectrum
Subtasks of Task: *Model and reengineer business process(es)* are less important for smaller projects
Perhaps disappointingly (from a theoretical software engineering perspective), proponents of both large and small projects see little value in the OPEN Task: *Write manuals and prepare other documentation* (O and D, respectively, for large and small projects)

Based on text in Henderson-Sellers et al. (2002a)

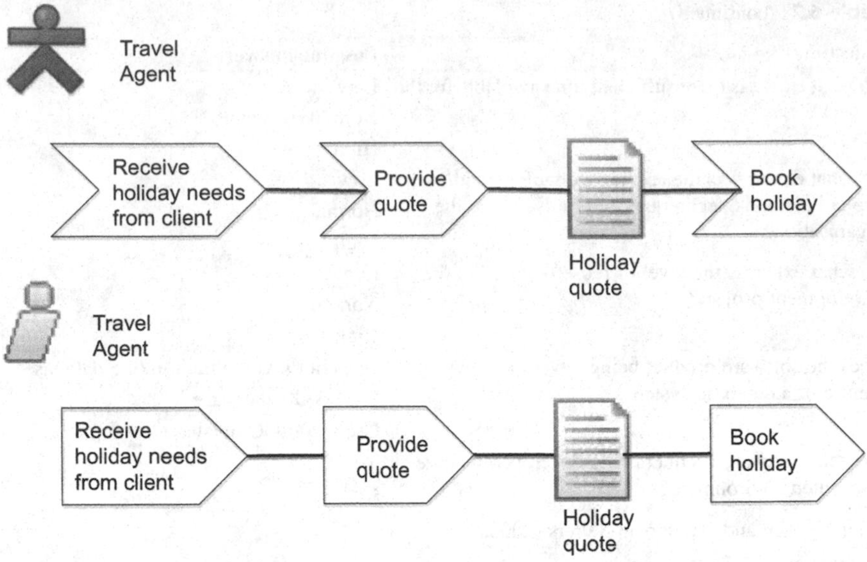

Fig. 6.8 Example of an SPEM-based Activity Diagram: (top) Version 1 (OMG 2005a) and (bottom) its newer counterpart in Version 2 (OMG 2008)

In an agent-oriented method engineering approach, Cossentino et al. (2007) utilise a similar approach in Activity Diagrams but base these on those described in SPEM Version 1 (OMG 2005a) since these ADs combine both the process and product parts into a single diagram (Fig. 6.8).

6.1.5 The Configuration-Based Approach[1]

The final option is that of using a configuration-based approach. Through extensive action research, Karlsson and Ågerfalk (2004, 2009b) observed that method engineers in practice often started with a company-wide development process, rather than constructing a situational method from scratch. Based on this observation, they proposed the Method for Method Configuration (MMC) (Fig. 6.9), which is founded on the concepts of method components and the impact of a characteristic of the method rationale (Chap. 3), expressed through the method components' interfaces. A characteristic can be thought of as a question related to one single aspect of the (type of) development situation under scrutiny. Such a question can have one or more possible answers. Together these form the 'dimension' of the characteristic. Configuration packages then correspond to these answers. Each characteristic addresses one or more method components and their reason for inclusion in the situational method. Table 6.4 shows the classification schema on

[1] We acknowledge contributions of Dr. Fredrik Karlsson to this section.

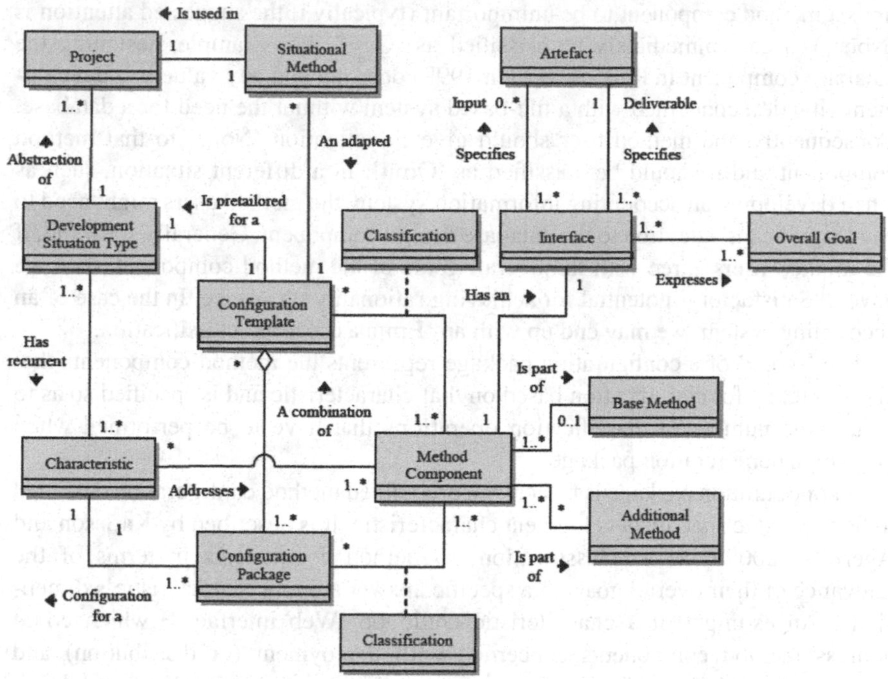

Fig. 6.9 Main concepts of the Method for Method Configuration (after Karlsson and Ågerfalk 2009b). Reprinted by permission of the publisher

Table 6.4 Classification schema for method components

		Potential to achieve rationality resonance		
		Satisfactory	**Unsatisfactory**	**Missing**
Attention given to method component	*None*	Omit	–	–
	Insignificant	Perform informal	Replace informal	Add informal
	Normal	Perform as is	Replace as is	Add as is
	Significant	Emphasise as is	Replace emphasised	Add emphasised

After Karlsson and Ågerfalk (2009b) (reprinted by permission of the publisher)

which the classification of method components is based. The vertical dimension quantifies the 'attention' that method users should devote to a particular method component. Based on empirical experience (Karlsson and Ågerfalk 2004, 2009b), the suggested values of this dimension are 'None', 'Insignificant', 'Normal' and 'Significant'. The three aspects of the horizontal dimension are 'Satisfactory', 'Unsatisfactory' and 'Missing'. These cut across the vertical dimension creating a two-by-two matrix. The vertical dimension expresses the potential for achieving 'rationality resonance' (see Chap. 3), based on the content of the base method and the method user's intentions. If, at this stage, the method user or the method engineer finds a method component to be unimportant (typically if the suggested attention is 'None'), it can immediately be classified as 'Omit'. For example, designing the database component in RUP (Kruchten 1999) does not add any value in a development situation concerned with a file-based system without the need for a database. Consequently, the method user should give the attention 'None' to that method component and it should be classified as 'Omit'. In a different situation, such as when developing an accounting information system, the method users might need to pay 'Significant' attention to the database design component. Generally speaking, if the method users agree with the overall goals of the method component, then we have a 'Satisfactory' potential for achieving rationality resonance. In the case of an accounting system, we may end up with an 'Emphasise as is' classification.

The 'scope' of a configuration package represents the method components that are of interest for classification based on that characteristic and is specified so as to reduce the number of classification operations that have to be performed when creating a configuration package.

A configuration package is basically a predefined method configuration designed to fit one single specific development characteristic. It is described by Karlsson and Ågerfalk (2009b) as a "classification of method components in terms of the relevance of their overall goals to a specific answer along a characteristic's dimension". An example of a characteristic could be 'Web interface?' which could address method components concerned with deployment (or distribution) and user interface design. The obvious two possible answers are 'Yes' and 'No'. Since the configuration package is a configuration of the base method suited to one characteristic value, the dimension in this case comprises two configuration packages. A configuration package would then include information about how such method components are to be selected with respect to this characteristic. Such a selection may also include components from complementary ISDMs in case the base method does not provide the necessary support.

Method configuration takes into account the need to combine structure with flexibility in SME and is defined as "the planned and systematic adaptation of a specific method via the use of 'reusable assets'". (Karlsson and Ågerfalk 2009b). A reusable asset, in this context, is a pre-configured version of a base method, which is used instead of creating a situational method from atomic fragments in a method base. To achieve this, MMC uses a three-layered reuse model comprising method components, configuration packages and configuration templates. These concepts are combined efficiently to produce a situational method that facilitates the work of method engineers.

Configuration packages and configuration templates are used in conjunction with method components, described in Chap. 4, to represent situational versions of an Information Systems Development Method (ISDM). The selection of method components to be included in a situational method is based on the belief that articulated goals (i.e., method rationale) are believed to be in line with the project members' intentions (i.e., rationality resonance). Method configuration must therefore consider to what extent it is important to achieve those goals prescribed by a method. If it is important to achieve certain goals, then significant attention should be paid to the method component, and the recommended classification may be 'Emphasise as is'. Unsatisfactory potential for achieving rationality resonance is associated with the replacement of existing method components by external method components that are more relevant. Finally, sometimes there are simply no grounds to believe that rationality resonance can be achieved. This could be the case when method components that support a particular aspect of the (type of) development situation are not to be found in the base method. The classification is then some variant of 'Add', depending on the required attention to the method component.

When modelling a configuration package, one typically begins by defining what parts of the base method are of interest when discussing this specific characteristic. When creating a new configuration package, all components of the base method are classified as *not applicable*. This indicates that they are outside the scope of the currently considered characteristic. Subsequently, relevant method components are brought into scope based on the method users' judgement. In this iterative process, each method component is discussed based on their method rationale (what it is supposed to do and why), as shown by their interface. Method users' requirements in relation to the constraints of the characteristics then decide the classification of existing method components.

The configuration package concept is used, together with characteristics, to simplify analysis of the base method, through narrowing the scope and reducing complexity. Nonetheless, configurations must reflect a more complicated picture, containing combinations of characteristics. For this purpose, one or more configuration packages for a common set of characteristics are combined into a configuration template.

Configuration templates are, in general, derivable from configuration packages and allow for the reuse of combined configuration packages that target development situation types common within the organisation. The task of combining configuration packages is not a completely mechanical process but requires judgement (Karlsson and Wistrand 2004). In some situations, configuration packages may even overlap. For example, two different configuration packages can address the same method component with contradictory classifications. Since configuration packages represent an analysis based on demarcated perspectives (one problem or aspect at a time), it is not surprising that conflicting classifications may occur when combining configuration packages. However, when these characteristics are combined, a decision has to be made regarding a method component's classification. These are decisions that cannot be represented within any single configuration package. Instead, such decisions must be represented in configuration templates.

The classification of method components in a configuration template follows the classification schema suggested in Table 6.4. When it comes to conflicting classifications, the recommendation (Karlsson and Ågerfalk 2009b) is to:

1. Decide which are the characteristic and configuration package that most essentially reflect the type of development situation at hand; and
2. Decide which configuration package requires the most method support. For example, when comparing the two classification alternatives 'Omit' and 'Perform as is', the latter suggests that more extensive method support is required.

The situational method is based on a selected configuration template and is the ISDM delivered for the project team to use. This method is then enacted by the team and turned into a 'method-in-action'. For various reasons, developers may choose not to follow the situational method to a tee, consciously or unconsciously. There is therefore a difference between the tailored version of the base method and the method-in-action (Ågerfalk and Fitzgerald 2006). Experiences from the actual method use should be fed back to the configuration process, in order to improve the configuration templates and/or configuration packages. The method users typically provide this feedback to the method engineer continuously throughout the project, at the ends of the iterations for example, or during project closeout.

Real-life development situations typically comprise a combination of several characteristics. A single project, for example, might involve diverse characteristics such as volatile requirements, a new technical platform, an inexperienced development team as well as Internet delivery. A configuration template then describes this more complex configuration and forms a pre-configured version of the complete organisation-wide ISDM for a typical project situation in the organisation. A configuration template is constructed out of a selection of configuration packages, each one addressing a specific characteristic. Consequently, a configuration template reflects a recurring development pattern within an organisation.

6.2 Requirements of the Intended Method

Before constructing a method, it is clearly beneficial to know what the requirements are for the intended method (Gupta and Prakash 2001). Identifying the requirements of the to-be-constructed method involve all members of the development team and the management team. This assumes that it is feasible that these people can identify the kind of method and its characteristics that will suit their forthcoming project and that the various perspectives can be integrated (Nuseibeh et al. 1996) and then communicated to the method engineer (Karlsson and Ågerfalk 2005). It is also typically assumed that these requirements do not change during the project. (Changing requirements are considered by, e.g., Rossi et al. (2004) in their study of evolutionary method engineering and Karlsson and Ågerfalk (2012) in what they refer to as method-user-centred method configuration. These approaches are discussed in more detail in Sects. 3.4 and 3.5, respectively.) This, of course, has many similarities with traditional requirements engineering in the context of software development (e.g., Glinz and Fricker 2013), rather than method construction. Analysing the needs of an organisation's method is examined by Vlaanderen et al. (2011) in the context of software process improvement (SPI) for software product management (see further discussion in Sect. 7.2). SPI is also the context for the analysis within Ericsson undertaken by Pareto et al. (2008). These authors utilise the ideas of technology road-mapping—an industry technique more often applied to facilitating decision making for strategic product development. Using an action research methodology, they contrast road-mapping with grounded theory and assessment-based approaches such as CMM (capability maturity model) and

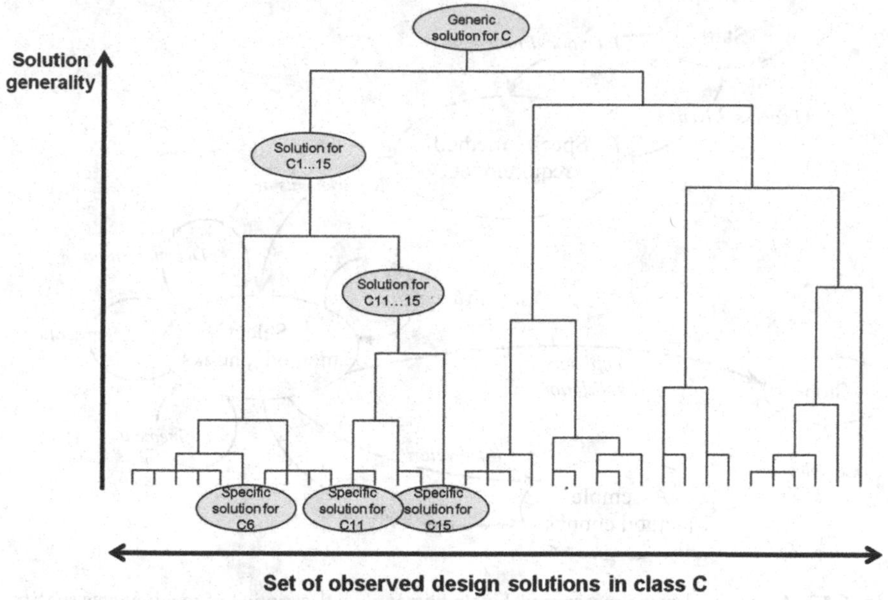

Fig. 6.10 Ultrametric tree visualisation for an exemplar data set (after Winter, figure 1, 2011) (With kind permission of Springer Science + Business Media)

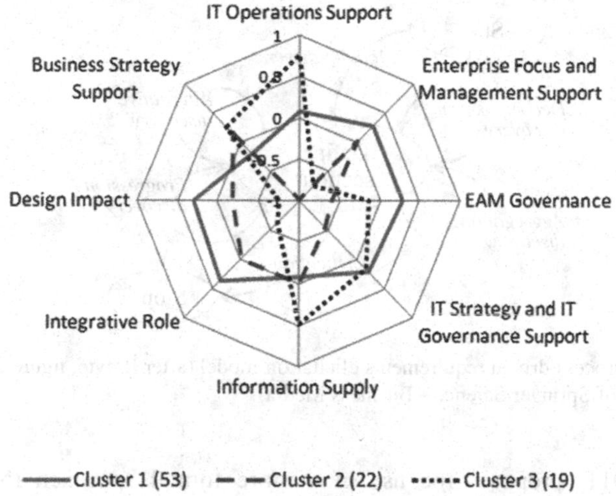

Fig. 6.11 Cobweb graphical representation of a three cluster solution with eight design factors (after Winter, figure 2, 2011) (With kind permission of Springer Science + Business Media)

SPICE (Software Process Improvement and Capability dEtermination), concluding that technology road-mapping can offer significant assistance for developing knowledge about SPI-related requirements in large organisations, as well as identifying options and opportunities (Pareto et al. 2008).

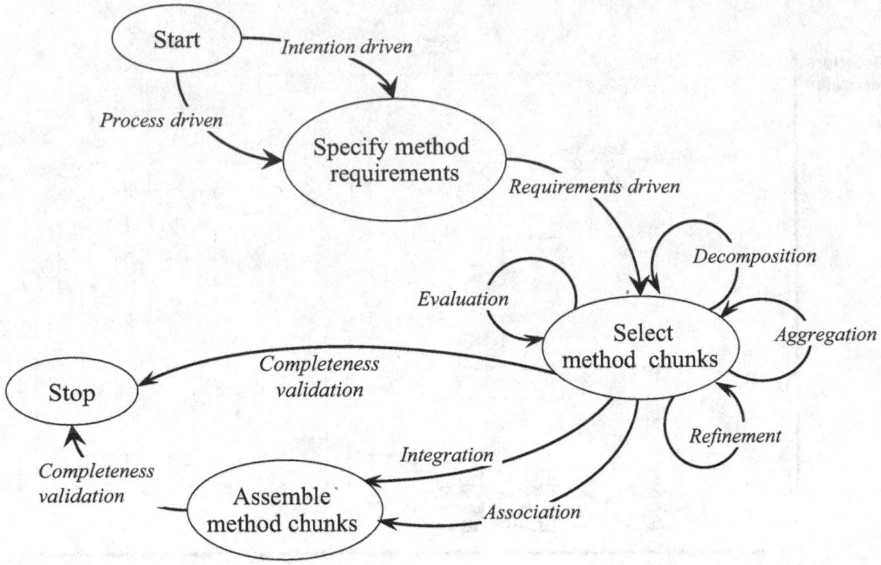

Fig. 6.12 Assembly-driven process model including explicit description of requirements specification (as a new intention plus two new strategies) (after Ralyté et al., figure 2, 2003) (With kind permission of Springer Science + Business Media)

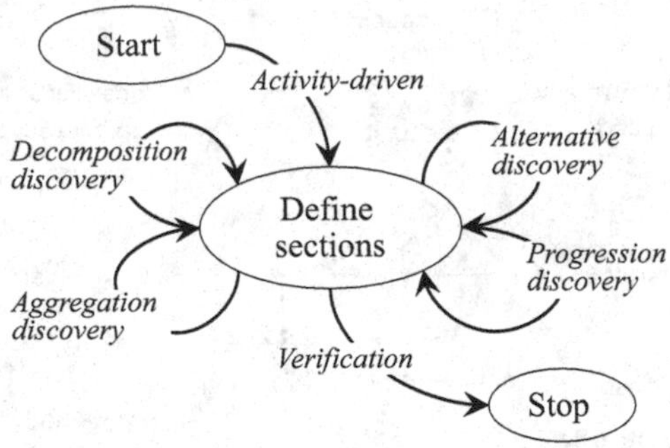

Fig. 6.13 The process-driven requirements elicitation model (after Ralyté, figure 2, 2002) (With kind permission of Springer Science + Business Media)

Winter (2011) proposes the use of a more formal approach to the design elements of method construction, an approach based on design science research. He argues that the sequence of events should follow:

1. Developing a rough idea of the design problem;
2. Conducting a literature analysis to identify possible contingency factors;
3. Conducting a field study and analysing the data with principal components;
4. Redefining the design problem based on the knowledge gained by point 3 above;

G1: <Project description; Define sections of the requirements map following activity-driven strategy>

G1.1: <Project description; Define the signature of the requirements map>

G1.2: <The map signature is defined; Identify the core and essential intentions necessary to achieve the intention specified in the map signature>

G1.3: <Intentions are elicited; Abstract intentions>

G1.4: <Intentions are elicited; Discover strategies>

G1.5: <Intentions and strategies are defined; Define sections>

Fig. 6.14 Guideline for Activity-driven strategy (based on text in Ralyté 2002) (With kind permission of Springer Science + Business Media)

5. Compute the ultrametric distances, which represent the degree of similarity between possible design solutions. These distances can be visualised in a dendogram-like graph (Fig. 6.10). Similar solutions are found at the lower end of the solution generality scale and dissimilar solutions at a high level of generality;
6. Clustering algorithms can then be applied to determine an optimal number of clusters for further examination;
7. Identify design situations from the clusters identified in point 6 above.

Winter (2011) notes that for each typical design problem, there should be 4–8 design factors identified. In his examination of exemplar data for enterprise architecture management, he found three clusters and eight design factors. These can be graphed, for example, as shown in Fig. 6.11. It can be seen that there are strong contrasts between the three design situations represented in this 'cobweb' diagram:

1. A balanced and active situation (solid line)
2. A business-focussed situation (dashed line)
3. An IT-focussed situation (dotted line).

This information gives added insights into the kind of fragments that might be most appropriate for the specific design situation.

The Requirements-driven strategy shown in Fig. 6.2 can itself be described by an additional intention (*Specify method requirements*) and different ways to achieve it. In the method chunk approach (Fig. 6.12), two possible strategies are proposed to specify requirements for a situational method (Intention-driven strategy and Process-driven strategy) (Ralyté et al. 2003). Both strategies use the map process modelling formalism.

In the process-driven strategy, applicable to the situation when the method engineer needs to construct a completely new method, a form of map called a requirements map is produced. This strategy applies the map construction guidelines proposed in Rolland et al. (1999), which were also adapted in the method chunk construction process (Ralyté and Rolland 2001a; Ralyté 2004) (see Fig. 5.3 in Sect. 5.2). As shown in Fig. 6.13, the requirements map construction process is limited to the identification of its sections without associating the corresponding guidelines. In fact, the guidelines will be associated to this map during the method chunk

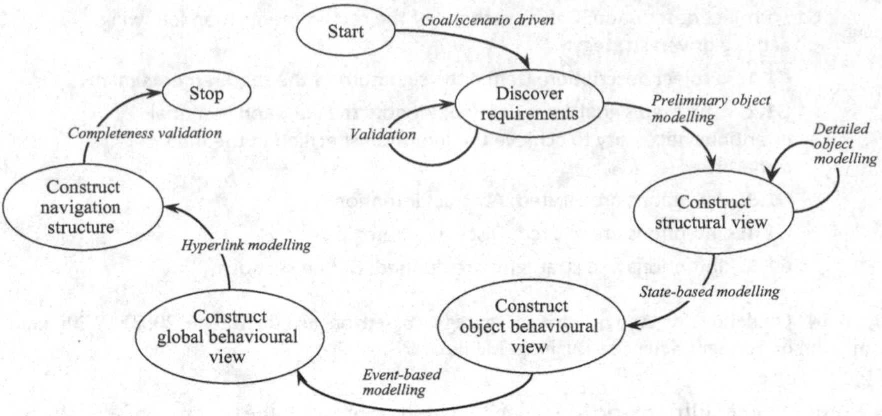

Fig. 6.15 Initial requirements map (after Ralyté, figure 3, 2002) (With kind permission of Springer Science + Business Media)

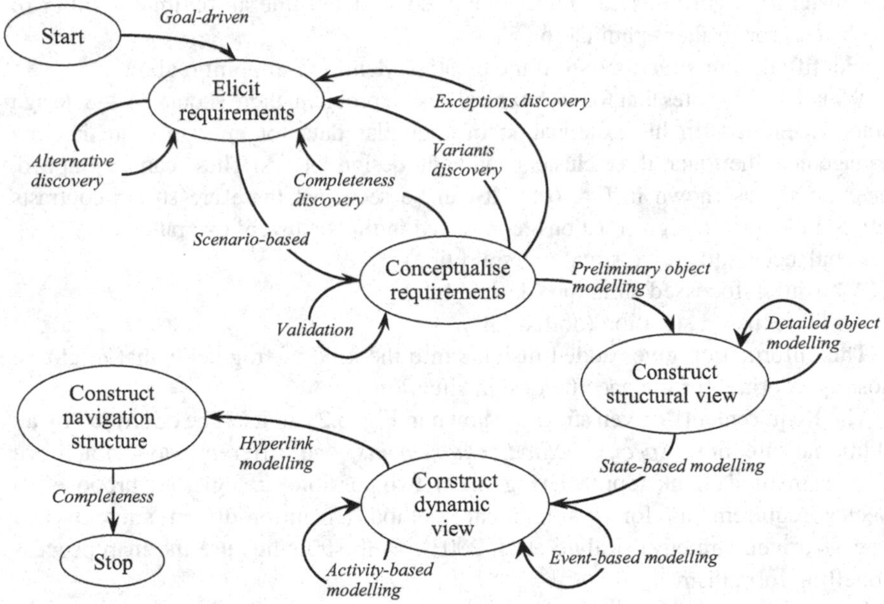

Fig. 6.16 Final requirements map (after Ralyté, figure 7, 2002) (With kind permission of Springer Science + Business Media)

selection process. The first set of sections is identified by using the Activity-driven strategy, which is based on the analysis and selection of the engineering activities to be supported by the method. Then, this collection of sections can be refined by decomposing or aggregating already identified sections or by discovering alternative or complementary sections. Finally, the Verification strategy helps to finalise and check the utility of the proposed requirements map. Ralyté (2002) shows by example how this map is used to create a requirements map. The example chosen is that of the construction of a method supporting the analysis and design of a B2B system. First the Activity-driven strategy is used, supported by its guideline (Fig. 6.14). Map sections are then defined based on Guideline G1.5 as:

For every intention I and one of its strategies S, identify $(I,S)_{pre}$ and $(I,S)_{post}$.

Connect sections using the following section construction predicate:

Map: Intention, Intention, Strategy $\rightarrow$ Section

$I_i, I_j, S_{ij} \rightarrow$ Section (I_i, I_j, S_i) if $(\exists\, S_{ki} \in$ Strategy:

$(I_i, S_{ki})_{post} \Rightarrow (I_j, S_{ij})_{pre}$ AND $(I_j, S_{ij})_{pre} \Rightarrow (I_j, S_{ij})_{post}$

This gives a set of six sections, as shown in Fig. 6.15. This is the initial requirements map. This is then modified using the four strategies of *Define sections* in Fig. 6.13; and a final requirements map is thus determined (Fig. 6.16). This final requirements map is then used as the basis for the method chunk selection and assembly process depicted in Figs. 6.2 and 6.12.

6.3 Identifying Useful Method Parts That Exist in the Repository

Method parts stored in a method base are very similar to reusable classes stored in a class repository or class library. Consequently, the issues of retrieval of method parts should be similar to those of finding reusable classes (Freeman and Henderson-Sellers 1991). Ter Hofstede and Verhoef (1997) identify the need to:

- Evaluate the contingency factors (circumstances special to this project)—in the context of a prototype CAME tool, these are discussed in Nguyen and Henderson-Sellers (2003a, b),
- Characterise required method part, e.g., with contingency factors and then
- Find it.

Identification of useful method parts is the remit of the intention *Select method parts* in the assembly-based process model of Fig. 6.2. For each retrieved method part, its potential usefulness is first evaluated (evaluation strategy)—this can be done using similarity measures as described by Ralyté and Rolland (2001a) and extended by Mirbel (2006), who describes three kinds of similarity: (1) the number of common aspects based on 'User Situation' and 'Reuse Context', (2) the forbidden aspects of 'User Situation' and 'Reuse Context' and (3) the number of necessary aspects in the 'User Situation'.

Refinement of the method part may be undertaken by one of three further strategies (Ralyté and Rolland 2001a):

- Decomposition strategy—where the method part is a compound chunk containing smaller parts not needed for the current method construction.
- Aggregation strategy—when the method part only partially covers the requirements.

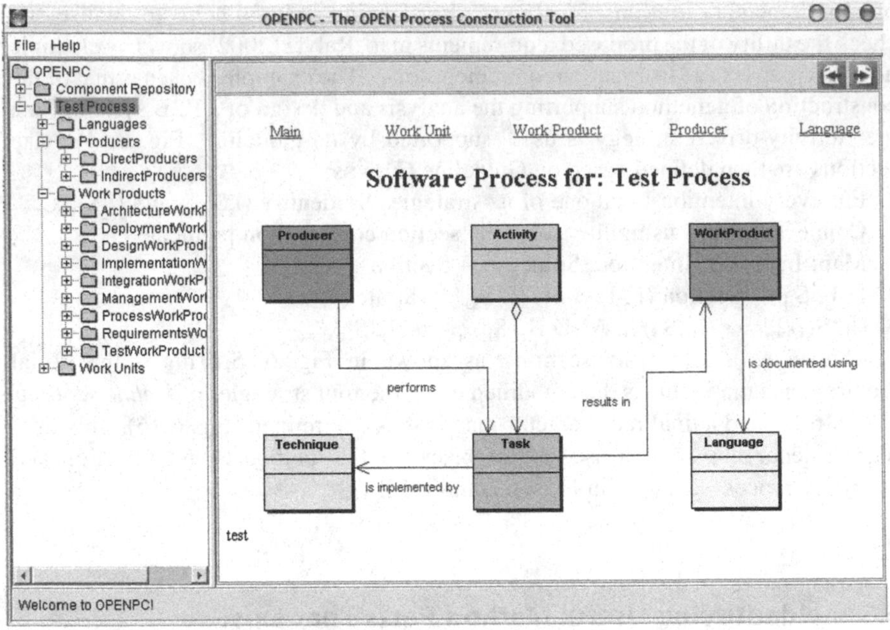

Fig. 6.17 Viewing the generated HTML page (after Henderson-Sellers and Nguyen 2004)

- Refinement strategy—suggests seeking another method part with a richer set of guidelines than the current selection.

As noted above, the deontic matrix approach (e.g., Graham et al. 1997) offers the capability of identifying appropriate method fragments (it is designed for use with fragments and not other kinds of method parts) that work well together. Although often thought of in terms of linking work units with work products and their producers, Nguyen and Henderson-Sellers (2003a) in fact identified seven possible deontic matrices: (1) Process/Activity, (2) Activity/Task, (3) Task/Technique, (4) Producer/Task, (5) Task/Work Product, (6) Producer/Work Product and (7) Work Product/Language. The values in these several matrices are determined by consideration of the situation in which the method will be created (hence the name 'situational method engineering'). The situational context consists of a number of factors such as project size, organisational culture, domain of the application to be developed and the skills and preferences of the development team that influence the method engineer in their evaluation of the most appropriate values for the deontic matrices. Nguyen and Henderson-Sellers (2003a) suggested that these values can best be elicited using a questionnaire along the lines suggested in Table 6.2. The values are then entered into a tool (see also Sect. 7.3) that offers a first estimate on the fragments that might be useful to the organisation's method construction enterprise.

Once completed, these matrices give guidance on the most appropriate selection of method fragments. As experiential data are gathered, a knowledge database is

Task	Activity 1	2	3	4	5	6	7	8	9	10
Undertake feasibility study									Y	
Undertake project planning									Y	
Manage human resources									Y	
Identify project roles and responsibilities									Y	
Analyse user requirements	Y									
Maintain trace between requirements and design	Y		Y			Y	Y		Y	Y
Create a software architecture		Y								
Prototype the architecture		Y								
Develop capacity plan		Y							Y	
Construct the object model			Y							
Identify classes, objects, roles, types, interfaces			Y							
Design the database model			Y							
Design the human interface			Y							
Refactor			Y							
Integrate components						Y				
Code				Y						
Plan integration						Y			Y	
Plan testing strategy					Y				Y	
Design test suite					Y					
Code test suite					Y					
Execute tests					Y					

Part of the activity/task matrix for a 'rigorous' or 'heavyweight' process

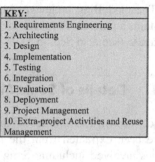

KEY:
1. Requirements Engineering
2. Architecting
3. Design
4. Implementation
5. Testing
6. Integration
7. Evaluation
8. Deployment
9. Project Management
10. Extra-project Activities and Reuse Management

Fig. 6.18 A portion of an OPF deontic matrix linking tasks to activities, completed with binary values for a heavyweight style of process/methodology

Table 6.5 Six steps of a possible top-down method construction process

Step number	Deontic matrix to be used
1	Select Activities
2	Select Tasks and allocate their usage to each selected Activity
3	Select Techniques and allocate their usage to each selected Task
4	Select Work Products and allocate them to the appropriate Task
5	Select Languages and allocate them for documenting each selected Work Product
6	Select Producers and allocate them for the performance of each selected Task

Adapted from Nguyen and Henderson-Sellers (2003a)

built up, which can then provide a 'first guess' (via an automated tool) on which the method engineer can then elaborate for the very specific situation (Nguyen and Henderson-Sellers 2003a). With an automated tool to help, not only can the method engineer be helped to identify appropriate method fragments, but web-based documentation can be automatically produced (Henderson-Sellers and Nguyen 2004)—see Fig. 6.17. Although five levels are suggested in Fig. 6.7 (the default), for a specific project often binary values are used (Fig. 6.18).

The series of selections (i.e., usage of each of these seven matrices) can be variable, as determined by the method engineer. As noted above, some prefer to start top-down, by first identifying Activities and then asking what Tasks are needed for those Activities and then what Techniques might be useful to implement the selected Tasks. And so on (Table 6.5).

The meta knowledge stored with the method fragment is highly relevant in ensuring a contextual retrieval. Suggestions on an appropriate query language are given by Rolland and Prakash (1996), e.g.,

Select method
for business system (area)
with risk-of project domain*structure = H
and with risk-of project domain*actors = H

The modelling language, MEL, proposed by Brinkkemper et al. (2001) also contains a portion useful for identifying and removing method fragments from the database (see also Sect. 5.5).

6.4 Details of Some Method Construction Options

Process construction relies on the assembly of a large number of method parts that have been extracted from the method base. Several authors have addressed the issues involved including Song (1995), Plihon et al. (1998), Ralyté et al. (1999), Ralyté (2001), Ralyté and Rolland (2001a) and Firesmith and Henderson-Sellers (2002).

In this section, we describe method construction options that veer away from the idea of a method as embodying a set of transformation engines, i.e., work units that transform work products in some way. The two approaches described in detail here both focus on identifying work products (Sect. 6.4.1) and goals (Sect. 6.4.2) and then using backward chaining to discover the work units. The section ends (Sect. 6.4.3) with a general discussion about these various approaches to method construction.

6.4.1 Using a Work Product Pool Approach

Gonzalez-Perez and Henderson-Sellers (2008a) introduce the 'work product pool' approach, which involves backward chaining in a structured but still non-automated fashion. They argue that, rather than building up a method from requirements through to implementation, a better approach is to ask "What is the final product?" and, consequently, "What are the penultimate products I need from which to construct this final product?" This questioning is done recursively. In other words, only work products vital to the construction of the final deliverable are identified rather than in a forward chaining approach that can easily lead to dead ends. Only after work products are defined are the processes identified by which these work products are created. This is in contrast, for instance, to the chunk

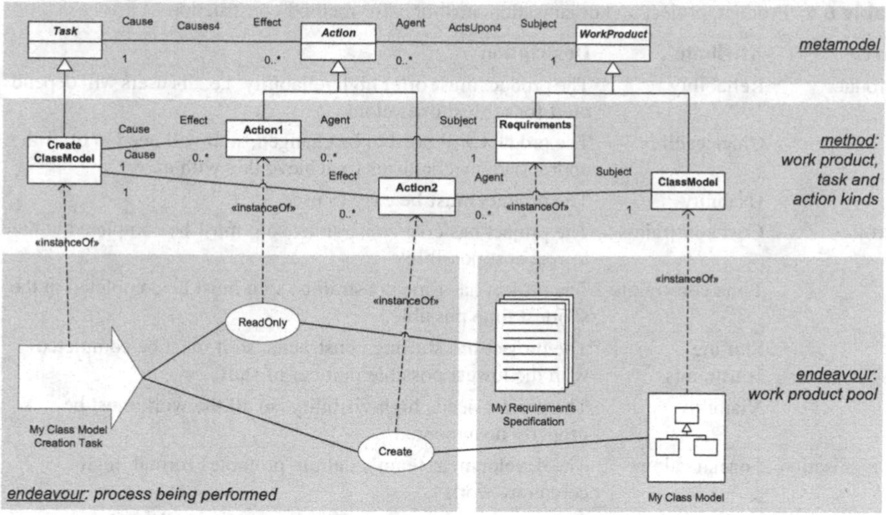

Fig. 6.19 The work product pool approach to method construction (reprinted from Gonzalez-Perez and Henderson-Sellers 2008a with permission from Elsevier)

approach in which product and process are inextricably linked or to the deontic matrix approach which tends to focus primarily on work units first and work products later (although the actual framework does not mandate this). Each of these method parts can then be related to both performance and to the metamodel (Fig. 6.19)—the specific use of the International Standard ISO/IEC 24744 (ISO/IEC 2007, 2010a) is demonstrated in detail in Gonzalez-Perez (2007).

6.4.2 A Goal-Based Approach

In a similar vein, Gonzalez-Perez et al. (2009) discuss the problems with method construction approaches that rely on expert opinion and subjective judgement and recommend, as an alternative, consideration of the *goal* of the method. They argue that any particular method part selection may critically affect the overall time consumed in the project performance, the rate of defect injection, etc. In other words, some apparently equivalently focussed method parts may not be similarly useful. They thus recommend attributing some attributes (Table 6.6) that may lead to an ability to create a more objective method part selection. These are then used in a goal analysis. In goal analysis, the final goal of each process step is considered from the point of view of a specific actor. There are three relevant reasoning techniques that are useful: means-ends analysis, contributions analysis and AND/OR decomposition (Bresciani et al. 2004). In means-ends analysis, the following are performed iteratively until an acceptable solution is reached: "Describe the current state, the desired state (the goal) and the difference between the two; Select a promising procedure for enabling this change of state by using this

Table 6.6 Product, project and organisation attributes for method construction

Area	Attribute	Description
Product	Reliability	The product must offer high reliability, i.e., its users will depend on it for critical operations
	Changeability	The product will need to be changed, so it will need to offer the appropriate mechanisms to achieve this with ease
	Usability	The product must be easy to use
Project	Cost constraints	The project has cost constraints, so it must be completed at the lowest cost possible
	Time constraints	The project has time constraints, so it must be completed in the shortest time possible
	Staffing constraints	The project has staffing constraints, so it must be completed with the lowest possible number of staff
	Visibility	The project needs high visibility, so all the work must be properly documented
Organisation	Formal culture	The development team's culture promotes formal, high-ceremony work
	Agile culture	The development team's culture promotes agile-style, low-ceremony work
	Experience	The development team has got extensive experience in the kind of project and product to be developed

After Gonzalez-Perez et al., table 5, 2009 (With kind permission of Springer Science + Business Media)

identified difference between present and desired states; Apply the selected procedure and update the current state" (Henderson-Sellers et al. 2004a). Contributions analysis helps to identify goals that may contribute towards the partial fulfilment of the final goal and is sometimes used as an alternative to means-ends analysis, particularly useful for soft goals. Positive or negative influences towards attainment of the goal are identified and quantified on a (usually 5 point) Likert scale. In particular, contribution analysis has been shown to be very effective for soft goals used for eliciting non-functional (quality) requirements. Finally, AND/OR decomposition changes a root goal into a finer goal structure, i.e., a set of subgoals—either alternatives (OR decomposition) or additive (AND decomposition).

In order to use goal analysis for method construction, we need to determine how each of the method fragments in the sample repository affects each of the above listed attributes. For example, we can say that performing a Quality Assurance process enhances product reliability. For each method fragment plus attribute pair, one of the five possible values has been determined: strongly enhances, enhances, neutral, deteriorates and strongly deteriorates. Table 6.7 shows these (non-neutral) mappings between method fragments and attributes. Gonzalez-Perez et al. (2009) note that they are not claiming that these mappings are optimal or even correct; these are a sample collection of reasonable mappings for the purpose of their explication. A separate study would be necessary in order to determine how each method fragment in a production repository affects each attribute of interest. Suppose we have two options for a software engineering process (SEP) and each

Table 6.7 Mappings between attributes and method fragments

Attribute		**Method fragment**		**Value**
Area	Name	Class	Name	
Product	Reliability	Process kind	Quality Assurance	Strongly enhances
		Task kind	Unit test class	Enhances
		Technique kind	Test-first development	Enhances
			In-house customer	Enhances
			Threat modelling	Strongly enhances
	Changeability	Process kind	Configuration Management	Enhances
		Task kind	Document requirements	Enhances
	Usability	Process kind	Acceptance Testing	Strongly enhances
		Task kind	Demonstrate the system	Enhances
			Obtain stakeholder feedback	Strongly enhances
Project	Cost constraints	Phase kind	System Definition	Deteriorates
		Process kind	Quality Assurance	Deteriorates
			Process Improvement	Deteriorates
	Time constraints	Phase kind	System Definition	Deteriorates
		Process kind	Process Improvement	Deteriorates
		Task kind	Unit test class	Deteriorates
		Technique kind	Prototyping	Deteriorates
			Automated builds	Enhances
	Staffing constraints	Process kind	Quality Assurance	Deteriorates
		Technique kind	Peer reviewing	Deteriorates
			Pair programming	Deteriorates
	Visibility	Task kind	Prepare defect report	Enhances
			Prepare process quality report	Enhances
Organisation	Formal culture	Phase kind	System Definition	Strongly enhances
		Task kind	Measure process quality	Enhances
	Agile culture	Phase kind	System Definition	Strongly deteriorates
		Process kind	Process Improvement	Deteriorates
		Task kind	Document requirements	Deteriorates
			Elicit requirements	Enhances
		Technique kind	In-house customer	Enhances
			Test-first development	Enhances
	Experience	Phase kind	System Definition	Strongly enhances
		Process kind	Requirements engineering	Enhances
			Acceptance Testing	Enhances
		Task kind	Elicit requirements	Enhances
		Technique kind	Focus groups	Strongly enhances
			Prototyping	Strongly enhances
			Walkthroughs	Enhances

(continued)

Table 6.7 (continued)

Attribute	Method fragment	Value
	In-house customer	Enhances

For each mapping, a value is included indicating how the choice of the method fragment affects the attribute (after Gonzalez-Perez et al., table 6, 2009) (With kind permission of Springer Science + Business Media)

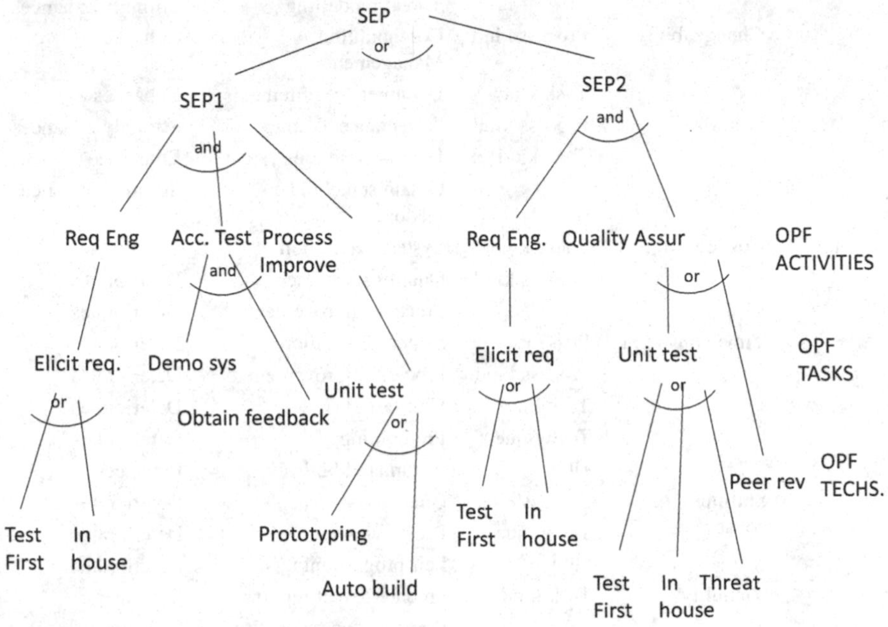

Fig. 6.20 Hierarchical tree depicting Activities, Tasks and Techniques for two hypothetical SEPs (after Gonzalez-Perez et al., figure 2, 2009) (With kind permission of Springer Science + Business Media)

has several Tasks, each implemented by a Technique chosen from a list. The two options are shown graphically in Fig. 6.20.

A table similar to that of Table 6.7 links Techniques to impact factors. The techniques are labelled there as X1–X6 where X1 = Test first; X2 = In-house customer; X3 = Prototyping; X4 = Automated builds; X5 = Threat modelling and X6 = Peer reviewing. Then the two processes can be described in terms of these terminal techniques as:

SEP1 is (X1 or X2); (X3 or X4)

SEP2 is (X1 or X2); (X1 or X2 or X5 or X6)

To illustrate this point, we consider the impact on two factors: Reliability and Agility (Table 6.8).

Table 6.8 Techniques used in the two SEP options of Fig. 6.20 and their impact on reliability and on agility

1. Reliability		
Test-first development (X1)	Enhances (+)	
In-house customer (X2)	Enhances (+)	
Prototyping (X3)	Neutral (o)	
Automated builds (X4)	Deteriorates (−)	
Threat modelling(X5)	Strongly enhances (++)	
Peer reviewing (X6)	Strongly enhances (++)	
2. Agility		
Test-first development (X1)	Enhances (+)	
In-house customer (X2)	Enhances (+)	
Prototyping (X3)	Deteriorates (−)	
Automated builds (X4)	Strongly deteriorates (−−)	
Threat modelling(X5)	Strongly deteriorates (−−)	
Peer reviewing (X6	Strongly enhances (++)	
Then the impact is as follows:		
Option	Reliability	Agility
SEP1 option 1 is X1; X3	+/0	+/−
SEP1 option 2 is X1; X4	+/−	+/−−
SEP1 option 3 is X2; X3	+/0	+/−
SEP1 option 4 is X2; X4	+/−	+/− −
SEP2 option 1 is X1; X1	+/+	+/+
SEP2 option 2 is X1; X2	+/+	+/+
SEP2 option 3 is X1; X5	+/+ +	+/− −
SEP2 option 4 is X1; X6	+/+ +	+/+ +
SEP2 option 5 is X2; X1	+/+	+/+
SEP2 option 6 is X2; X2	+/+	+/+
SEP2 option 7 is X2; X5	+/+ +	+/− −
SEP2 option 8 is X2; X6	+/+ +	+/+ +

Gonzalez-Perez et al. (2009) conclude that, from a reliability viewpoint, the best choice would be SEP2, options 3, 4, 7 or 8. On the other hand, from an agility perspective, the best choice would be SEP2, option 4 or 6.

The above analysis is fully supported and automated in Tropos (Giorgini et al. 2005). In particular, backward reasoning allows the analyst to search for possible method fragments from the repository that satisfy the desired goal. Moreover, by assigning a cost to each fragment, backward reasoning also produces the solution with the minimum cost. Nevertheless, even achieving these software-defined goals may be inadequate. Unless they are aligned and consistent with business goals, project success may be unachievable (Lepmets et al. 2012—see also Chap. 8).

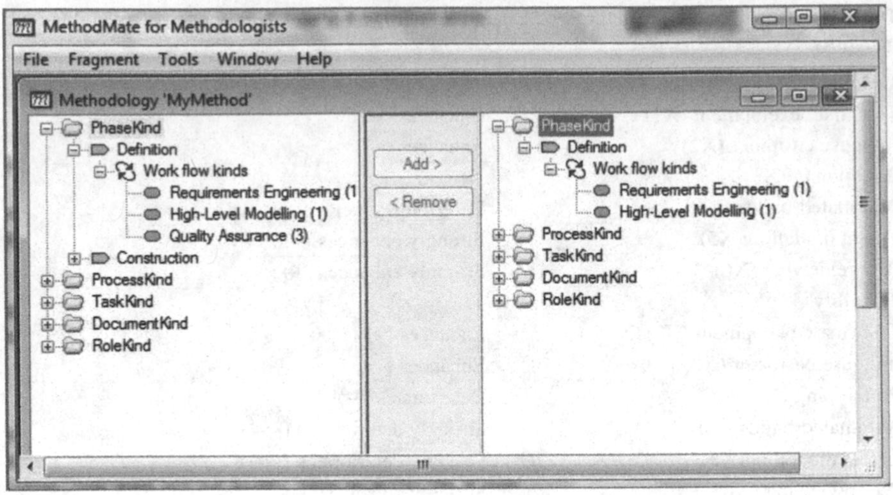

Fig. 6.21 Screen shot from MethodMate

6.4.3 Discussion of Various Approaches

Although much of our standard knowledge and understanding of SME was built up over a period from the early 1990s, the more recent (2007) publication of the ISO/IEC International Standard 24744 (ISO/IEC 2007) offers new possibilities for the 'glue' between fragments since this metamodel has a number of meta classes specifically designed to link the major method fragments together. These include the ActionKind and WorkPerformanceKind classes in the metamodel. As described in Chap. 4, this International Standard uses powertypes in its definition. Implementation of this standard provides useful tools for the method engineer; for instance, the research tool, MethodMate (based on the architecture described by Gonzalez-Perez (2005)—see screen shot in Fig. 6.21) and the commercial tools provided by the zAgile and MethodPark companies. The SPEM standard is also much utilised in tools like IBM's Method Composer but this standard does not fully support method enactment as does the ISO standard. CAME and CASE tools differ in their target applications in the sense that some support method construction, some method tailoring, whilst others are applicable for both. Consequently, we defer a detailed discussion (of two exemplar tools) until after our discussion of method tailoring (see Sect. 7.3).

In addition, increasingly sophisticated teams will wish to see their process mature commensurately. Using the deontic matrix approach, new method fragments are easily added to an organisation's existing methodology. Thus, the SME approach also provides implicit support for SPI (Henderson-Sellers 2006b; Henderson-Sellers et al. 2007a) and ISO/IEC 24744 has an explicit meta class to represent the capability level that will be used in such a software maturity evaluation, using, say, ISO 15504 (ISO/IEC 1998). Furthermore, the ISO metamodel is

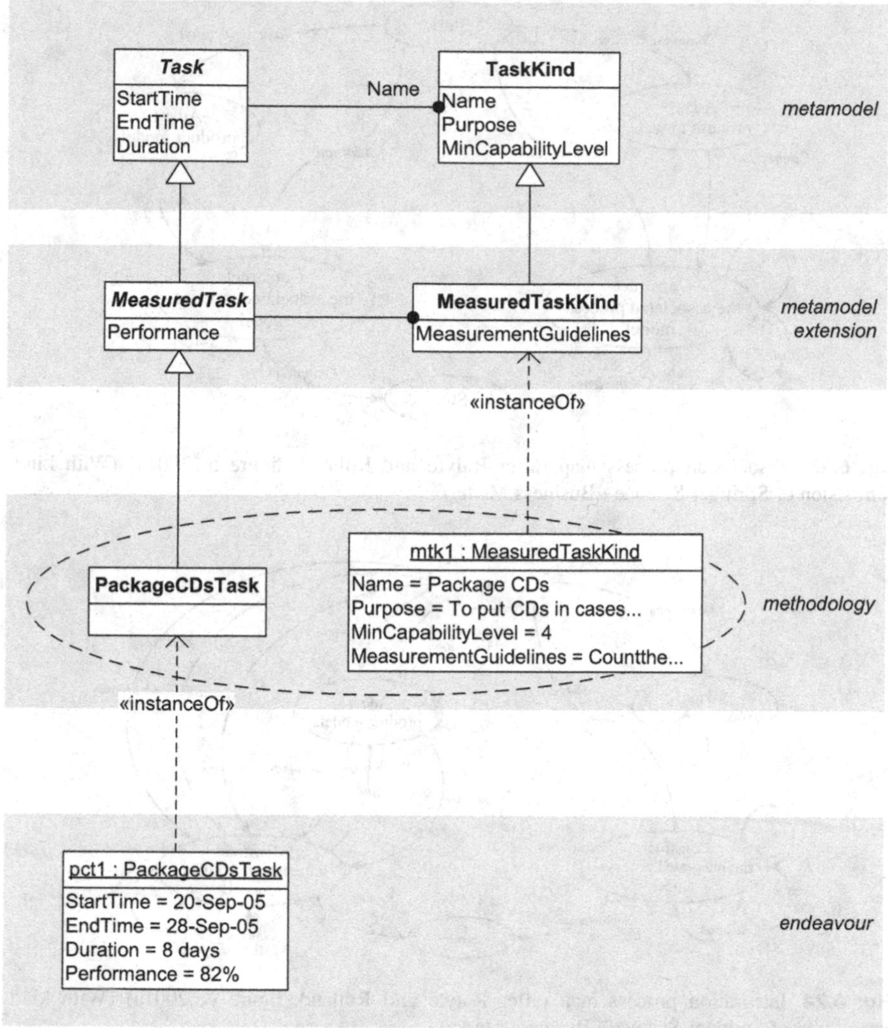

Fig. 6.22 Extending the ISO/IEC 24744 by the addition of a pair of extension classes (after Henderson-Sellers and Gonzalez-Perez 2006a)

also easily extended by the simple and straightforward addition of a subtype for each of the pair of class in the powertype pattern in the Metamodel domain (Fig. 6.22). In this example, MeasuredTask is subtyped from Task, and MeasuredTaskKind is subtyped from TaskKind. The powertype pattern relationship between the extension classes parallels the standard one in the metamodel. The additional attributes on these metamodel extension classes (MeasuredTask and MeasuredTaskKind) (Fig. 6.22) allow all measured tasks to have a performance value attached to them. Once this extension pattern has been introduced into the metamodel, the method engineer can use these extension classes in the creation

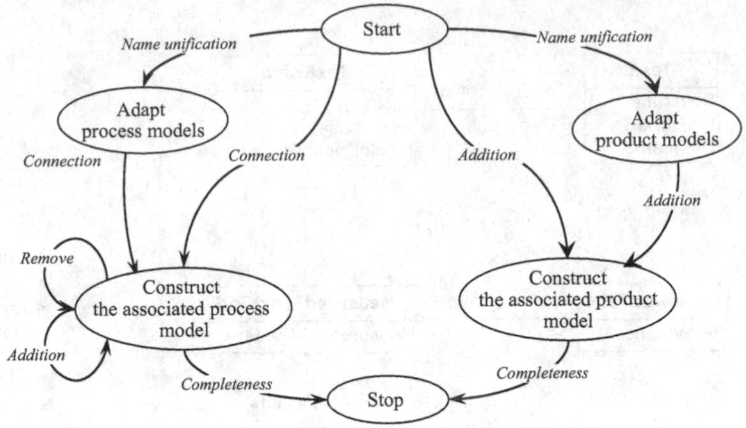

Fig. 6.23 Association process map (after Ralyté and Rolland, figure 5, 2001a) (With kind permission of Springer Science + Business Media)

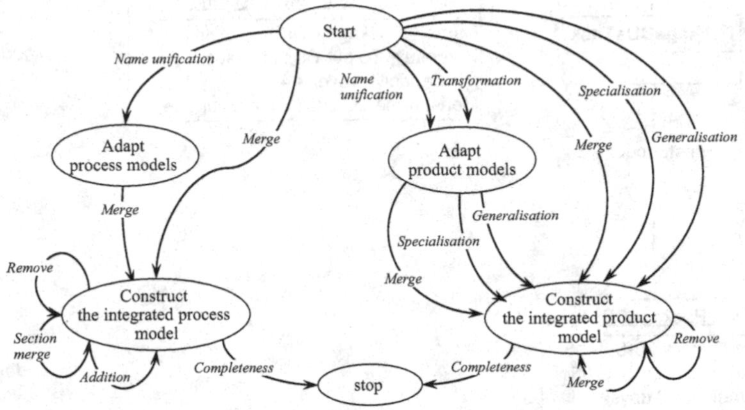

Fig. 6.24 Integration process map (after Ralyté and Rolland, figure 4, 2001a) (With kind permission of Springer Science + Business Media)

of method fragments in the normal way. (None of the other metamodels discussed in Chap. 4 can be used in this simple way—it requires artificial constructs such as UML profiles and stereotypes.)

In the context of the map-style of representation of process models, we can follow the intention in Fig. 5.3 of *Define a method part* (when completed over all method parts) with a section to describe the intention of *Select a method part*. This is accomplished using one or more strategies shown in Fig. 6.2, viz. decomposition, aggregation and refinement. Subsequently, we focus on part assembly as the focus of the intention *Assemble method parts* in the assembly-based process model of Fig. 6.2. Two strategies are suggested by Ralyté and Rolland (2001a): association and integration. The Association strategy is applicable when the parts fit together with no overlap. The parts then simply need connecting or associating via their well-defined interfaces. Typically one chunk will result—the production of a work product that is to be used as input to the second chunk. The map for this is shown in Fig. 6.23. Of note is the case when there is some overlap in terminology—hence the proposed *Name unification strategy* (Ralyté and Rolland 2001a). Two routes are shown: one via the adaptation of process models, one via the adaptation of product models. If no adaptation is necessary, then there are direct routes to the relevant construction intention.

The Integration strategy, on the other hand, offers the method engineer more challenges. In these cases, the two method parts (chunks) to be assembled contain common, or at least overlapping, material. Following the map of Fig. 6.24, which expands the *<Select method chunks, Assemble method chunks, Integration strategy>* section of Fig. 6.12, we see that there are two options. For chunks containing elements of both process and product, either aspect can be done first. Various strategies are expounded by Ralyté and Rolland (2001a), aimed at chunk unification. Following the Name unification strategy (if needed), an adaptation intention may be required followed by the relevant construction intention, as shown in Fig. 6.24. Pairs of fragments/chunks to be merged should, of course, have similar/complementary semantics and matching interfaces. It is also important to evaluate the degree of overlap—Ralyté and Rolland (2001a) suggest the use of similarity measures to evaluate the structural similarity of concepts (SSC) and the adjacent similarity of concepts (ASC) as product similarity measures; semantic affinity of intentions (SAI) and semantic affinity of sections (SAS) as process model similarity measures.

Both integration and association processes are supported by a set of assembly operators (Ralyté et al. 1999; Ralyté and Rolland 2001a) classified into product and process assembly operators. The product assembly operators deal with different product model elements (concept, property, link) and allow the operations of Add, Delete, Rename, Objectify, Specialise/Generalise and Merge of different elements. Similarly, the process assembly operators deal with different process model elements (intention, strategy, section), supporting their Add, Delete, Rename, Split and Merge.

Connection of method components via their defined interfaces is discussed briefly in Wistrand and Karlsson (2004). Ter Hofstede and Verhoef (1997) suggest the need to define a set of constructors, which are an (undefined) means of solving 'schema integration problems'. Their examples seem to focus on integrating two fragments from different metamodels; although this approach is equally valid for integrating two method fragments generated from the same metamodel as should generally be the case.

Rupprecht et al. (2000) note the need to use *constraints and requirements* to influence the particular design of the process under construction. These form the contextual basis. Coupled with this are the experience-derived construction rules, which consist of a condition part that refers to the constraints plus an execution part that triggers the construction operators (see Fig. 6.25 for a portion of their class-based ontology depicted in terms of a UML model). In this approach, the

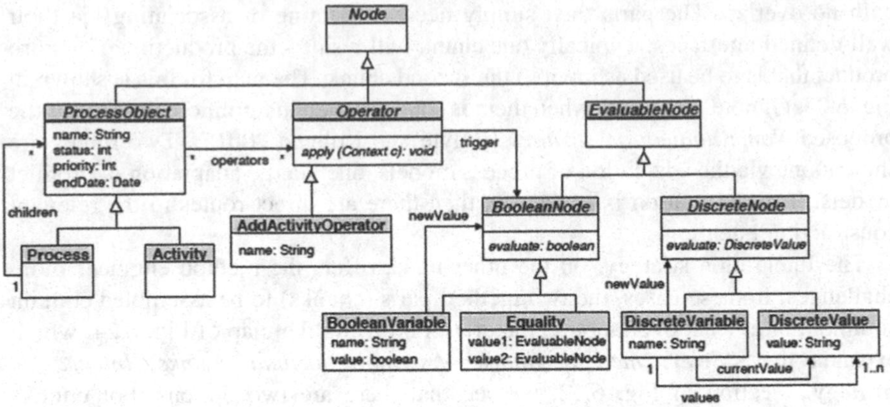

Fig. 6.25 A portion of the class-based ontology of Rupprecht et al. (figure 4, 2000) (With kind permission of Springer Science + Business Media)

application of specific operators on a process model is used to transform it to an adequate representation of a specific process. These authors use the following definitions (another example of the difficulty in comprehension caused by using the same terms as other authors but with different meanings—see also Sect. 1.3):

- Process = set of temporally or logically ordered activities used to reach a goal by using some resources.
- Task = definition of the goal plus information about all constraints needed to achieve the goal.
- Activity = performed by agents (people of machines). These are the things that are temporally ordered.
- Process model as the meta-level representation of an actual process. Process models can be decomposed into sub-processes. Ultimately, the atomic sub-process is the activity. Rupprecht et al. (2000) suggest that there are five basic categories of objectives for process modelling, viz. to facilitate human understanding and communication; to support process improvement; to support process management; to automate process guidance and to automate process execution support.
- Artefact = output of an activity (as suggested by Curtis et al. (1992) who unfortunately neglect the case of using an artefact as an *input* to an activity).

Using a formal language, Chroust (2000) argues that there are two operators needed for augmenting an existing methodology:

Union—which allows the combination of process models

Substitution—which substitutes one element of a method by a complete process (method) fragment.

Finally, based on the ideas introduced in detail in Chap. 3, Rossi et al. (2000) strongly urge that the construction process is well documented in terms of decisions taken: 'method rationale' (Oinas-Kukkonen 1996) and, in particular, 'method construction rationale'. Documenting decisions taken during method tailoring can assist in maintaining and incrementally advancing the method and its local use.

6.5 Summary

In this chapter, we have investigated several possible ways to construct a method from method parts. Some of these use the 'map' approach discussed earlier in the book. Others focus on identifying final goals and deliverables and then working backwards to identify appropriate method parts to be extracted from the repository or to be configured based on an existing organisation-wide method. Using a map formalism from Chap. 4, we identified seven possible process routes (Fig. 6.1), four of which were originally identified in the context of construction of a methodology from method chunks. To these we have added the approaches based on deontic matrices (e.g., Graham et al. 1997) and UML-style Activity Diagrams (Seidita et al. 2007) as well as the configuration-based approach used for method components (Karlsson and Ågerfalk 2009b).

In Sect. 6.2 we introduced the importance of having good requirements for the methodology before commencing its construction and introduced some ideas from design science in that context (Winter 2011). In Sect. 6.3 we focussed on the method base (or repository) and see how the method engineer can turn the requirements into identifiable and retrievable method parts. We then gave some advice on what drivers there should be for high quality method construction, including the idea of focussing on goals and their achievement rather than on the more traditional view of methodologies and processes as work units acting as transformation engines (Sect. 6.4).

In later chapters, we will see how these constructed methods can be further tailored (Chap. 7), how their quality can be assessed (Chap. 8) and how they have been used in practice (Chap. 9).

Tailoring a Constructed Method 7

Summary of What We Will Learn in Chapter 7

- What is meant by method tailoring
- What are the various styles of method tailoring
- New ideas regarding software process line engineering
- How to do method configuration with method components
- How SME and SPI can be linked
- Some of the software tools that are available to support SME

Having constructed a method using an SME approach, the first enactment should follow smoothly, since all situational constraints have been accommodated during its construction. However, on later endeavours, minor 'tweaking' may become necessary. Sometimes, management may decide to 'freeze' a base method upon which such modifications are to be made. Indeed, this thinking can also be imposed on an 'off-the-shelf' method, which requires project-specific customisation. These various kinds of modifications are generically known as 'tailoring'. For example, Fitzgerald et al. (2003) note, from empirical studies, that 'off-the-shelf' methods need to be tailored to fit the needs of a specific project, even if the method appears to be appropriate and suitable for the project in hand (Aydin and Harmsen 2002). Fitzgerald et al. (2003) focus on the usefulness of (a) contingency factors and (b) method engineering and show how this was successful within a Motorola case study. Kokol (1999) argues that the failure of IT in the medical area can be attributed to the inappropriateness of the methodology used—offering method engineering as a remedy. Arni-Bloch et al. (2006) show how a situational method engineering approach to the integration of COTS (commercial off-the-shelf) packages into more traditional information systems can be efficacious.

Industry experience leads Bajec et al. (2007b) to suggest Process Configuration as an effective tailoring approach to create situation-specific methods all based on a single base approach, which is itself allowed to continuously evolve. Evolution is

B. Henderson-Sellers et al., *Situational Method Engineering*,
DOI 10.1007/978-3-642-41467-1_7,

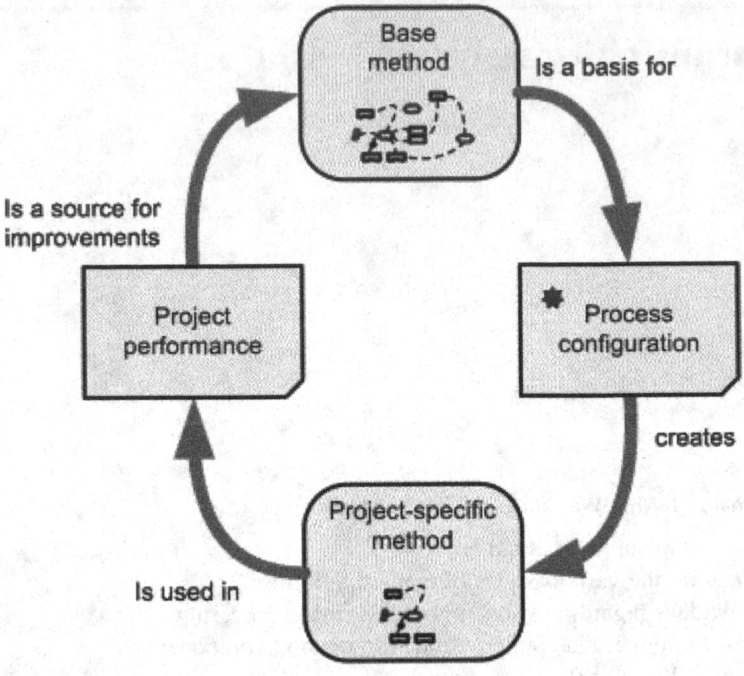

Fig. 7.1 Base method continuous evolution approach of Bajec et al. (2007b). Reprinted with permission from Elsevier

accomplished by means of the process configuration step to create a project-specific method, in the normal SME way; the difference here being the starting point: an extant base method (Fig. 7.1). Mirbel (2006) notes that tailoring can lead to multiple organisationally or project-specific methods for which the individual leads have no 'big picture' knowledge, only that of their 'own' methodology. As an antidote, therefore, to multiple tailored methods, Mirbel (2006) recommends the use of a 'federation' (as described in Chap. 2), a technique that also supports the use of quality metrics (see Chap. 8).

The tailoring of software methods and processes is seen by Pedreira et al. (2007) as being a mandatory part-activity but one that is usually done "without the proper dedication, following an ad-hoc approach and using neither guidelines nor rules". Their extensive literature review identifies a number of important issues:

- That tailoring can occur at one of many levels within an organisation including at the project level
- That tailoring may be formal or informal
- That often a case study within a real organisation can be valuable
- That the size of the organisation is influential in the approach adopted
- That there may be concerns about standards compliance
- That tools are needed to support the tailoring activity (see Sect. 7.3).

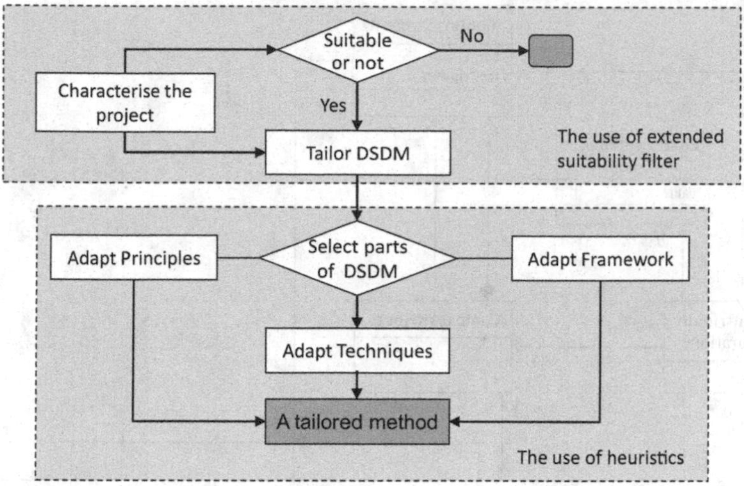

Fig. 7.2 Overall coaching activities used in method tailoring in an empirical study (after Aydin and Harmsen, figure 1, 2002) (With kind permission of Springer Science + Business Media)

The Motorola case study also provides an excellent depiction of how process tailoring works in practice. Fitzgerald et al. (2003) identified two types of tailoring at the project level: up front (recorded as part of the project plan) and dynamic (more ad hoc in light of modified perceptions of the project as it proceeds). In both cases, they found that capture and definition of tailoring criteria were essential in risk management and in terms of the overall success of the project. In the context of manufacturing processes, Rupprecht et al. (2000) discuss tailoring as 'process individualisation', i.e., adapting a process model for a specific context (see also Fig. 4.1). Patel et al. (2004) use, as an exemplar for their tailoring approach, the Rational Unified Process (Kruchten 1999; MacIsaac 2003), whereas Aydin and Harmsen (2002) and Aydin et al. (2005) utilise as their base methodology the DSDM (dynamic systems development method: Stapleton (1997)). Aydin and Harmsen (2002) undertook an empirical assessment with one specific large financial organisation, showing disparate levels of understanding across the management team. They instigated a set of coaching activities to assist in dissemination of this information and understanding of tailoring, in the context of aiming to achieve CMM level 3. The process that resulted is shown in Fig. 7.2.

An MDE approach to process tailoring is investigated by Hurtado Alegria et al. (2011) and Hurtado Alegria (2012) and evaluated in practice for the requirements engineering process of a medium-sized software company in Chile. In this approach, SPEM 2.0 (OMG 2008) is used to define the organisational process together with a context model based on the metamodel shown in Fig. 7.3. Tailoring transformation rules are then defined using a declarative language called ATL (the ATLAS Transformation Language) (Joualt et al. 2006).

There are also situations when a base method is kept but various versions of it are supported—as a 'family' of methods (e.g., Kornyshova et al. 2011). First addressed

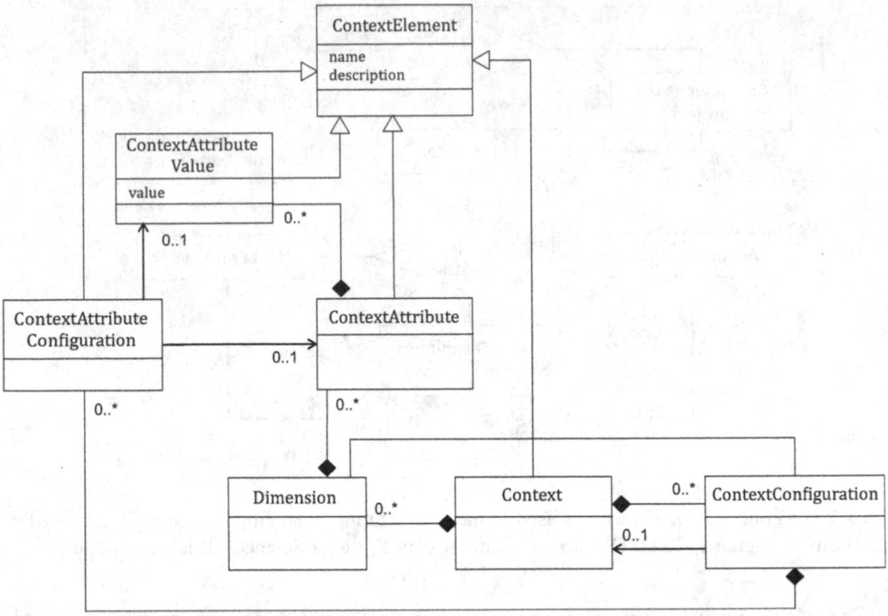

Fig. 7.3 Software process context metamodel (SPCM) (after Hurtado Alegria et al. 2011) Association for Computing Machinery, Inc. Reprinted with permission. doi: 10.1145/1987875.1987885

outside of SME (e.g., Rombach 2005; Simidchieva et al. 2007), process families were linked by Aharoni and Reinhartz-Berger (2008) to domain engineering. This was extended by Asadi et al. (2011), who proposed a parallel to software product line engineering (SPLE), which consists of domain engineering (for reuse) plus application engineering (with reuse), in order to create families of method-oriented architectures. These papers argue for the use of variants and variation points for creating method families; similar to the variability realisation techniques of Svahnberg et al. (2005) in SPLE, which aims to manage commonality of core software assets on the one hand and variability on the other (e.g., Asadi et al. 2011) and to profiles in the UML domain (a language for describing work products and not process-related). Examples of this software process line engineering approach are given by Rausch et al. (2005) with respect to the V-Modell XT used in German software houses and by Martinez-Ruiz et al. (2011) in SPEM-based projects. Rolland and Nurcan (2010) note that, in a business process family, a common goal may be met in a variety of different ways. This leads them to utilise the map approach (Sect. 4.3) to capture two possible kinds of adaptation and variability: (1) design time adaptation, resulting in a single path from Start to Stop and (2) run-time adaptation, in which desired features can be selected dynamically as part of the enactment. In all cases, there exists the challenge of managing the variability of a family of tailored approaches (plus the 'root' one) as they are used and applied.

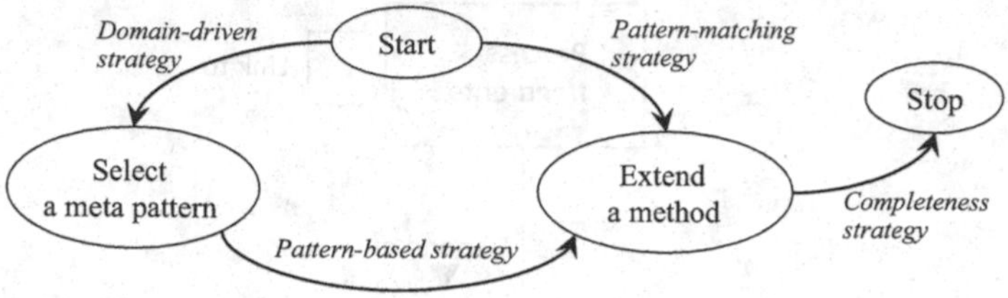

Fig. 7.4 Extension-based process model for SME (after Ralyté et al., figure 5, 2003) (With kind permission of Springer Science + Business Media)

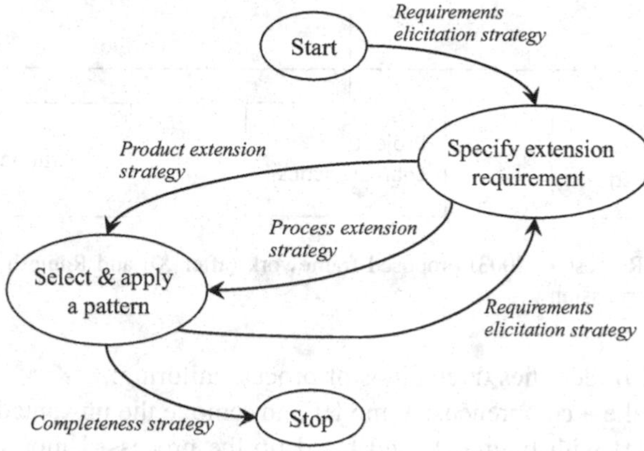

Fig. 7.5 Process model for pattern-matching-based method extension (after Ralyté et al., figure 5, 2003) (With kind permission of Springer Science + Business Media)

Wistrand and Karlsson (2004) discuss method configuration (MC) as a special case of ME. For them, MC has three strategies:

1. Selecting parts from an assumed pre-existing base method;
2. Integrating parts from other methods to fill gaps in the base method;
3. Developing new parts when (b) is not applicable

   (although it should be noted that this appears not to support restriction as they state!).

Wistrand and Karlsson (2004) state that, of Ralyté et al.'s (2003) three strategies (viz. assembly-based, extension-based and paradigm-based), extension-based is nearest to their SEM[1]-based MC strategy but (they claim) MC permits not just extension but also restriction (which they state is not possible using the Ralyté et al.'s extension strategy). This extension-based strategy can be expanded from Fig. 6.1 as shown in Fig. 7.4. Two strategies are shown: domain-driven in order to Select a meta pattern followed by a Pattern-based strategy or else a Pattern-matching strategy; the process model for pattern-matching-based method extension being depicted in Fig. 7.5.

[1] Systems engineering method.

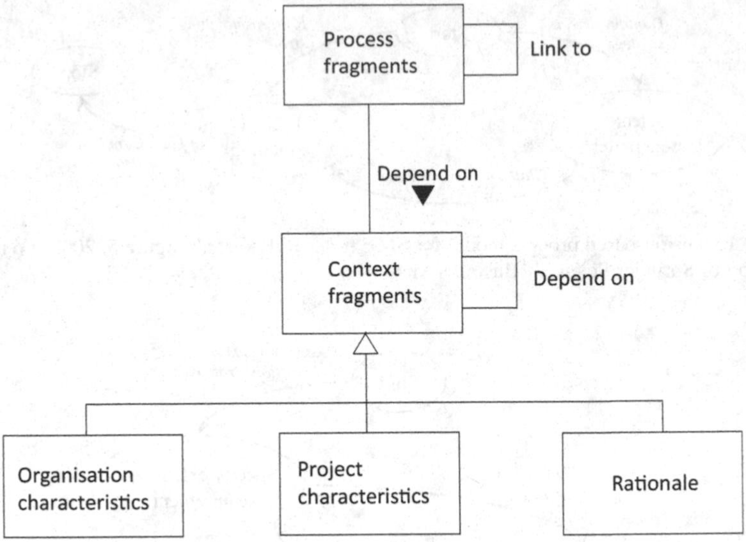

Fig. 7.6 Xu and Ramesh's (2003) proposed framework (after Xu and Ramesh 2003) ©IEEE reproduced with permission

Chroust (2000) identifies three kinds of process tailoring:

- *Reductive*. Take a comprehensive model and remove the unwanted pieces.
- *Synthetic*. Start with fragments and build up the process. Union operators are needed here.
- *Generic*. This is not clear in the original publication but appears to refer to the use of a fragment as a parameter for the generation of another fragment.

Tailoring usually involves removal of unwanted bits. Therefore useful operators are:

DIFFERENCE ($PM_1 - PM_2$)—returning those elements that are in one method but not the second. Elimination of an activity thus involves the subtraction of a unit set from the method by using this DIFFERENCE operator.

INTERSECTION ($PM_1 \cap PM_2$)—returning the common elements of the two process models.

EQUALITY ($PM_1 = PM_2$)—allowing the comparison of two models. The relation is true if $PM_1 - PM_2$ is the empty set. However, it should be noted that the empty set simply states that the method fragments in the two sets are identical. It does not guarantee that the configuration of those two method fragment sets is the same.

Process tailoring and process knowledge are discussed by Xu and Ramesh (2003) who propose a framework (described by the metamodel in Fig. 7.6) as a "first step in supporting the process reuse . . . to represent the elements needed to be captured in process tailoring". They go on to propose the design for a prototype tool developed to capture and use such process knowledge.

Table 7.1 Summary of different grounding processes (reprinted from Karlsson and Ågerfalk 2004 with permission from Elsevier)—based on ideas of Goldkuhl (1999)

Internal grounding	External theoretical grounding	Empirical grounding
Knowledge reconstruction	Conceptual grounding	Application and observation grounding
Conceptual grounding	Value grounding	
Value grounding	Explanatory grounding	
Evaluation of knowledge cohesion		

7.1 Process for Method Configuration

A configuration-based approach has been previously discussed (Sect. 6.1.5) in the context of 'greenfield' method construction. However, this approach is also useful for tailoring and improving previously constructed methods.

Karlsson (2002) focusses on one special aspect of SME, that of tailoring an existing or base method using Method for Method Configuration (MMC) (Karlsson et al. 2001). The scope is that of modifications to off-the-shelf software development methods like RUP (Kruchten 1999) to produce a situational method. MMC starts with a pre-selected base method, which could be a full method or a set of fragments, existing in some identifiable context. It is then broken down into a sequence of activities to be performed, perhaps grouped into sub-processes.

Karlsson (2002) argues that an essential activity in both MMC and SME should be grounding in order to assure quality, that grounding being performed in three parts: internal, external and empirical (Table 7.1). Internal grounding focusses on whether the concepts used are complete and consistent; external grounding relates this knowledge to other, external sources in the same domain, while empirical grounding tests and evaluates the method in everyday use. As a prerequisite to undertaking external grounding, he identifies five essential concepts: Base Method (the method that is used as the basis for the method tailoring); a Development Situation (an abstraction of one or more existing or future projects with common characteristics); Characteristic (a delimited part of a development situation); a Development Track (a method configuration suitable for some specific situation—renamed Configuration Package in Karlsson and Ågerfalk (2004)); a Generic Project Type (that predefines a combination of Development Tracks in order to facilitate reuse across commonly occurring situations—renamed as Configuration Template in Karlsson and Ågerfalk (2004)) (augmented by Prescribed Action, which represents a process fragment, in Karlsson and Ågerfalk (2004)). Karlsson (2002) then identifies the mappings between these five concepts in MMC and SME—summarised in Table 7.2 and exemplars presented by Karlsson and Ågerfalk (2005). More recently (Karlsson and Ågerfalk 2009b), the idea of a Configuration Package, which typifies the situational context for the tailoring (in terms of, for instance, co-location of project team, availability of customer(s),

Table 7.2 Summary of external grounding

Concept in MMC	Mapped concept in SME
Base method	SME usually (but not always) starts with fragments not a whole method so there is no corresponding concept in SME. The correspondence is to the finally constructed method rather than anything initially
Development situation	An equivalent concept is found in much of the SME literature
Characteristic	Although the concept exists in SME, MMC offers a more straightforward link to its effect on the configuration. In a bottom-up approach, the value of a characteristic value is potentially a method fragment. In MMC, however, there is a one-to-one mapping between the characteristic's value and a Development Track
Development Track	There are large differences in this concept. MMC focusses on screening of the base method rather than modularisation, which is the common focus in the SME literature. However, operationalised Development Tracks do have some similarities with, for example, method fragments and components, but with vaguer boundaries
Generic project type	Templates for systems engineering methods (SEMs) are not a new phenomenon in SME; for example, the use of paths in SEMs

project risk level, degree of management commitment), has been applied in an interesting analysis of empirical data from the use of MMC in agile computing domains. These authors conclude that MMC is useful as a quality assurance tool, and that goals can be useful as a reference point when extending the base method.

MMC and method configuration often utilise software tools—in particular MC Sandbox, described in detail in Sect. 7.3.2.

Ter Hofstede and Verhoef (1997) suggest that there should be two stages: customisation (of retrieved method fragments) followed by integration of the fragments. Customisation is seen in terms of generalisations/specialisations or simple additions or deletions such as:

- Add relationship
- Add role
- Add value
- Delete collection type

(for further details see Ter Hofstede and Verhoef 1997, p 415).

Perez et al. (1995) discuss congruence evaluation, arguing that this is the most important measure to be assessed. Congruence assesses how well the process model fits the intended usage/domain. They suggest that, in order to measure congruence, a contingency model must first be developed in order to define the relationships between the process model and its intended usage context. They introduce three variables: a dependent variable (the effectiveness of the process model), an independent variable (a characteristic of the process model) and a contingency variable (either a characteristic of the context or the process model). Attribute values must first be assigned, often subjectively by someone familiar with the situation, and then a congruence measure calculated based on the interrelationships established between the process model and the attributes of the process context. The derived congruence index is a real number in the closed interval [−1,1] with 1 indicating a perfect match and −1 the worst possible match. Low congruence values can thus be identified with the aim of improving the underlying values and thus increasing that specific value. A similar, contingency approach is also advocated by van Slooten and Hodes (1996), based on work of van de Hoef et al. (1995). Based on a banking example and field trial, van Slooten and Hodes (1996) recommend the following list of contingency factors:

- Management commitment
- Importance
- Impact
- Resistance and conflict
- Time pressure
- Shortage of human resources
- Shortage of means
- Formality
- Knowledge and experience
- Skills
- Size
- Relationships
- Dependency
- Clarity
- Stability
- Complexity
- Level of innovation.

Adaptation of processes is also discussed by Henninger et al. (2002) in the context of agile methodologies; in an empirical study in an industry in Ireland, Fitzgerald and Hartnett (2005) identified complementary features in XP (good support for the more technical aspects of software development) and Scrum (good support for project planning and tracking) and customised them, thus gaining overall benefit to the industry's projects.

7.2 Tailoring for Software Process Improvement

Tailoring and method configuration can be utilised not only in initial method design but also to support method/process improvement. Bajec et al. (2007a, b) create project-specific methods from a base method that is already in use in an organisation. They then build on these base methods by tailoring the process (a.k.a. process configuration) as discussed in Chap. 1 (Bajec 2011b), taking into account the method fragment's characteristics in the two dimensions of (1) technical suitability and (2) social suitability (where the latter represents whether people want to use the fragment) (Fig. 7.7). In the quadrant diagram of Fig. 7.7, each fragment is positioned in terms of its technical suitability and its social acceptability. The four quadrants are characterised as follows:

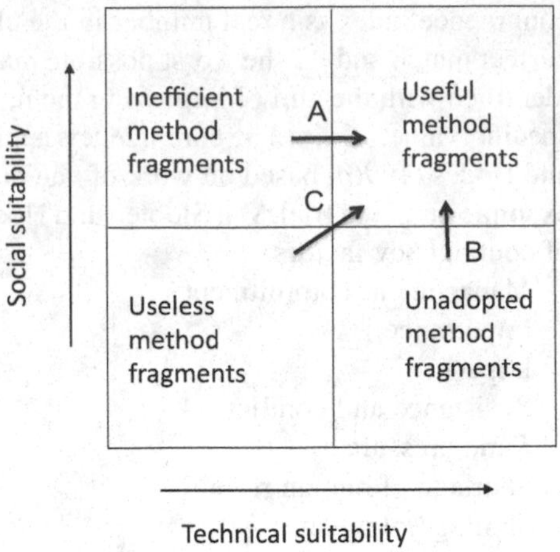

Fig. 7.7 Two-dimensional matrix for evaluating and improving the suitability of a method fragment (adapted from Vavpotic and Bajec 2009). Reprinted with permission from Elsevier

Useless: both technically and socially.

Inefficient: socially acceptable but of dubious technical worth. For example, fragments used on previous projects (and liked by team members) but not technically appropriate for the current project.

Unadopted: technically suitable but rejected on social acceptability grounds, e.g., a fragment that is overly complex or incompatible with personal bias or organisational culture.

Useful: both technically and socially.

Vavpotic and Bajec (2009) suggest that it may be possible to move fragments into the Useful quadrant. Arrow A in Fig. 7.7 denotes a socially acceptable fragment that, with technical improvement, could become 'useful'. Unadopted fragments (Arrow B) demand new consideration of why they are socially unacceptable. If lack of knowledge and understanding is the cause, then education and training may help. Arrow C depicts the greatest challenge; indeed, it may be best to discard such a 'useless' fragment and seek one that immediately sits in the top right quadrant.

Mirandolle et al. (2011) advocate an incremental method engineering approach to support software process improvement (SPI)—an approach introduced in van de Weerd et al. (2006) in their study of Product Software Knowledge Infrastructure. Although focussed on Software Product Management (SPM), the approach could be used for other domains with different entries in the matrices discussed below. In this approach, an individual fragment is changed—either by modification or by replacement. The target change is identified in terms of analysing the requirements of the company in terms of its situational factors and how these relate to candidate method fragments. For the SPM domain, Mirandolle et al. (2011) use the four business functions of the Software Product Management Competence Model of Bekkers et al. (2010), each of which has a small number of focus areas—a total of 15 across the four business functions of Requirements management, Release planning, Product planning and Portfolio management. For each of these focus

Table 7.3 SPM maturity matrix (after Mirandolle et al., table 1, 2011)

	0	1	2	3	4	5	6	7	8	9	10
Requirements management											
Requirements gathering		A		B	C		D	E	F		
Requirements identification			A			B		C			D
Requirements organising				A		B		C			
Release planning											
Requirements prioritisation			A		B	C	D			E	
Release definition			A	B	C				D		E
Release definition validation					A			B		C	
Scope change management				A		B		C		D	
Build validation					A			B		C	
Launch preparation		A		B		C	D		E		F
Product planning											
Road-map intelligence				A		B	C		D	E	
Core asset road-mapping					A		B		C		D
Product road-mapping			A	B			C	D		E	
Portfolio management											
Market analysis					A		B	C	D		E
Partnering and contracting						A	B		C	D	E
Product lifecycle management					A	B			C	D	E

areas, up to five levels of 'capability' are then identified. These capabilities do not, however, map directly to a Likert scale of 1–5 as in the CMMI (capability maturity model integration) and ISO/IEC 15504 but are mapped on to an extended scale of 'maturity' of 1–10 (Table 7.3). [Note that this is in conflict with the more usual meaning of maturity, which should be associated with differences in an organisation's concerns as they mature and gain wisdom (McBride 2011)—a term used since the 1950s. See also discussion in Chap. 8.]

Mirandolle et al. (2011) use 'Requirements prioritisation' as an exemplar (shaded in the table). In order to improve an organisation's constructed method in this particular focus area, the next step is to identify potential method fragments (here for Techniques). Each technique will encompass a subset of the 'capability levels'—the results for eight candidate techniques to improve the requirements prioritisation focus area in Table 7.3 are given in Table 7.4. This identifies which techniques might be useful for enhancing the maturity level of this focus area. Table 7.4 shows that to move to level E, only three techniques are candidates: integer linear programming approach, requirements triage and features prioritisation matrix. For each of these three, a list of its situational factors (from Bekkers et al. 2008), together with values for each of these factors, is constructed and compared to the situational factors for the target organisation. This gives a best fit for this focus area, which can be pictured by using a PDD (Chap. 4). For this example, the Features prioritisation matrix technique (the best fit for the case study company in Mirandolle et al. (2011)) is shown in Fig. 7.8 (shaded).

Table 7.4 Implemented 'capabilities' for the eight candidate techniques for the improvement of requirements prioritisation (slightly modified from Mirandolle et al., table 2, 2011)

Technique	Implemented capabilities				
Binary priority list	A	B			
Win–win requirements negotiation model	A	B	C		
Integer linear programming approach	A	B	C	D	E
Requirements triage	A	B	C		E
MOSCOW	A	B	C	D	
Cost value approach	A	B	C	D	
Quality function deployment	A	B	C		
Features prioritisation matrix	A	B	C	D	E

Incremental process improvement is also addressed by Vlaanderen et al. (2011). Although their domain is SPM, their results seem to be equally useful for software development. They combine an improvement cycle with an assessment cycle (Fig. 7.9). The assessment cycle begins with an analysis of the current situation, accomplished in terms of a PDD depiction (see Fig. 4.49 in Chap. 4 and Fig. 7.8) that shows the current processes and associated products. In order to determine motivation for improvement, questionnaires and interviews are used. In the second phase (analysis of needs), the situational factors are used in a determination of the optimal capability profile. This is then combined with a current capability profile to create an improvement matrix (Fig. 7.10). The difference (or 'gap'), shaded light grey in Fig. 7.10, indicates the capabilities that need to be implemented in the SPI process.

The third step is the selection of process alternatives (Fig. 7.9) in which each missing capability is connected to a potentially useful method fragment. They also suggest taking into account in this step a rating on the fragment in terms of, for instance, ease of use and satisfaction. Such information is documented in the full description of the method fragment or chunk as discussed in Chaps. 2 and 4. From all this information, an improvement road-map is created. Once accepted by all stakeholders, its implementation commences (Fig. 7.9).

Process improvement can also be viewed as responding to change requirements according to Etien et al. (2003). They propose a gap-based typology within the constraints of SME. The quality criteria they consider include completeness, consistency, minimality, exhaustiveness, fitness for use and correctness. This leads them to make modifications to the metamodel (Fig. 7.11) which they depict using the map concept (Fig. 7.12).

In the context of improving an agile method, Henderson-Sellers et al. (2007a) also advocate the use of SME practices for SPI, illustrating their proposal with results from two industry case studies (Serour and Henderson-Sellers 2004a, b)—essentially an application of the dual agility proposal of Henderson-Sellers and Serour (2005). Two different case studies (in a different country) but with a similar aim (of introducing an agile method into the organisation) are outlined in

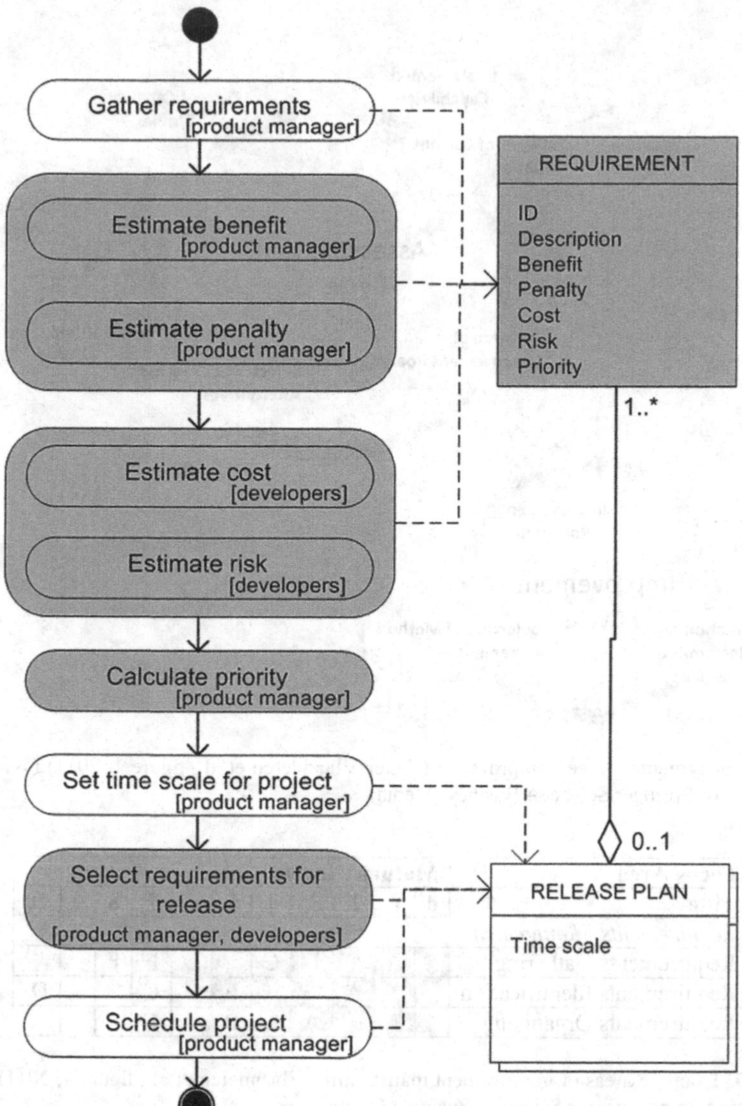

Fig. 7.8 Example PDD to illustrate the incorporation of the new technique for the requirements prioritisation focus area of Table 7.3 for the case study organisation (after Mirandolle et al., figure 5, 2011) (With kind permission of Springer Science + Business Media)

Henderson-Sellers and Qumer (2007). Agility is combined with service-orientation in the proposal of Hoppenbrouwers et al. (2011) in which they use SME principles to define a framework to support rule-based agile service development.

A slightly different challenge for SPI is to facilitate an organisation to move from a traditional software development environment, e.g., using a waterfall approach or

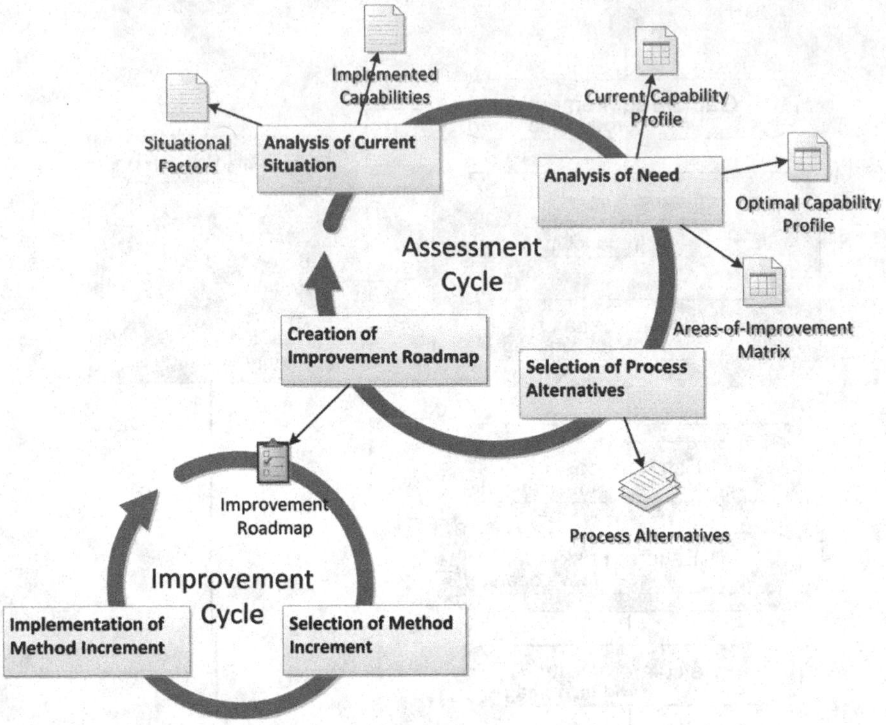

Fig. 7.9 Incremental process improvement (after Vlaanderen et al., figure 1, 2011) (With kind permission of Springer Science + Business Media)

Focus Area	**Maturity levels**										
Title	**0**	**1**	**2**	**3**	**4**	**5**	**6**	**7**	**8**	**9**	**10**
Requirements Management											
Requirements Gathering		A		B	C		D	E	F		
Requirements Identification			A			B		C			D
Requirements Organizing				A		B		C			

Fig. 7.10 Example areas of improvement matrix (after Vlaanderen et al., figure 4, 2011) (With kind permission of Springer Science + Business Media)

indeed no formal methodology, to a culture using a method engineering approach. Henderson-Sellers and Serour (2000) propose a method constructed from fragments that are themselves oriented to technology transition rather than software development. They create a method that they call TransOPEN from the fragments in the OPF repository (Firesmith and Henderson-Sellers 2002)—although in many cases these fragments are not retrieved from the method base but are rather added to it after construction from scratch, as described in Sect. 5.3. Other concerns regarding

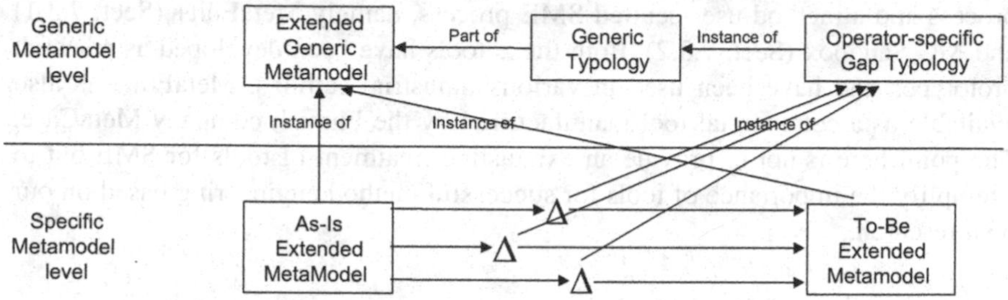

Fig. 7.11 Metamodel modification scheme (after Etien et al. 2003)

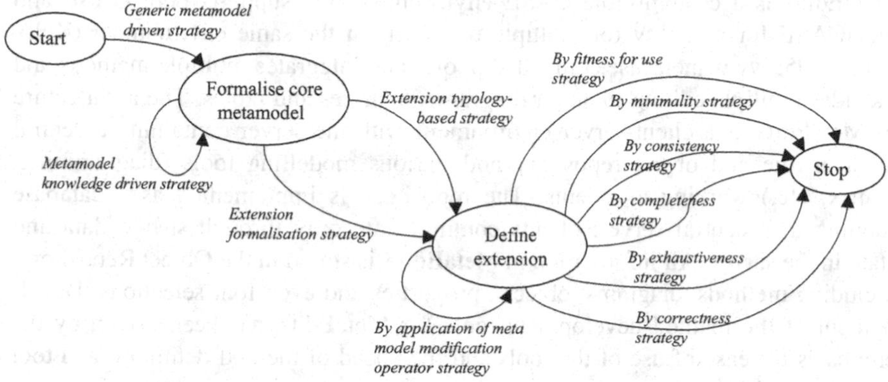

Fig. 7.12 Map formalism for the modification of an extended metamodel (as depicted in Fig. 7.11) (after Etien et al. 2003)

transition to a new methodology are discussed by Mohan and Ahlemann (2011c) in terms of the preferences of the individual team member (see also Chap. 1).

7.3 Tool Support

Tools for method construction—also useful for tailoring methods—have been around for some time and we can now talk about the 'fourth generation' tools. These tools allow users to specify methods within the CASE (computer-aided software engineering) environment by visual method development tools and often allow for flexible evolution of methods. These tools are no longer separate modules with complex method upgrade procedures and manual tailoring, but rather an integrated part of CASE tools.

These CASE tools range from simple diagramming and drawing tools to sophisticated environments that can derive complete method configurations based on user input such as situational characteristics and metamodels. In this section, we introduce two particular tools that exemplify a 'traditional' assembly-based SME process and a method-user-centred SME process, namely MetaEdit+ (Sect. 7.3.1) and MC Sandbox (Sect. 7.3.2). Both these tools have been developed as research prototypes and have been used in various industrial settings. MetaEdit+ is also available as a commercial tool manufactured by the Finnish company MetaCase. The point here is not to provide an exhaustive treatment of tools for SME but to exemplify the importance of tools for successful method engineering based on our own research.

7.3.1 Incremental Method Development with MetaEdit+

MetaEdit+ is a customisable CASE environment that supports both CASE and metaCASE functionality for multiple users within the same environment (Kelly et al. 2005; www.metacase.com). It supports and integrates multiple methods and includes multiple editing tools for diagrams, matrices and tables. The architecture of MetaEdit+ is a client-server environment with the server containing a central meta engine and object repository and various modelling tools (diagramming, matrix, etc.) working as clients. The repository is implemented as a database running in a central server: clients communicate only through shared data and state in the server. All information in MetaEdit+ is stored in the Object Repository, including methods, diagrams, objects, properties and even font selections. Development of the method development tools for MetaEdit+ has been driven by the emphasis for ease of use of the tools and the speed of method definition and tool implementation.

The core conceptual types of a method are defined at the repository level and can be modified by the method developers. Method engineers can change components of a method specification even while system developers are working with older versions of the method. The method can be developed and simultaneously tested on method engineers' workstations. The data continuity (i.e., that specification data remains usable even after method schema changes) is confirmed by a number of checks and limitations to the method evolution possibilities. The idea is that the user can always be guaranteed data continuity while working with partial methods.

7.3.1.1 Concepts in MetaEdit+

The core constructs of MetaEdit+ lie in its conceptual meta-metamodel called GOPRR (Graph-Object-Property-Relationship-Role).[2] The top-level GOPRR concept is the Graph. A Graph can contain Objects, which are linked together via bindings. The centre of each binding is a Relationship and it may have two or more Roles, allowing n-ary relationships. All of these concepts can have Properties, whose values can be simple (string, number, Boolean, text, etc.) or complex: references to another concept or collection of concepts. The methods can be modelled by using a graphical notation of the GOPRR formalism within the tool

[2] Recently updated to GOPPRR by including ports.

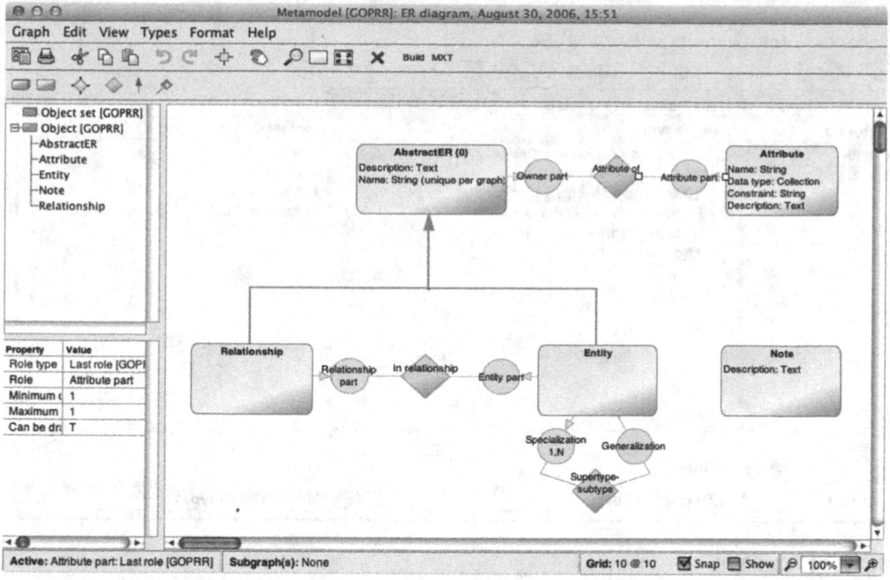

Fig. 7.13 ERA metamodel modelled with GOPRR in MetaEdit+

itself (see Fig. 7.13). The method definition can then be transformed into a method definition automatically.

Most rules and constraints in metamodels are to be found in the definition of Graph types. In GOPRR, an Object type does not specify which Relationship types it may take part in, nor vice versa. This is not a feature of an Object itself, but of a particular Graph type where that Object is used. A Graph type thus specifies the bindings of Objects, Relationships and Roles, including the cardinality of the Roles. In addition to bindings, other constraints can be expressed. Again, the specification of the constraints is simple and requires no programming.

MetaEdit+ is designed from its information model upwards to provide strong support for reuse. All GOPRR components can be reused, on both type and instance levels. In particular, graphs display a type-free interface to components, allowing them to be reused across different modelling languages, but still supporting the linking of interface relationships of an object in a higher-level graph to the objects within the lower level decomposition graph. This allows graphs to be reused using both black-box and white-box reuse techniques.

MetaEdit+ includes a comprehensive set of generic modelling tools that can adapt themselves to the metamodel currently being used. The tool's behaviour, menus, toolbars and dialogues all change to reflect the metamodel, without any work on the part of the metamodeller.

Tool support for reuse is built into the MetaEngine, and is thus available in all editors, browsers, etc. This includes the ability to select graphs, objects, relationships, roles and properties for reuse, selecting them based on their type or

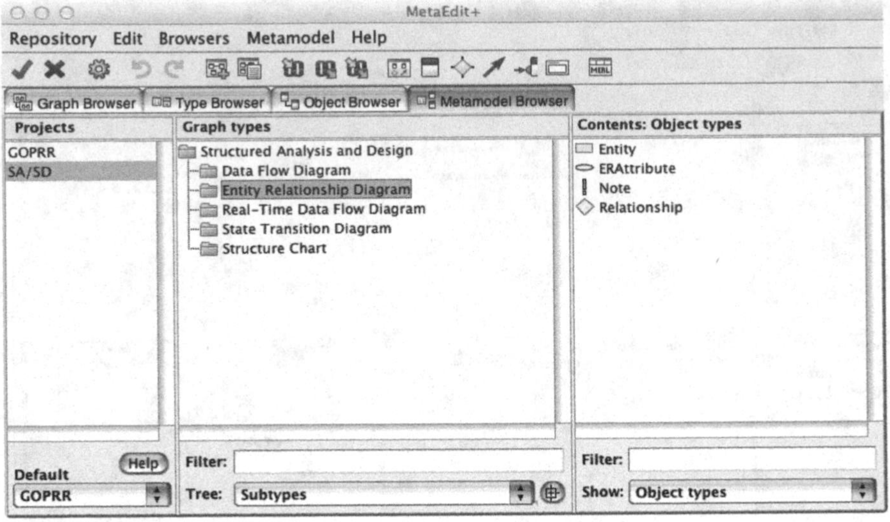

Fig. 7.14 MetaEdit+ type browser

via another component that already uses them. In addition, browsers offer wildcard string-based queries against type and identifying property (Fig. 7.14).

7.3.1.2 Defining a Situational Method

The types can be further modified with form-based tools and their symbols and property dialogues can be defined using special editors, as is shown for Entity type in Fig. 7.15. These tools can be used to modify the graphical and user interface properties of all the meta types in a uniform manner. The tools use the type definitions and tie the fields in the user interface to conceptual types automatically.

Code generation, documentation generation and model-checking reports are all performed in MetaEdit+ by running reports (Fig. 7.16). Reports access information in the repository and transform it into various text-based outputs. Reports can also output information in various graphical formats, call subreports, query information from the user with a dialogue or call external programs and commands.

MetaEdit+ includes a number of generic reports that will work with any metamodel, such as generating documentation in HTML, RTF or Word formats, or performing elementary checks on models. The library of existing metamodels that accompanies MetaEdit+ also includes appropriate code generators, e.g., for SQL from ER diagrams or for C++, Smalltalk, Java and other object-oriented languages from Class Diagrams and similar metamodels. There is also a tool available for debugging the generators (linking generated code and models). With the Report Browser, users can view and edit these and, most importantly, make their own new reports and queries on the repository.

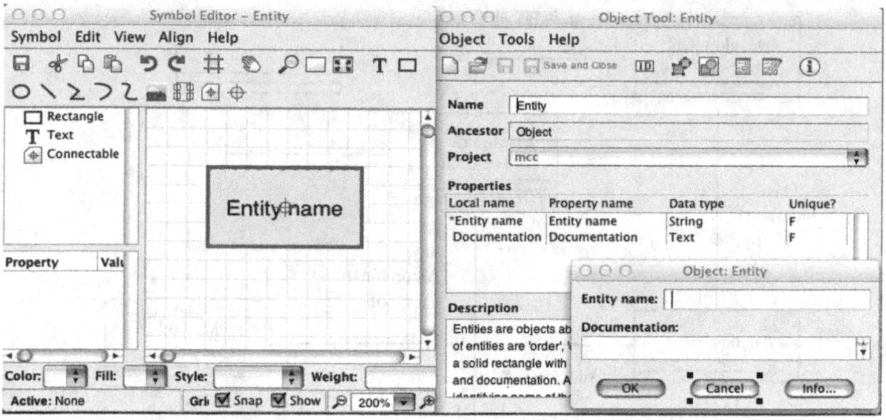

Fig. 7.15 Symbol and dialogue editor and type tool for entity meta type

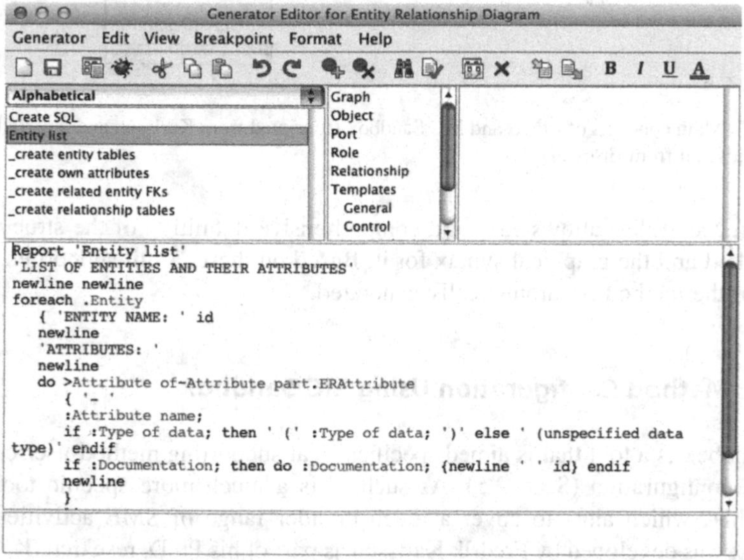

Fig. 7.16 MetaEdit+ report generator

The MetaEdit+ reporting language is a domain-specific language, designed specifically for the task of transforming the object structure of a model into text. While existing languages were considered, none seemed to fit the task well: there were languages for processing one text stream into another text stream (e.g., Perl), or for processing one object structure into another (e.g., any object-oriented language), but not for navigating an object structure and outputting text.

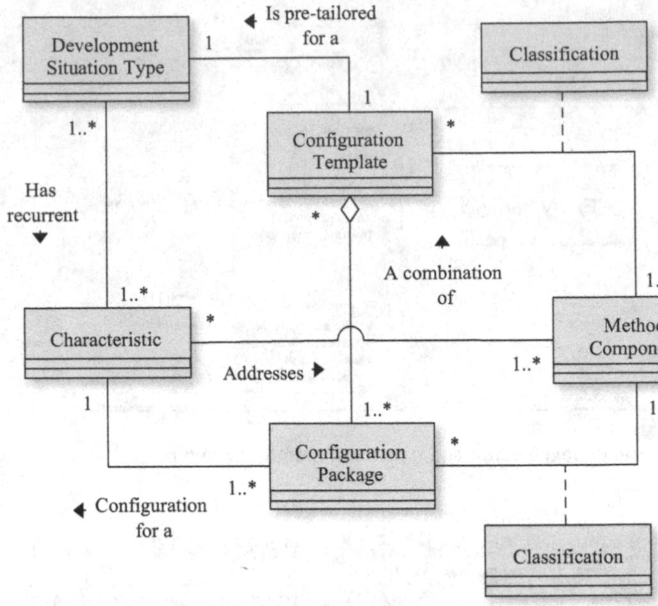

Fig. 7.17 Main concepts of MMC and MC Sandbox (reprinted from Karlsson and Ågerfalk 2012 with permission from Elsevier)

Thus, MetaEdit+ allows easy and comprehensive definition of the structure of the method and the graphical syntax for it. Based on these, a full support environment for the method is automatically generated.

7.3.2 Method Configuration Using MC Sandbox[3]

MC Sandbox is a tool that is aimed specifically at supporting method-user-centred method configuration (Sect. 3.5). As such, it is a much more specific tool than MetaEdit+, which aims to cover a much broader range of SME activities. MC Sandbox was developed by Fredrik Karlsson as part of his Ph.D. research (Karlsson 2005) and has been used and evaluated by him and colleagues in a number of industrial cases (e.g., Karlsson and Ågerfalk 2012). Method configuration according to the MMC approach is based on a set of concepts (see Fig. 7.17). These concepts form the basis of five sub-processes supported by MC Sandbox. In the following, we introduce these concepts with a special focus on the three core processes of method configuration: (1) define a configuration package, (2) define a configuration template and (3) define a situational method. The focus here is on how to involve method users, together with method engineers, in an interactive process

[3] We acknowledge contributions of Dr. Fredrik Karlsson to this section.

of tailoring the base method using MC Sandbox. We therefore assume that the MC Sandbox repository is already populated with method components and a base method composed of these components.

7.3.2.1 Concepts in MC Sandbox

MC Sandbox is designed to support the meta method MMC (Karlsson and Ågerfalk 2009a, b, 2012). The core parts of MMC are illustrated in Fig. 7.17 as a UML class diagram: development situation type, characteristic, method component, configuration package and configuration template.

As outlined in Sect. 2.3, a method component is a self-contained part of a method that expresses the transformation of one or several artefacts into a defined target artefact together with the rationale for such a transformation. Method components are non-hierarchical (as opposed to, for example, method fragments and method chunks) and their 'layer of granularity' is determined based on their output artefact. Thus, a method component covers a subsection of a method if the method has more than one type of deliverable. The content of a method component is described in terms of method elements that manifests the states of the component or facilitates the transformation from one defined state to another. A method component includes five different types of method elements: concept, notation, prescribed action, artefact and actor roles. A method component also includes the method rationale (see Chap. 3) of these elements, expressed as the goals to be achieved by using the method component, along with the values reflected by these goals.

A method component deliberately hides its content in order to reduce method engineers' and method users' cognitive load, i.e., the component is essentially treated as a 'black box'. A method component provides two views. The internal view contains all the required details and the external view provides a simplified view of these details, termed the interface (of the component). The interface shows the input and output artefacts of the component, together with the overall goals to be achieved by using the component. This is to facilitate achieving rationality resonance as discussed in Sect. 3.3. These parts of the method component provide an overview of the intended support that a method component provides and the intended results of the prescribed actions that it contains. Consequently, the complete method can be visualised as a storyboard of connected method components, where it is possible to navigate the components through input and output artefacts.

The basic idea of method configuration using MC Sandbox is to use characteristics and method rationale, as expressed by method components, when deciding whether or not to include a method component in a particular configuration. A characteristic describes a part of a recurrent development situation, focusing on a certain problem or aspect that the method configuration aims to solve or handle. Characteristics are analytical tools used to narrow down the focus to a delimited part of the overall method. Each characteristic addresses one or several method components and their purpose of existence in a situational method. In order to facilitate reuse, which improves the possibilities of prototyping situational methods, the concepts of configuration package and configuration templates are introduced and associated with the characteristic concept (Karlsson and Ågerfalk 2004).

A configuration package is a configuration of the base method suitable for one single value of a characteristic. Thus, a configuration package is a classification of method components based on overall goal relevance for a specific value of a characteristic. For example, a characteristic may be 'Type of testing' and a corresponding value the answer 'Automated'. In, for example, an organisation using RUP this could suggest the inclusion of method components such as Automated test scripts and Automation Architecture. In Fig. 7.17, tailoring decisions are illustrated by the association class Classification between Configuration Package and Method Component.

As noted in Sect. 6.1.5, a configuration package (as in MC Sandbox) covers a demarcated part of a situational method. Real-world projects, however, require situational methods that consider all parts of the base method. There is thus a need to combine common characteristics (and configuration packages) to capture complex situations. This is the purpose of the configuration template, which covers the complete set of method components required by a development situation and is a reusable pre-tailored version of the base method (Karlsson and Ågerfalk 2009b). The association class Classification between Configuration Template and Method Component captures these combined construction and tailoring decisions.

Configuration templates can be viewed as low-fi method prototypes for different types of development situations. These can be reused during method configuration as starting points for achieving a closer match between the situational method required by a project and the base method. A situational method, then, is a configuration template that has been fine-tuned and adapted to a specific project. The selection of a configuration template is based on a characterisation of the current project, where the existing set of characteristics is used as a foundation for formulating questions to ask project members.

These layers in MC Sandbox provide different starting points for method configuration. If a suitable configuration template can be found, it is fine-tuned and used as a situational method. In situations where no matching configuration template can be found, a new one can be constructed based on existing configuration packages. Method configuration using MC Sandbox can thus involve the selection of configuration packages as well as complementing them with new ones.

7.3.2.2 Defining Configuration Packages

All configuration packages inherit the structure of the base method. When a method component is added to the base method in MC Sandbox, it is added also to the set of configuration packages (see also earlier discussion on Method Configuration in Sect. 6.1.5). This activity serves as a starting point for a storyboard-inspired discussion about the base method, given a specific characteristic. Figure 7.18 illustrates the MC Sandbox graphical user interface (GUI) when working with configuration packages. As seen in the screen shot, the screen is divided horizontally. The lower section is the method modelling area and the upper section shows the status of selected method components. The right part of the upper section shows

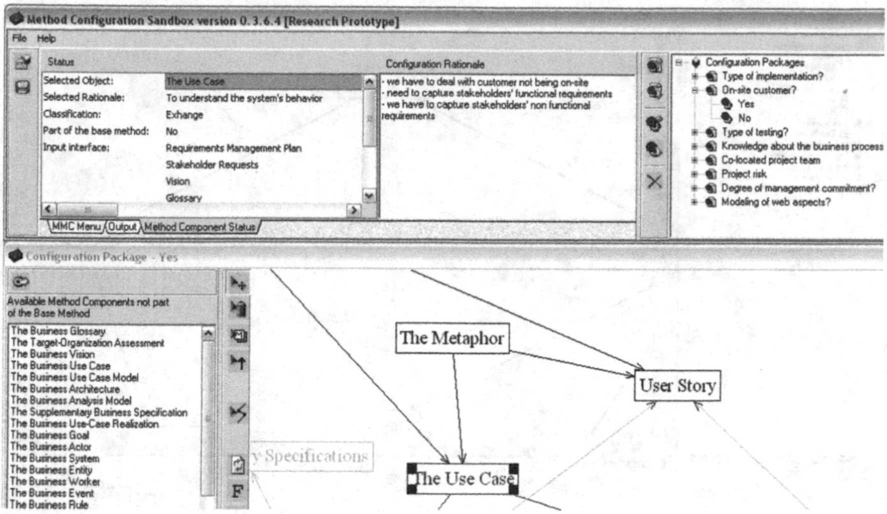

Fig. 7.18 Defining a configuration package (reprinted from Karlsson and Ågerfalk 2012 with permission from Elsevier)

the complete set of existing configuration packages based on the current base method. The tree structure is sorted by the characteristics to which the configuration packages belong. This part of the GUI also provides functionality for defining new characteristics.

The modelling area makes use of the external view of method components to visualise the current storyboard for these components. A method component is depicted as a rectangle in the modelling view. Arrows connecting method components show the uni- or bidirectional flow of artefacts between components. Different colours are used to illustrate the classification of method components. In this way, the base method can be viewed as a low-fi prototype, useful for discussing effects of skipping different components as well as introducing new ones.

The motivation for particular configurations is documented in MC Sandbox using the upper middle part of the GUI, which means that the arguments behind a specific classification can be recalled as required later in the process. Upon selection of a method component in the modelling view, the upper right section of the GUI presents the content of that method component interface. The interface contains information about recommended input, the deliverable (i.e., the output artefact produced by applying the component), the method component rationale and the current classification (*exchange* means that it is to be performed instead of a corresponding component suggested by the base method).

7.3.2.3 Defining Configuration Templates

A configuration template is essentially an aggregate of configuration packages. The selection of relevant configuration packages and their integration are therefore central to defining a configuration template. The GUI used for this shares its

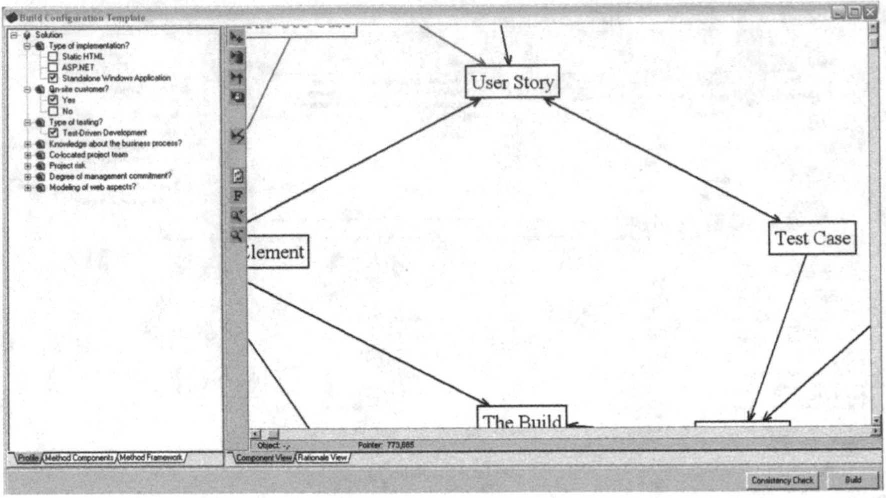

Fig. 7.19 Defining configuration template (reprinted from Karlsson and Ågerfalk 2012 with permission from Elsevier)

basic structure with the GUI for defining a configuration package. The upper part of the screen contains information about the currently selected item. Figure 7.19 illustrates the lower section, which is vertically divided. The left part presents the functionality offered to develop situation types and the right part is devoted to the modelling of the content of the configuration template.

A development situation type is characterised by means of the configuration packages that are selected for the existing range of characteristics. When the set of characteristics and configuration packages is updated, this list is changed. Each characteristic is formulated as a question, and the configuration packages act as possible answers. The method engineer clicks checkboxes to mark choices based on the ongoing discussion with the method users. It is possible to select 1 (or 0) configuration package per characteristic. If a characteristic is found to be irrelevant, it is typically ignored when selecting configuration packages and will thus not be part of the configuration template.

When all relevant selections have been made, the method engineer clicks the build button in the bottom right corner of the GUI, which causes MC Sandbox to build a configuration template. The base method and the classification of method components in the selected configuration packages are used as input to the combined tailoring. This is an automated process, although the method engineer needs to handle any classification conflicts. Such a conflict occurs when two or more configuration packages overlap and the classifications of a method component in that section differ. For example, a conflict occurs if a method component in the first configuration package is classified as 'omit' while in a second configuration package it is classified as 'perform as is'. Should such a conflict arise during a build, MC Sandbox lists them together with what it interprets as the reason for the conflict.

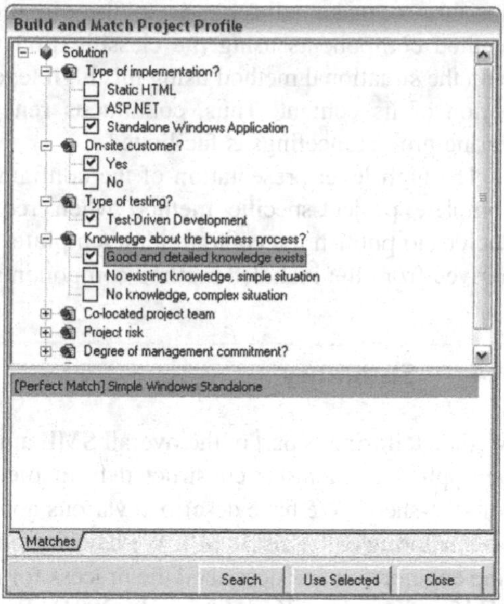

Fig. 7.20 Create project profile and search a configuration template (reprinted from Karlsson and Ågerfalk 2012 with permission from Elsevier)

The method engineer and the method users then have to resolve these conflicts in each specific case and give priority to one of the conflicting configuration packages.

The result of the building process is a prototype of a situational method, presented in the same low-fi fashion as when working with configuration packages. If the method users are not satisfied, modifications can be made either through selection of a different set of configuration packages and rebuilding the template, or through manual reclassifications of method components.

7.3.2.4 Defining a Situational Method

When using MC Sandbox, a situational method is always based on a configuration template. When defining a situational method, the range of characteristics is used to create a profile of the current project. The method engineer builds such a profile together with the method users. The screenshot in Fig. 7.20 shows the list of available characteristics and configuration packages. The choices are indicated through the use of checkboxes. One configuration package can be selected for each characteristic. If the characteristic is found to be irrelevant, it is ignored, just as when building a configuration template. The constructed project profile contains the criteria for searching in the repository for matching development situation types and corresponding configuration templates. The search returns the possible candidate configuration templates, which are shown at the bottom of the screen. MC Sandbox then builds a situational method based on the method engineer's and the method users' selection of configuration templates from the list. The configuration template built by MC Sandbox is a separate copy, so any changes to it will not affect the situational method. The situational method is presented in a view similar to that used for presenting configuration packages and templates. Even at this stage, it is possible to make adjustments to the situational method such as reclassifying method components using the classification schema mentioned above. Working with the situational method using this high level view facilitates continuous reevaluation of its content. Thus, continuous renegotiation of the situational method during project meetings is facilitated.

The high level presentation of the configuration template can be turned into a complete project-specific method when required. When the method engineer decides to publish the configuration template, a project-specific method website is derived from the included method components' internal views.

7.4 Summary

Method tailoring is part of the overall SME approach to method construction. It can be applied to methods constructed from method parts or to methods purchased 'off-the-shelf'. We have described various approaches to method configuration and how tailoring can assist in SPI. We have introduced the notions of software process line engineering and described the process for method configuration based upon the MMC approach of Karlsson et al. (2001). We then identified links between SME and SPI—elaborated on in a little more detail in the next chapter. Finally, we discussed the role of software support tools for SME; but, rather than a comprehensive review, we have described in full detail just two examples: MetaEdit+ (Sect. 7.3.1) and MC Sandbox (Sect. 7.3.2).

Assessing Quality

8

Summary of What We Will Learn in Chapter 8

- A framework for quality assessment for the SME context
- How to assess the quality of method parts
- How to assess constructed method quality
- What is meant by method enactment and why the enacted method's quality is important
- The contrast between process capability and process performance

One of the least understood aspects of situational method engineering is quality assessment. Here, we are concerned firstly about the quality of individual method parts (fragments, chunks, components) as they are stored in the method base, the overall quality of the method base itself in terms primarily of cohesion and the quality of the method that is constructed from these parts, extracted from the method base. This last concern has two aspects: (1) whether the overall method is cohesive and complete (i.e., it is a full method and not just a partial method) and that it contains no unrequired elements such as work products created but not used nor has any missing method elements; and (2) whether the constructed process is the right one for the industry application for which it is targeted. The quality of all these can be assessed statically. There is an additional, dynamical, quality concern: how well the method works in practice. Each of these aspects is covered in the succeeding subsections of this chapter, starting with a discussion of a framework into which all these aspects fit.

B. Henderson-Sellers et al., *Situational Method Engineering*,
DOI 10.1007/978-3-642-41467-1_8, © Springer-Verlag Berlin Heidelberg 2014

8.1 Framework for Quality Assessment

There have been a number of evaluation frameworks for methodologies (e.g., Monarchi and Puhr 1992; Hong et al. 1993; Jayaratna 1994; Henderson-Sellers et al. 2001). Some consist of a checklist of ideal methodology feature requirements (e.g., Kitchenham 1996; Tran and Low 2005; Grimán et al. 2006; Fung and Low 2009 and see further discussion below) or a theoretical evaluation or an empirical evaluation (Siau and Rossi 1998). Others have a specific focus such as MDE (Mohagheghi and Aagedal 2007) or requirements engineering (Coulin et al. 2006).

These published methodology evaluation frameworks assume a single technique for methodological quality assessment. More recently, McBride and Henderson-Sellers (2011) argue that the quality of a method can and should be assessed, possibly using different kinds of metrics, at three distinct points in the method's life cycle as identified in Fig. 1.8: when the method is designed (the 'process model' or 'method'), as well as considering two aspects of method enactment (the static aspects of the 'tailored process' and the dynamic aspects of the 'performed process').

Although the McBride and Henderson-Sellers (2011) framework is described in the context of SME, it neglects two other important SME-focussed qualities: the quality of the metamodel and the quality of the method parts (i.e., fragments, chunks and components). In the SME context, we can therefore add to Fig. 1.8 the need to include method parts within the intermediate 'layer' of Fig. 1.8 (see Fig. 8.1). This architecture is then well-aligned with the ISO architecture of Fig. 1.14.

The quality of the metamodel, although important, is really out of scope for SME practitioners (but see Ma et al. 2004; Bertoa and Vallecillo 2010). Nevertheless, since a metamodel is essentially a conceptual model as is the designed method (the process model), we include a discussion of conceptual model quality in Sect. 8.2.

Figure 8.1 highlights the two aspects of the 'Method domain' of Fig. 1.14, viz. fragments/chunks and the designed method (a.k.a. process model). Although the method part element is not discussed by McBride and Henderson-Sellers (2011), in our extended framework of Fig. 8.1 we need to seek techniques to evaluate the quality of individual method fragments and, when two fragments are conjoined, a method chunk or the slightly more complex method component (Sect. 8.3).

The other element of the Method domain, the process model or method, *is* discussed by McBride and Henderson-Sellers (2011). They argue that this designed or constructed method is aimed at achieving a specific purpose but in a limited range of circumstances. For example, a method engineer might design a new method to develop life critical software using medium to large teams under tight schedule and budget constraints. Thus, the first occasion when a complete method comes under quality control is as a process model or a designed/constructed method (Sect. 8.4). This designed method may also cover the situation of an organisationally standardised method although some authors prefer to refer this case for inclusion as an 'enacted method', following organisationally specific tailoring (see Chap. 7). All authors, however, include project-specific tailoring as part of

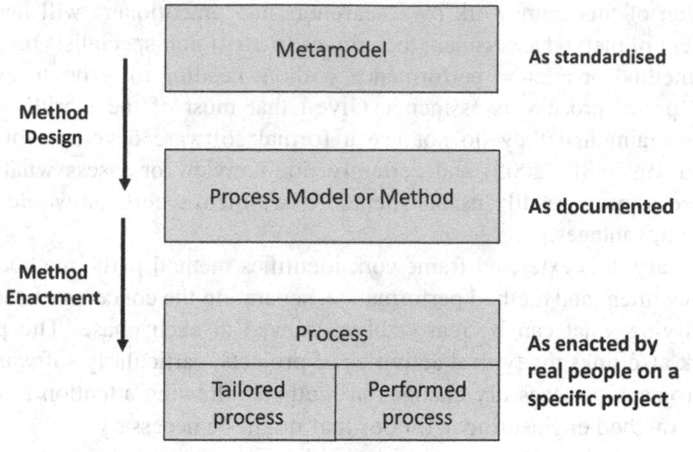

Fig. 8.1 A multilayer architecture, aligned with ISO/IEC 24744 (Fig. 1.14) that provides a framework for the various aspects of SME quality assessment (significantly modified from Henderson-Sellers 2006a)

enactment. Enactment here is taken to mean the instantiation of the process model for a particular situation or context. Method enactment (Sect. 8.5) has both a static and a dynamical aspect, as noted earlier. The static aspect denotes a method tailored to specific project parameters. At that time, decisions can be made to address the project constraints and contingencies. Individual values, for example, project team members' names, budgetary and scheduling constraints, are allocated as we move from the Method domain of Fig. 1.14 to the Endeavour domain. Other project-specific tailoring may also occur, thus requiring a reassessment of the method quality in the context of this specific project application. This may require similar, but not necessarily identical, metrics to those used for assessing the quality of the designed or constructed method (middle 'layer' of Fig. 8.1).

Whilst the tailored process component of the enactment can be measured statically (Sect. 8.5.1), once the project commences, the process unfolds in real time (Sect. 8.5.2). The performed process thus spans a period in calendar time, i.e., the period over which the method is in use. Quality assessment is sought both during the process (to correct any errant directions) as well as at the end of the project, e.g., as in a retrospective (Kerth 2001; Derby et al. 2006).

The framework of McBride and Henderson-Sellers (2011), as extended here, provides guidance about what could be assessed at each phase as well as the desirability of doing so. However, it should be noted that these authors purposefully do not attempt to answer the question regarding 'how' these recommended assessments should be undertaken, i.e., which software engineering metrics might be useful in each phase; rather they identify 'what' needs to be assessed and 'when'. The framework was designed primarily to provide a more rigorous and time-focussed approach to quality assessment than is currently undertaken through the more basic and more subjective means of expert opinion. It is thus anticipated that the adoption of this framework by researchers and practitioners will lead to the development of method assessment techniques to assist non-specialists review their intended method or method performance without needing to resort to expensive audits or formal process assessments. Given that most of the world's software developers claim that they do not use a formal software development method (Fitzgerald 1997; SEI 2005) and certainly don't review or assess what method they do use, a more readily usable method assessment technique would seem to offer some advantages.

In summary, this extended framework identifies method parts, method design, method enactment and method performance, separating the concerns of each phase and identifying what can be reasonably achieved at each phase. The proposed framework also links the typical activities of projects, particularly software development projects, to necessary changes in methods, drawing attention to different situational method engineering activities that might be necessary.

The proposed framework provides a guide to the development of assessment techniques and tools. Rather than try to develop a general assessment technique that attempts to require certainty where none is possible (method design) or fails to require rigour where some is possible (method enactment), tools can be developed to assess methods appropriately and as rigorously as possible, but no more. Similarly, existing assessment techniques can be positioned in relation to the type of method assessment they accomplish.

8.2 Conceptual Model Quality

Some of the quality aspects of models are discussed in Henderson-Sellers (1996, 2011a), by equating method part evaluation with assessment of the quality of conceptual models, for which there is a larger literature—see, for example, the literature review of Moody (2005). However, although large, the literature on conceptual model quality is not unambiguous (e.g., Unhelkar 2005). There are three key attributes of quality for conceptual models: syntactic, semantic and aesthetic (Unhelkar and Henderson-Sellers 2005; du Bois et al. 2007; special issue of the international journal *Information and Software Technology*—published in December 2009 (volume 51, issue 12)). Lindland et al.'s (1994) framework links these three concepts to four key aspects of modelling: language, domain, conceptual model and audience interpretation (Fig. 8.2). This framework and the extensions proposed by Krogstie and Sølvberg (2003) are discussed further by Siau and Tan (2005) who use it to analyse the role of human cognition in conceptual modelling. Siau and Tan (2005) suggest the use of a 'cognitive map' (Tolman 1948) to assist in quality assessment and quality improvement in this context.

With a large emphasis on the use of OMG models, typically documented using some version of UML (OMG 1997, 2001, 2005b, 2006, 2007, 2010; ISO/IEC 2005, 2012), much of the criticism of models and modelling languages and their application has been aimed at these OMG-based models and metamodels (e.g., Opdahl and Henderson-Sellers 2002; Ma et al. 2004; Unhelkar 2005; Moody and

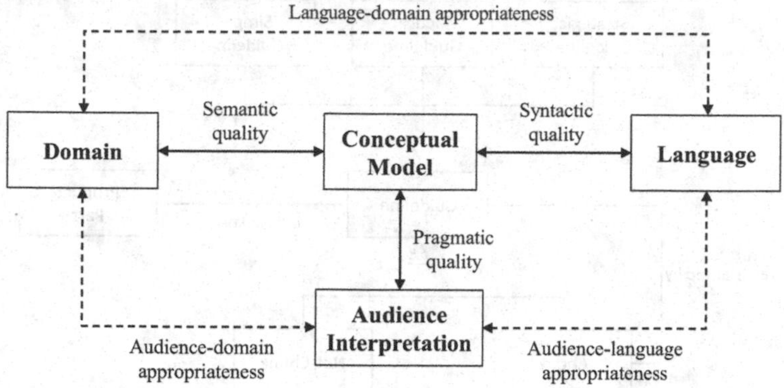

Fig. 8.2 Lindland et al.'s (1994) quality framework (reprinted from Siau and Tan 2005 with permission from Elsevier)

van Hillegersberg 2008; Esperanza Manso et al. 2009; Laarman and Kurtev 2010). These include concerns that:

- Domain models are (incorrectly) presented as metamodels These are often readily identified if they use UML Activity Diagrams with generic naming (Henderson-Sellers 2007).
- The representations of whole-part relationships are often incorrect (see, e.g., Barbier and Aretxandieta 2008). This is typically a result of the contradictions and ambiguities in the OMG documents themselves (see, e.g., Barbier et al. 2003).
- Inappropriate use of stereotypes (as discussed by Atkinson et al. 2003). Examples abound (e.g., Connallen 2002; Fuentes-Fernandez et al. 2007). Stereotype definitions are criticised in, for example, Gogolla and Henderson-Sellers (2002) and Henderson-Sellers and Gonzalez-Perez (2006b).
- Inappropriate use of specialisation; in particular, the use of multiple, overlapping subtypes (e.g., Fig. 8.3 in which the reader may not realise that a 'tactical guideline' must also be either a 'chunk' or a 'not-chunk'—and vice versa). Such diagrams need a discriminant (McGregor and Korson 1993; Henderson-Sellers and Edwards 1994)—although it should be noted that the appearance of a discriminant on a conceptual model is not readily implementable and often indicates a design that needs further quality improvement.

Henderson-Sellers (2007) notes that the quality of conceptual models, especially those that are standardised metamodels, is an important factor in ensuring successful use of contemporary design and development practices in industry worldwide. Even the four-layer architecture itself, especially when applied to methodologies rather than more straightforward modelling languages, is found to be problematic, as noted in earlier chapters (see full discussion in Gonzalez-Perez and Henderson-Sellers 2008b), in that an 'M2' metamodel (Fig. 1.11) cannot be used to support the 'M0' level elements.

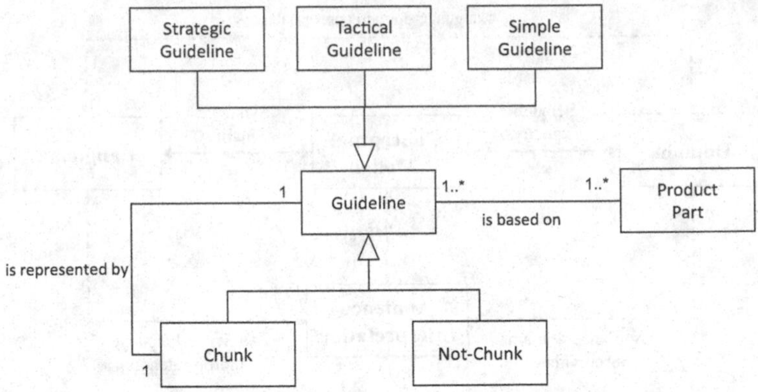

Fig. 8.3 A simple example of a published metamodel, expressed using UML's notation, in which OO/UML subtyping has been used poorly by creating two subtyping ranges: an arguably complete partition between three guidelines (suggested missing discriminant of 'purpose') together with a clearly complete partition based on chunk-ness (suggested missing discriminant of 'internal structure') (reprinted from Henderson-Sellers 2007, with permission from IOS Press)

Identifying appropriate metrics to apply in order to quantify the 'quality' of such models and metamodels is not easy. In their study of the quality of the UML metamodel, Ma et al. (2004) utilise a large number of metrics (Table 8.1) which are both applied directly to five versions of UML (V1.1, 1.3, 1.4, 1.5, 2.0) and used to calculate values of six external characteristics: reusability, flexibility, understandability, functionality, extensibility and effectiveness (Table 8.2).

The size and complexity of metamodels is also discussed in Henderson-Sellers et al. (2012) who compare UML, BPMN (Business Process Modeling Notation: OMG 2009a), SMM (Software Metrics Metamodel: OMG 2009b), ODM (Ontology Definition Metamodel: OMG 2009c), OSM (Organization Structure Metamodel: OMG 2009d) and SPEM (Software Process Engineering Metamodel: OMG 2008) by application of the Rossi and Brinkkemper (1996) metrics—see also Sect. 8.4. They conclude, from the numbers in Table 8.3, that complexity increases with each new version of the metamodel, and that BPMN and UML have similar complexity values although BPMN only offers functionality more like the scope of a UML Activity Diagram rather than the totality of the UML. They propose using this information in part of a project aimed at metamodel integration and interoperability (Qureshi 2012).

Furthermore, Garcia et al. (2006) argue that we still don't have a consistent set of terminology for software measurement. Although complexity metrics abound in the literature, few are well validated, both theoretically and empirically (e.g., Fenton 1994). Furthermore, metrics by themselves have little relevance to software quality improvement—unless underpinned by an appropriate conceptual model (Henderson-Sellers 1996). The linking of readily measured internal characteristics of software to the much more useful external characteristics remains a challenge.

Table 8.1 Architectural and meta class metrics (after Ma et al., tables 1 & 4, 2004) (With kind permission of Springer Science + Business Media)

Metric	Description
(1) Architectural metrics	
DSC	Design size in meta classes
NOH	Number of hierarchies. A count of the number of non-inherited classes that have children in the metamodel
MNL	Maximum number of the level of inheritance
NSI	Number of single inheritance meta classes
NMI	Number of multiple inheritance meta classes
ADI	Average depth of the meta class inheritance structure
AWI	Average width of the meta class inheritance structure
ANA	Average number of ancestors
ANDC	Average number of distinct meta classes that a meta class associates with
ANAT	Average number of meta attributes
ANAG	Average number of meta aggregations
ANS	Average number of stereotypes
AWF	Average number of well-formed rules
AAP	Average number of additional operations
NAC	Number of abstract meta classes
NCC	Number of concrete meta classes
NEK	Number of meta classes that have no parent and no child in the metamodel. Most of these standard for enumeration kinds
(2) Meta class metrics	
VPC	Parent meta classes
NAT	Number of meta attributes
DOI	Depth of the meta class inheritance
NOC	Number of directed children
NOA	Number of ancestors
NDC	Number of distinct meta classes that a meta class associates with
NAG	Number of the meta aggregations
NOS	Number of stereotypes
NWF	Number of well-formed rules
NOP	Number of additional operations

One problem is the propensity of researchers to invent a metric without consideration of how, or even if, it may be useful (e.g., Fenton 1994). Indeed, a better guiding framework is that of the GQM (Goal-Question-Metric) approach (Basili and Rombach 1988)—as was applied, for instance, in the empirical study of Nugroho and Chaudron (2009).

Whilst such observations can be useful, what is needed are objective software engineering metrics that can be applied to assess the quality of conceptual models. Some early work on complexity metrics (which is but one of the contributing factors to quality) was summarised in Henderson-Sellers (1996). Such metrics are reasonably well understood although still poorly validated in practice. Typical

Table 8.2 Quality attributes and their computation proposed by Ma et al. (table 8, 2004) (With kind permission of Springer Science + Business Media)

Quality attribute	Definition
Reusability	−0.25*Coupling + 0.25*Cohesion + 0.5*Messaging + 0.5*Design Size
Flexibility	0.25*Encapsulation − 0.25*Coupling + 0.5*Composition + 0.5*Polymorphism
Understandability	−0.33*Abstraction + 0.33*Encapsulation − 0.33*Coupling + 0.33*Cohesion − 0.33*Polymorphism − 0.33*Complexity − 0.33*Design Size
Functionality	0.12*Cohesion + 0.22*Polymorphism + 0.22*Messaging + 0.22*Design Size + 0.22*Hierarchies
Extensibility	0.5*Abstraction − 0.5*Coupling + 0.5*Inheritance + 0.5*Polymorphism
Effectiveness	0.2*Abstraction + 0.2*Encapsulation + 0.2*Composition + 0.2*Inheritance + 0.2*Polymorphism

Table 8.3 Size and complexity measures for six OMG metamodels (after Henderson-Sellers et al. 2012)

	Size measures			
Metamodel	No. of individual object types	No. of different relationship types	No. of different property types	Total complexity
UML V1.4.1 Activity Diagram	8	5	6	11.18
UML V1.4.1 (full)	57	53	72	106.00
UML V2.3 (superstructure)	288	23	154	327.40
BPMN 1.0	22	10	85	88.30
BPMN 1.2	90	6	143	169.07
BPMN 2.0	159	17	294	334.70
ODM	100	27	21	105.69
OSM	11	6	13	18.05
SMM	38	6	41	56.22
SPEM	101	16	56	116.59

measures are of coupling and cohesion (Stevens et al. 1974), fan-in/fan-out (Henry and Kafura 1981), inheritance (e.g., Chidamber and Kemerer 1994) and reusability (Yap and Henderson-Sellers 1993). Fan-out is also a metric used by Eberle et al. (2009) in their determination of the quality of a fragment in terms of its compactness (a compact fragment being one with minimum fan-out value).

However, current OO metrics, especially those for complexity (e.g., Henderson-Sellers 1996), only deal with structural issues. Saeki (2003a) points out that without semantic considerations, these metrics can never be accepted as measuring the real

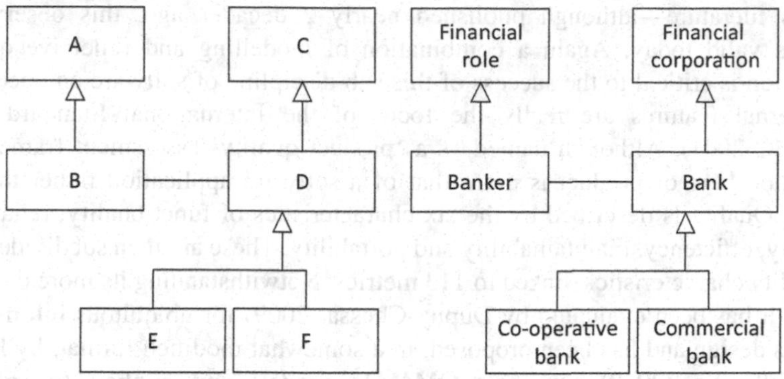

Fig. 8.4 Comparison of a low (left) and high (right) quality model fragment where both models have identical values of traditional software metrics

'quality' of the model or model element. For example, in Fig. 8.4, it is obvious that the model on the right hand side is of higher quality (i.e., it will be more easily understood and utilised) than that of the left hand side although both have identical values for any structural metric. Saeki's (2003a) proposal is to include a link to a Metric class in the metamodel that then permits semantic information to be included in a measurable model.

Consistency in terminology of software measurement is urged by de los Angeles Martin and Olsina (2003) and Garcia et al. (2006) in terms of proposals for an ontology as a first step in terminological harmonisation.

Other recent compendium works include Genero et al. (2005) and Lanza and Marinescu (2006). There are also many individual papers attempting to introduce quality assessment into conceptual modelling although these are as yet far from definitive in terms of a large-scale and accepted body of software engineering metrics that can be applied by conceptual modellers. Interesting recent examples include Aggarwal et al. (2007a, b) and Franch (2009).

Any metrics/measures that are derived must be mathematically sound, usually being based upon measurement theory (see, e.g., Zuse 1994) and must have appropriate mathematical qualities (some of these are outlined in Weyuker (1988) although some are disputed, e.g., Cherniavsky and Smith 1991; Mayer and Hall 1999). If the measure is theoretically sound, then it can be evaluated for utilisation in some prediction chain. Fenton (1991) outlines how a simple metric, which is typically a count of some internal feature (such as lines of code and decision points) of the target software unit, can be linked, via a model, to an external feature of interest—these external features usually being called the '-ilities' since they include features such as maintainability and reliability. External features are not, in general, immediately deducible from internal features unless an appropriate conceptual model linking them is determined. Typically, some empirical analysis is needed here—although simple statistics, especially correlation analysis, is rarely sufficient. Fenton (1994) notes the poor quality of much of the metrics literature—although published nearly 2 decades ago, this observation remains valid today. Again a combination of modelling and reflective quality evaluation is critical to the success of this sub-discipline of software engineering.

External features are really the focus of the International Standard 9126 (ISO/IEC 2001). Although named as a 'product quality' assessment framework, the notion here of product is more that of a software application rather than its design. Quality is described by the six characteristics of functionality, reliability, usability, efficiency, maintainability and portability. These are then subdivided into 24 quality characteristics, linked to 113 metrics. Notwithstanding its more dynamic nature, it has been evaluated by Dupuy-Chessa (2009) for ubiquitous information systems design and has been proposed, in a somewhat modified format, by Bertoa and Vallecillo (2010) (as their QM4MM model) and applied to software metamodels—an interesting study that analyses metamodels both from the viewpoint of a model and the viewpoint of a language (for further information on the relationship between models, metamodels and languages see Henderson-Sellers 2012 and Henderson-Sellers et al. 2013).

Finally, as we noted earlier, since a metamodel is just one specific kind of model, often depicted as a UML class diagram, its quality can be evaluated like that for any other design model, e.g., the quality of a class model for a banking information system (Henderson-Sellers 2007). However, one additional and much-neglected factor is important both here and for fragment quality (Sect. 8.3)—that of the granularity of the model (but see Yang and Unhelkar 2010). Whilst granularity theory is well advanced, its application to metamodels is scant (see, e.g., Henderson-Sellers and Gonzalez-Perez 2010).

8.3 Quality of Method Parts

Method parts (method fragments and method chunks) are typically defined by classes in a metamodel. Thus each fragment is a model of some domain concept. Furthermore, the meta class to which this fragment is conformant is also (part of) a model. Thus, from all viewpoints, we can consider method part quality as being assessable by any metrics that are applicable to models (or elementary parts of models).

Although method part quality can indeed be linked to conceptual model quality, in reality a method part is atomic or, as with a method chunk, a conglomerate of a very small number (usually two) of atomic entities. Thus, conceptual modelling metrics, which tend to focus on the complexity of large system models, are not all that helpful. Instead, the basic building block of SME—the method fragment, chunk or component—needs to be considered as a single entity. We thus seek quality assessment techniques at the 'atomic' level.

The two crucial characteristics of a method part are its granularity and its size (assuming that we have already determined that it accurately conforms to the appropriate element in the defining metamodel—see also Sect. 8.2). If fragments are too coarse-grained, thus containing restricted information and/or detail, it is likely that they will be highly specific to a single situation (organisational context), i.e., their reusability may be limited and there may be partial overlaps between the specifications of fragment pairs (Henderson-Sellers et al. 2008). In addition, it is arguable that fragments coming from repositories constructed on top of metamodels with very different granularities would suffer from interoperability and composability issues, since the abstraction levels at which they have been defined are naturally different. These three granularity issues are highly relevant to issues of SME, e.g., in terms of method construction, fragment storage, fragment interoperability and composability. In particular, a strategic, long-term research goal is an evaluation of the quality of the method fragments and the consequent quality of any methodology constructed from the fragments within the SME approach. Here, we concentrate on a precursor for a future quality evaluation by focussing on the granularity of method fragments in the context of their conformance to a metamodel (Henderson-Sellers and Gonzalez-Perez 2011).

8.3.1 Granularity Theory

Granularity is a kind of abstraction (see Chap. 1); indeed, it is often called a 'granularity abstraction' (Mani 1998). In more general but formal terms, an abstraction can be defined as a mapping between two 'systems', each of which may be described by the same or a different language (e.g., Mani 1998). Formally, this is expressed (Giunchiglia and Walsh 1992) as:

$$f : \sum_1 \Rightarrow \sum_2 \textit{ is a pair of formal systems } \left(\sum_1, \sum_2\right) \textit{ with languages } \Lambda_1 \textit{ and } \Lambda_2 \textit{ respectively and an effective total function } f_\Lambda : \Lambda_1 \rightarrow \Lambda_2 \tag{8.1}$$

or more simply (Ghidini and Giunchiglia 2004) as

$$\textit{given two languages } L_o \textit{ and } L_1, abs : L_o \rightarrow L_1 \textit{ is an abstraction.} \tag{8.2}$$

where *abs* is an abstraction function, L_0 is known as the ground language and L_1 the abstract language.

A granularity abstraction is then formally defined (Mani 1998; citing Hobbs 1985; Giunchiglia and Walsh 1992) as:

$$\begin{aligned}&\textit{An abstraction F is a granularity abstraction iff}\\&(i)\ \textit{F maps individual constants in } \Lambda \textit{ to their equivalence class under the}\\&\textit{indistinguishability relation} \sim \textit{in } \Lambda.\ (\textit{thus, for an individual x in } \Lambda,\\&F(x) = K(x) \textit{ where } K(x) = \{y \textit{ such that } x \sim y\}.)\\&(ii)\ \textit{F maps everything else, including the predicates in } \Lambda, \textit{ to itself.}\end{aligned} \tag{8.3}$$

Alternatively, granularity is formally defined in Ghidini and Giunchiglia (2004) as

$$x_1, \ldots\ldots x_n \in L_o, x \in L_1 \text{ and } abs(x_i) = x \text{ for all } i \in [1, n] \tag{8.4}$$

(where x is either a constant, a function or a predicate).

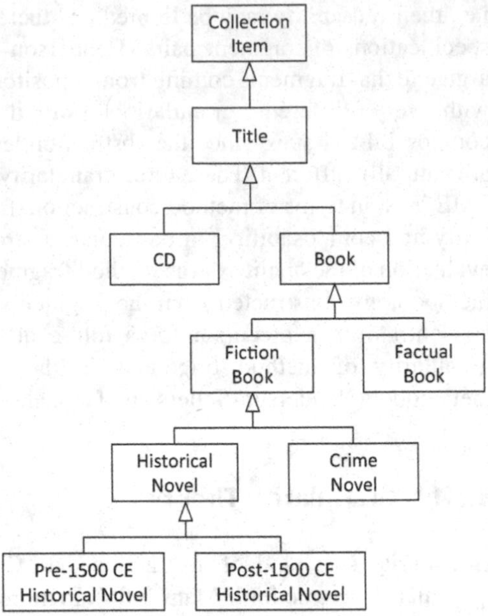

Fig. 8.5 Example of granularity levels in a generalisation/specialisation hierarchy (after Henderson-Sellers and Gonzalez-Perez, figure 1, 2010) (With kind permission of Springer Science + Business Media)

In other words, for a number of elements (x_i), *all* of them are mapped on to a single element. Examples are classification, aggregation and generalisation.

This formal definition accords well with our own, human interpretation of the world around us. Mani (1998, quoting Hobbs 1985), argues that when we conceptualise the world, we do so at different levels of granularity, these levels being determined by the number of characteristics that are seen as relevant to a particular purpose. For example, a forest is composed of trees; that means the forest (the composite) can be used as a granular abstraction of the trees in it (the components). Ask someone standing at the edge of a forest to say what they see. Likely they will say 'trees' or maybe 'a forest'. However, a surprising answer would be leaves or even cells or at the other granularity extreme 'part of the biosphere'. Such answers result from the fact that our brains are better tuned to the tree granularity than the granularity of a leaf or of the holistic Earth. The tree is our 'gestalt' (defined as a collection perceived as a whole). Other animals will no doubt have different gestalts, e.g., a worm will see leaf litter but not the trees and never the forest.

The above example discusses granularity in terms of whole-part relationships. Another example is in the application of granularity to the generalisation and specialisation relationships that are often used in modelling. For example, at a fine granularity, we might have *walkfrom(location)*, *drivefrom(location)* and *flyfrom(location)*, which are equivalent to the coarse granularity *gofrom(location)* (Ghidini and Giunchiglia 2004). We might browse in a library collection through all the titles, some of which are CDs, some books (Fig. 8.5). In the fiction section, we might find historical novels and crime novels. Historical novels might be further classified as pre- and post-1500 CE. Individual books that are classified as, say, pre-1500 Historical Novels are members of the set thus defined, yet are also members of the set at the coarse granular level as specified by Collection Item (Henderson-Sellers and Gonzalez-Perez 2010).

As noted earlier, several authors consider that method fragments/chunks may be any level of granularity such that even the full methodology can be considered as a method fragment. Ter Hofstede and Verhoef (1997) identify a number of such levels of abstraction: product level (milestone documents, major process stages)—the project manager's level; model level, e.g., class diagrams, task hierarchies (the modeller's level); component level (invariant rules, graphical conventions, etc.). These are all interrelated; for example, choosing a class diagram means that at the component level only certain conceptual entities and relationships are available for use.

As noted above, the third application area for granularity is found in the classification structures commonly used in modelling and metamodelling—and hence in SME. Since granularity is a kind of abstraction and since abstraction is to do with the loss of detail during a transformation, we can observe that, when an object is created as an instance of a class, detail is added and, conversely, when we map from a (fine granular) set of objects into a single class, we lose information, i.e., we purposefully omit details in order to gain a simpler, and hence more comprehensible, model. This kind of abstraction leads to the common (but not totally accurate) appellation of 'levels of abstraction' as applied to the multi-level architecture as promulgated in the OMG for standards such as UML, MOF and SPEM (see discussion of Fig. 1.11 in Chap. 1 and more detailed discussion in Chap. 4).

Henderson-Sellers and Gonzalez-Perez (2010) have proposed a measure of the system granularity, G_S, as being related to the number of entities, n, in each system. Since it is reasonable to propose that the fine-grained system should have a smaller value for G_S than for a coarse-grained system, they propose that the grain size (system granularity value) is a reciprocal measure of the number of granularity abstraction mappings (Eq. 8.3 or 8.4) between two entities (Lakoff 1987). Thus

$$G_S = 1/n \tag{8.5}$$

This measure refers to entities represented in a single system/model, i.e., it can only be used in a comparative and evaluative sense if there are two versions of the *same* system. Thus, for example, applying Eq. 8.5 to the entities along the main 'chain' in Fig. 8.5, x_1 = *Collection Item*, x_2 = *Title*, x_3 = *Book*, x_4 = *Fiction Book*, x_5 = *Historical Novel* and x_6 = *Pre-1500 CE Historical Novel*, it is possible to compare the granularity of this system (G_S = 1/6) with a similarly functioned system consisting of just one class called simply Library Collection Item, i.e., *abs*(x_i) = *Library Collection Item* for all x_i in the original fine-grained system (L_1) (and hence G_S = 1/1). (A similar argument applies if the fine-grained system uses aggregation relationships rather than the generalisation relationships of Fig. 8.5.)

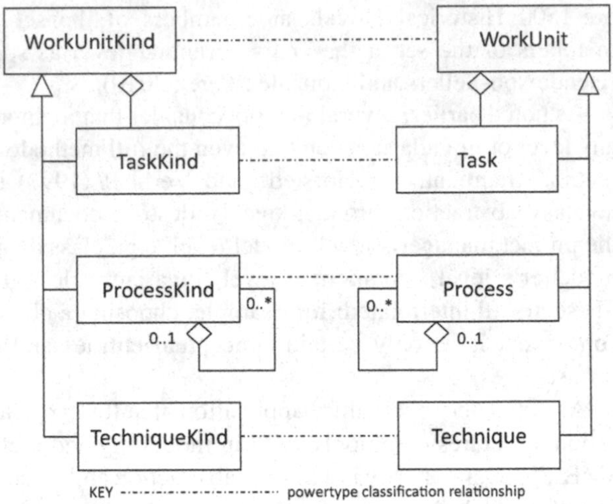

Fig. 8.6 The WorkUnit/WorkUnitKind meta-level classes together with the subtypes as defined in ISO/IEC 24744. (A more coarse granular metamodel representation is given in Fig. 4.10) (after Henderson-Sellers and Gonzalez-Perez, figure 3, 2011) (With kind permission of Springer Science + Business Media)

One problem is that this approach, by itself, cannot guarantee anything about the comparative sizes of individual entities. For the example in Fig. 8.5, we have no information about the consistency or otherwise of entities such as Historical Novel, Fiction Book and Book. We must therefore ask: "What is the influence of these theories of granularity for method fragments?" Firstly, there is the granularity of the defining metamodel (Chap. 4). In fact, our earlier examples are strictly metamodels rather than models. For example, Fig. 2.11 in Chap. 2 shows two different granularities for a process element. Clearly, by default, a fragment conformant to the more coarse granular metamodel must itself be coarse granular. In contrast, using the finer granularity metamodel permits a finer granular method fragment since, using the mapping of Eq. 8.4, we can clearly see that we could have fragments mapped to any of these three classes, not just the one of the coarse granular metamodel. Secondly, even when a fragment is conformant to a fine granular metamodel element, there is no guarantee that it will have atomic granularity. It is quite possible that it may be a conglomerate of two or more atomic concepts (Rogers and Henderson-Sellers 2014). Here, we explain this latter idea in terms of fragments conformant to the TaskKind model element in the metamodel (see Fig. 8.6).

Based on the evaluation (Henderson-Sellers and Gonzalez-Perez 2010) of the granularity of a number of methodology metamodels, a more recent evaluation of method fragment granularity in relation to metamodel granularity was presented in Henderson-Sellers and Gonzalez-Perez (2011). In their analysis, they assumed an overall system size, S. For this system, if only one fragment were to be generated conformant with each meta element, then for n meta elements, the overall size would be related to the fragment sizes by

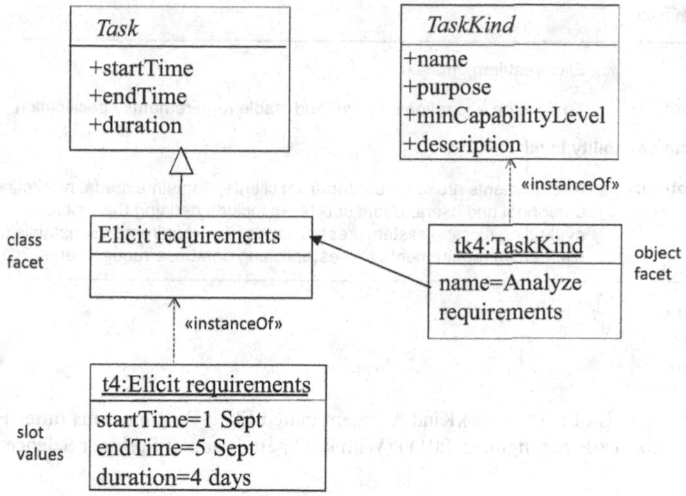

Fig. 8.7 Powertype pattern for Task/TaskKind and the class and object facets created together with an example of the process 'object' in the Endeavour domain (after Henderson-Sellers and Gonzalez-Perez, figure 4, 2011) (With kind permission of Springer Science + Business Media)

$$S = \sum_{i=1}^{n} f_i \tag{8.6}$$

where f_i is the size of the i-th fragment. To compare the effect of granularity they consider two representations of the one system at different granularities. Thus, for a constant size, S, the fragment size must be bigger for smaller n. Since it is likely that larger fragments are not atomic and therefore of less than optimal quality, this size evaluation could be contributory to an overall evaluation of the quality of the method fragments in a repository and, by inference, the quality of the constructed methodology, as discussed elsewhere in this chapter.

A method fragment conformant to the Task/TaskKind powertype pattern must contain the exact same number of fields as defined in the SEMDM. Many of these fields are likely to have short values—all except the Description field of TaskKind (Fig. 8.7). Henderson-Sellers and Gonzalez-Perez (2011) evaluated possible strategies to answer the question "How long (number of words/number of concepts, etc.) should a method fragment (such as Task/TaskKind in Fig. 8.8) be in order for the fragment to be regarded as of 'good quality'?" They argued that determining whether the value (a string) of the Description field belied an atomic Task/TaskKind or not. Atomicity is hard to discern, of course, being a determination regarding whether or not the entity can be decomposed into smaller entities (within the vocabulary dictated by the concomitant metamodel). They suggested inverting

Task Kind

Name:	Elicit requirements
Purpose:	To develop and refine a formal and stable requirements specification.
Minimum capability level:	1
Description:	Requirements are to be elicited from clients, domain experts, marketing personnel and users. Usual sub-tasks include defining the problem, evaluating existing systems, establishing user requirements, establishing distribution requirements and establishing database requirements.

startTime
endTime
duration

Fig. 8.8 The details of a Task/TaskKind fragment called Elicit Requirements (after Henderson-Sellers and Gonzalez-Perez, figure 5, 2011) (With kind permission of Springer Science + Business Media)

Eqs. 8.4 and 8.5 in order to seek (a) a maximum value of n and, in parallel, (b) a minimum value for each f_i; in other words, the set with the largest number of elements that satisfies Eq. 8.4 and a parallel set $\{f_1 \ldots\ldots f_n\}$ such that each f_i is a minimum, whilst retaining a conformance of each of these elements to the relevant class in the metamodel.

8.3.2 Application of Granularity Theory

In the following example, we illustrate the relationship between a fragment and its defining meta-level class with the subclass of WorkUnit/WorkUnitKind named Task/TaskKind. Using ISO/IEC 24744 (ISO/IEC 2007), each concept is depicted in the metamodel using a powertype pattern (Henderson-Sellers and Gonzalez-Perez 2005c and Chap. 1) as shown in Fig. 8.7. Powertype instantiation then depicts, at the model level (i.e., in the Method domain), an entity with both a class facet (here ElicitRequirements) and an object facet (here t4:TaskKind). As we saw in Chap. 4, the powertype pattern is powerful because it not only permits representations at the model level but also, by instantiating the class facet of the method fragment (in the Model domain), permits the allocation of project-specific values in the Endeavour domain (Gonzalez-Perez and Henderson-Sellers 2006a). The method fragment is thus a combination of allocated values (from the object facet) and specified but unallocated attributes (from the class facet) (Fig. 8.8).

As noted above, it is clear from Figs. 8.7 and 8.8 that any method fragment conformant to the Task/TaskKind powertype pattern that is defined in the ISO/IEC 24744 metamodel will, by definition, contain the exact same number of fields. The long-term research question therefore devolves to an evaluation of "How long should a method fragment be in order for the fragment to be regarded as of 'good quality'?"—remembering that the value of the method part is in its content not merely its length.

To begin to answer this question, rather than simply a length evaluation, one should consider whether the Description really describes an atomic concept or not (Rogers and Henderson-Sellers 2014). In other words, can the text (of the Description attribute) be broken down into two non-interdependent pieces? In the case of a TaskKind description field (as in Fig. 8.8), are there multiple actions that can be disambiguated?

As a concrete example, Henderson-Sellers and Gonzalez-Perez (2011) analyse the case of a 'Draw a use case diagram' method fragment. As a Task/TaskKind fragment this could well be considered to be atomic. If the metamodel's most fine granular class is Task, then this is likely to be an appropriate conclusion. On the other hand, if the metamodel were to support finer grained classes (cf. the discussion of Fig. 2.11 in Chap. 2), such as Step, then the 'Draw a use case diagram' *as a Task/TaskKind* would not be atomic. In this case, *not* breaking down 'Draw a use case diagram' into Steps would be a reflection of a (poor quality) coarse granular system—as compared to the same fragment but viewed as atomic (and good quality) in the former context. In this latter case, it may be possible to break down the 'Draw a use case diagram' into steps such as 'Draw a symbol for each use case' and 'Add actors to use case diagram'.

In contrast, one could argue that 'Create a design for an atomic reactor control system' will necessarily involve a large number of (sub)tasks. Thus, if we are able to break down the fragment into a larger number of other fragments, we can readily deduce that the original fragment was not atomic and hence of poor quality. Adding a quantitative value to that 'quality' does not, however, seem possible at this time.

This discussion also has some historical relevance in the area of metrics when, over 2 decades ago, people were asking "What is the best size for a class in any given object-oriented programming language?" Haynes and Henderson-Sellers (1996), based on empirical data from industry, suggested strongly that there can never be an absolute cut-off threshold number but rather that there is a distribution that can be analysed statistically such that the larger the size, the lower the probability (but not zero) that the class (and, by extension here, the method fragment) is of good quality.

8.3.3 Chunk Quality

Chunk quality is addressed by Mirbel (2006) who recommends using the similarity metrics of Ralyté and Rolland (2001a) to compare individual chunks—either proposed or already in the method base—both between each other and between the chunk and the user requirements. Ralyté and Rolland (2001a) introduce structural and semantic measures for work products as well as similarity measures for the process part of a method chunk. Semantic similarity is measured in terms of a *name affinity* (NA) metric based on both synonymy and hyperonymy relationships. As well, they argue it is necessary to complement this with a measure of structural similarity using a *global structural similarity of concepts* (GSSC) measure, which comprises a *structural similarity of concepts* (SSC) and an *adjacent similarity of concepts* (ASC) metric. These metrics are calculated using the following formulae:

$$NA\ \left(\mathrm{n}(\mathrm{e}_{\mathrm{ij}}), \mathrm{n}(\mathrm{e}_{\mathrm{kl}})\right) = \begin{cases} 1 & \text{if} < \mathrm{n}(\mathrm{e}_{\mathrm{ij}})\ \mathrm{SYN}\ \mathrm{n}(\mathrm{e}_{\mathrm{kl}}) > \\ \sigma_{1R} * \cdots * \sigma_{(m-1)R} & \text{if}\, \mathrm{n}(\mathrm{e}_{\mathrm{ij}}) \rightarrow^{\mathrm{m}} \mathrm{n}(\mathrm{e}_{\mathrm{kl}}) \\ 0 & \text{else} \end{cases}$$

where σ_R is a weight, SYN is the synonymy relationship and $n(e_{ij}) \rightarrow {}^{m}n(e_{kl})$ is the length of the path between e_{ij} and e_{kl} in a thesaurus and $m \geq 1$

$$\mathrm{GSSC}(c_1, c_2) = \frac{\mathrm{SSC}(c_1, c_2) + \mathrm{ASC}(c_1, c_2)}{2}$$

$$\mathrm{SSC}(c_1, c_2) = \frac{2 * (\text{Number of common properties in } c_1 \text{ and } c_2)}{\sum_{i=1}^{2} \text{Number of properties in } c_1}$$

$$\mathrm{ASC}(c_1, c_2) = \frac{2 * (\text{Number of common adjacent concepts to } c_1 \text{ and } c_2)}{\sum_{i=1}^{2} \text{Number of adjacent concepts to } c_1}$$

Their process-focussed semantic similarity measures utilise elements of the MAP approach (Chap. 4). The *semantic affinity of intentions* (SAI) and the *semantic affinity of sections* (SAS) measure the closeness of two intentions (in a map) and the closeness of two map sections. These are calculated by:

$$\mathrm{SAI}(\mathrm{i}_\mathrm{i}, \mathrm{i}_\mathrm{j}) = \begin{cases} 1 & \text{if}(\mathrm{i}_\mathrm{i} \cdot \text{verb}\,\mathrm{SYN}\,\mathrm{i}_\mathrm{i} \cdot \text{verb}) \wedge (\mathrm{i}_\mathrm{i} \cdot \text{target}\,\mathrm{SYN}\,\mathrm{i}_\mathrm{j} \cdot \text{target})) \\ 0 & \text{else} \end{cases}$$

$$\mathrm{SAS}(\langle \mathrm{i}_\mathrm{i}, \mathrm{i}_\mathrm{j}, \mathrm{s}_{\mathrm{ij}} \rangle, \langle \mathrm{i}_\mathrm{k}, \mathrm{i}_\mathrm{l}, \mathrm{s}_{\mathrm{kl}} \rangle) = \begin{cases} 1 & \text{if } \mathrm{SAI}(\mathrm{i}_\mathrm{l}, \mathrm{i}_\mathrm{k}) = 1 \wedge \mathrm{SAI}(\mathrm{i}_\mathrm{j}, \mathrm{i}_\mathrm{l}) = 1 \wedge \mathrm{s}_{\mathrm{ij}}\,\mathrm{SYN}\,\mathrm{s}_{\mathrm{kl}} \\ 0 & \text{else} \end{cases}$$

For process-focussed structural similarity, Ralyté and Rolland (2001a) propose the use of two kinds of measure that may be useful for comparing the structure of two maps and to identify any overlaps between these two maps. The *structural similarity by intentions* (SSI) measures the proportion of similar intentions in the two maps, based on the calculation of the SAI values of their respective intentions. The proportion of similar map sections, the *structural similarity by sections* (SSS), is complemented by the PSS (*partial structural similarity*) measure, which looks at pairs of intentions. Mathematically, these three metrics are given as:

$$\mathrm{SIS}(m_1, m_2) = \frac{2 * \text{Number of similar intentions in } m_1 \text{ and } m_2}{\sum_{i=1}^{2} \text{Number of intentions in } m_1}$$

$$\mathrm{SSS}(m_1, m_2) = \frac{2 * \text{Number of similar sections in } m_1 \text{ and } m_2}{\sum_{i=1}^{2} \text{Number of sections in } m_1}$$

$$\mathrm{PSSS}\left(m_1 : \langle i_{1i}, i_{1j} \rangle,\ m_2 : \langle i_{2k}, i_{2l} \rangle\right)$$
$$= \frac{2 * \text{Nb. of similar sections between } \langle i_{1i},\ i_{1j} \rangle \text{ and } \langle i_{2k}, i_{2l} \rangle}{\text{Nb. of sect. between } \langle i_{1i},\ i_{1j} \rangle + \text{Nb. of sect. between } \langle i_{2k},\ i_{2l} \rangle}$$

m_1, m_2 : the maps; $m_1 : \langle i_{1i},\ i_{1j} \rangle$: a couple of intentions in the map m_1

In utilising these earlier similarity metrics, Mirbel (2006) recommends that although a value of 1 indicates a perfect match, it is also possible that useful matches may result when the similarity measure has a value less than unity.

8.3.4 Method Base Quality

There is a second important quality aspect of method parts and that relates to the method base in which the parts are stored. It is important that any method part accepted into the inventory of the method base be compatible (or else documented as non-compatible) with other elements in the method base. A method base that contains contradictory elements or elements that have different granularities, unless extremely carefully documented, is next to useless.

Henderson-Sellers and Gonzalez-Perez (2011) apply the ideas described in Sect. 8.3.2 to fragments contained in the method base of the OPF (Firesmith and Henderson-Sellers 2002). They make recommendations for revisions based on these granularity ideas. This study, however, only addressed the size and granularity aspects of method parts (in this case, atomic method fragments). When one moves away from a method part focus, it is important to be able to assess the quality of method parts in terms of how they fit into the larger picture. In particular, we need to investigate metrics for evaluating the cohesion and the semantic consistency of method parts across the method base. To the best of our knowledge this has not been undertaken in the SME context.

Note that this is a difficult balancing act for the quality control of the method base. Here, we can leverage the work done on object-class documentation as reported in the early 1990s by, e.g., Henderson-Sellers and Freeman (1992). These authors discuss various storage and retrieval approaches. Although not designed for method bases, their proposals can be immediately applied to SME. It is of course desirable that the suite of method parts in the method base can be used in creating methodologies of very different characters. In other words, we might wish to support incremental delivery styles of methodologies, agile methodologies, waterfall methodologies and so on. This requires a suite of method parts that initially seem incompatible with each other. It is therefore vital to document the characteristics and areas of application for each method part so that a user of the method base (human or software tool) can be sure of extracting only those method parts that are relevant to the particular SME context.

8.3.5 Other Quality Issues

Saeki (2003a) observes that structural characteristics of individual elements or small systems can be measured by some of the Chidamber and Kemerer (1994) metrics—but note later criticisms by, e.g., Henderson-Sellers et al. (1996). Using the Method Engineering Language (MEL) of Brinkkemper et al. (2001), Saeki (2003a) recommends the incorporation into the design modelling language's metamodel elements to directly support such measurement (Fig. 8.9). He then uses MEL together with this revised metamodel to calculate, as an example, the quality characteristics of UML use case diagrams.

Wistrand and Karlsson (2004) suggest six criteria for the evaluation of method components (applicable to all their three scenarios):

- Self-contained
- Internally consistent and coherent
- Rationality[1]
- Connectivity
- Applicability
- Implementability.

Whilst not strictly SME-related, Bertoa et al. (2006) measure the usability of software components (in the CBSE sense). They use an adaptation of ISO/IEC 9126. They stress that proposing measures is insufficient since it is vital to (a) show how these are computed, (b) are both objective and reproducible and (c) effectively assess the target sub-characteristic of quality (in this study, usability).

A slightly different argument is put by Vavpotic and Bajec (2009)—as discussed earlier (Sect. 7.2): viz. that the technical quality of the methodology must be complemented by the social quality of the methodology. Their approach offers a formalisation and justification for many of the aims of SME, i.e., that it should be socially appropriate for a particular set of *humans*—the members of the development team and the management culture (e.g., Constantine and Lockwood 1994). In order to ensure effectiveness of the to-be-constructed methodology, they advocate a socio-technical evaluation of all potential method fragments. Quality improvement results from encouraging method fragments in the lower three quadrants of Fig. 7.8 to migrate into the upper right quadrant (Fig. 8.10).

---

[1] For further details on rationality, see, e.g., Oinas-Kukkonen (1996) and Rossi et al. (2000).

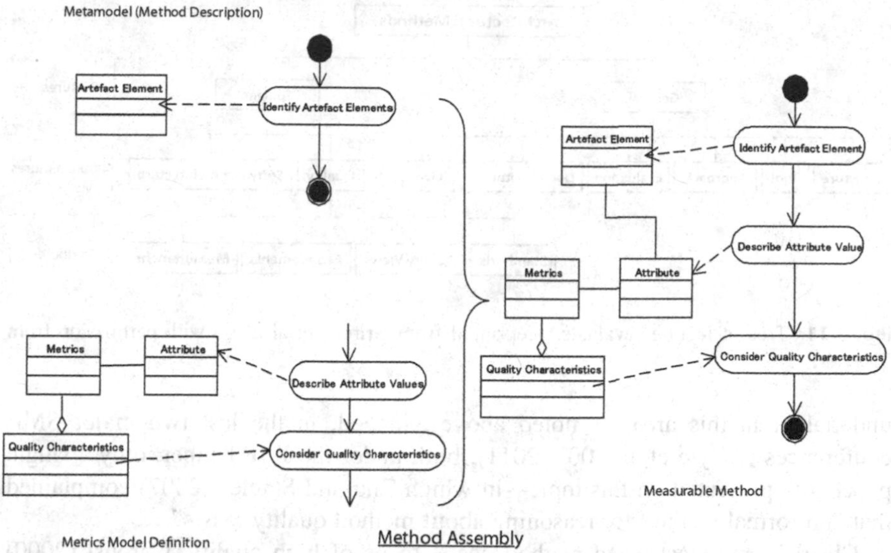

Fig. 8.9 Method assembly metamodel fragment for measureable methods (after Saeki, figure 3, 2003a) (With kind permission of Springer Science + Business Media)

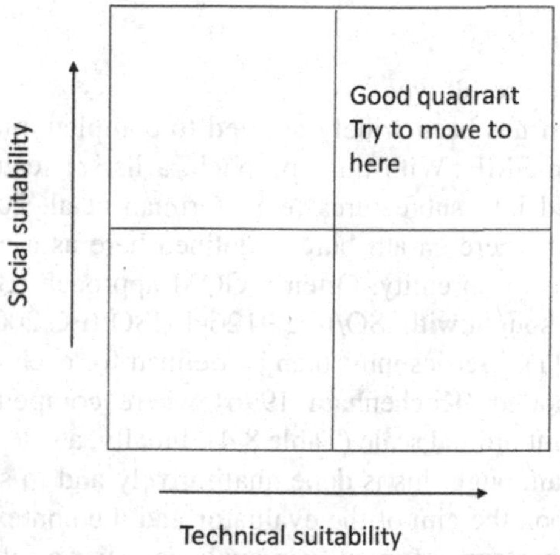

Fig. 8.10 Two-dimensional matrix for the suitability of a method fragment (derived from presentation of Bajec 2011b)

8.4 Constructed Method Quality

Although Tolvanen et al. (1996) raised the question of how to standardise the quality of engineered methods and Brinkkemper et al. (1998) proposed 12 heuristic rules for achieving quality (see below), almost no research has since been

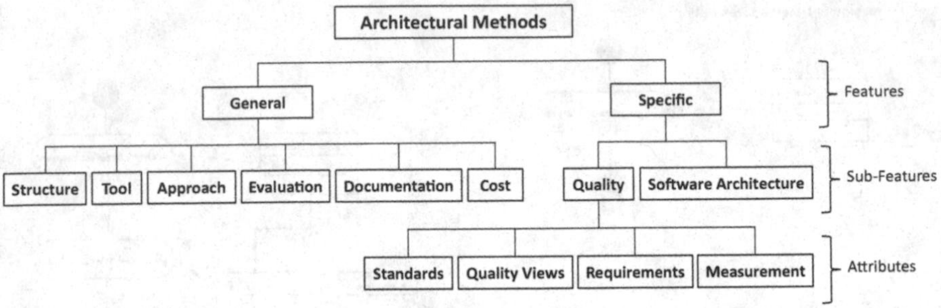

Fig. 8.11 Tree of features evaluated (reprinted from Grimán et al. 2006 with permission from Elsevier)

undertaken in this area (as noted above). Indeed, in the last two major SME conferences (Ralyté et al. 2007, 2011), both under the IFIP banner, only a single paper was presented on this topic—in which Zhu and Staples (2007) complained that "no formal method for reasoning about method quality exists".

Clearly, any constructed method needs to be of high quality. Chroust (2000) suggests five well-formedness characteristics for all process models:

- Source and sink for all result types
- Connectivity of activity types
- Connectivity of model
- Cycle-freeness
- Unique source for a result type.

Feature evaluation has been widely applied to complete methodologies, albeit not in the context of SME. With this approach, a list of features is constructed, possibly decomposed into subfeatures (e.g., Grimán et al. 2006) and again into attributes (Fig. 8.11) where an attribute is defined here as a measurable property (physical or abstract) of an entity. Often a GQM approach (Basili et al. 1994) is used or alignment is sought with ISO/IEC 9126-1 (ISO/IEC 2001) or with ISO/IEC 25010 (ISO/IEC 2011). Metrics must then be defined for each attribute—these can be simple or compound (Kitchenham 1996) where compound metrics can be assessed on a six-point ordinal scale (Table 8.4). Finally, a side-by-side comparison can be undertaken, although this is done qualitatively and to some degree subjectively, depending upon the aim of the evaluator and the context of the evaluation. An alternative is to perform a formal 'gap analysis'. (For a fully worked example, see, for example, Tran and Low 2005.)

One concern, frequently voiced, is that typically such an evaluation is done by one of the authors of one of the methodologies under investigation. Although such a framework, by its nature, is objective, typically the values assigned to any particular methodology against the ideal (Table 8.4) have a subjective element. As an antidote, Iivari and Kerola (1983) suggest using a Delphi-based approach (Okoli and Pawlowski 2004); alternatively, an external review committee could be created (e.g., Stojanovic et al. 2004). [Various approaches to feature-based evaluation are discussed in detail in Fung (2011).]

Table 8.4 Ordinal scale used in the feature analysis of Grimán et al. (2006). Reprinted with permission from Elsevier

Value given	Description	Definition
5	Excellent	The estimation of the feature is over and above the expectations
4	Very good	The estimation of the feature exceeds the expectations
3	Good	The estimation of the feature covers all the expectations
2	Poor	The estimation of the feature does not cover the expectations
1	Very poor	The estimation of the feature does not cover the expectations or even come near to doing so
0	Does not apply	The estimation of the feature cannot be undertaken as it does not apply for the feature evaluated

Brinkkemper et al. (1998) stress the need to assemble a *meaningful* method from the retrieved fragments by, for example, using two fragments at the same granularity. It is not usually appropriate to assemble a method for industrial usage from, say, a class diagram and an ER diagram because of the extensive overlap between these two fragments, although there are some situations (e.g., in a research mode, creating a method for doing parallel modelling of the same information using class diagrams and ER diagrams, and then exploring the commonalities and differences or for purposes of teaching the differences between the two approaches).

Brinkkemper et al. (1998) focus on possible defects that might occur as a result of the assembly process. These include:

- Internal incompleteness. There is a reference to a second fragment that has not been included in the constructed method.
- Inconsistency. Contradictions[2] between a pair of selections—for example, the selection of two similar techniques to fulfil one particular task without due consideration or rationale being given, i.e., thoughtless selection of highly similar method fragments.
- Inapplicability. Fragments selected cannot be applied by project team members due, usually, to insufficient capability.

These defects may occur in the context of the internal or situation-independent quality (van de Hoef et al. 1995) for which the most important criteria are:

- Completeness. All fragments are connected to some other fragment.
  - Input/output completeness
  - Content completeness
  - Process completeness
  - Association completeness
  - Support completeness.

[2] Brinkkemper et al.'s use of the word contradiction here is perhaps too strong since inconsistencies reflect suboptimal selection rather than actual contradictions.

Table 8.5 Rules proposed in Brinkkemper et al. (1998) for ensuring constructed process quality (after Henderson-Sellers and Ralyte 2010)

1. There should be at least one concept newly introduced in each method fragment
2. There should be at least one concept linking the two fragments to be assembled
3. When adding new concepts, there should be connections between them and existing fragments
4. When adding new associations, both new fragments should be participants
5. In the resultant combined fragment, there should be no isolated elements
6. There should be no name duplication for different method fragments
7. Identification of added concepts should occur after the associated concepts have been identified
8. When two fragments are assembled, it is necessary that the output of one is used as the input to the other
9. Every work product must be identifiable as the output of a particular process fragment
10. When a work product has been created from other work products, then the process fragments producing the individual work products are summed to the process producing the amalgamated work product
11. Any technical method fragment should be supported by a conceptual method fragment
12. When there is an association between two product fragments, there should be at least one association between their respective components

- Consistency. There are no unnecessary clashes.
  - Precedence consistency
  - Perspective consistency
  - Support consistency
  - Granularity consistency
  - Concurrence consistency.

(others being efficiency, reliability and applicability: Harmsen (1997)).

However, Nuseibeh et al. (1996) note that full consistency is not generally achievable. They discuss means of providing partial consistency and provide some suggestions for rules for consistency management. In some contrast, Brinkkemper et al. (1998) note the obvious ease with which meaningless constructions of 'methods' can be made by unthinking combination of fragments. To ensure its meaningfulness, they suggest using a framework of three dimensions (perspective, abstraction, granularity—see Sect. 4.1).

Brinkkemper et al. (1998) propose 12 rules (Table 8.5) to ensure that the constructed methodology is of high quality. Rules 1–6 refer to method fragments in the conceptual layer and the diagram layer. Rule 7 relates to the diagram layer and Rules 9–11 with the conceptual modelling fragments. (It should be noted that (1) these rules assume that a process element acts merely as a transformation engine, i.e., it has of necessity one input and one output and (2) Rule 9 has some exceptions—some work products, especially the first work product input to the first process element, may be supplied externally, having been created outside the software development environment and used as a 'seed input' to initiate the method.)

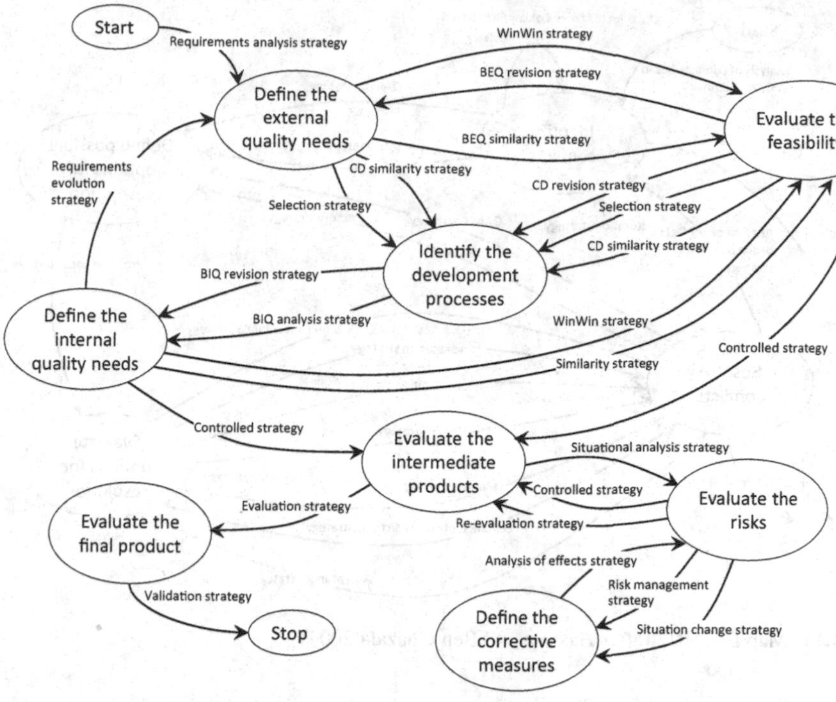

Fig. 8.12 Map for SQA (after Hassine and Ben Ghazala 2004)

Contingency models are proposed by Perez et al. (1995) and van Slooten and Hodes (1996)—discussed here in Chap. 7. Similarity measures proposed by Ralyté and Rolland (2001a) were discussed briefly above in Chap. 6.

Hassine and Ben Ghazala (2004) also use the map (see Sect. 4.3) as a means of discussing how to incorporate quality fully into a method engineering approach. Figure 8.12 depicts the various intentions and strategies to support software quality assurance (SQA) using the three standard guidelines discussed earlier (IAG, ISG, SSG). These guidelines are used to decompose the SQA process into sub-processes. Hassine and Ben Ghazala (2004) then underpin this with a metamodel based, *inter alia*, upon that of Ralyté and Rolland (2001a) (Fig. 4.16). They then use this situation-specific SQA approach to create an exemplar, called WinWin, exemplified in Fig. 8.13 by the map depicting an IAG for the section <Define external quality needs, Evaluate the feasibility of these needs, WinWin>. WinWin identifies and provides a negotiation framework for the resolution of conflicts between the quality requirements.

The process assessment framework of McBride and Henderson-Sellers (2011) (Sect. 8.1) can now be used to evaluate the quality of the 'constructed method'. Since the constructed method must have some primary purpose, such as to develop

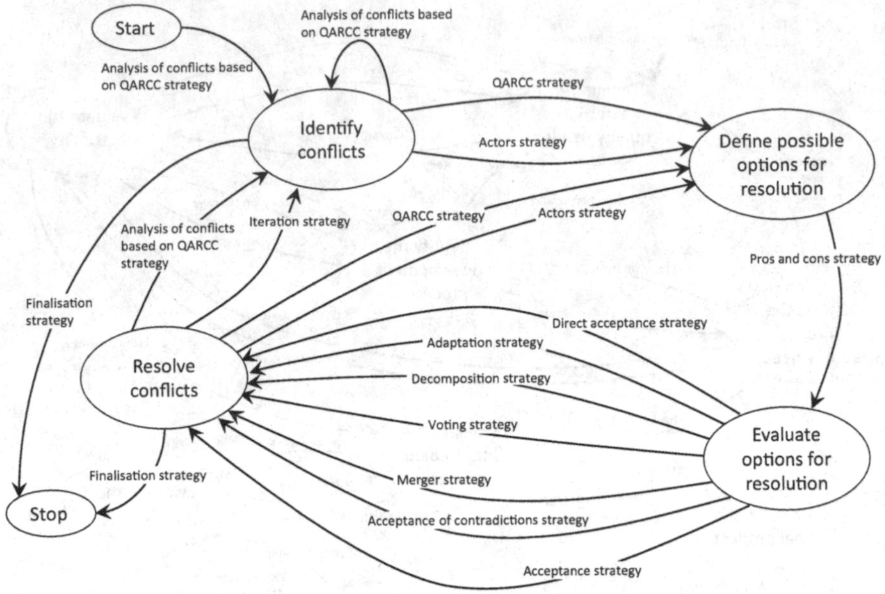

Fig. 8.13 Map for ARI2 (after Hassine and Ben Ghazala 2004)

software or to maintain a system, then, clearly, that constructed method must contain all the method fragments, but no more, that are required for the constructed method to meet its target. Indeed, identifying these fragments is a major component of any SME approach (Brinkkemper 1996; Ralyté and Rolland 2001a; Ralyté et al. 2003; Rolland 2009).

Processes can, of course, be examined to determine if they contain the expected activities (Goldkuhl and Lind 2008). However, a method is not a random collection of processes nor does it consist only of the processes that support the primary activities. The interaction between processes required to support project management or other forms of coordination can also be examined, as can the process interactions necessary for performance management. For the purposes of this discussion, performance management will include those activities involved in setting performance expectations and constraints such as delivery dates, budget and project scope, then managing those expectations and constraints throughout the lifetime of the project.

The software development work must be coordinated, so the method must contain the means to achieve or impose coordination. Coordination is usually achieved through developing a work breakdown structure, a schedule for its completion and reintegration, plans of how the work is to be completed, standards of how the work is to be done and standards relating to what work needs to be produced (Kraut and Streeter 1995; Nidumolu 1996; McBride 2008). Since software development is inherently uncertain, there is usually a need for dynamic coordination, achieved through meetings, reviews and other exchanges. As with performance, the method needs to provide for coordination and, furthermore, it should be adequate for the range of circumstances encountered.

Suggestions for the improvement of software processes, albeit for one specific approach (processes based on the SPEM metamodel), are provided by Pereira et al. (2011). They extend SPEM by modifying and adding a suite of well-formedness rules that they then use to check the consistency of processes derived from SPEM. They apply this to one specific example (the Inception Iteration of the OpenUP process) and identify some inconsistencies. They also, incidentally, identify a source of possible error in the SPEM metamodel itself, which, they observe, "allows the specification of a *Task* that does not consume, produce and/or modify any *Work Product*". From these studies they suggest that process errors typically result from the use of a UML class diagram-based metamodel that is only capable of representing single multiplicity constraints. They also recommend that the consistency checking they advocate should be undertaken before enactment.

Bogg et al. (2010) undertook a pilot project to assess the efficacy of using the work product pool approach (see Sect. 6.4) to method construction (Gonzalez-Perez and Henderson-Sellers 2008a) to evaluate the quality of the agent-oriented MOBMAS methodology (Tran and Low 2008). This approach was proposed as being useful for either providing a simple quality check for a newly constructed methodology or to determine whether an extant methodology has either too few or too many methodological elements. Bogg et al. (2010) recommend a four-step assessment process:

1. Identifying work product types and their interdependencies;
2. Using the work product pool approach, undertake backward chaining to recreate the target methodology;
3. Analyse the recreated methodology for problems, e.g., missing elements;
4. Write a report to be presented to the decision makers responsible for the methodology.

In much of the literature, as discussed above, there is an implicit assumption that the assessment of the quality of the method is being undertaken with respect to some already stated set of requirements for the methodology. Typically, the reader understands these requirements to be those of the functional requirements. However, there are also likely to be non-functional requirements, as pointed out by Zhu and Staples (2007), and, furthermore, the shared understanding of these requirements is a balance between implicit and explicit understanding (see Fig. 3.2 and Glinz and Fricker 2013). These authors introduce the notion of a 'method tactic' by which a method part or a whole method can undergo improvement with respect to some stated non-functional requirement. They define a tactic[3] as a technique for SME intended to achieve some specific method quality. They argue that these are

[3] This is a different meaning to the use of the word 'tactic' earlier in the book—especially in Chap. 4.

Table 8.6 Some example method tactics as suggested by Zhu and Staples (2007)

Use verbal communication and 'light' informal documentation
Use formal documentation
Downstream-driven input (feedback)
Upstream-driven input (feedforward)
Introduce continuous feedback/auditing
Introduce staged feedback/auditing
Allow a single method chunk to be carried out incrementally
Use configuration management
Reduce task dependencies between multiple resources

unlikely to be definable as individual method parts but, rather, highlight crosscutting constraints. Examples of their method tactics are given in Table 8.6. Many are paired, representing two ends of a spectrum. Others, despite the authors' assertions, can often be found as method parts in an existing method base; for example, the use of configuration management (Table 8.6) as an Activity method part in the OPF method base (Firesmith and Henderson-Sellers 2002). Of the four non-functional requirements they identify (agility, scalability, interoperability and usability), Zhu and Staples (2007) only consider the first two. In particular, they evaluate the agility of eight leading agile methods, and note that agility and scalability are often at odds with each other.

With the more recent interest in agile methodologies comes a need to evaluate their quality. For pre-constructed agile methods, quality evaluation can follow a similar path to that for traditional methods (as discussed above)—with one exception: the evaluation of the degree of agility attained by the method. Using a framework called the 4-DAT (Qumer and Henderson-Sellers 2006), these authors assess the degree of agility of six well-known agile methods and two non-agile methods (spiral and waterfall) (Qumer and Henderson-Sellers 2008). Figure 8.14 shows that in all cases the agile methods significantly outperform waterfall and spiral methods in terms of the agility of both their phases and their practices.

In their analysis of the quality of pre-constructed object-oriented methodologies (as opposed to SME-constructed methods), Rossi and Brinkkemper (1996) proposed a suite of 17 metrics based on the four key elements of OPRR (Smolander 1992): object, properties, relationship and role. These are elements in a metamodel that is then used to characterise a number (11) of methodologies (process models). First, each 'technique' in the method is evaluated with these metrics. Then, these values are cumulated to give a measure of the complexity of the overall methodology. However, it is unclear whether a large value of complexity indicates some 'error' in the method design (i.e., viewed as negative) or whether a more positive interpretation is that a more complex method leads to greater expressive power. Rossi and Brinkkemper (1996) argue that there needs to be a balance between learnability (low complexity) and expressiveness (high complexity).

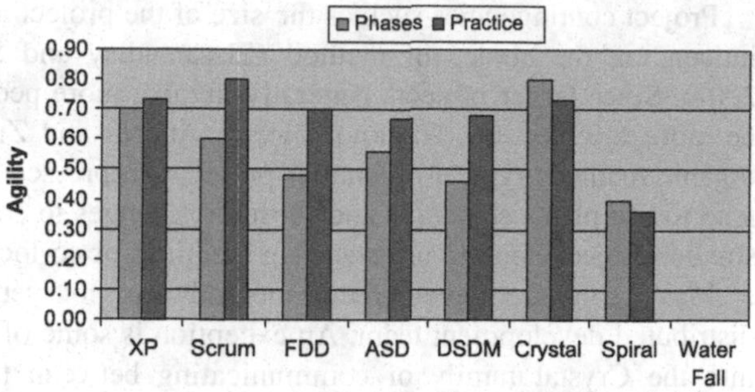

Fig. 8.14 Comparison of 4-DAT values (phases and practices) for six agile methodologies as compared to spiral and waterfall approaches (reprinted from Qumer and Henderson-Sellers 2008 with permission from Elsevier)

A non-technical approach to evaluating the practical use of a method is presented by Mohan and Ahlemann (2011c) using a psychoanalytical approach (see discussion in Chap. 1).

8.5 Method Enactment

Method enactment focusses on the SME-*constructed* process both in terms of the process as tailored (for a specific endeavour) and as it is executed on a specific project. This is the 'enacted method' that must be quality assessed—first statically and then dynamically.

8.5.1 Evaluating the Quality of the Tailored Process

When projects are being planned, it is with considerable knowledge of the expected project contingencies and constraints. Some constraints are fixed, like the delivery date of software required for a specific event. Some are negotiable, like the number of people in the development team or the actual scope of the project. Whilst such constraints are normally considered as part of project planning, they also contribute to method tailoring during that planning. Method enactment uses tailoring to describe the association of parameters in the designed method to actual project-specific resources, such as actual team members, real deadlines and available funding, and the subsequent method tailoring.

There is a considerable body of information on contingency theory relating to software development some of which is discussed in McBride and Henderson-Sellers (2011) and outlined below. However, there is little consensus on the contingencies of importance in different circumstances. Additionally, other fields such as product development (Reinertsen 2009) have the potential to open discussion on method enactment to a much wider treatment than the current concerns of software project planning. For these reasons, here, we will not attempt a rigorous examination of specific contingency factors that may impact software development projects, but simply summarise them.

Project contingencies such as the size of the project are generally recognised as influencing the choice of method (Elssamadisy and Schalliol 2002; Cockburn 2004). Since larger projects generally involve more people, coordination tends to be more mechanistic (Nidumolu 1996; Andres and Zmud 2002) than the more organic methods typical of smaller projects. Expressed differently, larger projects tend to use plans, standards and formal exchanges to coordinate their work whilst smaller projects tend to use stand-up meetings or co-location.

Many software development methods do not yet address the effect of a distributed development team. An exception is some of the practices incorporated into the Crystal family of communicating between team members. These are significant in agile development methods (Cockburn 2006) where the problems of communicating between team members are acknowledged and different techniques are proposed to overcome barriers to communication. Other less agile development methods seem to be unaffected by team distribution implying that the projects concerned were already using techniques that were less affected by distance (McBride et al. 2006). It is also possible that some methods are more susceptible to communication barriers than others and that compensation is sometimes possible.

Various authors have identified sources of uncertainty including platform and market uncertainty (MacCormack and Verganti 2003), requirements uncertainty (Nidumolu 1996), outcome uncertainty and task programmability (Eisenhardt 1989) as significantly influencing choice of method and its tailoring. Whilst specific relationships between different types of uncertainty and method may need some investigation, the general connection seems to be well accepted.

Safety critical or security critical applications may demand extra processes (in the ISO sense, i.e., a second meaning to the one depicted in Fig. 8.1), intended to augment an otherwise less critical method (ISO/IEC 2010b; Davis 2005). In this case, the contingency is addressed by extra processes and activities rather than a selection among equivalent activities in a process already included in the method. A project with stringent quality requirements will need to meet those requirements through more rigorous verification activities which may, in turn, affect the selection of personnel on the verification team and the distribution of other tasks. Method enactment involves more than mere adjustment to parts of the method. It may require wholesale redistribution of activities within the method.

Although the project management literature does not specifically identify such project planning activities as method tailoring, it nevertheless has significant method tailoring characteristics. For example, a project manager may be faced with a demand to outsource some of the development, leading to a question of where verification of the outsourced development is to be performed. Verification of the work could be performed by the developers, if they were known and trusted, or by the acquirer after delivery. Such decisions will be reflected in the method as different ways in which activities are grouped together to form processes and the allocation of those processes to organisations.

The main contingencies of software development projects, described above, are those that are normally considered when a project is planned. In the parlance of method engineering, the method is configured. Method configuration through the selection of specific activities suited to the circumstances has been discussed in Ralyté and Rolland (2001b) and Henderson-Sellers and Nguyen (2004).

In contrast to assessment at the method design stage, method assessment at enactment has specific information about the project constraints and contingencies so that it can be expected to determine the utility of the method with greater certainty than previously possible. Assessment at enactment is unlikely to be significantly different from assessment at design but has greater immediacy. An assessment would be expected to determine whether or not the proposed means of monitoring and managing performance is likely to be effective in the specific circumstances. For example, if the project is large and distributed, oversight of the distributed organisations cannot rely on the same oversight processes as would be employed if all parties belonged to the same organisation. Similarly, coordination processes at the low range of project size, where co-location may be possible, would be different from coordination processes needed at the high end of project size.

A method assessment at enactment would help avoid a tendency to use a familiar but possibly inappropriate method. It would help direct attention to parts of the method affected by the constraints and contingencies and help remove subjective judgement about whether or not the method 'feels' right.

8.5.2 Assessing the Effectiveness of the Constructed Method in Practice

The whole point about tailoring a method for specific constraints and contingencies is to achieve the best possible outcome in practice. A tailored method represents a hypothesis that the best outcome possible will be achieved under the specific constraints and contingencies. Like all hypotheses, it should be possible to gather evidence to prove or disprove it. Yet so far there seems to have been little attempt to do so. An assessment should be able to identify two distinct issues: the right method but the wrong performance and the wrong method with the right performance (e.g., McBride and Henderson-Sellers 2011). An assumption that the first case is, by default, true seems to dominate existing process assessment methods (SEI 2001; ISO/IEC 2004c) and also seems to underlie quality management approaches (ISO/IEC 2000). However, the argument of situational method engineering is that the method may possibly be unsuited to the circumstances leading to poor outcomes no matter how the method is performed.

Performance is usually negotiated during project planning as the scope of the project, the available personnel, quality and other requirements, budget and delivery milestones are considered and resolved (Hughes and Cotterell 1999; Cleland and Ireland 2002; Burke 2003). Performance monitoring and management would normally be achieved through some unspecified means, e.g., project review meetings, to inform the project of changes in the constraints and as a means to collect and report performance data. A method assessment would need to examine whether these activities were present and adequate for the expected range of circumstances.

8.5.2.1 Process Capability

Method assessment to date has focussed on what is commonly called capability, independently of whether the process is off-the-shelf or constructed using SME practices. Capability assessment is used to evaluate the method as it is used on a particular project, based largely on whether pre-stated deliverables are actually delivered. It is then inferred from this evaluation whether (or not) the process elements used to produce these work products have been successfully executed.

One well-known approach is that of the capability maturity model (CMM: Paulk et al. 1993) and its successors like CMMI, which are based on quality management principles and the observation that organisations tend to solve their process problems in a particular sequence. The original software capability and maturity model (SW-CMM: Humphrey 1988, 1989) was succeeded by a model that integrated software and systems development (CMMI). This general approach has been broadly copied by other assessment models including COBIT (ITGI 2007), OPM3 (Fahrenkrog et al. 2004) and, in the International Standard, ISO/IEC 15504, commonly known as SPICE, an acronym for Software Process Improvement and Capability dEtermination (ISO/IEC 2004b), the last of these currently under revision as the ISO/IEC 33000 series. Other emerging International Standards are those in the 25000 series known as SQuaRE (systems and software quality requirements and evaluation). These ideas are also reflected in the Business Development domain (Business Development Institute International 2005).

Underpinning these assessment models is a collection of the so-called processes,[4] each with a stated purpose together with several activities that would achieve that purpose. During an assessment exercise, objective evidence is sought that each activity has been performed before concluding that the process purpose has been achieved. A rigorous assessment requires that multiple items of evidence be found for each activity for each process. In order to maximise the assessment's reliability, each process is assessed across several projects within the organisation. One distinguishing feature between the two most common approaches used in software engineering (CMM/CMMI and SPICE) is that the result of the evaluation in the former case is a single number (on a scale of 1–5) derived from an assessment of *all* aspects of the software engineering methodology/process, whilst, in the latter case, the SPICE results are given for each priority process area (on a scale of 0–5). Although this gives a profile rather than a single number, it has the advantage that only those process aspects of interest to the organisation are assessed, thus obviating having to factor in low scores from irrelevant processes (as happens with CMM assessments).

[4] The use of the word 'process' in software engineering is problematical—as we noted in Sect. 1.3. Here, it is used in the same sense as the ISO/IEC software engineering standards such as 12207 and 15504 where it can be taken as a synonym for 'method fragment' as defined in earlier chapters.

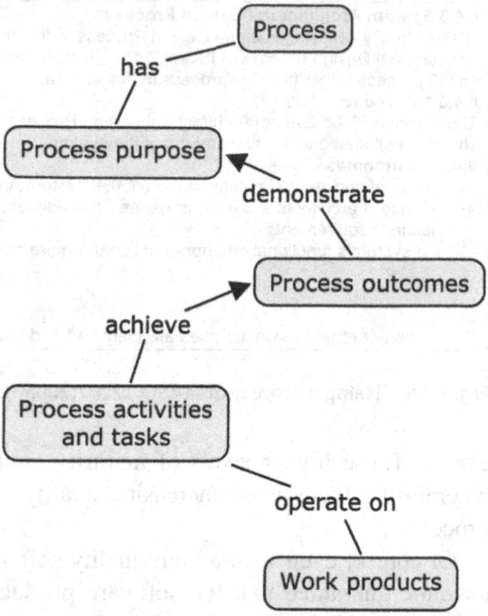

Fig. 8.15 Process model used for capability assessment (kindly supplied by T. McBride)

In general, it takes an assessment team of four or more assessors about 1 week to carry out a capability assessment along the lines outlined above. Even on a very approximate calculation, each assessment will cost tens of thousands of dollars. This may be inconsequential when the cost of the project is in the millions of dollars. However, it means that this type of assessment, rigorous though it may be, is unlikely to be used by small organisations seeking to put some objectivity into their process improvement efforts.

Current assessment methods are activity-based and depend on causal or associative connections between a set of activities and their outcomes (Fig. 8.15). Although there is considerable open-mindedness among assessment experts, to be adjudged as having achieved an outcome requires evidence that some appropriate activities have been performed and that those activities will achieve the outcome. There is no direct assessment of the outcomes and no direct assessment that the process purpose has been achieved, only this indirect evidence.

These types of process assessment can also underpin software process improvement (SPI) efforts. An assessment 'before' and 'after' such an initiative is often used to reflect improvements in an industry's software production. Strategies for high maturity organisations (e.g., levels 4 or 5) are proposed by Barcellos et al. (2012), in which they highlight some problems in implementing software process control (SPC), a technique often utilised in such high maturity organisations (e.g., Chatfield 1975). In such organisations, the focus is on identifying means by which to overhaul the process itself, replacing activities where appropriate, tightening up reviews where appropriate. Level 5 specifically should call the entire method into question, reconstructing it in response to external

6.4.3 System Architectural Design Process
NOTE The System Architectural Design Process in this International Standard is a specialisation of the Architectural Design Process of ISO/IEC 15288. Users may consider claiming conformance to the 15288 process rather than the process in this standard.
6.4.3.1 Purpose
The purpose of the System Architectural Design Process is to identify which system requirements should be allocated to which elements of the system.
6.4.3.2 Outcomes
As a result of successful implementation of the System Architectural Design Process:
a) a system architecture design is defined that identifies the elements of the system and meets the defined requirements
b) the system's functional and non-functional requirements are addressed;
.
.
.and
j) human-centred design activities are identified and performed.

Fig. 8.16 Example process from ISO 12207:2008 (kindly supplied by T. McBride)

events. These higher levels of maturity contrast with the lower levels (up to 3) wherein the focus is on increasing quality and productivity as facilitated by the process.

Of course, even with a high quality software development process, there is no absolute guarantee that the software product will be of equivalent high quality (Pfleeger 1999, p. 34) although without such a process the cause(s) of errors are hard to trace and hence hard to correct (Firesmith et al. 1997; Fung 2011). Indeed, Fung (2011) points out, in the context of dynamic evolution of software systems, that attempting to evolve a system whilst still running may prove highly detrimental should that software be of insufficiently high quality.

Processes are situated in the circumstances in which they are performed; thus, the process purpose also needs to be situated in the same circumstances. In terms of specifying a rigorous process assessment method, such situatedness is unsatisfactory. Not only is it impossible to specify what would be considered as a satisfactory process purpose achievement in advance of knowing the circumstances, the process purpose itself is quite subjective. For example, the purpose given for the System Architectural Design Process found in ISO/IEC 12207 (2008) (Fig. 8.16) illustrates this subjectiveness since it does not identify a test that would determine which system requirements should be allocated to which elements of the system. Furthermore, each of the outcomes is subjective because, although each identifies an artefact or event that can be verified, there is no test of the acceptability of that artefact or event. For example, for outcome (a) (Fig. 8.16), how is it determined that the design identifies elements of the system and how is it determined that the architectural design meets the defined requirements? This quandary does not resolve itself through considering the process activities and tasks (or practices and sub-practices) because there is considerable judgement necessary about what would be appropriate activities. In process models such as ISO 12207 that underpin the ISO process assessment method (i.e., SPICE), the activities and tasks are worded quite openly in order that organisations, and assessors, can decide what specific activities are appropriate in the specific circumstances. Overall, this model of process assessment depends on the domain knowledge and training of the process assessor.

Software process assessment has so far assessed capability rather than performance because the motivation has been to assess the capabilities of potential software systems developers and not to assess their current performance. Rather than imply the goals from the performed activities, it should be possible to imply the performed activities from the achieved goals. Rather than determine if specific activities are or will be performed and subsequently deduce that there is a high probability that the process purpose and other goals will be achieved, it should be possible to assess the achievement of the goals or process purposes such that it would be possible to deduce that appropriate activities are being performed. This has not been attempted to date because, as shown above, the purpose of each process is also situated and its achievement subjective. However, the overall goal of software development methods remains constant—to produce a software product with required functional and non-functional qualities and to achieve other organisational goals. In their study of the alignment between business goals and software development goals, Lepmets et al. (2012) note that there is no coherent approach to ensure that these are connected and little experience in practice on how to achieve such compatibility.

Thus, we can see that traditional method quality assessments are focussed on the notion of capability, for example, of an organisation, to undertake a method enactment in a commensurately quality way (remembering that these assessments evaluate the organisation on a scale of (usually) one to five). These approaches do *not* address questions more relevant to SME (as outlined above) such as whether the method, per se, is either complete or appropriate for the target project(s). In this chapter, we therefore deviate from the traditional ideas of capability assessment by first adopting a framework for the various stages of a process (design and enactment) and then seeing what sort of evaluative metrics might be needed at each of these stages.

8.5.2.2 Process Performance

As noted above, available process assessment methods such as SPICE (ISO/IEC 2004a) and CMMI (SEI 2006) are assessments of process capability, not of performance. Moreover, they assess processes and not the overall performance of the method. Process capability attempts to measure the degree to which a given process is likely to achieve its stated purpose (ISO/IEC 2004b). By itself, that says nothing about how well suited the process is to the circumstances. That determination relies on the knowledge and experience of the process assessor to decide whether the process itself is flawed and needs improvement or whether the process is being incorrectly performed for one reason or another. Other forms of assessment, such as a process audit, generally rely on the judgement of the auditor. This dependence on the well-intended judgement of an experienced auditor or assessor is unsatisfactory for a number of reasons. The first is that the assessor may not be sufficiently knowledgeable about software development or the particular circumstances, leading to well intended but harmful findings. The second is that such assessors tend to be expensive, out of reach for any but large software developers with project budgets able to absorb the high cost of a rigorous assessment.

Informal assessments are done all the time. People learn and adjust what they do. For example, Scrum practice includes a retrospective at the end of each sprint (Schwaber 1997; Rising and Janoff 2000) and most methods have some sort of post-mortem or other form of audit; the need for continual improvement is built into ISO 9001. However, these general imperatives to improve do not provide guidance on what to look for or how to recognise the need for improvements.

During method performance, information is available about how well the method is achieving its intended purpose. It is necessary to compare actual performance to expected performance in order to determine where changes to the method (e.g., in the case of the wrong process performed correctly) are required or where changes to method performance (the right process performed incorrectly) are needed.

However, it is apparent that most of the method attributes of method performance, the quality of both the fragments and the constructed method are evaluated in real time. Feedback may well suggest a dynamic replacement or the addition of new method fragments in order to ensure that the project is successfully completed. Of special interest are compound attributes for which there are no direct measures. Nor do there seem to be generally agreed-upon models of effectiveness, efficiency, coordination or governance. Like project success, it may be difficult to say what is required to achieve it, but relatively easy to determine if it is not being achieved. Rather than try to show that these are present and being achieved, it should be possible to detect their absence through errors or other symptoms of failure.

Method performance assessment would prompt a review of the project constraints and contingencies. Conversely, a change in project contingencies or constraints may prompt a method performance assessment. Additionally, a method performance assessment would provide an additional means to detect and justify changes to the method or to the manner of performing the method. It is not proposed that method performance assessment is equivalent to or should replace other, more rigorous, process assessments. The proposed method performance assessment is intended to directly and objectively assess the appropriateness of the method rather than imply it through the subjective knowledge and experience of a process assessor.

During assessment of method performance, the quality of both the fragments and the constructed method are evaluated in real time. Feedback may well suggest a dynamic replacement or the addition of new method fragments in order to ensure that the project is successfully completed.

8.6 Summary

Perhaps the greatest SME research challenge is to consolidate a proven set of metrics for quality assessment: the quality of method parts (fragments, chunks, components, patterns, etc.), the quality of the constructed method and the quality of the method-in-action. In this chapter, we have presented a framework for quality assessment (Sect. 8.1) and then examined quality metrics at various scales and target applications. Conceptual model quality is the best understood, although mostly in contexts other than SME. Nonetheless, these metrics are equally applicable to SME models, as we demonstrated in Sect. 8.2. We then introduced some initial discussions about the quality of individual method parts (Sect. 8.3) before we considered, in Sect. 8.4, how we might measure the quality of the constructed method. Issues regarding the internal quality and the fitness for purpose, as two distinct interpretations of 'quality of the constructed method', have been little discussed in the literature. A similar dearth of knowledge exists when we consider how to measure method enactment (Sect. 8.5). Method enactment also led to a brief discussion on process capability, in terms of SPICE (ISO/IEC 15504) and the SEI's CMMI as well as SPI. These areas are most likely to provide new additions to our SME body of knowledge over the next few years. One suggestion (Bajec 2012) is that of method weight which is defined as a product between its size (measured by the number of elements of which the method is composed) and its density, which states in how much detail each element is described.

Examples of Constructed Processes

9

Summary of What We Will Learn in Chapter 9

- What a constructed process looks like: (a) a hypothetical SME methodology; (b) an agile methodology as tailored from XP in an actual industry situation; (c) a method constructed using the MAP approach and (d) a MetaEdit+-based construction of a method for developing mobile applications.

In this chapter, we present four different examples of the application of the ideas of SME presented in the first eight chapters. Situational method construction often begins with team members identifying 'on paper' method fragments from a repository. In our first example (Sect. 9.1), we do just that by constructing a medium-sized methodology using the deontic matrices strategy of Fig. 6.1. This illustrates the mechanics of choosing appropriate fragments for a hypothetical situation and mirrors the approach we actually took with one software company in Spain.

We then ask how these ideas are applied in practice. There are several documented case studies of SME-created methodologies (e.g., Serour et al. 2002; Henderson-Sellers and Serour 2005; Henderson-Sellers and Qumer 2007). For example, Henderson-Sellers and Serour (2005) undertook an extensive action research study of several organisations who chose to create an agile method from method fragments. The resulting method of one of those organisations is depicted in Fig. 9.1 where each ellipse represents a high-level Work Unit (called Activity in the OPF) and connecting lines embody the chosen links based on a contract-driven life cycle model (Graham 1995a). There are also several published examples of SME-created methods starting from a base method, thus emphasising the tailoring capabilities of SME (e.g., Bajec et al. 2007b; Vavpotic and Bajec 2009; Žvanut and Bajec 2010). In Sect. 9.2, we sketch how these base-method tailoring ideas have been applied in a real-life industrial situation: that of a small Swedish company

B. Henderson-Sellers et al., *Situational Method Engineering*,
DOI 10.1007/978-3-642-41467-1_9, © Springer-Verlag Berlin Heidelberg 2014

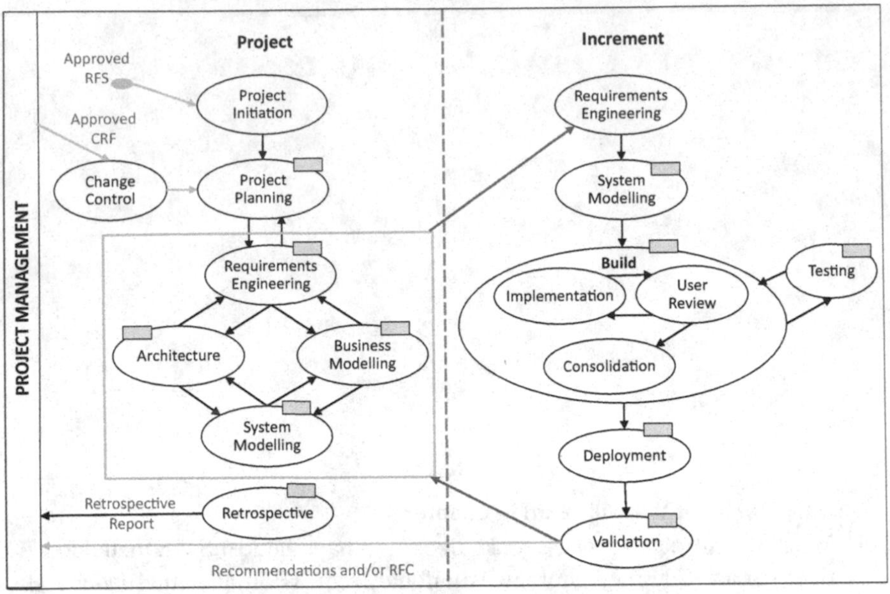

Fig. 9.1 The engineered method for the study organisation (after Henderson-Sellers and Serour 2005, Reprinted by permission of the publisher)

requiring the construction of an agile methodology, created using the MC Sandbox approach described in detail in Sect. 7.3.2.

Section 9.3 reports on the creation of a situation-specific method created for a small company operating in the domain of e-commerce. In this case study, the MAP formalism was used to provide the industry with a method that permitted the production of semi-formal documentation of enterprise business and unified employees' awareness of company's business structure and activities. In addition, use of the Empathy map technique permitted the identification of new ways to improve customers' loyalty and gave them new skills.

Finally, in Sect. 9.4, we describe construction of a method for developing mobile applications using the critical success chains (CSC) method and the MetaEdit+ tool environment, essentially creating a domain-specific modelling approach.

To date, the choice of approach has been most influenced by the individuals involved. This book, and particularly this chapter, is the first to bring together these various approaches, both illustrating how they are applied and how they can be aligned. In general terms, bottom-up construction works best for migrating an organisation from no process (as, for instance, described in Henderson-Sellers and Serour 2005). When any method is in place already, migration more usefully follows a tailoring approach. These four exemplar case studies, although described briefly, encompass this wide range of organisational situations for which SME can provide a solution.

Table 9.1 Example 1: Process at SPICE capability level 1 (after Henderson-Sellers et al. 2004b)

Purpose: To establish a managed and evolving repository of knowledge about the domain
Outline: A strategy to guide the management of the repository of domain knowledge is developed. The scope and characteristics of the domain are defined and standard terminology is established. Finally, the domain status is assessed
Outcomes
1 A domain engineering strategy is developed
1 The domain is defined
1 Standard terminology is established
1 Domain characteristics are identified
1 The domain status is assessed
Specific tasks
1 Develop a strategy for domain engineering
Identify the stakeholders and their objectives, organisational constraints and applicable organisational policies. Identify how to achieve the desired outcomes while satisfying the stakeholders' objectives within the identified constraints. Identify what needs to be done and when, the required resources and how to overcome deficits in those resources. Identify how the organisation will decide the strategy is working
Actions
Domain strategy: Create
Business objectives: ReadOnly
Techniques
Strategy development: Optional
1 Define domain
A description of the type of problem that systems in the domain solve and the external environment with which systems interact is produced. The observable behaviour that systems exhibit in solving the problem is described. The behavioural aspects of the system should be viewed from a black-box perspective. Any significant constraints concerning how the systems operate in terms of performance, reliability or distribution concerns are also included. The primary functions performed by every system in the domain and any important functions performed by only some systems are defined
Actions
Domain specification: Create
Domain strategy: ReadOnly
1 Establish standard terminology
Definitions of all significant terms used by domain experts in discussing the requirements or engineering of systems in the domain. Cross references to related terms and references to definitions from standard glossaries should be included
A structure should be created that shows term specialisations and relationships among similar concepts to reveal missing terms that represent generalisations of specialisations of known terms. In addition, a structure should be created that shows the composition of terms and the interrelationship of independent concepts in the formation of logical structures to reveal missing terms that are necessary to complete the definition of other terms or terms that tie other terms together into more complex concepts
Actions
Domain specification: Modify
1 Identify domain characteristics
Assumptions, constraints and core characteristics of the domain are identified

(continued)

Table 9.1 (continued)

Actions
Domain specification: Modify
1 Assess domain status
An evaluation of the technical maturity of the domain in terms of Domain Objectives and plans for domain development and evolution is performed. The Assess Domain Status task is defined in terms of its sub-activities
Determine marketability
Determine implement ability and risk
These sub-activities comprise a Viability Analysis. Each of the sub-activities results in an endorsement and commitment to the defined Domain Scope
Actions
Domain assessment: Create
Domain specification: ReadOnly
Domain strategy: ReadOnly

9.1 A Mid-Sized Plan-Based Methodology

The construction of any methodology using an SME approach depends upon the availability of a good quality method base that has a scope appropriate for the software development context under consideration. In this example, we focus on a context where software capability, process assessment and process improvement are judged as important. In the late 1990s, an EU-funded project, called OOSPICE (Stallinger et al. 2003; Henderson-Sellers et al. 2003, 2004c), aimed to develop such a methodological context and, in 2004, Henderson-Sellers et al. (2004b) presented two examples that show the same process: the first being a process containing the tasks needed to achieve SPICE capability level 1 (Table 9.1) and the second a depiction of how the process would look for the achievement of SPICE capability level 5 (Table 9.2).

Fragment selection can be undertaken using any of the approaches of Sect. 6.1. A software tool created within the OOSPICE project was used to generate the documentation for each task from the method base, ensuring that appropriate integrity constraints, as discussed in earlier chapters, were met. These constraints ensure, for instance, that any work product that a task produces as output is used as an input to another task.

It is both clear and not surprising that the level 5 method depicted in Table 9.2 is significantly larger (in terms of number of fragments) than the level 1 method (Table 9.1). The level 1 methodology has only five specific tasks (in this artificial example). At level 5, these five specific level 1 tasks are enhanced by several tasks at levels 2–5. In both examples, for some tasks, specific techniques are suggested and for all tasks at both levels, actions are specified.

Table 9.2 Example 2: Process at SPICE capability level 5 (after Henderson-Sellers et al. 2004b)

Purpose: To establish a managed and evolving repository of knowledge about the domain
Outline: A strategy to guide the management of the repository of domain knowledge is developed. The scope and characteristics of the domain are defined and standard terminology is established. Finally, the domain status is assessed
Outcomes
1 A domain engineering strategy is developed
1 The domain is defined
1 Standard terminology is established
1 Domain characteristics are identified
1 The domain status is assessed
2 The objectives for the performance of the process are identified. (2.1)
2 Resources required for performing the process are made available, allocated and used. (2.1)
2 The responsibility and authority for performing the process activities is assigned. (2.1)
2 The performance of the process is planned. (2.1)
2 The performance of the process is controlled. (2.1)
2 The process work product requirements are defined. (2.2)
2 The documentation and control requirements for the process work products are defined. (2.2)
2 Any dependencies among controlled work products are identified. (2.2)
2 Work products are appropriately identified, documented and controlled. (2.2)
2 Work products are verified and, if necessary, adjusted to meet the defined requirements. (2.2)
3 A standard process including appropriate guidance on tailoring is defined, that supports the execution of the process. (3.1)
3 Performance of the defined process is conducted in accordance with an appropriately selected and/or tailored standard process. (3.1)
3 Process performance data is collected and used as a basis for understanding the behaviour of the defined process. (3.1)
3 Experiences of using the defined process are collected and used to refine the standard process and tailoring guidance. (3.1)
3 The standard process identifies the competencies, roles and responsibilities required for enacting the defined process. (3.2)
3 The process infrastructure required for performing the defined process is identified and documented as part of the standard process. (3.2)
3 The required resources are made available, allocated and used to support the performance of the defined process. (3.2)
4 Objectives for process performance are established. (4.1)
4 Product and process measures are identified in line with relevant process objectives. (4.1)
4 Product and process measures are collected to monitor the extent to which the defined process objectives are met. (4.1)
4 Process capability is measured and maintained across the organisational unit. (4.1)
4 Suitable analysis and control techniques are identified. (4.2)
4 During process enactment, product and process measures are analysed to support control of process performance within defined limits. (4.2)
4 Process performance trends across the organisational unit are analysed. (4.2)
4 Effective actions are taken to address special causes of variation in performance. (4.2)
5 The process improvement goals for the process are defined that support the relevant business goals of the organisation. (5.1)

(continued)

Table 9.2 (continued)

5 The causes of real and potential variations are identified. (5.1)
5 Improvement opportunities are identified. (5.1)
5 An implementation strategy is established and deployed to achieve the process improvement goals across the organisation. (5.1)
5 The impact of all proposed changes is assessed against the objectives of the defined process and standard process. (5.2)
5 The implementation of all agreed changes is managed to ensure that any disruption to the process performance is understood and acted upon. (5.2)
5 The effectiveness of process change on the basis of actual performance is evaluated against the defined product requirements and process objectives to determine whether results are due to common or special causes. (5.2)
Specific tasks
1 Develop a strategy for domain engineering
Identify the stakeholders and their objectives, organisational constraints and applicable organisational policies. Identify how to achieve the desired outcomes while satisfying the stakeholders' objectives within the identified constraints. Identify what needs to be done and when, the required resources and how to overcome deficits in those resources. Identify how the organisation will decide the strategy is working
Actions
Domain strategy: Create
Business objectives: ReadOnly
Techniques
Strategy development: Optional
1 Define domain
A description of the type of problem that systems in the domain solve and the external environment with which systems interact is produced. The observable behaviour that systems exhibit in solving the problem is described. The behavioural aspects of the system should be viewed from a black-box perspective. Any significant constraints concerning how the systems operate in terms of performance, reliability or distribution concerns are also included. The primary functions performed by every system in the domain and any important functions performed by only some systems are defined
Actions
Domain specification: Create
Domain strategy: ReadOnly
1 Establish standard terminology
Definitions of all significant terms used by domain experts in discussing the requirements or engineering of systems in the domain. Cross references to related terms and references to definitions from standard glossaries should be included. A structure should be created that shows term specialisations and relationships among similar concepts to reveal missing terms that represent generalisations of specialisations of known terms. In addition, a structure should be created that shows the composition of terms and the interrelationship of independent concepts in the formation of logical structures to reveal missing terms that are necessary to complete the definition of other terms or terms that tie other terms together into more complex concepts
Actions
Domain specification: Modify
1 Identify domain characteristics
Assumptions, constraints and core characteristics of the domain are identified

(continued)

Table 9.2 (continued)

Actions
Domain specification: Modify
1 Assess domain status
An evaluation of the technical maturity of the domain in terms of Domain Objectives and plans for domain development and evolution is performed. The Assess Domain Status task is defined in terms of its sub-activities
Determine marketability
Determine implement ability and risk
These sub-activities comprise a Viability Analysis. Each of the sub-activities results in an endorsement and commitment to the defined Domain Scope
Actions
Domain assessment: Create
Domain specification: ReadOnly
Domain strategy: ReadOnly
2 Develop a plan for the process
Identify the process objectives, input and output work products, resources required to achieve the process objectives and the resources necessary to achieve them. Identify responsibilities and authorities necessary for performing the process
Actions
Process plan: Create
Business objectives: ReadOnly
Project plan: ReadOnly
Techniques
Timeboxing
Optional
Workflow analysis: Optional
2 Identify work product control requirements
For all process work product, identify requirements related to their control and management through the product's life cycle
Actions
Process plan: ReadOnly
Work product requirements: ReadOnly
2 Identify work product dependencies
Identify and document dependencies among work products
Actions
Process plan: Modify
Process work product: Modify
2 Identify work product requirements
For each process work product, identify its content and project requirements
Actions
Work product requirements: Create
Process plan: ReadOnly
2 Manage work products

(continued)

Table 9.2 (continued)

Identify, document and control work products. Work products should be appropriately identified by name, status and version. Changes to work products should be managed and updated versions of work products communicated to stakeholders
Actions
Process work product: Modify
2 Modify controlled work product
A controlled work product is modified and the modifications recorded. Updated versions are placed under control and distributed as necessary
Actions
Process work product: Modify
2 Monitor and manage the process plan
Monitor a planned process according to its plan. Detect deviations from the plan are detected and resolved. Issues arising from performing the process are communicated to stakeholders
Actions
Process plan: Modify
2 Verify work products
Work products are verified against their requirements
Actions
Work product requirements: ReadOnly
3 Collect process performance data
Collect and analyse process performance data. Use the analysed data to contribute to understanding and improving the standard process
Actions
Defined process: ReadOnly
Process plan: ReadOnly
3 Define a standard process
A standard process that supports the execution of the process is defined. Tailoring guidelines and constraints on such tailoring are written to describe how the standard process could be modified to suit the particular project or circumstances. The definition should cover roles, responsibilities and infrastructure necessary to perform the process
Actions
Defined process: Create
3 Improve the standard process
Data from and experiences with performed processes are used to develop improvements to the standard processes
Actions
Defined process: Modify
3 Perform defined process
The defined, and possibly tailored, process is performed as defined and planned. All required work products will be produced
Actions
Defined process: ReadOnly
3 Support process performance
Required resources are made available, allocated and used to support the performance of the process. Another critical aspect of this process attribute is ensuring that enabling conditions for

(continued)

Table 9.2 (continued)

successful deployment (implementation) of the defined process are present. Enabling conditions include
Defining the specific attributes of human resources who implement the process
Understanding the process infrastructure required for performing the defined process
Successful allocation and deployment of the required human resources and process infrastructures
A common documented understanding of roles, responsibilities and competencies for performing the defined process
The process infrastructure encompasses tools, methods and special facilities that are required for performing the defined process
Actions
Defined process: ReadOnly
Process plan: ReadOnly
4 Analyse process performance data
Industry best practice and process performance data are analysed to identify potential opportunities for process improvement
Actions
Process performance analysis: Create
Process performance data: ReadOnly
4 Analyse process performance trends
Analyse process performance data from across the organisational unit to determine causes of variation of process performance and the extent to which the process supports the business objectives
Actions
Process performance analysis: Create
Process measurement plan: ReadOnly
Process performance data: ReadOnly
4 Assess process capability
Measure and record process capability across the organisational unit
Actions
Process capability assessment: Create
Defined process: ReadOnly
4 Control the process performance
Use statistical process control or other suitable quantitative technique to monitor and control the process. The analysis and control techniques chosen will be influenced by the nature of the process as well as by the overall context of the organisational unit being assessed. For example, not all processes are equally suited to statistical control, and alternative techniques can be selected that demonstrate a qualitative understanding of the process
Actions
Process measurement plan: ReadOnly
Process performance data: ReadOnly
4 Correct process performance
Actions are identified to correct causes of process performance variation and to better achieve the process objectives

(continued)

Table 9.2 (continued)

Actions
Defined process: Modify
Process performance analysis: ReadOnly
4 Define process analysis and control techniques
Define process analysis and control techniques that are capable of identifying root causes of variation in process performance
Actions
Process measurement plan: Modify
4 Define process performance measures
Measures that support the process objectives are identified and documented
Actions
Process measurement plan: Create
4 Define process performance objectives
Relevant business goals are understood and clearly identified, and some form of correspondence is established between the business goals and the specific goals and measures for product and process
Actions
Process measurement plan: Modify
4 Quantitatively monitor process performance
Data for the identified process measures is collected and analysed to determine the extent to which the defined process supports the objectives for that process
Actions
Defined process: ReadOnly
Process measurement plan: ReadOnly
Process performance data: ReadOnly
5 Assess proposed process changes
Assess the potential impact of proposed process changes against the process objectives
Actions
Process improvement plan: ReadOnly
Process improvements: ReadOnly
5 Define process improvement goals
Define process improvement goals that support business goals
Actions
Process improvement plan: Create
5 Develop and implement improvement strategy
Develop a strategy to implement process improvements. Implement the strategy across the organisation to achieve the identified improvements
Actions
Process improvement plan: Modify
5 Develop process improvement strategy
The implementation timing and sequencing of agreed changes is carefully planned so as to ensure a minimal amount of disruption to process performance. This planning will typically consider factors such as project criticality and status, process change effectiveness evaluation and new business generation
Actions
Process improvement plan: ReadOnly

(continued)

Table 9.2 (continued)

Project plan: ReadOnly
5 Evaluate process change effects
The effectiveness of changes is evaluated against actual results and adjustments are made as necessary to achieve relevant process improvement objectives
Actions
Defined process: ReadOnly
Process improvement plan: ReadOnly
Process improvements: ReadOnly
5 Identify process improvements
Identify potential process improvements
Actions
Process improvements: Create
Process improvement plan: ReadOnly
5 Identify real and potential task variation causes
Examine processes to anticipate and identify real or potential causes of variations in process
Actions
Business objectives: ReadOnly
Defined process: ReadOnly
Process performance data: ReadOnly
5 Manage process change implementation
The implementation timing and sequencing of agreed changes is carefully planned so as to ensure a minimal amount of disruption to process performance. This planning will typically consider factors such as project criticality and status, process change effectiveness evaluation and new business generation
Actions
Defined process: Modify
Process improvement plan: ReadOnly
Process improvements: ReadOnly

9.2 An Agile Method[1]

Here, we focus on a case study in which one particular agile method, eXtreme Programming (XP) (Beck 2000), was configured using MC Sandbox (Sect. 7.3.2) to suit particular project characteristics. The case study, originally reported by Karlsson and Ågerfalk (2008, 2009a), was performed in collaboration with a small Swedish software company with a global market. The case study involved three projects. This section will discuss two of these as detailed in Table 9.3—further details can be found in Karlsson and Ågerfalk (2009a) together with an explicit analysis of how the configured method adhered to agile values as per the Agile Manifesto (www.agilemanifesto.org).

[1] We acknowledge contributions of Dr. Fredrik Karlsson to this section.

Table 9.3 Characteristics of projects in the case study (after Karlsson and Ågerfalk 2009a)

Project	Type of information system	Person-hours	Duration (calendar months)	No. of developers
1	Web-based inventory system	1,500	4	5
2	Web-based time report system	800	2	4

Instead of providing a detailed description of all the method configurations, we make a brief overview of the two configurations and provide a selection of examples based on two configuration packages covering the two types of configuration situations where the potential to achieve rationality resonance is unsatisfactory or missing (see Table 6.7, Chap. 6 of this book). Karlsson and Ågerfalk (2009a) extend this discussion to include also a case in which the potential to achieve rationality resonance is satisfactory.

In the following, we draw on several data sources from the projects, including configurations stored in MC Sandbox, logbooks from method configuration workshops and interviews with developers. Through the method configuration workshops, all project members were involved in the configuration work where configuration packages and templates were either created or reused. The starting point for the configuration work was XP implemented as a base method in MC Sandbox (see Sect. 7.3.2) with some additional method components, mainly adopted from the Rational Unified Process. The developers could also add configuration packages and templates along the way. In the configuration work, the project members used the external view of the method components to discuss the components and implications of different configuration choices. The internal view had to be consulted only in cases where the method component content was unknown to the project members. The objective was to increase understanding of each participant's specific method needs as a basis for consensus decisions regarding method configuration. One project member was in charge of documenting the configuration decisions in MC Sandbox. However, depending on what method parts were in focus, different people took the responsibility of driving the work forward. As outlined in Sect. 7.3.2, MC Sandbox offers a facility to store information about configuration decisions along with comments that explain why the decisions were made. Information about decisions is stored in a structured format while comments are stored as free text. The latter facilitated storing of arguments as quotations from the configuration workshops.

9.2.1 Configuration Templates

An important characteristic of MMC (the Method for Method Configuration) is its focus on reuse of configurations, which was useful since the projects showed a number of similarities. For example, they all involved development of web-based systems. Table 9.4 shows the characteristics and configuration packages resulting from the method configuration work. The two rightmost columns in the table show

Table 9.4 Examples of configurations (after Karlsson and Ågerfalk 2009a)

Characteristic	Configuration package	Project 1	2
Knowledge about business process	High	•	
	Low		•
On-site customer	Yes	•	
	No		•
Co-located project team	Yes		•
	No	•	
Type of testing	Automated		•
	Manual		

the combination of configuration packages for each project, i.e., they illustrate the suggested configuration templates.

9.2.2 Configuration Packages

The content of configuration templates builds on the content of configuration packages. We chose to illustrate and exemplify the configuration content in this case study with two different configuration packages covering two of the three degrees of potential to achieve rationality resonance (see Table 6.7, Chap. 6 of this book):

- 'Knowledge about business process = Low'
- 'On-site customer = No'.

The first configuration package illustrates how the base method was complemented with aspects that are not present in standard XP. When this happens, rationality resonance cannot be achieved without extending the base method with additional components. The second configuration package illustrates how the developers questioned the operationalisation of a basic value in XP (to have a high degree of interaction with the end user), i.e., the potential to achieve rationality resonance was limited (unsatisfactory) in this scenario.

9.2.2.1 Knowledge About Business Process = Low

The first configuration package (Knowledge about business process = Low) concerns how the project teams plan to go about increasing their knowledge of the business process. Based on their knowledge of the base method, the developers determined that business modelling is not supported by standard XP. Consequently, they turned to additional methods to find something that could be used as a complement. It turned out that some of the developers had earlier experience of the Rational Unified Process so they chose to adopt parts of its business modelling discipline. Table 9.5 shows the four method components that the developers decided to add to this configuration package.

Table 9.5 Configuration package: Knowledge about business process = Low

Method component	Method component's rationale	Classification
c1: Business Vision	To capture and communicate very high-level objectives of a business effort	Added as is
c2: Business Use Case	To describe the value-added aspect of the business process	Added as is
c3: Business Use Case Model	To provide an overview of the direction and intent of the business	Added as is
c4: Business Glossary	To understand the terms that are specific to the project	Added as is

The first method component was the 'Business vision'. The developers expressed that achieving "a high-level view" of the business was important. As one developer puts it, "it [the Business vision] can work much like the Vision [card], but for business modelling" (Karlsson and Ågerfalk 2009a). From the system developers' comments in MC Sandbox, we find the following, "Necessary to provide a comprehensive landmark, but still being fairly simple" (Karlsson and Ågerfalk 2009a). Thus, it was perceived to tie in with the overall way of working as suggested by XP.

The second component addressed was the Business Use Case. The project members found it essential to be able to capture business process details in order to know "where to plug the [information] system into the business", in order "not to push a cube through a round whole". They thus expressed a need to understand how the business could be supported by a new information system.

The third component added is the Business Use Case Model. It became clear from the workshops that this component is closely associated with the Business Use Case component: "it is needed to create an overview", "you get that [the Business Use Case Model] into the bargain when working with Business Use Cases".

Finally, the Business Glossary component was selected, although opinions differed. Two developers regarded the Business Glossary "unnecessary". However, counterarguments were provided by other developers: "concepts tend to become important" and "when you are unskilled in a business, terms are difficult [to remember]". Once the dust had settled, it was decided to add the component.

Considering rationality resonance, we find that such exists between the first three method components and each of the system developers in the two project teams that used the configuration packages. Table 9.6 illustrates this. Here A2.1 means that the rationale of project member one in the second project resonated with Method component c1. When it comes to the last method component, the Business Glossary, however, rationality resonance is not achieved with two of the developers—one in the second team and one in the third team.

9.2.2.2 On-site Customer = No

The focus of the second configuration package (On-site customer = No) is on how the project teams plan to handle the situation when no customer will be on-site. Table 9.7 shows the included method components and their classifications.

Table 9.6 Experienced rationality resonance: knowledge about business process = Low

Method component	Rationality resonance
c1: Business Vision	A2.1-A2.4
c2: Business Use Case	A2.1-A2.4
c3: Business Use Case Model	A2.1-A2.4
c4: Business Glossary	A2.1, A2.2, A2.4

Table 9.7 Configuration package: on-site customer = No

Method component	Method component's rationale	Classification
c5: Vision card	To capture the purpose of the system	Perform as is
c6: Metaphor	To describe the system's likeness	Perform informal
c7: User story	To describe a path through the system	Omit
c8: Use case	To understand the system's behaviour	Exchanges as is

Table 9.8 Experienced rationality resonance: on-site customer = No

Component	Rationality resonance
c5: Vision Card	A2.1-A2.4
c6: Metaphor	A2.1-A2.4
c8: Use case	A2.1-A2.4

The first component of this configuration package is the Vision card. The system developers suggested that it was important for the customer to be able to "depict the future system" and that the feasibility of this method component "does not change with this kind of relationship to the customer". Hence, the method component was to be performed as described in the base method (XP).

The second method component was the Metaphor, which was suggested to be used on an informal basis. As noted by one of the system developers in a method configuration workshop, "we use them frequently but usually we do not document them". According to the MMC classification scheme, this is an example of 'Perform informal'.

The final two method components in Table 9.7 illustrate the replacement of User stories with Use cases. The rationale for replacing the method component was that User stories were not detailed enough since, according to the developers, "we need to compensate [the increased distance] with more details", "one needs tools that are not that interaction intense" and "I view it [the use case] as a more suitable way".

Table 9.8 shows the analysis of rationality resonance for this configuration package. Two of the three method components found in the configuration package are original method components from XP. Rationality resonance is found between all three method components and the developers. Everyone agreed that these were suitable to include in the configuration package.[2]

[2] Note, however, that Karlsson and Ågerfalk (2009a) report on a third project within the same organisation where this was not the case, and analyse the consequences.

9.2.3 Discussion

In this section, we have explored MMC as a tool for method configuration. With regard to the configurations made in the two projects some notable insights can be drawn.

In the examined cases, MMC was very much used as a vehicle for quality assurance. Derived from the notion of method rationale, each method component contains the goals that it operationalises. This selection mechanism worked well in the case described here. Throughout the method configuration process, all changes were mapped to agile goals as per the Agile Manifesto. According to the developers, this worked well as a way to understand better their own work practices and rationale: "we have discussed our needs", "now everybody ought to know why these things [the selected method components] are important" and "though we did not change it [the method], we discussed why". MMC thus facilitated a discussion of the association between actors, method components and agile goals in this case. This is a unique aspect of method engineering approaches that embrace method rationale. One critical way to implement that focus is the use of interfaces. The case study indicates that an interface/body model is useful when adopting method-user-centred method configuration.

An interesting distinction between this study and previous research on tailoring of agile methods is the project members' awareness of their tailoring decisions. The empirical material shows that the developers made deliberate choices with regard to higher level principles such as agile goals and values. In situations where method parts were exchanged, these changes were carefully designed with regard to the overall agile goals of the team. In the specific case above, where the customer was not on-site, the studied projects revealed difficulties in fulfilling the agile goal that business people and developers should work together daily throughout the project. This initiated a discussion on how to choose a different operationalisation, and on what part of the goal was the root-cause of the problem: "it [method rationale] created awareness", "we came to discuss how to mitigate this risk [increased distance]" and "we were able to check against the different goals".

The study also shows that rationality resonance is not something that can easily be discussed at the project team level. Therefore, the method rationale framework facilitates the tracing of rationality resonance to individual combinations of project members and method components. Rationality resonance did not exist between all system developers and the focussed method components. That is, not all project members agreed that the choices made led to the achievement of important goals. One of the developers who did not want to include a business glossary, for example, expressed: "Though we disagree I understand what they want to achieve . . . I just do not find it that important". Another developer disagreed with replacing user stories with use cases: "use cases do not compensate [for the increased distance] . . . I think it was an unnecessary exchange". Thus, although MMC does not always generate consensus decisions, it facilitates the creation of awareness of different project members' opinions.

9.3 A Method for Business Formalisation and Innovation

In this section, we report on the elaboration of a situation-specific method created for a small company operating in the domain of e-commerce. The objective of this work was to provide the company with methodological support allowing the specification of its business model and business processes and then to explore their potential evolution and related innovations. This objective emerged during a brainstorming session with the company's employees about their daily activities, potential evolution and business. This session clearly demonstrated that the understanding and opinions of different persons concerning this subject are divergent; one of the reasons being that the company does not have any documentation of its business activities and applications. We followed the assembly-based SME approach (Ralyté et al. 2003; Mirbel and Ralyté 2006), discussed in Chap. 6, to construct a project-specific method dedicated to specify the company's business situation with a set of models. According to this approach, the SME process consists of three main steps: method requirements specification, method chunks selection and assembly of selected method chunks (see Fig. 9.2).

9.3.1 Method Requirements Specification

As shown in Fig. 9.2, there are two strategies for specifying situation-specific method requirements: *intention-driven* and *process-driven*. The *intention-driven* strategy is especially suitable for an existing method adaptation by adding new intentions and/or strategies while the *process-driven* strategy is relevant in the case of a brand new method construction. In this case study, a new method was necessary because the company did not use any particular method and we could not identify any existing method fully satisfying the project's situation. This strategy requires the assessment of the enterprise/project situation first and then the identification of a set of engineering intentions that are required to be fulfilled by the new method and then to order them by using the Map formalism (Rolland et al. 1999)—discussed in Chap. 4.

In this case, the evaluation of company's situation was characterised by a set of criteria; some of them are shown in Table 9.9.

The characterisation above demonstrates that, in order to stay competitive in the market, this company has to constantly increase its offerings and to innovate its business strategy. However, it does not have any well-structured documentation concerning its business model, activities and data. In a few years, this company will not be a start-up anymore and having an appropriate documentation will therefore be key for the evolution of the enterprise. Therefore, we have identified two main objectives (representing two phases of method application) that should be satisfied by the new method: (1) to document the enterprise business situation and (2) to discover potential business evolution options based on the analysis of the produced models. In particular, it was decided to use three modelling perspectives: business, business process and information (data) models in both method phases with

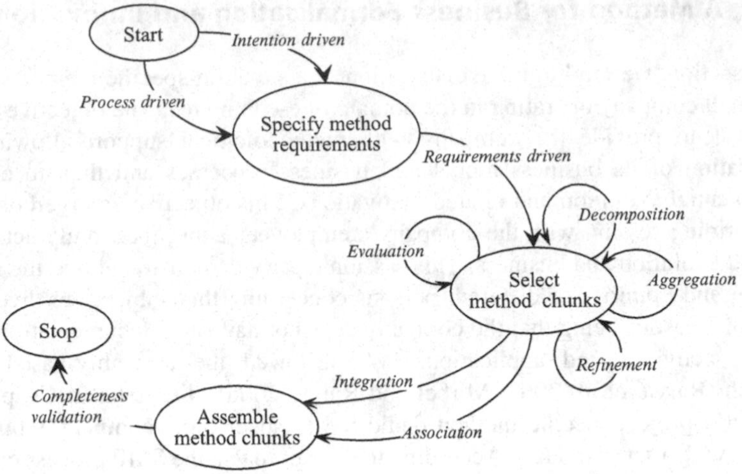

Fig. 9.2 Process model for assembly-based situational method engineering (Ralyté et al., figure 2, 2003) (With kind permission of Springer Science + Business Media)

Table 9.9 Characterisation of the enterprise situation

Criteria	Evaluation
Size of the company	Very small enterprise (seven employees) with an aim to grow
Maturity	Founded in 2010 with one specialised e-commerce web store. In 2011, the company grows to nine web stores. The objective for 2012–2020 stores
Market	Niche market based on the 'market to demand' model
Need for innovation and evolution	High: the company has to permanently look for new niche products to increase their offer—to create new web stores
Need for strategic watch	High: the company has to watch technology and business innovations to stay competitive on the market
Management of growth	By project: the creation of each new store is managed as a project
Impact and risk of each new project	High
IS/business documentation	No formal or semi-formal documentation available concerning business activities, information system and applications

potentially different strategies to manipulate these models. During the first phase of the method application, these models should serve to specify the As-Is situation, while in the second phase they should be used to discover and evaluate the potential To-Be situations. The requirements map for the new method construction is illustrated in Fig. 9.3. It says that the method will be based on two main intentions (*Document enterprise business situation* and *Discover business evolutions*) and identifies the types of approaches/techniques that should be used to achieve these intentions in terms of generic strategies (e.g., *Business modelling techniques*,

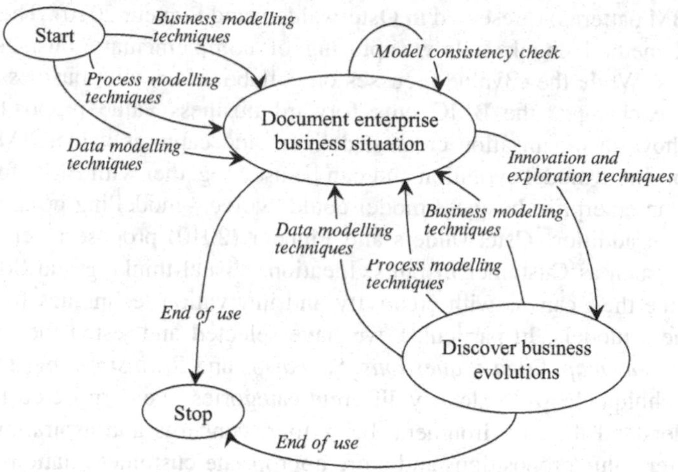

Fig. 9.3 Requirements map for the new method construction (after Ralyté 2013)

Process modelling techniques). In the next step, we use this requirements map to select appropriate method chunks.

9.3.2 Method Chunks Selection

Once the method requirements have been specified, the selection of the method chunks matching these requirements can start. The *Requirements-driven strategy* (see Fig. 9.2) helps to formulate method chunk selection queries by giving values to the attributes of the descriptors and interfaces of method chunks (see method chunk definition in Chap. 4). For example,

> Select method chunks where
> Design activity = 'Process modelling'
> AND Situation = 'Activity description'
> AND Intention = 'Define process model'

At least one method chunk has to be selected for each requirements map section (i.e., <source intention, target intention, strategy>). *Evaluation*, *Decomposition*, *Aggregation* and *Refinement* strategies can be used to refine the candidate chunk selection by refining the selection query and analysing more in depth if the chunk matches the requirements.

In our case, we did not have a fully operational repository and the selection of method chunks was mainly based on literature review. For example, for business model construction, we have selected three method chunks: e3value (Gordijn and Akkermans 2001), business model canvas (BMC) and related business model patterns (BM patterns) (presented in Osterwalders and Pigneur 2010). The e3 value and BMC method chunks allow capturing of complementary business model perspectives. While the e3value focusses on collaborations with business partners and value exchanges, the BMC puts forward business value propositions and describes how an organisation creates, delivers and captures value. BM patterns facilitate business model evolution and can be used together with BMC for discovering how an enterprise business model could evolve—modelling possible To-Be situations. In addition, Osterwalders and Pigneur (2010) propose a set of design approaches such as Customer insights, Ideation, Visual thinking and Storytelling that combine their canvas with creativity and innovation techniques for creating new business models. In particular, we have selected and tested the techniques named *Empathy map*, *What-if questions*, *Scenarios* and *Brainstorming*. The *Empathy map* technique helps to identify different categories of enterprise customers, to better understand their environment, behaviour, concerns and aspirations and to design better value propositions and more appropriate customer relationships. The *What-if questions* help team members to break free of constraints imposed by current models, while *Scenarios* allow the imagining of new ways of realising business activities. We recommend completing the application of these techniques with concluding brainstorming sessions. Table 9.10 lists the method chunks selected for each requirements map section.

9.3.3 Method Chunks Assembly

As shown Fig. 9.2, the assembly-based SME approach identifies two strategies, named *Association* and *Integration,* to assemble selected method chunks into a new method. The integration strategy has to be applied if selected method chunks have similar engineering goals, their process and/or product models overlap (i.e., contain same or similar elements) and they are used to produce the same deliverable (e.g., the same model). Otherwise, the association strategy is used to position the method chunks in the new method and provide guidelines for their execution. In our case, the method chunks representing two business modelling techniques—e3value and BMC—have the same engineering goal—to construct a business model, but they produce different and complementary business models. Therefore, the association strategy is sufficient to indicate that these two method chunks can be applied in parallel without any particular ordering. In contrast, BMC and BM patterns are overlapping method chunks because they use the same canvas model. However, the integration of these two method chunks already exists because they are extracted from the same approach (Osterwalders and Pigneur 2010). Other selected method chunks deal with complementary engineering goals and simple association is sufficient to combine them into the desired method. Figure 9.4 illustrates the process model of the assembled method.

Table 9.10 Selection of method chunks according to the method requirements

Requirements map sections	Selected method chunks
<Start, Document enterprise business situation, Business modelling techniques>	e3value (Gordijn and Akkermans 2001)
<Discover business evolutions, Document enterprise business situation, Business modelling techniques>	Business model canvas (Osterwalders and Pigneur 2010)
	Business modelling patterns (Osterwalders and Pigneur 2010)
<Define Business Model, Define Process Model, Process modelling techniques>	BPMN is selected for modelling enterprise activities in terms of process models. In particular, we recommend using guidelines provided in (Silver 2009)
<Discover business evolutions, Document enterprise business situation, Process modelling techniques>	
<Start, Document enterprise business situation, Data modelling techniques>	UML class diagrams fit very well for producing data models
<Discover business evolutions, Document enterprise business situation, Data modelling techniques>	
<Document enterprise business situation, Document enterprise business situation, Model consistency check>	The objective here is to validate the consistency between the three types of models (business, process and data models). We could not identify an existing method chunk supporting this task and have to define a set of consistency validation rules to cover this method requirement
<Document enterprise business situation, Discover business evolutions, Innovation and exploration techniques>	Extracted form (Osterwalders and Pigneur 2010)
	Empathy map
	What-if questions
	Scenarios
	Brainstorming
<Document enterprise business situation, Stop, End of use>	The application of the method stops when the enterprise decides to stop the use of the documentation obtained by applying this method
<Discover business evolutions, Stop, End of use>	

9.3.4 Concluding Remarks Concerning the Method Application

Several collaboration and modelling sessions have been organised together with company's employees in order to specify the initial business documentation. In particular, we have developed e3 value and BMC models to represent the company's business model. Enterprise activities were formalised with business process models by using BPMN notation and the data models with class diagrams. This project permitted the production of semi-formal documentation of enterprise business and unified employees' awareness of company's business structure and activities.

The second phase of our method was tested by applying the Empathy map technique, which permitted the identification of new ways to improve customers' loyalty and even to transform them into purchasing advisors.

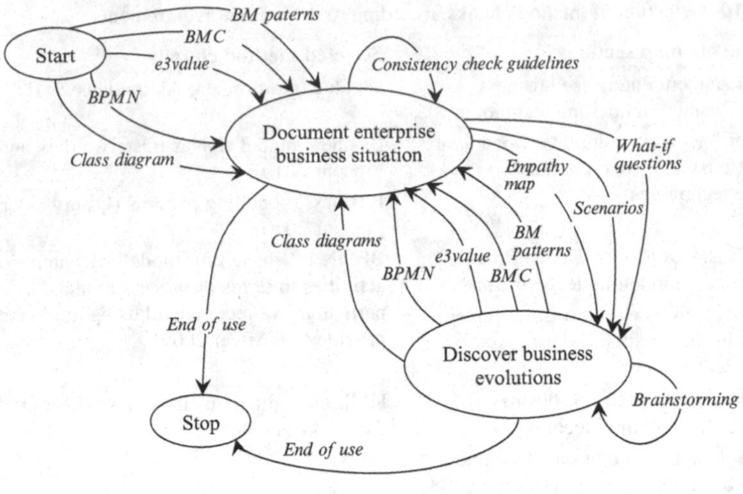

Fig. 9.4 Process model of the constructed method (after Ralyté 2013)

9.4 A Method for Rapid Prototyping of Mobile Applications

In this section, we describe construction of a method for developing mobile applications using the CSC method. Mobile applications are one of the growth areas of the software industry and, since there is little previous experience by the developers and the applications are often rather small and made for specific purposes, they are very suitable for method development using SME.

In this section, we describe the development of a user- and needs-centred rapid prototyping method that employs a well-known requirements gathering method from marketing, CSC and ties that together with a prototyping method for Symbian phones, allowing for fast prototyping and agile development with testing in demo or production settings of mobile applications.

9.4.1 Conceptual Specification of the Approach Used

The selected conceptual structure and process, CSC, is described in Fig. 9.5 (the CSC metamodel) and in Table 9.11 where we provide a step-by-step description of the method.

The process of CSC starts by selection of participants for the elicitation process. After the selection process, the prospects are contacted and, during, for example, a telephone conversation, stimuli for the system are collected informally. These are later used in the requirement elicitation phase where the method utilises a variation of in-depth interview called laddering. This has been used successfully in marketing to define features of consumer products. Laddering tries to perceive how people see

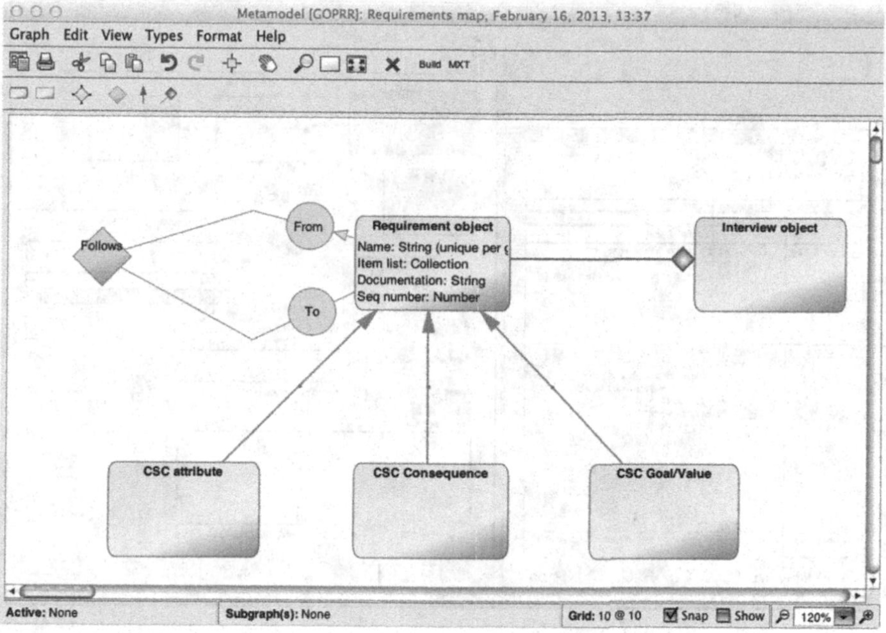

Fig. 9.5 Metamodel of CSC

Table 9.11 Critical success chains process description

CSC process	Objectives
Pre-study preparation Determine scope and participants. Collect project idea stimuli	*Determine scope to manage complexity* Select participants to represent views you need to understand, e.g., employees at various levels, suppliers, customers and experts Arrange for data collection Collect interview stimuli
Data collection Elicit personal constructs from organisational members	*Ask participant to rank-order stimuli on importance* Ask series of "Why would this system be important...?" questions to collect consequence and value data Ask series of "What is it about this system that makes you think it would do that...?" questions to collect attribute data Record answers as linked chains Collect several chains from each participant
Analysis Aggregate personal constructs into CSC models	*Interpret individual statements and label consistently across participants* Cluster chains Map clusters into network models
Ideation workshops Elicit feasible strategic IS from technical and business experts and customers	*Recruit workshop participants with technical and business skills* Evaluate CSC network models and develop 'back-of-the-envelope' ideas for IS projects that satisfy the relationships implicit in the models

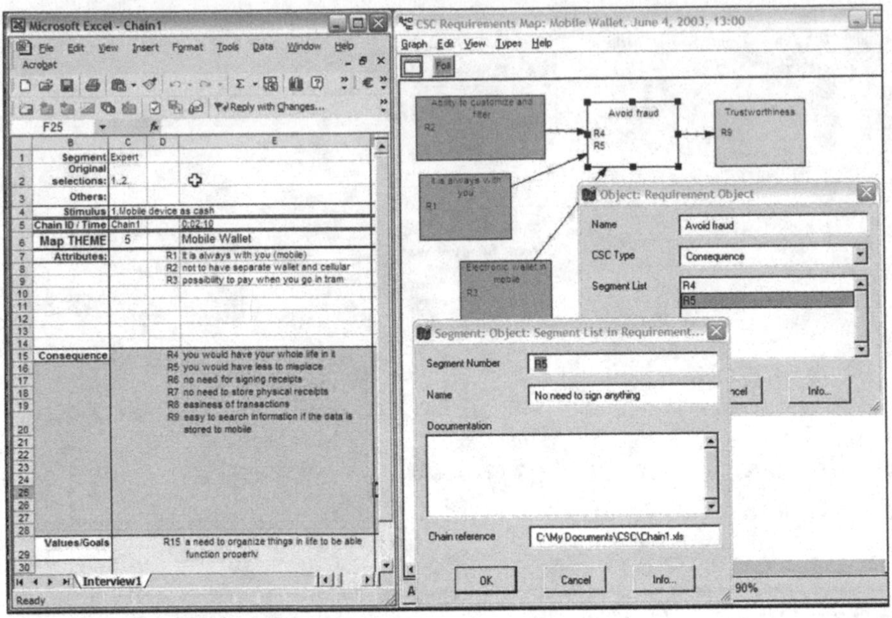

Fig. 9.6 The implemented CSC environment

and understand the surrounding world. Hence, by using laddering, implicit requirements can be made explicit in order to understand what the end-users actually want. The ladders can be collected during the interview, or in a post-process of transcribing the interviews and reconstructing the ladders. The individual ladders form chains.

In the analysis phase of CSC, identified chains are clustered. A partial example of a chain is presented in Fig. 9.6 that describes a mobile wallet application for mobile phone. It can be seen that 'trustworthiness' and 'no need to sign anything' are important system features, one of the key reasons being to avoid fraud. These, in turn, result in a greater level of trust and economic security. The purpose of these 'CSC maps' is to show managers within few minutes what are the most beneficial features.

A simplified version of the CSC model using GOPRR metamodelling language within MetaEdit+ was then constructed. The formal metamodel (Fig. 9.5) allows the analysis of the method's conceptual structure, as well as immediate tool support for modelling systems using the method; see Fig. 9.6 for an example of this. The SME-constructed method can be regarded as a domain-specific method (DSM).

Figure 9.5 shows part of the conceptual definition of the CSC method according to GOPRR. The method definition is done by identifying the key objects of the method, connecting them by the relationship types and adding properties to those. Roles define how different object types can participate in the relationships; in our model, it describes the interaction connection between the CSC metamodel and the

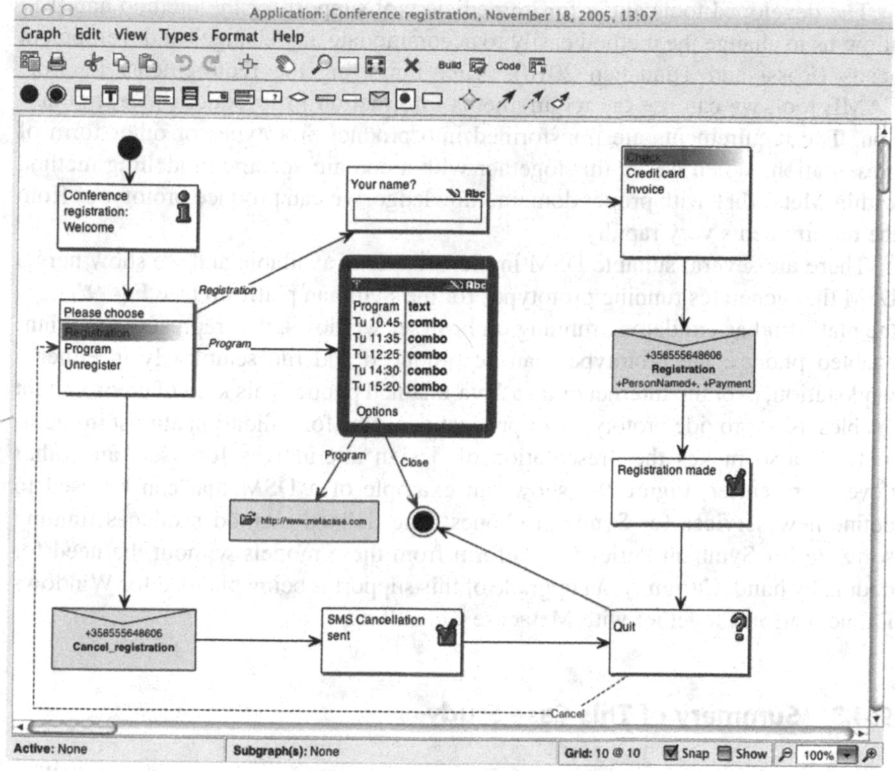

Fig. 9.7 Example of a method for developing Symbian applications

data collected by an in-depth interviewing method stored in a spreadsheet. When the objects and relationships are defined with their graphical representations, we have a complete conceptual specification of the method, which can be used immediately for modelling.

9.4.2 Constructed Method Support Environment

When the conceptual and graphical presentation of the CSC method has been completed, they can be used to analyse chains. In Figs. 9.6 and 9.7, the developed method in use is shown within MetaEdit+. An example model was created that constitutes a part of the CSC map, and the ladders mapped back to this specific diagram. The model includes objects (attributes, consequences and values) with references to the individual segments, i.e., the ladders in the chain. Additionally, we can show how it is possible to enable hyper linking to the original spreadsheet containing the actual interview data. The given example chain also includes a hyperlink into the interview recording that is indexed according to the chain's starting time.

The developed tools allow for immediate tool support for the method and they allow us to change the method easily to accommodate any changes in development needs (Rossi and Tuunanen 2010). After importing the requirements into the CAME tool, we can use the requirements information for product concept definition. The requirements are transformed into product prototypes or other form of presentation. When we tie this together with a domain-specific modelling method within MetaEdit+ with proper domain knowledge, we can produce prototypes from the requirements very rapidly.

There are several suitable DSM implementations available and we show here a DSM that generates running prototypes for the Symbian platform (see Fig. 9.7). As the platform has emulators, running on browser windows, that represent Symbian-enabled phones, the prototypes can be produced and run seamlessly in either a workstation, over the Internet or on a Java-enabled phone. This kind of environment enables us to provide prototypes or product concepts for validation almost immediately. It also makes the presentation of design alternatives for users and other developers easier. Figure 9.7 shows an example of a DSM that can be used to define new services for Symbian phones. The defined method produces running software for Symbian Series 60 platform from these models without the need for coding by hand. Currently, an upgrade of this support is being planned for Windows Phone platform together with Metacase Consulting.

9.4.3 Summary of This Case Study

In this section, we have shown how to develop a domain-specific modelling language and its supporting environment for a mobile platform. The described case study shows how a situational method engineering environment is not only suitable for large companies, but for any size of company that has a novel development situation and a good understanding of what the needs are of the domain. The DSM approach is particularly suitable when the domain is new and a target run-time platform (such as a mobile operating system and its APIs) is available (for further details see Rossi and Tuunanen 2010).

9.5 Summary

In this chapter, we have presented in brief four case studies of how SME ideas have been used ‘for real’. The various method construction techniques discussed earlier in this book have all been used to assist an organisation to create a quality method for its software development endeavours.

We have purposefully highlighted different aspects of SME: from bottom-up construction of a new method to tailoring an existing one; for mobile and agile development environments; and using a CAME tool as an integral part of the method construction, evaluation and utilisation.

Part III

The Future of SME

Recent Advances in SME

10

Summary of What We Will Learn in Chapter 10

- How SOA can be merged with the ideas of SME
- How the underpinning ideas of SME that relate to method construction and tailoring can also be applied to the construction and tailoring of metamodels
- How recent discussions on the relationship between metamodels and modelling languages might impact SME

In the earlier chapters of this book, we have introduced a comprehensive review of the state-of-the-art in situational method engineering. However, over the last few years, there have been published a number of new ideas that are highly relevant to SME. In particular, we highlight in this chapter just three of these: how SME support service-oriented architectures (SOA), the application of SME to metamodels known as situational metamodel engineering (SMME) and recent discussions regarding the overall metamodelling architecture and how modelling languages might be a better focus than metamodels.

10.1 SOA Addressed by SME

Recently there has been an upsurge in SOA that has led to a new focus within the SME community (Guzélian and Cauvet 2007; Deneckère et al. 2008; Rolland 2009; Ralyté et al. 2011). Rolland (2009) has elaborated on the idea of applying the service-oriented approach notions to SME and has defined the underpinning concepts of Method as a Service (MaaS) and method-oriented architecture (MOA). Gholami et al. (2011) have developed new atomic method fragments suitable for inclusion in the OPF repository. Despite its novelty and vision, currently this idea has been explored in only a very limited way. We can mention two

B. Henderson-Sellers et al., *Situational Method Engineering*,
DOI 10.1007/978-3-642-41467-1_10, © Springer-Verlag Berlin Heidelberg 2014

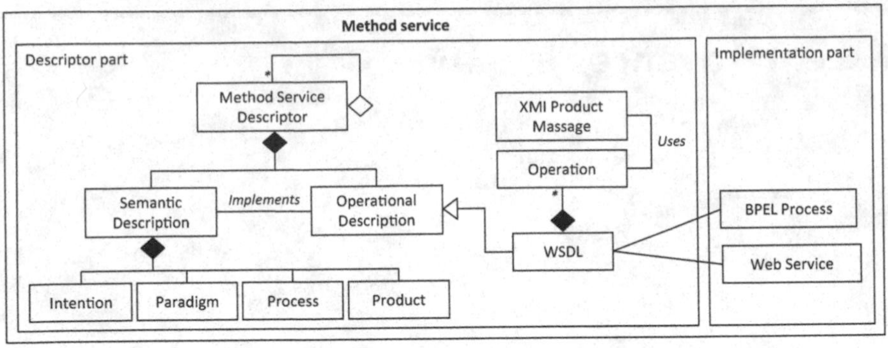

Fig. 10.1 Metamodel for a method service chunk (after Deneckère et al. 2008)

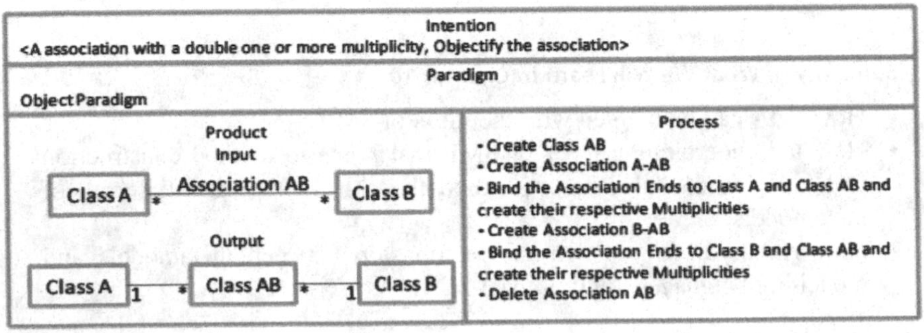

Fig. 10.2 Example method service chunk: descriptor for the 'Objectify' fragment (after Deneckère et al. 2008)

approaches: MaaS (Deneckère et al. 2008; Iacovelli et al. 2008) and SO2M (Guzélian and Cauvet 2007; Cauvet 2010).

Deneckère et al. (2008) analysed the drawbacks of existing metamodels of method fragments and chunks and then, based on the MaaS idea, proposed a new concept for method fragment implementation, called *method service*. According to their definition, a method service comprises two basic parts: (1) the 'method service descriptor' documenting the method chunk/fragment implemented by the method service (the semantic description of the method service goal and operational description of the method service activities) and (2) the 'implementation part' containing the executable code for method service application (Fig. 10.1). An example, for an 'Objectify' chunk is shown in Fig. 10.2. Iacovelli et al. (2008) further discuss the implementation of MaaS and the adaptation of SOA technology to MOA.

The SO2M approach proposes the notion of method service as a means to implement method components and to enable the construction of new methods by discovering, adapting and dynamically composing existing method services. Formally, a method service is defined as having three parts: (1) the 'identification part' defining the goal of the method service, (2) the 'process part' describing the

Table 10.1 Contextual variables and their possible values (after Börner, table 1, 2011, With kind permission of Springer Science + Business Media)

Context variable	Parameter values
Company size	Small or medium-sized enterprise
	Large company
Service consumers	Internal consumer
	External consumer
	Internal and external consumers
Budget	Generous funding
	Low budget
Skills and experience	SOA skills available
	BPM skills available
	Both skills available
	None available
SOA maturity level	SIMM level 1–3
	SIMM level 4–7
Compliance	Standard legal compliance
	Special regulations
	Internal policies
IT department	Existent
	Non-existent
Interaction	Customer interaction
	Employee interaction
	Customer and employee interaction
Organisational structure	One product company
	Multiple product company

preconditions and postconditions and the structure of the process for achieving the service goal and (3) the 'resource part' defining the solution offered by the service, which is an executable process described in terms of activities and objects and corresponds to a process fragment in other approaches.

Another representation of coarser granularity method elements is seen in the metamodel element called 'conglomerate' in ISO/IEC 24744 (a.k.a. SEMDM). This is defined as follows: "A conglomerate is *a collection of related methodology elements that can be reused in different methodological contexts*. Conglomerates provide the basic reuse mechanism in the SEMDM." For example, "In a given methodology, the process kind 'Quality Assurance', the document kinds 'Quality Standard' and 'Quality Report' and the team kind 'Quality Assurance Team' (all of them methodology elements) are put into a conglomerate named 'Quality-Related Fragments' so that a methodologist can, easily and in a single step, incorporate it to a customised methodology or remove it from a methodology" (ISO/IEC 2007, p. 20).

Börner (2011) identifies nine major situational factors for method fragments as services—the possible values for which are depicted in Table 10.1. Comparison of this table with the generic table for situational factors discussed in Chap. 1 (Table 1.1) indicates the difference in the target audience sought in these SOA studies.

Yet another coarser grained approach is the use of 'practices'. Despite there being a lack of a concise definition for this approach, it may in the future be an appropriate coarse-grained method part that will be of value to some industries. It is argued that this is a good way to divert the focus of attention from the method engineer to the software developer (see, e.g., OMG 2011).

10.2 Situational Metamodel Engineering

As we have seen, situational method engineering creates, stores and uses method fragments via a method base or repository of method parts (fragments, chunks, patterns, etc.). An SME user then extracts method parts and combines them with situational characteristics in order to create a situationally specific method. Sometimes, there is a pre-existing method that is to be modified (rather than a method being created) during the SME process.

In the same way that any one organisation is unlikely to wish to use *all* the elements of any method base, however tightly focussed it is on their domain (such as the enterprise architecture management method base of Buckl et al. 2011), it is unlikely that they will wish to use all the facilities embodied in one of the standard metamodels—or perhaps wish to use parts of several. This has led to two research lines: an investigation into the interoperability between metamodels (e.g., Henderson-Sellers et al. 2012; Qureshi 2012) and the creation of the subdiscipline (to SME) of SMME as proposed by Hug et al. (2009)—a highly similar approach to SME but focussed on the creation and modification of metamodels rather than methods (a.k.a. process models—see Fig. 1.8). They named this 'situational metamodel engineering' or SMME.

In SMME, the repository stores one (or possibly more) metamodel—but a metamodel that is comprehensive in nature, i.e., much larger than needed in any one situation. (Part-metamodels may also be stored here.) Assuming this exists (which it currently doesn't but will in the very near future, e.g., Henderson-Sellers et al. 2012), then a smaller and highly situationally specific metamodel is 'carved out' from this much larger metamodel (Fig. 10.3). In the situation when a metamodel is currently in use, then the slightly modified approach (parallel to Fig. 1.5) merges situationally specific metamodel parts into an existing model as shown in Fig. 10.4.

There now arises the question regarding how a method engineer can create a metamodel most appropriate for her/his needs. Hug et al. (2009) examine these issues based on earlier work on metamodel patterns (Hug et al. 2007b). Furthermore, the majority of the process metamodels do not offer any extension or adaptation mechanism, the exceptions being SPEM (OMG 2005a) and ISO/IEC 24744 (Henderson-Sellers and Gonzalez-Perez 2006a; ISO/IEC 2007). To do this, Hug et al. (2008) devised a two-phase method consisting of the selection of a metamodel (or metamodel part), followed by refinement, in which metamodelling

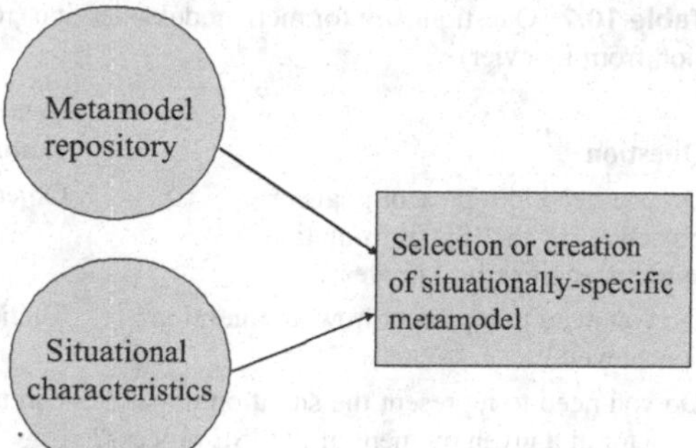

Fig. 10.3 Engineering a situational metamodel

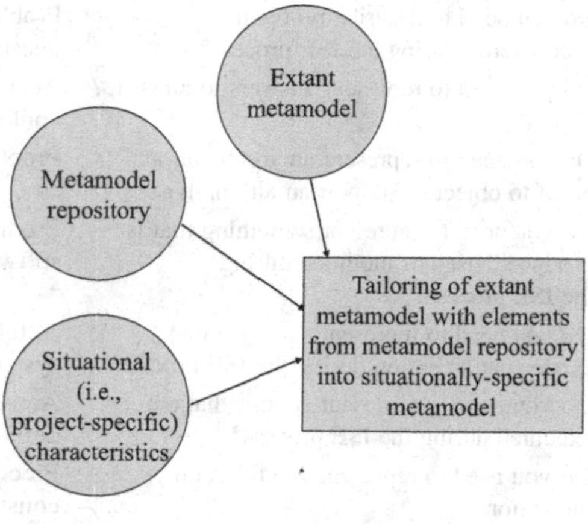

Fig. 10.4 Engineering a situationally specific metamodel from an existing one

patterns and business patterns (Hug et al. 2007b) are applied (see also Hug 2009). The metamodel pattern, called Concept–Concept Category (Hug et al. 2007a), builds on earlier patterns of Coad (1992) and on the Deep Instantiation idea of Atkinson and Kühne (2001a) together with the powertype pattern (Odell 1994; Gonzalez-Perez and Henderson-Sellers 2006a).

In the selection phase, a questionnaire similar to that of Henderson-Sellers and Nguyen (2004) has to be completed (Table 10.2) where each question corresponds to one of the concepts of the Process domain metamodel. The answers to the questionnaire will help to determine which concepts are included in the draft process metamodel and which are to be excluded. For example, if the method engineer answers 'yes' to the first question, the draft process metamodel will include the Intention concept.

Hug et al. (2009) note that by selecting one metamodel part, it is often inevitable that another must accompany it. For instance, if the concepts of Work Unit and Work Product are chosen, then there must also be associations of 'in' and 'out'. Sometimes, there is a more direct existence dependency. Depender–dependee relationships are shown in Table 10.3. As before, the selected draft metamodel can be depicted with the MAP formalism of Rolland et al. (1999).

Table 10.2 Questionnaire for metamodel selection (reprinted from Hug et al. 2009, with permission from Elsevier)

Question	Synonyms, also known as, examples	Concept
Do you need to represent goals or objectives of the ISE (information systems engineering) process?	Objective, goal, subgoal	Intention
Do you need to represent how an intention is achieved?	Tactics, approach, manner	Strategy
Do you need to represent the situation of an actor at a given moment of the ISE process?	Circumstance	Situation
Do you need to represent both intention and situation?		Context
Do you need to describe problems encountered during the ISE process?	Problem, toughness, question, difficulty	Issue
Do you need to represent answers to an issue?	Answer, choice, possibility, contingency, option, dilemma	Alternative
Do you need to represent an argument, a proof to object or support an alternative?	Proof, reason	Argument
Do you need to represent something that is produced, used or modified during the ISE process?	Product, document, model, software, program	Work Product
Do you need to represent someone that carries out an action during the ISE process?	Actor, developer, analyst, system	Role
Do you need to represent actions that are executed during the ISE process?	Activity, phase, task, work definition	Work Unit
Do you need to represent condition on the action?	Precondition, postcondition, constraint	Condition

Table 10.3 The depender concepts and their dependee concepts (reprinted from Hug et al. 2009, with permission from Elsevier)

Depender	Dependee
Strategy	{Source Intention ∧ Target Intention}
Context	{Situation ∧ Intention}
Argument	Alternative
Alternative	Issue
Condition	Work Unit
Role	{Alternative ∨ Work Unit ∨ Work Product}

During the refinement phase, the method engineer selects the concepts needed to ensure that all organisational requirements have been met. For each concept, they can choose to reuse an existing metamodelling pattern or a business pattern, selecting them appropriately by consideration of the situational factors (Figs. 10.4 and 10.5). The result of this second phase can also be depicted with the MAP formalism.

Hug et al. (2009) also suggest the use of a P-Sigma formalism (Conte et al. 2002) (Table 10.4) as a standardised and more formal representation of the patterns, thus forming a pattern system. It offers a way of expressing the semantics common to the majority of formalisms proposed in the literature, in order to support a quality

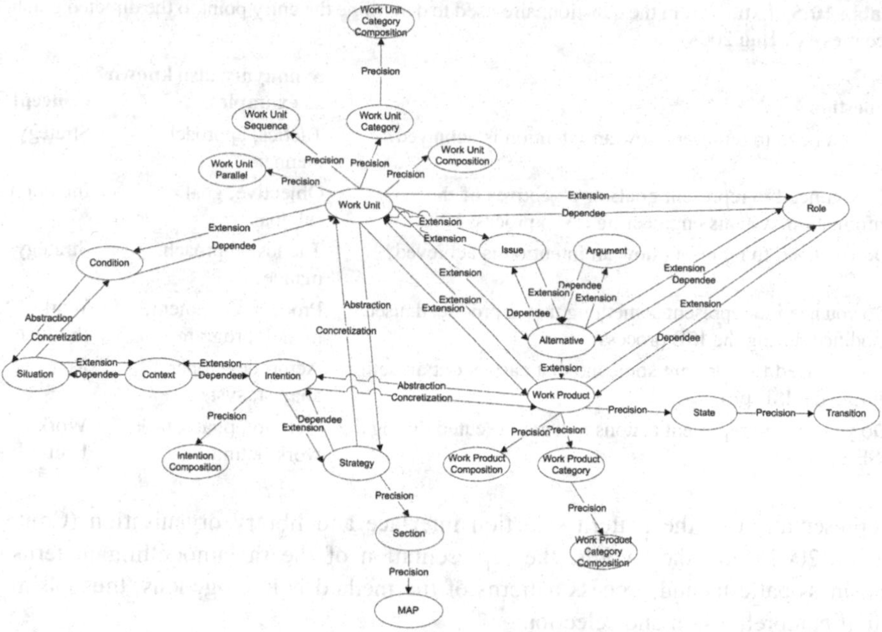

Fig. 10.5 Directed graph for process metamodel construction (courtesy C. Hug 2008)

Table 10.4 The P-Sigma formalism (reprinted from Hug et al. 2009, with permission from Elsevier)

Pattern interface	
Identification	Defines the couple (problem, solution) that references the pattern
Classification	Defines the pattern function through a collection of domain keywords (domain terms)
Context	Describes the precondition of pattern application
Problem	Defines the problem solved by the pattern
Force	Defines the pattern contributions through a collection of quality criteria associated to a technology
Pattern realisation	
Process solution	Indicates the problem solution in terms of a process to follow. An activity diagram allows representing the process
Model solution	Describes the solution in terms of expected products (a class diagram and optionally a set of sequence diagram)
Application case	Describes application examples of the Model Solution. This item is optional, but recommended in order to facilitate the understanding of the pattern solution
Consequence	Gives the consequence induced by the pattern application
Patterns relations	
Uses, refines, requires, alternative	

Table 10.5 Extract from the questionnaire used to determine the entry point to the directed graph (courtesy C. Hug 2008)

Question	Synonyms, also known as examples	Concept
Do you need to represent how an intention is achieved?	Tactics, approach, manner	Strategy
Do you need to represent goals or objectives of the information systems engineering (ISE) process?	Objective, goal, subgoal	Intention
Do you need to represent how an intention is achieved?	Tactics, approach, manner	Strategy
Do you need to represent something that is produced, used or modified during the ISE process?	Product, document, model, program	Work Product
Do you need to represent someone that carries out an action during the ISE process?	Actor, developer, analyst, system	Role
Do you need to represent actions that are executed during the ISE process?	Activity, phase, task, work definition	Work Unit

representation of the pattern selection interface and library organisation (Conte et al. 2002). In other words, the representation of the metamodelling patterns, business patterns and process patterns of the method is homogenous, thus easing their comprehension and selection.

The pattern interface part comprises the items that help the selection of patterns; the pattern realisation part gives the model solution or the process solution; while the relation part describes the relationship with other patterns. Not all the items can be filled for every pattern, particularly process solution and model solution.

The procedure for creating the process metamodel under construction (PMUC) can be represented as a directed graph (Fig. 10.5). The entry point to this graph is determined by the answers to a set of questions (Table 10.5). When the method engineers have answered 'yes' to a question, they can enter into the graph and move around it by following the edges (Fig. 10.6). For example, one of the questions of the questionnaire is "Do you need to represent actions that are executed during the information systems engineering process?" If the method engineers answer 'yes', the Work Unit concept will be added into the PMUC, and the method engineers will begin moving around the graph from the node *Work Unit* that corresponds to the Work Unit concept. Had the method engineer answered 'no', he/she would have had to move on to the next question. The method engineers then choose an edge that corresponds to their goal concerning the source node. Each time the method engineers choose an edge, they will be asked whether they want to add the target node on the PMUC. If they do not wish to add the target node upon reflection, they return to the source node. The rules governing movement around the graph can be defined using appropriate logics. This SMME approach has been subject to empirical validation in Hug et al. (2010).

The use of SMME gives method engineers wider flexibility in terms of extension, refinement and adaptation for the underpinning metamodel. In constructing a situationally specific metamodel from scratch, a minimalistic metamodel can be created that is therefore much more readily understandable than a comprehensive

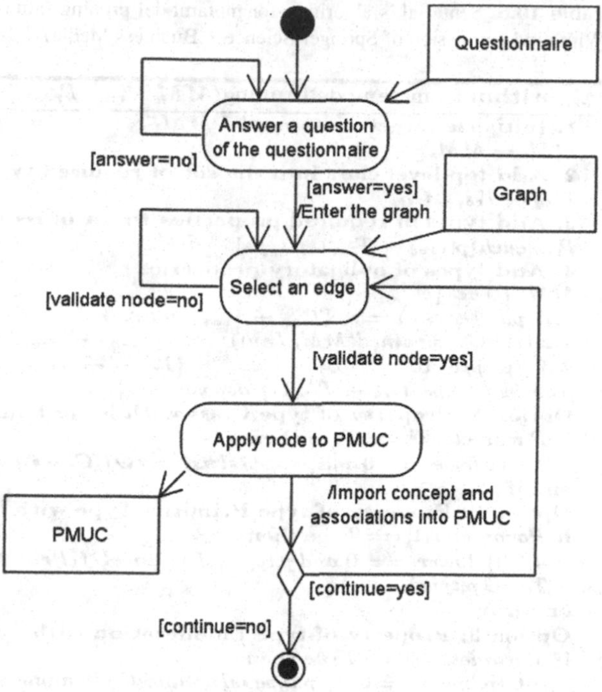

Fig. 10.6 Procedure for PMUC (courtesy C. Hug 2008)

metamodel such as SPEM (OMG 2005a). In other words, it is a bottom-up construction process rather than a top-down pruning process.

Hug et al. (2009) argue that SMME offers a number of advantages as follows:

- A lower cost of maintaining the Process domain metamodel;
- A lower cost in maintaining the pattern system;
- A lower cost of education for method engineers (metamodel users);
- Unlimited extensibility, refinement and adaptation for underpinning metamodels.

Sen et al. (2009) note similar concerns with overly large metamodels, citing the UML 2.0 metamodel. Their approach is focussed on their notion of 'metamodel pruning' by which a large metamodel is reduced in size to an 'effective metamodel', i.e., changing a large graph to a smaller graph. The first phase of their 'pruning algorithm', shown in Table 10.6, is to compute the entire set of required types (steps 1–5). In the second phase (step 6), the set of all required properties is computed. In the final phase (steps 7 and 8), extraneous properties and types are removed resulting in a final metamodel.

10.3 Metamodels and Modelling Languages

The second metamodel-linked focus provides a challenge to existing multilevel architectures (described here in Chap. 1). Some of the ideas have been discussed in terms of their mathematical underpinning (see also Henderson-Sellers 2012) but more recently (Henderson-Sellers et al. 2013) a more dramatic suggestion is that it

Table 10.6 Sen et al.'s algorithm for metamodel pruning (after Sen et al., algorithm 1, 2009, With kind permission of Springer Science + Business Media)

Algorithm 1. metamodelPruning(MM_s, T_{req}, P_{req}, C_{top}, $Parameter$)

1. Initialize target meta-model MM_t
$MM_t \leftarrow MM_s$
2. Add top-level class into the set of required types
$T_{req} \leftarrow T_{req} \cup C_{top}$
3. Add types of required properties to set of required types
$P_{req}.each\{p|T_{req} \leftarrow T_{req} \cup p.type\}$
4. Add types of obligatory properties
$MM_t.P.each\{p|$
4.1 $(p.lower > 0) \implies \{T_{req} \leftarrow T_{req} \cup p.type\}$
4.2 $(p.isConstrained(MM_t.Inv)) \implies \{T_{req} \leftarrow T_{req} \cup p.type\}$
4.3 $(p.opposite! = \phi) \implies \{T_{req} \leftarrow T_{req} \cup p.type, T_{req} \leftarrow T_{req} \cup p.opposite.type, T_{req} \leftarrow T_{req} \cup p.opposite.oC\}$
Option 1: Property of type Class with lower bound 0
if $Parameter[0] == True$ **then**
4.4 $(p.lower == 0\, and\, p.type.isInstanceOf(Class)) \implies \{T_{req} \leftarrow T_{req} \cup p.type\}$
end if
Option 2: Property of type PrimitiveType with lower bound 0
if $Parameter[1] == True$ **then**
4.5 $(p.lower == 0\, and\, p.type.isInstanceOf(PrimitiveType)) \implies \{T_{req} \leftarrow T_{req} \cup p.type\}$
end if
Option 3: Property of type Enumeration with lower bound 0
if $Parameter[2] == True$ **then**
4.6 $(p.lower == 0 andp.type.isInstanceOf(Enumeration)) \implies \{T_{req} \leftarrow T_{req} \cup p.type\}\}$
end if
5. Add all multi-level super classes of all classes in T_{req}
$MM_t.T.each\{t \mid t.isInstanceOf(Class) \implies t.allSuperClasses.each\,\{s|T_{req} \leftarrow T_{req} \cup s\}\}$
6. Add all required properties to P_{req}
$MM_t.P.each\{p|$
6.1 $(p.type \in T_{req}) \implies \{P_{req} \leftarrow P_{req} \cup p\}$
6.2 $(p.oC \in T_{req}) \implies \{P_{req} \leftarrow P_{req} \cup p\}$
6.3 $(p.lower > 0) \implies P_{req} \leftarrow P_{req} \cup p\}$
6.4 $(p.isConstrained(MM_t.Inv)) \implies \{P_{req} \leftarrow P_{req} \cup p\}$
6.5 $(p.opposite! = \phi) \implies \{P_{req} \leftarrow P_{req} \cup p, P_{req} \leftarrow P_{req} \cup p.opposite\}$
Option 1: Property of type Class with lower bound 0
if $Parameter[0] == True$ **then**
6.6 $(p.lower == 0\, and\, p.type.isInstanceOf(Class)) \implies \{P_{req} \leftarrow P_{req} \cup p\}$
end if
Option 2: Property of type PrimitiveType with lower bound 0
if $Parameter[1] == True$ **then**
6.7 $(p.lower == 0\, and\, p.type.isInstanceOf(PrimitiveType)) \implies \{P_{req} \leftarrow P_{req} \cup p\}$
end if
Option 3: Property of type Enumeration with lower bound 0
if $Parameter[2] == True$ **then**
6.8 $(p.lower == 0 andp.type.isInstanceOf(Enumeration)) \implies \{P_{req} \leftarrow P_{req} \cup p\}\}$
end if
7. Remove Properties
$MM_t.P.each\{p|$
7.1 $p \notin P_{req} \implies (t.P \leftarrow t.P - p)$
7.2 $p.type \notin T_{req} \implies (t.P \leftarrow t.P - p)\}$
}
8. Remove Types
$MM_t.T.each\{t|t \notin T_{req} \implies MM_t.T \leftarrow MM_t.T - t\}$

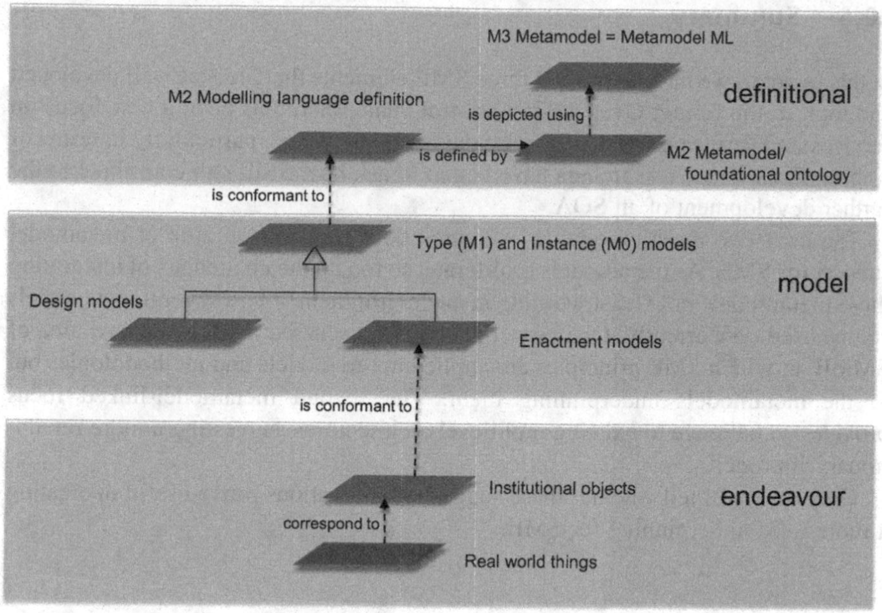

Fig. 10.7 A newly proposed architecture that focusses on language use rather than metamodels for the creation of a conceptual modelling environment (after Henderson-Sellers et al. 2013, reprinted by permission of the publisher)

is time for a 'revolution' in multilevel architectures rather than further evolution. Drawing parallels with astronomy, they argue that there have been a number of the so-called 'Ptolemaic fixes' to the OMG architecture of Fig. 1.11 to permit it to support enactment of processes. These fixes have been identified by these authors as including potency and deep instantiation (Atkinson and Kühne 2001b), clabjects and powertypes (e.g., Gonzalez-Perez and Henderson-Sellers 2008b; Atkinson et al. 2009) and the Orthogonal Classification Architecture (Atkinson and Kühne 2003, 2005). Although these all provide pragmatic value to SME, it is suggested that by utilising speech act theory (e.g., Searle 1969) it is possible to replace the OMG strict metamodelling architecture by one focussing on modelling languages (Fig. 10.5) that also include a foundational ontology, consequently providing a more theoretically valid and practically acceptable framework can be provided to the modelling community, including of course the SME community (Eriksson et al. 2013) (Fig. 10.7).

Other challenges relevant to SME include whether the philosophical underpinnings of modelling and metamodelling is consistent (Partridge, 2012, personal communication); in particular, what is understood by modellers by the term 'concept' (see Smith 2004 and Partridge et al. 2013 for more detailed discussion of this topic).

The increasing focus on cloud computing (e.g., Yau and An 2011), despite the risk of accommodating sensitive corporate data in the cloud (e.g., Reinicke 2012), is another contemporary factor that could have a direct bearing on the use of SME.

10.4 Summary

In this chapter, we have identified three SME elements that are less well developed and look to the future. Over the last several years, there has been a new focus on services and service provision in everyday software usage, particularly in terms of web services. Thus, researchers have begun to ask how SME can contribute to the further development of an SOA.

The next two research-oriented ventures both concern the area of metamodel support for SME. As metamodels proliferate, so too do the challenges of integrating those metamodels or at least working in an environment where several metamodels can be used concurrently. One aspect of that, as discussed here, is the new area of SMME in which SME principles are applied not to models and methodologies but to the metamodels underpinning them. The second metamodel-linked focus provides a challenge to existing multilevel architectures suggesting a more revolutionary approach.

Only time will tell whether these suggested innovations prove useful in creating a more solid underpinning for SME.

Final Summary and Future Work 11

The history of situational method engineering as a subdiscipline of software engineering is around 20 years old. Increasing recognition that a one-size-fits-all methodology has led to increased interest in other options—specifically, the construction of a methodology from smaller method parts, those parts being chosen with the specific context or situation in mind. That situation may include the style of software being developed (e.g., real-time, information system), the resources and personal skills available in the team and the organisational culture. It may be organisation-specific or project-specific and may change over time. Changes are easily accommodation by the selection of new method parts (e.g., as team maturity increases—perhaps measured by CMMI or ISO/IEC 15504) or by the replacement of method parts (e.g., as individuals' skills mature or as a result of technology changes). SME is highly flexible both in terms of its ability to construct various styles of method (from bureaucratic plan-based to highly agile) and in terms of it being able to provide a basic method that can morph in time.

In this book, we have not only synopsised the state-of-the-art in situational method engineering, we have also drawn together the various research strands for which we, the authors, have been personally responsible over the past years, initially leading independent groups with slightly different axiomatic bases and, more recently, through the recognition originally espoused in Ågerfalk et al. (2007) that, for future widespread industry adoption, a single 'voice' is needed from our research communities to be heard by industry vendors and developers. This book draws together those various strands into a single conceptual basis for the advancement of situational method engineering into the future.

Although we present in this book a state-of-the-art (as of mid-2013), further research will occur together with experiential evidence of these 'methods in action'. The SME topics that are likely to be investigated in the next few years would seem to us to need to include the following:

- How best to collect the organisation's requirements for constructing an SME method.

B. Henderson-Sellers et al., *Situational Method Engineering*,
DOI 10.1007/978-3-642-41467-1_11, © Springer-Verlag Berlin Heidelberg 2014

- How to extend the theory to redress the current imbalance in some SME approaches between method parts relating to product and process and method parts relating to producers.
- How to measure the quality of individual method parts—for storage in the method base.
- How best to glean from these requirements the appropriate set of method parts, if possible in a semi-automated way (some preliminary work is to be found in Henderson-Sellers and Nguyen 2004) and what metrics are appropriate for checking this selection.
- How to measure the quality of a constructed method (1) as a method and (2) as being appropriate for the organisational requirements.
- How to avoid clashes of mindset, e.g., using an agile fragment together with a bureaucratic (high ceremony) fragment or, when appropriate, construct a hybrid methodology.
- How to evaluate the quality of method-in-action.
- How to use SME in the context of existing (legacy) methods (most of the SME literature assumes greenfield projects).
- What sort of tools can be created to support industry adoption of an SME approach (some initial ideas, commensurate with ISO/IEC 24744 metamodel, are to be found in Gonzalez-Perez (2005) and others are discussed in Chap. 7).

We look forward to an exciting few years ahead when SME provides industry with provably enhanced capacity for software development by use of a specifically and situationally created and tailored method.

References

Ågerfalk PJ (1999) Pragmatization of information systems: a theoretical and methodological outline. Licentiate thesis. Department of Computer and Information Science, Linköping University. Printed in Sweden by Linköping University. ISBN: 91-7373-628-7

Ågerfalk PJ (2003) Information systems actability: understanding information technology as a tool for business action and communication. Doctoral dissertation. Department of Computer and Information Science, Linköping University, Printed in Sweden by UniTryck, ISBN: 91-7373-628-7

Ågerfalk PJ (2004) Grounding through operationalization: constructing tangible theory in IS research. Paper presented at the 12th European conference on information systems (ECIS 2004), Turku, Finland

Ågerfalk PJ (2006) Towards better understanding of agile values in global software development. In: Krogstie J, Halpin TA, Proper HA (eds) Proceedings of the workshop on exploring modeling methods for systems analysis and design (EMMSAD '06), held in conjunction with the 18th conference on advanced information systems (CAiSE '06), Luxembourg, Luxembourg. Namur University Press, Namur, pp 375–382

Ågerfalk PJ, Åhlgren K (1999) Modelling the rationale of methods. In: Khosrowpour M (ed) Managing information technology resources in organizations in the next millennium. Proceedings of the 10th information resources management association international conference. IDEA Group, Hershey, PA, pp 184–190

Ågerfalk P, Fitzgerald B (2006) Exploring the concept of method rationale: a conceptual tool for method tailoring. In: Siau K (ed) Advanced topics in database research, vol 5. IGI, Hershey, PA

Ågerfalk PJ, Goldkuhl G (2001) Business action and information modelling: the task of the new millennium. In: Rossi M, Siau K (eds) Information modeling in the new millennium. Idea Group, Hershey, PA, pp 110–136

Ågerfalk PJ, Wistrand K (2003) Systems development method rationale: a conceptual framework for analysis. Paper presented at the 5th international conference on enterprise information systems (ICEIS 2003), 23–26 April 2003, Angers, France

Ågerfalk PJ, Goldkuhl G, Fitzgerald B, Bannon L (2006) Reflecting on action in language, organisations and information systems. Eur J Inform Syst 15(1):4–8

Ågerfalk PJ, Brinkkemper S, Gonzalez-Perez C, Henderson-Sellers B, Karlsson F, Kelly S, Ralyté J (2007) Modularization constructs in method engineering: towards common ground? In: Ralyté J, Brinkkemper S, Henderson-Sellers B (eds) Situational method engineering: fundamentals and experiences. Springer, New York, NY, pp 359–368

Aggarwal KK, Singh Y, Kaur A, Malhotra R (2007a) Software design metrics for object-oriented software. J Object Tech 6(1):121–138

Aggarwal KK, Singh Y, Kaur A, Malhotra R (2007b) Investigating effect of design metrics on fault proneness in object-oriented systems. J Object Tech 6(10):127–141

Aharoni A, Reinhartz-Berger I (2008) A domain engineering approach for situational method engineering. In: Li Q, Spaccapietra S, Yu E, Olivé A (eds) ER 2008. Lecture notes in computer science, vol 5231. Springer, Berlin, pp 455–468

B. Henderson-Sellers et al., *Situational Method Engineering*,
DOI 10.1007/978-3-642-41467-1,

Ambler S (1998) Process patterns: building large-scale systems using object technology. SIGS Press, New York, NY

Ambler S (1999) More process patterns: building large-scale systems using object technology. SIGS Press, New York, NY

Andres HP, Zmud RW (2002) A contingency approach to software project coordination. J Manag Inform Syst 18(3):41–70

ANSI (1989) Information resource dictionary system (IRDS). American National Standards Institute, New York, NY

Araujo T, Rossi M (1993) Process models for CASE shell environments. In: Brinkkemper S, Harmsen F (eds) Proceedings of the fourth workshop on the next generation of CASE tools. Memoranda Informatica 93.3, Universiteit Twente, pp 90–99

Argyris C, Schön D (1978) Organisational learning: a theory of action perspective. Jossey-Bass, San Francisco, CA

Arni-Bloch N, Ralyté J, Léonard M (2006) Integrating information systems components: a situation-driven approach. In: Latour T, Petit M (eds) CAiSE '06: 18th conference on advanced information systems engineering—trusted information systems: proceedings of the workshops and doctoral consortium, Luxembourg, 5–9 June 2006. Namur University Press, Namur, pp 433–444

Asadi M, Mohabbati B, Gaševic D, Bagheri E (2011) Developing families of method-oriented architecture. In: Ralyté J, Mirbel I, Deneckère R (eds) ME 2011. IFIP AICT, vol 351. IFIP, Paris, pp 168–183

Aßmann U, Zschaler S, Wagner G (2006) Ontologies, meta-models, and the model-driven paradigm. In: Calero C, Ruiz F, Piattini M (eds) Ontologies for software engineering and software technology. Springer, Berlin, pp 249–273

Atkinson C (1997) Metamodelling for distributed object environments. First international enterprise distributed object computing workshop (EDOC '97), Brisbane, Australia

Atkinson C (1999) Supporting and applying the UML conceptual framework. In: Bézivin J, Muller P-A (eds) «UML» 1998: beyond the notation, vol 1618. Springer, Berlin, pp 21–36

Atkinson C, Kühne T (2001a) The essence of multilevel metamodeling, UML '01. Lecture notes in computer science, vol 2185. Springer, Heidelberg, pp 19–33

Atkinson C, Kühne T (2001b) Processes and products in a multi-level metamodeling architecture. Int J Software Eng Knowl Eng 11(6):761–783

Atkinson C, Kühne T (2003) Model-driven development: a metamodelling foundation. IEEE Software 20(5):36–41

Atkinson C, Kühne T (2005) Concepts for comparing modeling tool architectures. Model driven engineering languages and systems. Lecture notes in computer science, vol 3713. Springer, Berlin, pp 398–413

Atkinson C, Kühne T, Henderson-Sellers B (2003) Systematic stereotype usage. Software Syst Model 2(3):153–163

Atkinson C, Gutheil M, Kiko K (2006) On the relationship of ontologies and models, in meta-modelling and ontologies. Proceedings of the 2nd workshop on meta-modelling, WoMM 2006, LNI, vol P-96, pp 47–60

Atkinson C, Gutheil M, Kennel B (2009) A flexible infrastructure for multilevel language engineering. IEEE Trans Software Eng 35(6):742–755

Atkinson C, Kennel B, Goß B (2010) The level-agnostic modeling language. In: Malloy B, Staab S, van den Brand M (eds) SLE 2010. Lecture notes in computer science, vol 6563. Springer, Berlin, pp 266–275

Avison DE (1996) Information systems development methodologies: a broader perspective. In: Brinkkemper S, Lyytinen K, Welke RJ (eds) Method engineering. Principles of method construction and tool support. Proceedings of IFIP TC8, WG8.1/8.2 working conference on method engineering, 26–28 August 1996, Atlanta, USA. Chapman & Hall, London, pp 263–277

Avison DE, Fitzgerald G (2003) Where now for development methodologies? Comm ACM 46 (1):79–82

Avison DE, Wood-Harper AT (1991) Information systems development research: an exploration of ideas in practice. Comput J 34(2):98–112

Aydin M (2007) Examining key notions for method adaptation. In: Ralyté J, Brinkkemper S, Henderson-Sellers B (eds) Situational method engineering: fundamentals and experiences. Proceedings of the IFIP WG 8.1 working conference, 12–14 September 2007, Geneva, Switzerland. IFIP series, vol 244. Springer, Berlin, pp 49–63

Aydin MN, Harmsen F (2002) Making a method work for a project situation in the context of CMM. In: Oivo M, Komi-Sirviö S (eds) Product-focused software process improvement: 14th international conference, PROFES 2002, Rovaniemi, Finland, 9–11 December 2002. Lecture notes in computer science, vol 2559. Springer, Berlin, pp 158–171

Aydin MN, Harmsen F, van Slooten K, Stegwee RA (2005) A model for a method adaptation process. In: Vasilecas O, Caplinskas A, Wojtkowski G, Wojtkowsi W, Zupanicic J (eds) Information systems development. Advances in theory, practice and education. Kluwer Academic/Springer, New York, NY, pp 477–487

Baddoo N, Hall T (2003) De-motivators for software process improvement: an analysis of practitioners' views. J Syst Software 66:23–33

Bajec M (2011a) Application of method engineering principles in practice: lessons learned and prospects for the future. In: Ralyté J, Mirbel I, Deneckère R (eds) Engineering methods in the service-oriented context. Proceedings of the 4th IFIP WG8.1 working conference on method engineering, ME 2011, Paris, France, April 2011. Springer, Heidelberg, pp 2–3

Bajec M (2011b) Keynote presentation at ME '11, Paris, 20–22 April 2011

Bajec M (2012) Personal communication

Bajec M, Vavpotič D, Furlan S, Krisper M (2007a) Software process improvement based on the method engineering principles. In: Ralyté J, Brinkkemper S, Henderson-Sellers B (eds) Situational method engineering: fundamentals and experiences. Proceedings of the IFIP WG 8.1 working conference, 12–14 September 2007, Geneva, Switzerland. IFIP series, vol 244. Springer, Berlin, pp 283–297

Bajec M, Vavpotič D, Krisper M (2007b) Practice-driven approach for creating project-specific software development methods. Inform Software Tech 49(4):345–365

Barbier F, Aretxandieta X (2008) State-based composition in UML 2. Int J Software Eng Knowl Eng 18(7):1–25

Barbier F, Henderson-Sellers B, Le Parc-Lacayrelle A, Bruel J-M (2003) Formalization of the whole-part relationship in the Unified Modeling Language. IEEE Trans Software Eng 29 (5):459–470

Barcellos M, Falbo R, Rocha AR (2012) Using a reference domain ontology for developing a software measurement strategy for high maturity organizations, presented at VORTE 2012 workshop, Beijing, 11 September 2012. Available from the IEEE Xplore Digital Library

Basili VR, Rombach HD (1987) Tailoring the software process to project goals and environments. In: Proceedings of the ninth international conference on software engineering, 30 March–2 April 1987, Monterey, CA

Basili VR, Rombach HD (1988) The TAME project: towards improvement-orientated software environments. IEEE Trans Software Eng 14(6):758–773

Basili VR, Caldiera G, Rombach HD (1994) The goal-question-metric approach, encyclopedia of software engineering. Wiley, Chichester, NY, pp 528–532

Beck K (2000) Extreme programming explained. Embrace change. Addison-Wesley, Boston, MA, p 190

Becker J, Kugeler M, Rosemann M (2003) Process management—a guide for the design of business processes. Springer, Berlin

Becker J, Janiesch C, Pfeiffer D (2007) Reuse mechanisms in situational method engineering. In: Ralyté J, Brinkkemper S, Henderson-Sellers B (eds) Situational method engineering:

fundamentals and experiences. Proceedings of the IFIP WG 8.1 working conference, 12–14 September 2007, Geneva, Switzerland. IFIP series, vol 244. Springer, Berlin, pp 79–93
Bekkers W, van de Weerd I, Brinkkemper S, Mahieu A (2008) The influence of situational factors in software product management: an empirical study. In: Proceedings of the second international workshop on software product management, IWSPM '08, IEEE Computer Society, Los Alamitos, CA, pp 41–48
Bekkers W, van de Weerd I, Spruit M, Brinkkemper S (2010) A framework for process improvement in software product management. In: Riel A, O'Connor R, Tichkiewitch S, Messnarz R (eds) EuroSPI 2010, CCIS, vol 99. Springer, Heidelberg, pp 1–12
Belbin RM (1981) Management teams. Why they succeed or fail. Butterworth-Heinemann, Oxford, p 171
Belbin RM (1993) Team roles at work. Butterworth-Heinemann, Oxford, p 141
Bergstra J, Jonkers H, Obbink J (1985) A software development model for method engineering. In: Roukens J, Renuart J (eds) ESPRIT '84: status report of ongoing work. Elsevier Science B.V., North-Holland
Berki E, Georgiadou E, Holcombe M (2004) Requirements engineering and process modelling in software quality management—towards a generic process metamodel. Software Qual J 12:265–283
Bertoa MF, Vallecillo A (2010) Quality attributes for software metamodels. In: Proceedings of QAOOSE 2010, Malaga, Spain, 2 July 2010
Bertoa MF, Troya JM, Vallecillo A (2006) Measuring the usability of software components. J Syst Software 79:427–439
Beydoun G, Low G, Tran N, Henderson-Sellers B (2005) Preliminary basis for an ontology-based methodological approach for multi-agent systems. In: Akoka J, Liddle SW, Song I-Y, Bertolotto M, Comyn-Wattiau I, van den Heuvel W-J, Kolp M, Trujillo J, Kop C, Mayr HC (eds) Proceedings of the perspectives in conceptual modeling: ER2005 workshops CAOIS, BP-UML, CoMoGIS, eCOMO and QoIS, Klagenfurt, Austria, 24–28 October 2005. Lecture notes in computer science, vol 3770. Springer, Berlin, pp 131–140
Beydoun G, Tran N, Low G, Henderson-Sellers B (2006) Foundations of ontology-based methodologies for multi-agent systems. In: Kolp M, Bresciani P, Henderson-Sellers B, Winikoff M (eds) Lecture notes in computer science, vol 3529. Springer, Berlin, pp 111–123
Bézivin J, Gerbé O (2001) Towards a precise definition of the OMG/MDA framework. In: Proceedings of ASE '01, IEEE Computer Society, Los Alamitos, CA, pp 273–280
Bézivin J, Lemesle R (1998) Ontology-based layered semantics for precise OA&D modeling. In: Bosch J, Mitchell S (eds) Object-oriented technology: ECOOP '97 workshop reader. Lecture notes in computer science, vol 1357. Springer, Berlin, pp 287–292
Boar BH (1984) Application prototyping: a requirements definition strategy for the 80s. Wiley, New York, NY
Bogg P, Low G, Henderson-Sellers B, Beydoun G (2010) Work product-driven software development methodology improvement, ICSOFT 2010. In: Cordeiro J, Virvou M, Shishkov B (eds) Proceedings of the fifth international conference on software and data technologies, 22–24 July 2010, Athens, Greece, vol 2. SciTePress, Lisbon, pp 5–13
Börner R (2011) Towards construction of situational methods for service identification. In: Ralyté J, Mirbel I, Deneckère R (eds) Engineering methods in the service-oriented context. Proceedings of the 4th IFIP WG8.1 working conference on method engineering, ME 2011, Paris France, April 2011. Springer, Heidelberg, pp 204–218
Bresciani P, Perini A, Giorgini P, Giunchiglia F, Mylopolous J (2004) Tropos: an agent-oriented software development methodology. Auton Agent Multi Agent Syst 8(3):203–236
Brinkkemper S (1990) Formalisation of information systems modelling. Ph.D. Thesis, University of Nijmegen, Thesis Publishers, Amsterdam, The Netherlands
Brinkkemper S (1996) Method engineering: engineering of information systems development methods and tools. Inform Software Tech 38(4):275–280
Brinkkemper S (2006) Personal email communication to authors

Brinkkemper S, Saeki M, Harmsen F (1998) Assembly techniques for method engineering. In: Pernici B, Thanos C (eds) Advanced information systems engineering. Proceedings of the 10th international conference, CAiSE '98, Pisa, Italy, June 8–12 1998. Lecture notes in computer science, vol 1413. Springer, Berlin, pp 381–400

Brinkkemper S, Saeki M, Harmsen F (1999) Meta-modelling based assembly techniques for situational method engineering. Inform Syst 24(3):209–228

Brinkkemper S, Saeki M, Harmsen F (2001) A method engineering language for the description of systems development methods (extended abstract). In: Dittrich KR, Geppert A, Norrie MC (eds) Advanced information systems engineering: proceedings of the 13th international conference, CAiSE 2001, Interlaken, Switzerland, 4–8 June 2001. Lecture notes in computer science, vol 2068. Springer, Berlin, pp 473–476

Brooks FP (1987) No silver bullet: essence and accidents of software engineering. IEEE Comput 20(4):10–19

Bucher T, Klesse M, Kurpjuweit S, Winter R (2007) Situational method engineering: on the differentiation of "context" and "project type". In: Ralyté J, Brinkkemper S, Henderson-Sellers B (eds) Situational method engineering: fundamentals and experiences. Proceedings of the IFIP WG 8.1 working conference, Geneva, Switzerland, 12–14 September 2007. IFIP series, vol 244. Springer, Berlin, pp 33–48

Buckl S, Ernst AM, Lankes J, Schneider K, Schweda CM (2007) A pattern based approach for constructing enterprise architecture management information models. In: Wirtschaftsinformatik 2007. Universitätsverlag Karlsruhe, Karlsruhe, pp 145–162

Buckl S, Matthes F, Schweda CM (2011) A method base for enterprise architecture management. In: Ralyté J, Mirbel I, Deneckère R (eds) Engineering methods in the service-oriented context. Proceedings of the 4th IFIP WG8.1 working conference on method engineering, ME 2011, Paris France, April 2011. Springer, Heidelberg, pp 34–48

Bunge M (1977) Treatise on basic philosophy: vol. 3: ontology I: the furniture of the world. Reidel, Boston

Bunge M (1979) Treatise on basic philosophy: vol. 4: ontology II: a world of systems. Reidel, Boston

Burke R (2003) Project management: planning and control techniques. Burke Publishing, Tokai

Buschmann F, Meunier R, Rohnert H, Sommerlad P (1996) Pattern-oriented software architecture volume 1: a system of patterns. Wiley, Chichester, NY

Business Development Institute International (2005) Capability maturity model for business development, version 1.0. Business Development Institute International, Phoenix, AZ

Calero C, Ruiz F, Piattini M (eds) (2006) Ontologies in software engineering and software technology. Springer, Berlin, p 339

Cameron J (2002) Configurable development processes: keeping the focus on what is being produced. Comm ACM 45(3):72–77

Carroll JM (1994) Making use a design representation. Comm ACM 37(12):29–35

Cato J (2001) User-centred web design. Addison Wesley, Harlow

Cauvet C (2010) Method engineering: a service-oriented approach. In: Nurcan S, Salinesi C, Souveyet C, Ralyté J (eds) Intentional perspectives on information systems engineering. Springer, Berlin, pp 335–354

Cervera M, Albert M, Torres V, Pelechano V (2011) Turning method engineering support into reality. In: Ralyté J, Mirbel I, Deneckère R (eds) Engineering methods in the service-oriented context. Proceedings of the 4th IFIP WG8.1 working conference on method engineering, ME 2011, Paris France, April 2011. Springer, Heidelberg, pp 138–152

Chakraborty S, Sarker S, Sarker S (2010) An exploration into the process of requirements elicitation: a grounded approach. J Assoc Inform Syst 11(4):212–249

Chatfield C (1975) The analysis of time series: an introduction. Chapman & Hall, London

Checkland PB (1981) Systems thinking, systems practice. Wiley, New York, NY

Cherniavsky JC, Smith CH (1991) On Weyuker's axioms for software complexity measures. IEEE Trans Software Eng 17(6):636–638

Chidamber S, Kemerer C (1994) A metrics suite for object-oriented design. IEEE Trans Software Eng 20(6):476–493

Chou S-C (2002) A process modeling language consisting of high level UML-based diagrams and low level process language. J Object Tech 1(4):137–163

Chroust G (2000) Software process models: structure and challenges. In: Feng Y, Notkin D, Gaudel MC (eds) Software: theory and practice—proceedings, IFIP congress 2000. Kluwer, Amsterdam, pp 279–286

Cleland DI, Ireland LR (2002) Project management: strategic design and implementation. McGraw-Hill, New York, NY

Coad P (1992) Object-oriented patterns. Comm ACM 35(9):152–159

Cockburn A (2000) Selecting a project's methodology. IEEE Software 17(4):64–71

Cockburn A (2004) http://alistair.cockburn.us/crystal/crystal.html

Cockburn A (2006) Agile software development: the cooperative game, 2nd edn. Addison-Wesley, Boston, MA

Coleman D, Hayes F, Bear S (1992) Introducing objectcharts or how to use statecharts on object-oriented design. IEEE Trans Software Eng 18(1):9–18

Conklin J, Begeman ML (1988) gIBIS: a hypertext tool for exploratory policy discussion. ACM Trans Office Inform Syst 6(4):303–331

Conklin EJ, Yakemovic KB (1991) A process-oriented approach to design rationale. Hum Comput Interact 6:357–394

Conklin J, Selvin A, Shum SB, Sierhuis M (2003) Facilitated hypertext for collective sensemaking: 15 years on from gIBIS. In: Weigand H, Goldkuhl G, de Moor A (eds) Proceedings of the 8th international working conference on the language-action perspective on communication modelling (LAP 2003). Tilburg University, Tilburg, pp 1–22

Connallen J (2002) Building web applications with UML, 2nd edn. Addison-Wesley, Boston, MA

Conradi R (2001) Personal communication to first author

Conradi R, Fernström C, Fuggetta A (1993) A conceptual framework for evolving software processes. ACM SIGSOFT Software Eng Notes 18(4):26–35

Constantine LL (1996) Usage-centered design for embedded systems: essential models. In: Proceedings of the embedded systems conference '96. Miller Freeman, San Francisco, CA

Constantine LL, Lockwood LAD (1994) One size does not fit all: fitting practices to people. Am Program 7(12):30–38

Constantine LL, Lockwood LAD (1999) Software for use. A practical guide to the models and methods of usage-centered design. ACM Press, New York, p 579

Conte A, Fredj M, Hassine I, Giraudin J-P, Rieu D (2002) A tool and a formalism to design and apply patterns. OOIS, Lecture notes in computer science, vol 2425. Springer, Berlin, pp 135–146

Corcho O, Fernandez-Lopez M, Gomez-Perez A (2006) Ontological engineering: principles, methods, tools and languages. In: Calero C, Ruiz F, Piattini M (eds) Ontologies for software engineering and software technology. Springer, Berlin, pp 1–48

Cortes Cornax M, Dupuy-Chessa S, Rieu D (2011) Bridging the gap between business processes and service composition through service choreographies. In: Ralyté J, Mirbel I, Deneckère R (eds) Engineering methods in the service-oriented context. Proceedings of the 4th IFIP WG8.1 working conference on method engineering, ME 2011, Paris France, April 2011. Springer, Heidelberg, pp 190–203

Cossentino M (2006) Personal communication to first author

Cossentino M, Gaglio S, Henderson-Sellers B, Seidita V (2006a) A metamodelling-based approach for method fragment comparison. In: Latour T, Petit M (eds) CAiSE '06. 18th Conference on advanced information systems engineering—trusted information systems, Luxembourg, 5–9 June 2006. Proceedings of the workshops and doctoral consortium. Namur University Press, Namur, pp 419–432

Cossentino M, Gaglio S, Seidita V (2006b) A repository of fragments for agent systems design. In: Proceedings of the WOA06, pp 130–137

Cossentino M, Gaglio S, Garro A, Seidita V (2007) Method fragments for agent design methodologies: from standardization to research. Int J Agent-Oriented Software Eng 1 (1):91–121

Coughlan J, Lycett M, Macredie RD (2003) Communication issues in requirements elicitation: a content analysis of stakeholders experiences. Inform Software Tech 45(8):525–537

Coulin C, Zowghi D, Sahraoui A-E-K (2006) A situational method engineering approach to requirements elicitation workshops in the software development process. A situational approach to requirements elicitation workshops. Software Process Improv Pract 11(5):451–464

Cunin P-Y, Greenwood RM, Francou L, Robertson I, Warboys B (2001) The PIE methodology—concept and application. In: Ambriola V (ed) Software process technology. Proceedings of the 8th European workshop, EWSPT 2001. Lecture notes in computer science, vol 2077. Springer, Berlin, pp 3–26

Curtis B, Kellner MI, Over J (1992) Process modelling. Comm ACM 35(9):75–90

D'Souza D, Wills AC (1998) Objects, components, and frameworks with UML: the catalysis approach. Addison-Wesley, Boston, MA

Davis N (2005) Secure software development life cycle processes: a technology scouting report (CMU/SEI-2005-TN-024)

De Antonellis V, Pernici B, Samarati P (1991) F-ORM METHOD: a methodology for reusing specifications. In: van Assche F, Moulin B, Rolland C (eds) Object-oriented approach in information systems, North-Holland

de los Angeles Martin M, Olsina L (2003) Towards an ontology for software metrics and indicators as the foundation for a cataloguing web system. In: Proceedings of the first conference on Latin American web congress, IEEE Computer Society, Los Alamitos, CA, pp 103–113

Deneckère R (2001) Approche d'extension de methods fondée sur l'utilisation de composants génériques. Ph.D. Thesis, University of Paris 1-Sorbonne, France

Deneckère R, Souveyet C (1998) Patterns for extending an OO model with temporal features. In: Rolland C, Grosz G (eds) Proceedings of OOIS '98. Springer, London, pp 201–218

Deneckère R, Iacovelli A, Kornyshova E, Souveyet C (2008) From method fragments to method services. In: Halpin T, Krogstie J, Proper E (eds) Proceedings of EMMSAD '08 thirteenth international workshop on exploring modeling methods for systems analysis and design. CEUR, pp 80–96

Deneckère R, Kornyshova E, Rolland C (2009) Enhancing the guidance of the intentional model "MAP": graph theory application. In: Proceedings of the third IEEE international conference on research challenges in information science, RCIS 2009, Fès, Morocco, 22–24 April 2009. IEEE Computer Society, Los Alamitos, CA, pp 13–22

Derby E, Larsen D, Schwaber K (2006) Agile retrospectives: making good teams great. Pragmatic Bookshelf, Raleigh, NC, p 200

Devedzic V (2002) Understanding ontological engineering. Comm ACM 45(4):136–144

Dorling A (1993) SPICE: software process improvement and capability determination. Inform Software Tech 35(6/7):404–406

Dourish P (2001) Where the action is: the foundations of embodied interaction. MIT Press, Cambridge

du Bois B, Lange CFJ, Demeyer S, Chaudron MRV (2007) A qualitative investigation of UML modelling conventions. In: Kühne T (ed) MoDELS 2006 workshops. Lecture notes in computer science, vol 4364. Springer, Berlin, pp 91–100

Dupuy-Chessa S (2009) Quality in ubiquitous information system design. In: Proceedings of the third international conference on research challenges in information sciences 2009 (RCIS 2009). IEEE Computer Society, Los Alamitos, CA, pp 343–352

Eberle H, Unger T, Leymann F (2009) Process fragments. In: Meersman R, Dillon T, Herrero P (eds) OTM 2009, part I. Lecture notes in computer science, vol 5870. Springer, Berlin, pp 398–405

Eisenhardt KM (1989) Agency theory: an assessment and review. Acad Manage Rev 14(1):57–74

Elssamadisy A, Schalliol G (2002) Recognizing and responding to "bad smells" in extreme programming. In: 24th International conference on software engineering, pp 617–622

Eriksén S (2002) Designing for accountability. In: Proceedings of the second Nordic conference on human-computer interaction (NordiCHI 2002). ACM Press, New York, NY, pp 177–186

Eriksson O, Henderson-Sellers B, Ågerfalk PJ (2013) Ontological and linguistic metamodelling revisited—a language use approach. Inform Software Tech 55(12):2099–2124

Esperanza Manso M, Cruz-Lemus JA, Genero M, Piattini M (2009) Empirical validation of measures for UML class diagrams: a meta-analysis study. In: Chaudron MRV (ed) MODELS 2008 workshops. Lecture notes in computer science, vol 5421. Springer, Berlin, pp 303–313

Espinosa A, Garbajosa J (2011) A study to support agile methods more effectively through traceability. Innovat Syst Software Eng 7:53–69

Etien A, Deneckère R, Salinesi C (2003) Extending methods to express change requirements. In: Ralyté J, Rolland C (eds) Proceedings of the first international workshop on 'engineering methods to support information systems evolution (EMSISE'03). In conjunction with OOIS'03 (9th international conference on object-oriented information systems), Université de Genève, pp 15–28

Fahrenkrog S, Abrams F, Haeck WP, Whelbourn D (2004) Organizational project management maturity model (OPM3). Project Management Institute, Newtown Square, PA

Favre J-M (2004) Foundations of meta-pyramids: languages vs. metamodels. Episode II. story of thotus the baboon. In: Proceedings of Dagstuhl seminar 04101 "language engineering for model-driven software development"

Fayad ME, Tsai WT, Fulghum ML (1996) Transition to object-oriented software development. Comm ACM 39(2):108–121

Fenton N (1991) Software metrics: a rigorous approach. Chapman and Hall, London, p 337

Fenton N (1994) Software measurement: a necessary scientific basis. IEEE Trans Software Eng 20:199–206

Finkelstein A, Kramer J, Goedicke M (1990) ViewPoint oriented software development. Proceedings of Conférence Le Génie Logiciel et ses applications, Toulouse, pp 337–351

Finkelstein A, Kramer J, Nuseibeh B (1994) Software process modelling and technology. Research Studies Press Ltd., Taunton

Fiorini ST, Leite JCSP, De Lucena CJP (2001) Process reuse architecture. In: Dittrich KR, Geppert A, Norrie MC (eds) Proceedings of CAiSE2001. Lecture notes in computer science, vol 2068. Springer, Berlin, pp 284–298

Firesmith DG, Henderson-Sellers B (1999) Improvements to the OPEN process metamodel. JOOP/ROAD 12(7):30–35

Firesmith DG, Henderson-Sellers B (2002) The OPEN process framework. An introduction. Addison-Wesley, London, p 330

Firesmith D, Henderson-Sellers B, Graham I (1997) OPEN modeling language (OML) reference manual. SIGS Books, New York, NY, p 276

Firesmith D, Krutsch S, Stowe M, Hendley G (1998) Documenting a complete Java application using OPEN. Addison-Wesley, Harlow, p 494

Fitzgerald B (1997) The use of systems development methodologies in practice: a field study. Inform Syst J 7(3):201–212

Fitzgerald B, Hartnett G (2005) A study of the use of agile methods within Intel. In: Baskerville RL, Mathiassen L, Pries-Heje, J, DeGross JI (eds) Business agility and information technology diffusion. Springer, Berlin, pp 187–202

Fitzgerald B, Russo NL, Stolterman E (2002) Information systems development: methods in action. McGraw-Hill, Berkshire

Fitzgerald B, Russo NL, O'Kane T (2003) Software development method tailoring at Motorola. Comm ACM 46(4):65–70

Fitzgerald B, Hartnett G, Conboy K (2006) Customising agile methods to software practices at Intel Shannon. Eur J Inform Syst 15:197–210

Flatscher RG (2002) Metamodeling in EIA/CDIF—meta-metamodel and metamodels. ACM Trans Model Comput Simul 12(4):322–342

Franch X (2009) A method for the definition of metrics over i* models. In: van Eck P, Gordijn J, Wieringa R (eds) Advanced information systems engineering. Proceeding of the 21st international conference, CAiSE2009. Lecture notes in computer science, vol 5565. Springer, Berlin, pp 201–215

Freeman C, Henderson-Sellers B (1991) OLMS—an object library management support system. In: Potter J, Tokoro M, Meyer B (eds) TOOLS 6. Prentice Hall, Sydney, pp 175–180

Fuentes-Fernandez R, Gomez-Sanz JJ, Pavon J (2007) Integration in agent-oriented development. Int J Agent-Oriented Software Eng 1(1):2–27

Fung KH (2011) A method engineering approach to support dynamic evolution in composition-based distributed applications. Ph.D. Thesis, University of New South Wales, Sydney, Australia

Fung KH, Low G (2009) A methodology evaluation framework for dynamic evolution in composition-based distributed applications. J Syst Software 82(12):1950–1965

Gamma E, Helm R, Johnson R, Vlissides JM (1994) Design patterns: elements of reusable object-oriented software. Addison-Wesley, Boston, MA

Garcia F, Bertoa MF, Calero C, Vallecillo A, Ruiz F, Piattini M, Genero M (2006) Towards a consistent terminology for software measurement. Inform Software Tech 48:631–644

Garciá-Magariño I (2013) A collection of method fragments automated with model transformations in agent-oriented modeling. Eng Appl Artif Intel 26:1131–1148

Garfinkel H (1967) Studies in ethnomethodology. Polity Press, Cambridge

Gašević D, Kaviani N, Hatala M (2007) On metamodeling in megamodels. In: Engels G, Opdyke B, Schmidt DC, Weil F (eds) MoDELS 2007. Lecture notes in computer science, vol 4735. Springer, Berlin, pp 91–105

Genero M, Piattini M, Calero C (eds) (2005) Metrics for software conceptual models. Imperial College Press, London

Gericke A, Fill, H-G, Karagiannis D, Winter R (2009) Situational method engineering for governance, risk and compliance information systems. In: Proceedings of DESRIST '09, Malvern, PA, USA, 7–8 May 2009. ACM Press, New York

Ghidini C, Giunchiglia F (2004) A semantics for abstraction. In: Lopez de Mantaras R, Saitta L (eds) Proceedings of ECAI 2004. IOS Press, Amsterdam, pp 343–352

Gholami MF, Sharifi M, Jamshidi P (2011) (online), Enhancing the OPEN process framework with service-oriented method fragments. Software Syst Model. doi: 10.1007/s10270-011-0222-z

Giorgini P, Mylopoulous J, Sebastiani R (2005) Goal-oriented requirements analysis and reasoning in the Tropos methodology. Eng Appl Artif Intell 18(2):159–171

Giunchiglia F, Walsh T (1992) A theory of abstraction. Artif Intell 57(2–3):323–390

Glass RL (2000) Process diversity and a computing old wives'/husbands' tale. IEEE Software 17 (4):127–128

Glass RL (2003) Questioning the software engineering unquestionables. IEEE Software 20 (3):119–120

Glass RL (2004) Matching methodology to problem domain. Comm ACM 47(5):19–21

Glinz M, Fricker S (2013) On shared understanding in software engineering. In Proceedings of GI conference on software engineering, Aachen, Germany, 2013. GI lecture notes in informatics, vol 213, pp 19–35

Gnatz M, Marschall F, Popp G, Rausch A, Schwerin W (2001) Towards a living software process development process based on process patterns. In: Ambriola V (ed) Software process technology. Proceedings of the 8th European workshop, EWSPT 2001. Lecture notes in computer science, vol 2077. Springer, Berlin, pp 182–202

Gogolla M, Henderson-Sellers B (2002) Analysis of UML stereotypes within the UML metamodel. In: Jezequel J-M, Hussman H, Cook S (eds) «UML»2002, Dresden, Germany, 30 September–4 October 2002 UML 2002—the Unified Modeling Language. Lecture notes in computer science, vol 2460. Springer, Berlin, pp 84–99

Goldkuhl G (1999) The grounding of usable knowledge: an inquiry in the epistemology of action knowledge. Linköping University, Linköping. CMTO Research Papers 1999:03

Goldkuhl G, Lind M (2008) Coordination and transformation in business processes: towards an integrated view. Bus Process Manag J 14:761–777

Goldkuhl G, Lind M, Seigerroth U (1998) Method integration: the need for a learning perspective. IEE Proc Software 145(4):113–118

Gonzalez-Perez C (2005) Tools for an extended object modelling environment. In: Proceedings of the 10th IEEE international conference on engineering of complex computer systems. IEEE Computer Society, Washington, DC, pp 20–23

Gonzalez-Perez C (2007) Supporting situational method engineering with ISO/IEC 24744 and the work product pool approach. In: Ralyté J, Brinkkemper S, Henderson-Sellers B (eds) Situational method engineering: fundamentals and experiences. Proceedings of the IFIP WG 8.1 working conference, Geneva, Switzerland, 12–14 September 2007. IFIP series, vol 244. Springer, Berlin, pp 7–18

Gonzalez-Perez C, Henderson-Sellers B (2005) Templates and resources in software development methodologies. J Object Tech 4(4):173–190

Gonzalez-Perez C, Henderson-Sellers B (2006a) A powertype-based metamodelling framework. Software Syst Model 5(1):72–90. doi:10.1007/210270-005-0099-9

Gonzalez-Perez C, Henderson-Sellers B (2006b) An ontology for software development methodologies and endeavours. In: Calero C, Ruiz F, Piattini M (eds) Ontologies in software engineering and software technology. Springer, New York, NY, pp 123–152

Gonzalez-Perez C, Henderson-Sellers B (2006c). On the ease of extending a powertype-based methodology metamodel. In: Meta-modelling and ontologies. Proceedings of the 2nd workshop on meta-modelling, WoMM 2006, LNI, vol P-96, pp 11–25

Gonzalez-Perez C, Henderson-Sellers B (2007) Modelling software development methodologies: a conceptual foundation. J Syst Software 80(11):1778–1796

Gonzalez-Perez C, Henderson-Sellers B (2008a) A work product pool approach to methodology specification and enactment. J Syst Software 81(8):1288–1305. doi:10.1016/j.jss.2007.10.001

Gonzalez-Perez C, Henderson-Sellers B (2008b) Metamodelling for software engineering. Wiley, Chichester, p 210

Gonzalez-Perez C, Giorgini P, Henderson-Sellers B (2009) Method construction by goal analysis. In: Barry C, Conboy K, Lang M, Wojtkowski G, Wojtkowski W (eds) Information systems development. Challenges in practice, theory, and education. Springer, New York, NY, pp 79–92

Gordijn J, Akkermans H (2001) E3-value: design and evaluation of e-business models. IEEE Intell Syst 16(4):11–17

Gould JD, Lewis C (1985) Designing for usability: key principles and what designers think. Comm ACM 28(3):300–311

Graham I (1995a) A non-procedural process model for object-oriented software development. Rep Object Anal Des 1(5):10–11

Graham I (1995b) Migrating to object technology. Addison-Wesley, Wokingham, p 552

Graham I, Henderson-Sellers B, Younessi H (1997) The OPEN process specification. Addison-Wesley, London, p 314

Green P, Rosemann M (2005) Business systems analysis with ontologies. IGI Group, Hershey, PA

Greenwood RM, Balasubramaniam D, Kirby G, Mayes K, Morrison R, Seet W, Warboys B, Zirintsis E (2001) Reflection and reification in process system evolution: experience and opportunity. In: Ambriola V (ed) Software process technology. Proceedings of the 8th European workshop, EWSPT 2001. Lecture notes in computer science, vol 2077. Springer, Berlin, pp 27–38

Greiffenberg S (2003) Methodenentwicklung in Wirtschaft und Verwaltung. Verlag Dr. Kovac, Hamburg

Grimán A, Pérez M, Mendoza L, Losavio F (2006) Feature analysis for architectural evaluation methods. J Syst Software 79(6):871–888

Grosz G, Rolland C (1990) Using artificial intelligence techniques to formalize the information system design process, DEXA. Springer, Berlin, pp 374–380

Gruber TR (1993) A translation approach to portable ontology specifications. Knowl Acquis 5:199–220

Guarino N (1998) Formal ontology and information systems. In: Proceedings of the International conference on formal ontology in information systems—FOIS '98, Trento, Italy

Guizzardi G (2005) Ontological foundations for structural conceptual models. University of Twente, Enschede

Guizzardi G (2007) On ontology, ontologies, conceptualizations, modeling languages, and (meta) models. In: Frontiers in artificial intelligence and applications volume 155. Proceedings of the 2007 conference on databases and information systems IV: selected papers from the seventh international Baltic conference DB&IS 2006. IOS Press, Amsterdam, pp 18–39

Guizzardi G, Wagner G (2005a) On the ontological foundations of agent concepts. In: Bresciani P, Giorgini P, Henderson-Sellers B, Low G, Winikoff M (eds) Agent-oriented information systems II, vol 3508. Springer, Berlin, pp 113–128

Guizzardi G, Wagner G (2005b) Some applications of a unified foundational ontology in business modeling. In: Green P, Rosemann M (eds) Business systems analysis with ontologies. IGI Group, Hershey, PA, pp 345–367

Gupta D, Prakash N (2001) Engineering methods from method requirements specifications. Requir Eng 6:135–160

Guzélian G, Cauvet C (2007) SO2M: towards a service-oriented approach for method engineering. In: Proceedings of IKE '07, Las Vegas, NV, USA

Haire B (2000) Web OPEN: an extension to the OPEN framework, Capstone project, Faculty of Engineering. University of Technology, Sydney, p 122

Hall RR (2001) Prototyping for usability of new technology. Int J Hum Comput Stud 55(4):485–501

Han T, Purao S, Storey VC (2008) Generating large-scale repositories of reusable artifacts for conceptual design of information systems. Decis Support Syst 45(4):665–680

Harel D (1987) Statecharts: a visual formulation for complex systems. Sci Comput Program 8 (3):231–274

Harmsen AF (1997) Situational method engineering. Moret Ernst & Young, Amsterdam

Harmsen AF, Saeki M (1996) Comparison of four method engineering languages. In: Brinkkemper S, Lyytinen K, Welke RJ (eds) Method engineering. Principles of method construction and tool support. Chapman & Hall, London, pp 209–231

Harmsen AF, Brinkkemper S, Oei H (1994) Situational method engineering for information systems projects. In: Olle TW, Verrijn-Stuart AA (eds) Methods and associated tools for the information systems life cycle. Proceedings of the IFIP WG8.1 working conference CRIS/94, North Holland, Amsterdam, pp 169–194

Hasher L, Zacks RT (1984) Automatic processing of fundamental information: the case of frequency of occurrence. Am Psychol 39(12):1372–1388

Hassine L, Ben Ghazala H (2004) Une approche pour la definition de methods situationelle d'assurance de la qualité logicielle. Génie Logiciel 70:29–37

Haynes P, Henderson-Sellers B (1996) Cost estimation of OO projects: empirical observations, practical applications. Am Program 9(7):35–41

Heineman GT, Councill W (eds) (2001) Component-based software engineering: putting the pieces together. Addison-Wesley, Reading, MA

Henderson-Sellers B (1995) Who needs an OO methodology anyway? Guest editorial. J Object-Orient Prog 8(6):6–8

Henderson-Sellers B (1996) Object-oriented metrics. Measures of complexity. Prentice Hall, Upper Saddle River, NJ, p 234

Henderson-Sellers B (2002) Process metamodelling and process construction: examples using the OPEN process framework (OPF). Ann Software Eng 14:341–362

Henderson-Sellers B (2003) Method engineering for OO system development. Comm ACM 46 (10):73–78

Henderson-Sellers B (2005) Creating a comprehensive agent-oriented methodology—using method engineering and the OPEN metamodel. In: Henderson-Sellers B, Giorgini P (eds) Agent-oriented methodologies. Idea Group, Hershey, PA, pp 368–397

Henderson-Sellers B (2006a) Method engineering: theory and practice. In: Karagiannis D, Mayr HC (eds) Information systems technology and its applications. Proceedings of the 5th international conference ISTA, 30–31 May 2006, Klagenfurt, Austria. Lecture notes in informatics (LNI), vol P-84. Gesellschaft für Informatik, Bonn, pp 13–23

Henderson-Sellers B (2006b) SPI—a role for method engineering. In: EUROMICRO 2006. Proceedings of the 32nd EUROMICRO conference on software engineering and advanced applications (SEAA). IEEE Computer Society, Los Alamitos, CA, pp 4–5

Henderson-Sellers B (2007) On the challenges of correctly using metamodels in method engineering, keynote paper. In: Fujita H, Pisanelli D (eds) New trends in software methodologies, tools and techniques. Proceedings of the sixth SoMeT_07. Frontiers in artificial intelligence and applications, vol 161. IOS Press, Amsterdam, pp 3–35

Henderson-Sellers B (2009) Agent-oriented methods and method engineering, chapter 8. In: Chiang R, Siau K, Hardgrave B (eds) Systems analysis and design: techniques, methodologies, approaches, and architectures. M.E. Sharpe, Armonk, NY, pp 118–138

Henderson-Sellers B (2011a) Random thoughts on multi-level conceptual modelling. In: Delcambre L, Kaschek R (eds) The evolution of conceptual modeling. Lecture notes in computer science, vol 6520. Springer, Berlin, pp 93–116

Henderson-Sellers B (2011b) Bridging metamodels and ontologies in software engineering. J Syst Software 84(2):301–313. doi:10.1016/j.jss.2010.10.025

Henderson-Sellers B (2012) On the mathematics of modelling, metamodelling, ontologies and modelling languages (SpringerBriefs in computer science). Springer, Heidelberg, p 106

Henderson-Sellers B, Bulthuis A (1996) The COMMA project. Object Magazine 6(4):24–26

Henderson-Sellers B, Bulthuis A (1998) Object-oriented metamethods. Springer, New York, NY, p 158

Henderson-Sellers B, Edwards JM (1994) BOOKTWO of object-oriented knowledge: the working object. Prentice-Hall, Sydney, p 594 + xxvii

Henderson-Sellers B, Freeman C (1992) Cataloguing and classification for object libraries. ACM SIGSOFT Software Eng Notes 17(1):62–64

Henderson-Sellers B, Gonzalez-Perez C (2005a) The rationale of powertype-based metamodelling to underpin software development methodologies. In: Hartmann S, Stumptner M (eds) Conferences in research and practice in information technology 43. Australian Computer Society, pp 7–16

Henderson-Sellers B, Gonzalez-Perez C (2005b) A comparison of four process metamodels and the creation of a new generic "standard". Inform Software Tech 47(1):49–65

Henderson-Sellers B, Gonzalez-Perez C (2005c) Connecting powertypes and stereotypes. J Object Tech 4(7):83–96

Henderson-Sellers B, Gonzalez-Perez C (2006a) On the ease of extending a powertype-based methodology metamodel, keynote paper. In: Meta-modelling and ontologies. Proceedings of the 2nd workshop on meta-modelling, WoMM 2006. LNI, vol P-96, pp 11–25

Henderson-Sellers B, Gonzalez-Perez C (2006b) Uses and abuses of the stereotype mechanism in UML1.4 and 2.0. In: Nierstrasz O, Whittle J, Harel D, Reggio G (eds) Model driven engineering languages and systems, 9th international conference, MoDELS 2006, Genoa, Italy, October 2006. Lecture notes in computer science, vol 4199. Springer, Berlin, pp 16–26

Henderson-Sellers B, Gonzalez-Perez C (2010) Granularity in conceptual modelling: application to metamodels. In: Proceedings of ER 2010. Lecture notes in computer science, vol 6412. Springer, Berlin, pp 275–288

Henderson-Sellers B, Gonzalez-Perez C (2011) Towards the use of granularity theory for determining the size of atomic method fragments for use in situational method engineering. In:

Ralyté J, Mirbel I, Deneckère R (eds) Engineering methods in the service-oriented context. Proceedings of the 4th IFIP WG8.1 working conference on method engineering, ME 2011, Paris France, April 2011. Springer, Heidelberg, pp 49–63

Henderson-Sellers B, Graham IM with additional input from Atkinson C, Bézivin J, Constantine LL, Dué R, Duke R, Firesmith D, Low G, Mckim J, Mehandjiska-Stavrova D, Meyer B, Odell JJ, Page-Jones M, Reenskaug T, Selic B, Simons AJH, Swatman P, Winder R (1996) OPEN: toward method convergence? IEEE Comput 29(4):86–89

Henderson-Sellers B, Nguyen VP (2004) Un outil d'aide à l'ingénierie de méthodes reposant sur l'approche OPEN. Génie Logiciel 70:17–28

Henderson-Sellers B, Qumer A (2007) Using method engineering to make a traditional environment agile. Cutter IT J 20(5):30–37

Henderson-Sellers B, Ralyte J (2010) Situational method engineering: state-of-the-art review. J Univers Comput Sci 16(3):424–478

Henderson-Sellers B, Serour M (2000) Creating a process for transitioning to object technology. In: Proceedings of the seventh Asia-Pacific software engineering conference. APSEC 2000, IEEE Computer Society, Los Alamitos, CA, pp 436–440

Henderson-Sellers B, Serour MK (2005) Creating a dual agility method—the value of method engineering. J Database Manag 16(4):1–24

Henderson-Sellers B, Unhelkar B (2000) OPEN modeling with UML. Addison-Wesley, Harlow, p 245

Henderson-Sellers B, Constantine LL, Graham IM (1996) Coupling and cohesion (towards a valid metrics suite for object-oriented analysis and design). Object Oriented Syst 3:143–158

Henderson-Sellers B, Simons AJH, Younessi H (1998) The OPEN toolbox of techniques. Addison-Wesley, London, p 426 + CD

Henderson-Sellers B, Dué RT, Graham I, Collins G (2001) A qualitative comparison of two processes for object-oriented software development. Inform Software Tech 43(12):705–724

Henderson-Sellers B, Haire B, Lowe D (2002a) Using OPEN's deontic matrices for e-business. In: Rolland C, Brinkkemper S, Saeki M (eds) Engineering information systems in the internet context. Kluwer Academic, Boston, MA, pp 9–30

Henderson-Sellers B, Lowe D, Haire B (2002b) OPEN process support for web development. Ann Software Eng 13:163–201

Henderson-Sellers B, Stallinger F, Lefever B (2003) The OOSPICE methodology component: creating a CBD process standard, chapter 8. In: Barbier F (ed) Business component-based software engineering. Kluwer Academic, Dordrecht, pp 135–149

Henderson-Sellers B, Giorgini P, Bresciani P (2004a) Enhancing agent OPEN with concepts used in the Tropos methodology. In: Omicini A, Pettra P, Pitt J (eds) Engineering societies in the agents world IVL: 4th international workshop, ESAW 2003. LNAI, vol 3071. Springer, Berlin, pp 328–345

Henderson-Sellers B, Serour M, McBride T, Gonzalez-Perez C, Dagher L (2004b) Process construction and customization. J Univers Comput Sci 10(4):326–358

Henderson-Sellers B, Bohling J, Rout T (2004c) Creating the OOSPICE model architecture—a case of reuse. Software Process Improv Pract 8(1):41–49

Henderson-Sellers B, Serour MK, Gonzalez-Perez C, Qumer A (2007a) Improving agile software development by the application of method engineering practices. In: Hasselbring W (ed) SE'07 Proceedings of the 25th conference on IASTED international multi-conference: software engineering, Innsbruck, 13–15 February 2007. ACTA Press, Anaheim, CA, pp 55–60

Henderson-Sellers B, Gonzalez-Perez C, Ralyté J (2007b) Situational method engineering: chunks or fragments? In: Eder J, Tomassen SL, Opdahl AL, Sindre G (eds) Proceedings of the CAiSE Forum, pp 89–92

Henderson-Sellers B, France R, Georg G, Reddy R (2007c) A method engineering approach to developing aspect-oriented modelling processes based on the OPEN process framework. Inform Software Tech 49(7):761–773. doi:10.1016/j.infsof.2006.08.003

Henderson-Sellers B, Gonzalez-Perez C, Ralyté J (2008) Comparison of method chunks and method fragments for situational method engineering. In: Proceedings 19th Australian software engineering conference. ASWEC2008, IEEE Computer Society, Los Alamitos, CA, pp 479–488

Henderson-Sellers B, Qureshi MA, Gonzalez-Perez C (2012) Towards an interoperable metamodel suite: size assessment as one input. Int J Softw Inform 6(2):111–124 (special issue)

Henderson-Sellers B, Eriksson O, Gonzalez-Perez C, Ågerfalk PJ (2013) Ptolemaic metamodelling? The need for a paradigm shift. In: Cueva Lovelle JM, Pelayo García-Bustelo C, Sanjuán Martínez O (eds) Progressions and innovations in model-driven software engineering. IGI Global, Hershey, PA, pp 90–146

Henninger S, Ivaturi A, Nuli K, Thirunavukkaras A (2002) Supporting adaptable methodologies to meet evolving project needs. In: Proceedings of the 1st ICSE workshop on iterative, adaptive, and agile processes, Orlando, FL, 25 May 2002

Henry S, Kafura D (1981) Software structure metrics based on information flow. IEEE Trans Software Eng 7(5):510–518

Hesse W (2008a) Engineers discovering the "real world"—from model-driven to ontology-based software engineering. In: Kaschek R, Kop C, Steinberger C, Fliedl G (eds) UNISCON 2008. LNBIP vol. 5. Springer, Berlin, pp 136–147

Hesse W (2008b) From conceptual models to ontologies—a software engineering approach, paper presented at Dagstuhl seminar on conceptual modelling, 27–30 April 2008 (preprint on conference website: http://drops.dagstuhl.de/opus/volltexte/2008/1598)

Higgins JM (1995) Storyboard your way to success. Train Dev 49(6):13–18

Hobbs J (1985) Granularity. In: Proceedings of the international joint conference on artificial intelligence (IJCAI-85)

Holmström J, Sawyer S (2011) Requirements engineering blinders: exploring information systems developers' black-boxing of the emergent character of requirements. Eur J Inform Syst 20:34–47

Hong S, van den Goor G, Brinkkemper S (1993) A formal approach to the comparison of object-oriented analysis and design methodologies. In: Proceedings of the 26th Hawaii international conference on system science, vol IV. IEEE Computer Society, Los Alamitos, CA, pp 689–698

Hoppenbrouwers SJBA, Proper HA, van der Weide ThP (2005) A fundamental view on the process of conceptual modelling. In: Delcambre L, Kop C, Mayr HC, Mylopoulos J, Pastor O (eds) ER 2005. Lecture notes in artificial intelligence, vol 3716. Springer, Berlin, pp 128–143

Hoppenbrouwers S, Zoet M, Versendaal J, van de Weerd I (2011) Agile service development: a rule-based method engineering approach. In: Ralyté J, Mirbel I, Deneckère R (eds) Engineering methods in the service-oriented context. Proceedings of the 4th IFIP WG8.1 working conference on method engineering, ME 2011, Paris France, April 2011. Springer, Heidelberg, pp 184–189

Hruby P (2000) Designing customizable methodologies. JOOP 2000:22–31

Hug C (2009) Méthode, modèles et outil pour la méta-modélisation des processus d'ingénierie de systèmes d'information. Ph.D. Thesis, Université Joseph Fourier—Grenoble I, France, p 222

Hug C, Front A, Rieu D (2007a) Un patron pour la méta-modélisation de concepts et de catégories de concepts. INFORSID, p X

Hug C, Front A, Rieu D (2007b) Ingénierie des processus: une approche à base de patrons. INFORSID, pp 471–486

Hug C, Front A, Rieu D (2008) A process engineering method based on ontology and patterns. ICSOFT (ISDM/ABF), pp 29–36

Hug C, Front A, Rieu D, Henderson-Sellers B (2009) A method to build information systems engineering process metamodels. J Syst Software 82(10):1730–1742

Hug C, Mandran N, Front A, Rieu D (2010) Qualitative evaluation of a method for information systems engineering processes. In: Proceedings of RCIS 2010, IEEE Computer Society, Los Alamitos, CA, pp 257–268

Hughes B, Cotterell M (1999) Software project management. McGraw-Hill, London
Hughes J, Reviron E (1996) Selection and evaluation of information system development methodologies: the gap between the theory and practice. In: Jayaratna N, Fitzgerald B (eds) Lessons learned from the use of methodologies (proceedings of the 4th conference on information system methodologies). British Computer Society, London, pp 309–319
Humphrey WS (1988) Characterizing the software process: a maturity framework. IEEE Software 5(2):73–79
Humphrey WS (1989) Managing the software process. Addison-Wesley, Reading, MA
Humphrey WS, Kellner MI (1989) Software process modeling: principles of entity process models, ICSE 1989. IEEE Computer Society/ACM Press, Los Alamitos, CA, pp 331–342
Hurtado Alegria JA (2012) A meta-process for defining adaptable software processes. Ph.D. Thesis, University of Chile
Hurtado Alegria JA, Bastarrica MC, Quispe A, Ochoa SF (2011) An MDE approach to software process tailoring. In: Proceedings of ICSSP '11, 21–22 May 2011, ACM, Waikiki, Honolulu, HI
Iacovelli A (2011) Personal communication to first author
Iacovelli A, Souveyet C (2011) Towards common ground in SME: an ontology of method descriptors. In: Ralyté J, Mirbel I, Deneckère R (eds) Engineering methods in the service-oriented context. Proceedings of 4th IFIP WG8.1 working conference on method engineering, ME 2011, Paris France, April 2011. Springer, Heidelberg, pp 77–90
Iacovelli A, Souveyet C, Rolland C (2008) Method as a service (MaaS). In: Proceedings of international conference on research and challenges of information systems—RCIS 2008, IEEE
Iivari J, Kerola P (1983) A sociocybernetic framework for the feature analysis of information systems design methodologies. In: Olle TW, Sol H, Tully C (eds) Information system design methodologies: a feature analysis. Elsevier, Amsterdam, pp 87–140
Iivari J, Maansaari J (1998) The usage of systems development methods: are we stuck to old practice? Inform Software Tech 40(9):501–510
Introna LD, Whitley EA (1997) Against method-*ism*: exploring the limits of method. Inform Tech People 10(1):31–45
ISO/IEC (1995) Software life cycle processes. ISO/IEC 12207. International Standards Organization/International Electrotechnical Commission, Geneva
ISO/IEC (1998) TR15504—information technology: software process assessment. Technical report. International Standards Organization/International Electrotechnical Commission, Geneva
ISO/IEC (2000) Quality management systems—requirements. ISO/IEC 9001. ISO, Geneva
ISO/IEC (2001) Software engineering—product quality—part 1. Quality model. ISO/IEC 9126–1. International Organization for Standardization, Geneva
ISO/IEC 15504-1 (2004a) Software process assessment—part 1: concepts and vocabulary. ISO/IEC 15504-1:2004. International Standards Organization/International Electrotechnical Commission, Geneva
ISO/IEC 15504-2 (2004b) Information technology—software process assessment—a reference model for processes and process capability. International Standards Organization/International Electrotechnical Commission, Geneva
ISO/IEC 15504-3 (2004c) Information technology—process assessment—part 3: guidance on performing an assessment. International Standards Organization/International Electrotechnical Commission, Geneva
ISO/IEC (2005) Unified Modeling Language (UML) version 1.4.2. ISO/IEC 19501. International Organization for Standardization/International Electrotechnical Commission, Geneva
ISO/IEC (2007) Software engineering: metamodel for development methodologies. ISO/IEC 24744. International Standards Organization/International Electrotechnical Commission, Geneva

ISO/IEC (2008) Systems and software engineering—software life cycle processes. ISO/IEC 12207:2008. International Standards Organization/ International Electrotechnical Commission, Geneva

ISO/IEC (2010a) Software engineering: metamodel for development methodologies. Annex A—notation. International Standards Organization/International Electrotechnical Commission, Geneva

ISO/IEC (2010b) Information technology—process assessment—part 10: safety extension. ISO/IEC 15504–10. ISO, Geneva

ISO/IEC (2011) Systems and software engineering—systems and software quality requirements and evaluation (SQuaRE)—system and software quality models. FDIS 25010. ISO, Geneva

ISO/IEC (2012) OMG Unified Modeling Language (UML2.1.2)—part 1 infrastructure and part 2 superstructure. ISO/IEC 19505. International Organization for Standardization/International Electrotechnical Commission, Geneva

ITGI (2007) COBIT 4.1. IT Governance Institute, Rolling Meadows

Jacobson I, Christerson M, Jonsson P, Övergaard G (1992) Object-oriented software engineering: a use case driven approach. Addison-Wesley, Reading, MA, p 524

Jarke M, Pohl K (1992) Information systems quality and quality information systems. In: Proceedings of the IFIP 8.2 working conference on the impact of computer-supported techniques on information systems development, Minneapolis, MN, June 1992

Jarke M, Mylopoulos J, Schmidt JW, Vassiliou Y (1992) DAIDA: an environment for evolving information systems. ACM Trans Inform Syst 10(1):1–50

Jarke M, Pohl K, Weidenhaupt K, Lyytinen K, Marttiin P, Tolvanen J-P, Papazoglou M (1998) Meta modelling: a formal basis for interoperability and adaptability. In: Krämer B, Schmidt H-W (eds) Information systems interoperability. Research Studies Press Ltd./Wiley, Chichester, pp 229–263

Jarke M, Rolland C, Sutcliffe A, Domges R (1999) The NATURE requirements engineering. Shaker, Aachen

Järvi A, Hakonen H, Mäkilä T (2007) Developer driven approach to situational method engineering. In: Ralyté J, Brinkkemper S, Henderson-Sellers B (eds) Situational method engineering: fundamentals and experiences. Proceedings of the IFIP WG 8.1 working conference, Geneva, Switzerland, 12–14 September 2007. IFIP series, vol 244. Springer, Berlin, pp 94–99

Jayaratna N (1994) Understanding and evaluating methodologies, NIMSAD: a systemic approach. McGraw-Hill, London

Jeffery DR, Basili VR (1988) Validating the TAME resource data model. In: Proceedings of the 10th international conference on software engineering, Singapore, 11–15 April 1988

Jeusfeld MA (2011) A deductive view on process-data diagrams. In: Ralyté J, Mirbel I, Deneckère R (eds) Engineering methods in the service-oriented context. Proceedings of the 4th IFIP WG8.1 working conference on method engineering, ME 2011, Paris France, April 2011. Springer, Heidelberg, pp 123–137

Jørgensen KA (2004) Modelling on multiple abstraction levels. In: Proceedings of the 7th workshop on product structuring—product platform development, Chalmers University of Technology, Göteborg, 24–25 March 2004

Jouault F, Allilaire F, Bezivin J, Kurtev I, Valduriez P (2006) ATL: a QVT-like transformation language. In: Companion to the 21st annual ACM SIGPLAN conference on OOPSLA 2006, ACM, pp 719–720

Karlsson F (2002) Bridging the gap—between method for method configuration and situational method engineering. In: Proceedings of promote IT 2002, 22–24 April 2002, Skövde, Sweden

Karlsson F (2005) Method configuration: method and computerized tool support. Linköping studies in information science. Dissertation no. 11, Linköping University. ISBN: 91-85297-48-8

Karlsson F (2013) Longitudinal use of method rationale in method configuration: an exploratory study. Eur J Inform Syst 22:690–710

Karlsson F, Ågerfalk PJ (2004) Method configuration: adapting to situational characteristics while creating reusable assets. Inform Software Tech 46:619–633

Karlsson F, Ågerfalk PJ (2005) Method-user-centred method configuration. In: Ralyté J, Ågerfalk PJ, Kraiem N (eds) Proceedings of the first international workshop on situational requirements engineering processes: methods, techniques and tools to support situation-specific requirements engineering processes (SREP '05), Paris France, August 2005. In Conjunction with the thirteenth IEEE requirements engineering conference (RE '05), pp 31–43

Karlsson F, Ågerfalk PJ (2007) Multi-grounded action research in method engineering: the MMC case. In: Ralyté J, Brinkkemper S, Henderson-Sellers B (eds) Situational method engineering: fundamentals and experiences. Proceedings of the IFIP WG 8.1 working conference, Geneva, Switzerland, 12–14 September 2007. IFIP series, vol 244. Springer, Berlin, pp 19–32

Karlsson F, Ågerfalk PJ (2008) Method configuration: the eXtreme programming case. Proceedings of the 9th international conference on agile processes in software engineering and extreme programming (XP 2008), Limerick, Ireland, June 10–14, 2008. LNBIP, vol 9. Springer, Berlin, pp 32–41

Karlsson F, Ågerfalk PJ (2009a) Exploring agile values in method configuration. Eur J Inform Syst 18(4):300–316

Karlsson F, Ågerfalk PJ (2009b) Towards structured flexibility in information systems development: devising a method for method configuration. J Database Manag 20(3):51–75

Karlsson F, Ågerfalk PJ (2012) MC Sandbox: devising a tool for method-user-centered method configuration. Inform Software Tech 54(5):501–516

Karlsson F, Wistrand K (2004) MC sandbox—tool support for method configuration. In: Grundspenkis J, Kirikova M (eds) CAiSE '04 workshops in connection with the 16th conference on advanced information systems engineering, Riga, Latvia, 7–11 June 2004. Knowledge and model driven information systems engineering for networked organisations, proceedings. Faculty of computer science and information technology, vol 1. Riga Technical University, Riga, Latvia, pp 199–210

Karlsson F, Wistrand K (2006) Combining method engineering with activity theory: theoretical grounding of the method component concept. Eur J Inform Syst 15:82–90

Karlsson F, Agerfalk P, Hjalmarsson A (2001) Method configuration with development tracks and generic project types. In: Sixth CAiSE/IFIP8.1 international workshop on evaluation of modeling methods in systems analysis and design

Kaschek R (2005) Modelling ontology use for information system. In: Althoff K-D, Dengel A, Bergmann R, Nick M, Roth-Berghofer Th (eds) Professional knowledge management. Lecture notes in computer science, vol 3782. Springer, Berlin, pp 609–622

Keet M (2007) Enhancing comprehension of ontologies and conceptual models through abstractions. In: Basili R, Pazienza MT (eds) AI*IA 2007. LNAI, vol 4733. Springer, Berlin, pp 813–821

Kelly S (1993) A matrix editor for a MetaCASE environment. In: Brinkkemper S, Harmsen F (eds) Proceedings of fourth workshop on the next generation of CASE tools. Memoranda Informatica 93.3, Universiteit Twente, 1–14 May 1993

Kelly S (1997) Towards a comprehensive MetaCASE and CAME environment: conceptual architectural, functional and usability advances in MetaEdit+ dissertation, Jyväskylä studies in computer science, economics and statistics, vol 41, University of Jyväskylä, Finland

Kelly S, Lyytinen K, Rossi M (1996) MetaEdit+: a fully configurable multi-user and multi-tool CASE and CAME environment. In: Vassiliou Y, Mylopoulos J (eds) Proceedings of the 8th conference on advanced information systems engineering. Springer, Berlin

Kelly S, Rossi M, Tolvanen J-P (2005) What is needed in a MetaCASE environment. Enterprise Modell Inform Syst Architect 1(1):25–35

Kerth NL (2001) Project retrospectives: a handbook for team reviews. Dorset House, New York, NY, p 268

Kitchenham BA (1996) Evaluating software engineering methods and tool part 1: the evaluation context and evaluation methods. ACM SIGSOFT Software Eng Notes 21(1):11–14

Klein H, Hirschheim R (2001) Choosing between competing design ideals in information systems development. Inform Syst Front 3(1):75–90
Kokol P (1999) Method engineering and unified paediatric health care encounter design. Int J Healthc Tech Manag 1(3/4):401–408
Kornyshova E, Deneckère R, Salinesi C (2007) Method chunks selection by multicriteria techniques: an extension of the assembly-based approach. In: Ralyté J, Brinkkemper S, Henderson-Sellers B (eds) Situational method engineering: fundamentals and experiences. Proceedings of the IFIP WG 8.1 working conference, 12–14 September 2007, Geneva, Switzerland. IFIP series, vol 244. Springer, Berlin, pp 64–78
Kornyshova E, Deneckère R, Claudepierre B (2010) Contextualization of method components. In: Proceedings of RCIS, IEEE Computer Society, Los Alamitos, CA, pp 235–246
Kornyshova E, Deneckère R, Rolland C (2011) Method families concept: application to decision-making methods. In: Halpin T, Nurcan S, Krogstie J, Soffer P, Proper E, Schmidt R, Bider I (eds) BPMDS 2011 and EMMSAD 2011. LNBIP, vol 81. Springer-Verlag, Berlin, pp 413–427
Kraut RE, Streeter LA (1995) Coordination in software development. Comm ACM 38(3):69–81
Krogstie J, Sølvberg A (2003) Information systems engineering—conceptual modeling in a quality perspective. Kompendiumforlaget, Trondheim
Kruchten PH (1999) The rational unified process: an introduction. Addison-Wesley, Reading, MA
Kühne T (2006) Matters of (meta-) modelling. Software Syst Model 5:369–385
Kumar K, Welke RJ (1992) Methodology engineering: a proposal for situation-specific methodology construction. In: Cotterman WW, Senn JA (eds) Challenges and strategies for research in systems development. Wiley, Chichester, pp 257–269
Kunz W, Rittel HWJ (1970) Issues as elements of information systems. Working paper 131. Institute for Urban and Regional Development, University of California, Berkeley
Laarman A, Kurtev I (2010) Ontological metamodelling with explicit instantiation. In: van den Brand M, Gašević D, Gray J (eds) Software language engineering, second international conference, SLE 2009, revised selected papers. Lecture notes in computer science, vol 5969. Springer-Verlag, Berlin, pp 174–183
Lakoff G (1987) Fire, women, and dangerous things. What categories reveal about the mind. University of Chicago Press, Chicago, IL
Lanza M, Marinescu R (2006) Object-oriented metrics in practice. Springer, Berlin, p 205
Lapouchnian A (2005) Goal-oriented requirements engineering: an overview of the current research. Department of Computer Science, University of Toronto, Toronto, p 30
Lepmets M, McBride T, Ras E (2012) Goal alignment in process improvement. J Syst Software 85 (6):1440–1452
Leppänen M (2006) Towards an ontology for information systems development. In: Krogstie J, Halpin T, Proper E (eds) The 9th international workshop on exploring modeling methods in systems analysis and design (EMMSAD '06), Luxemburg, 5–6 June 2006, in conjunction with the 18th international conference on advanced information systems engineering (CAiSE '06), published in Latour T. and Petit M (eds) Proceedings of workshops and doctoral consortium, Presses Universitaires de Namur, pp 363–374
Leppänen M (2007) An ontological framework of method engineering: an overall structure. In: Proper E, Halpin T, Krostie J (eds) 10th International workshop on exploring modeling methods in systems analysis and design (EMMSAD '07), 11–12 June 2007, Trondheim, Norway. Proceedings of workshops and doctoral consortium. CEUR-WS, vol 365, pp 41–51
Lindland OI, Sindre G, Sølvberg A (1994) Understanding quality in conceptual modeling. IEEE Software 11(2):42–49
Lings B, Lundell B (2004) Method-in-action and method-in-tool: some implications for CASE. Paper presented at the 6th international conference on enterprise information systems (ICEIS 2004)
Low G, Mouratidis H, Henderson-Sellers B (2010) Using a situational method engineering approach to identify reusable method fragments from the secure TROPOS methodology. J Object Tech 9(4):93–125

Lyytinen K (1987) Different perspectives on information systems: problems and solutions. ACM Comput Surv 19(1):5–46
Lyytinen K, Robey D (1999) Learning failure in information systems development. Inform Syst J 9:85–101
Lyytinen K, Kerola P, Kaipala J, Kelly S, Lehto J, Liu H, Marttiin P, Oinas-Kukkonen H, Pirhonen J, Rossi M, Smolander K, Tahvanainen V-P, Tolvanen J-P (1994) MetaPHOR: metamodeling, principles, hypertext, objects and repositories. Computer science and information systems reports, technical report TR-7. Department of Computer Science and Information Systems, University of Jyväskylä, Finland, p 39
Ma H, Shao W, Zhang L, Ma Z, Jiang Y (2004) Applying OO metrics to assess UML meta-models. In: Baar T, Strohmeier A, Moreira A, Mellor SJ (eds) UML 2004. Lecture notes in computer science, vol 3273. Springer, Berlin, pp 12–26
MacCormack A, Verganti R (2003) Managing the sources of uncertainty: matching process and context in software development. J Prod Innovat Manag 20(3):217–232
MacIsaac B (2003) An overview of the RUP as a process engineering platform. In: Gonzalez-Perez C, Henderson-Sellers B, Rawsthorne D (eds) Proceedings of the OOPSLA 2003 workshop on process engineering for object-oriented and component-based development, Anaheim, CA, 26–30 October 2003. COTAR, Sydney, pp 43–52
MacLean A, Young RM, Bellotti VME, Moran TP (1991) Questions, options, and criteria: elements of design space analysis. Hum Comput Interact 6(3/4):201–250
Madhavji NH (1991) The process cycle. Software Eng J 6(5):234–242
Maiden NAM, Gizikis A, Robertson S (2004) Provoking creativity: imagine what your requirements could be like. IEEE Software 21(5):68–75
Malcolm E (2001) Requirements acquisition for rapid applications development. Inform Manag 39:101–107
Mani I (1998) A theory of granularity and its application to problems of polysemy and underspecification of meaning. In: Cohn AG, Schubert LK, Shapiro SC (eds) Principles of knowledge representation and reasoning: proceedings of the sixth international conference (KR '98). Morgan Kaufmann, San Mateo, CA, pp 245–257
Martínez LG, Castro JR, Licea G, Rodríguez-Díaz A, Alvarez CF (2011) Knowing software engineer's personality to improve software development. In: Escalona MJ, Shishkov B, Cordeiro J (eds) Proceedings of the 6th international conference on software and database technologies (ICSOFT 2011), vol 2, Seville, Spain, 18–21 July 2011. SciTePress, Lisbon, pp 99–104
Martinez-Ruiz T, Garcia F, Piattini M, Münch J (2011) Modelling software process variability: an empirical study. IET Software 5(2):172–187
Marttiin P, Koskinen M (1998) Similarities and differences of method engineering and process engineering approaches. In: Khosrowpour M (ed) Effective utilization and management of emerging information technologies. IRMA international conference, pp 420–424
Marttiin P, Lyytinen K, Rossi M, Tahvanainen V-P, Tolvanen J-P (1995) Modeling requirements for future CASE: issues and implementation considerations. Inform Resour Manag J 8(1):15–25
Mayer T, Hall T (1999) A critical analysis of current OO design metrics. Software Qual J 8:97–110
McBride T (2008) The mechanisms of project management of software development. J Syst Software 81(12):2386–2395
McBride T (2011) Personal communication to first author
McBride T, Henderson-Sellers B (2011) A method assessment framework. In: Ralyté J, Mirbel I, Deneckère R (eds) Engineering methods in the service-oriented context. Proceedings of the 4th IFIP WG8.1 working conference on method engineering, ME 2011, April 2011, Paris France. Springer, Heidelberg, pp 64–76
McBride T, Henderson-Sellers B, Zowghi D (2006) Managed outsourced software development: does organisational distance demand different project management? In: Proceedings of UKAIS 2006, Cheltenham, 10–11 April 2006, CD

McGregor JD, Korson T (1993) Supporting dimensions of classification in object-oriented design. J Object-Orient Prog 5(9):25–30

McIlroy MD (1968) Mass produced software components. Paper presented at the North Atlantic Treaty Organisation (NATO) conference on software engineering, Garmisch-Partenkirchen, Germany

Mellor SJ, Scott K, Uhl A, Weise D (2004) MDA distilled. Principles of model-driven architecture. Addison-Wesley, Boston, MA, p 150

Meyer B (1997) Object-oriented software construction, 2nd edn. Prentice-Hall, Upper Saddle River, NJ

Mirandolle D, van de Weerd I, Brinkkemper S (2011) Incremental method engineering for process improvement—a case study. In: Ralyté J, Mirbel I, Deneckère R (eds) Engineering methods in the service-oriented context. Proceedings of the 4th IFIP WG8.1 working conference on method engineering, ME 2011, Paris France, April 2011. Springer, Heidelberg, pp 4–18

Mirbel I (2006) Method chunk federation. In: Latour T, Petit M (eds) CAiSE '06. 18th Conference on advanced information systems engineering—trusted information systems, Luxembourg 5–9 June 2006. Proceedings of the workshops and doctoral consortium. Namur University Press, Namur, pp 407–418

Mirbel I (2007) Connecting method engineering knowledge: a community based approach. In: Ralyté J, Brinkkemper S, Henderson-Sellers B (eds) Situational method engineering: fundamentals and experiences. Proceedings of the IFIP WG 8.1 working conference, 12–14 September 2007, Geneva, Switzerland. IFIP series, vol 244. Springer, Berlin, pp 176–192

Mirbel I, De Rivieres V (2002) Adapting analysis and design to software context: the JECKO approach. In: Bellahsène Z, Patel D, Rolland C (eds) Proceedings of the 8th international conference on object-oriented information systems (OOIS '02), Montpellier, France, 2–5 September 2002. Lecture notes in computer science, vol 2425. Springer, Berlin, pp 223–228

Mirbel I, Ralyté J (2006) Situational method engineering: combining assembly-based and roadmap-driven approaches. Requir Eng 11:58–78

Mohagheghi P, Aagedal J (2007) Evaluating quality in model-driven engineering, international workshop on modeling in software engineering (MISE '07), IEEE Computer Society

Mohan K, Ahlemann F (2011a), Understanding acceptance of information system development and management methodologies by actual users: a review and assessment of existing literature. In: Proceedings of the 10th international conference on Wirtschaftsinformatik, Zurich, Switzerland, 16–18 February 2011, AIS Electronic Library (AISeL), paper 41, http://aisel.aisnet.org/wi2011/41

Mohan K, Ahlemann F (2011b) A theory of user acceptance of IS project management methodologies: understanding the influence of psychological determinism and experience. In: Proceedings of the 10th international conference on Wirtschaftsinformatik, Zurich, Switzerland, 16–18 February 2011, AIS Electronic Library (AISeL), paper 24, http://aisel.aisnet.org/wi2011/24

Mohan K, Ahlemann F (2011c) What methodology attributes are critical for potential users? Understanding the effect of human needs, In: Mouratidis H, Rolland C (eds) Advanced information systems engineering. 23rd International conference, CAiSE 2011, London, UK, June 2011. Lecture notes in computer science, vol 6741. Springer, Berlin, pp 314–328

Monarchi D, Puhr GI (1992) A research typology for object-oriented analysis and design. Comm ACM 35(9):35–47

Monarchi D, Booch G, Henderson-Sellers B, Jacobson I, Mellor S, Rumbaugh J, Wirfs-Brock R (1994) Methodology standards: help or hindrance? Proceedings of the ninth annual OOPSLA conference, ACM SIGPLAN, vol 29, no. 10, pp 223–228

Moody DL (2005) Theoretical and practical issues in evaluating the quality of conceptual models: current state and future directions. Data Knowl Eng 55:243–276

Moody D, van Hillegersberg J (2008) Evaluating the visual syntax of UML: an analysis of the cognitive effectiveness of the UML family of diagrams. In: Software language engineering,

SLE 2008, revised selected papers. Lecture notes in computer science, vol 5452. Springer, Berlin, pp 16–34

Nandhakumar J, Avison DE (1999) The fiction of methodological development: a field study of information systems development. Inform Tech People 12(2):176–191

Naumann JD, Jenkins AM (1982) Prototyping: the new paradigm for systems development. MIS Q 6(3):29–44

Nehan Y-R, Deneckère R (2007) Component-based situational methods. A framework for understanding SME. In: Ralyté J, Brinkkemper S, Henderson-Sellers B (eds) Situational method engineering: fundamentals and experiences. Proceedings of the IFIP WG 8.1 working conference, Geneva, Switzerland, 12–14 September 2007. IFIP series, vol 244. Springer, Berlin, pp 161–175

Nguyen VP, Henderson-Sellers B (2003a) Towards automated support for method engineering with the OPEN approach. In: Proceedings of the 7th IASTED SEA conference. ACTA Press, Anaheim, CA, pp 691–696

Nguyen VP, Henderson-Sellers B (2003b) OPENPC: a tool to automate aspects of method engineering. In: Proceedings of ICSSEA 2003, Paris, France, vol 5, p 7

Nguyen L, Swatman PA (2000) Complementary use of ad hoc and post hoc design rationale for creating and organising process knowledge. In: Proceedings of HICSS 2000

Nickols FW (1993) Prototyping: systems development in record time. J Syst Manag 44(9):26–30

Nidumolu SR (1996) A comparison of the structural contingency and risk-based perspectives on coordination in software development projects. J Manag Inform Syst 13(2):77–113

Niknafs A, Ramsin R (2008) Computer-aided method engineering: an analysis of existing environments. In: Proceedings of the 20th international conference on information systems engineering (CAiSE '08). Lecture notes in computer science, vol 5074. Springer, Berlin, pp 525–540

Niknafs A, Asadi M, Abolhassani H (2007) Ontology-based method engineering. Int J Comput Sci Netw Secur 7(8):282–287

Nonaka I (1994) A dynamic theory of organizational knowledge creation. Organ Sci 5(1):14–37

Nugroho A, Chaudron MRV (2009) Evaluating the impact of UML modeling on software quality: an industrial case study. In: Schürr A, Selic B (eds) MoDELS 2009. Lecture notes in computer science, vol 5795. Springer, Berlin, pp 181–195

Nuseibeh B, Finkelstein A, Kramer J (1996) Method engineering for multi-perspective software development. Inform Software Tech 38(4):267–274

Odell JJ (1994) Power types. J Object-Orient Prog 7(2):8–12

Odell JJ (1995) Introduction to method engineering. Object Magazine 5(5):69–72, 91

Odell JJ (1996) Keynote paper: a primer to method engineering. In: Brinkkemper S, Lyytinen K, Welke RJ (eds) Method engineering. Principles of method construction and tool support. Chapman & Hall, London, pp 1–7

Oinas-Kukkonen H (1996) Method rationale in method engineering and use. In: Brinkkemper S, Lyytinen K, Welke RJ (eds) Method engineering. Principles of method construction and too support. Proceedings of IFIP TC8, WG8.1/8.2 working conference on method engineering, Atlanta, USA, 26–28 August 1996. Chapman & Hall, London, pp 87–93

Oivo M, Basili VR (1992) Representing software engineering models: the TAME goal oriented approach. IEEE Trans Software Eng 18(10):886–898

Okoli C, Pawlowski SD (2004) The Delphi method as a research tool: an example, design considerations and applications. Inform Manag 42(1):15–29

OMG (1997) UML semantics. Version 1.1, 15 September 1997, OMG document ad/97-08-04

OMG (2001) OMG Unified Modeling Language specification, version 1.4. OMG documents formal/01-09-68 through 80 (13 documents). http://www.omg.org. Accessed 12 July 2002

OMG (2002) Software process engineering metamodel specification, formal/2002-11-14. Object Management Group

OMG (2003) MDA guide version 1.0.1, OMG document omg/03-06-01

OMG (2005a) Software process engineering metamodel specification, version 1.1. formal/05-01-06. Object Management Group

OMG (2005b) Unified Modeling Language: superstructure, version 2.0, formal/05-07-04, p 709

OMG (2006) Unified Modeling Language: infrastructure. Version 2.0. formal/05-07-05, p 218

OMG (2007) Unified Modeling Language: superstructure. Version 2.1.1, OMG document formal/07-02-03

OMG (2008) Software & systems process engineering meta-model specification. Version 2.0, OMG document number: formal/2008-04-01

OMG (2009a) Business process model and notation (BPMN) FTF beta 1 for version 2.0, OMG document no dtc/2009-08-14

OMG (2009b) Architecture-driven modernization (ADM): software metrics meta-model (SMM) FTF—beta 1. OMG document no ptc/2009-03-03

OMG (2009c) Ontology definition metamodel version 1.0, OMG document no formal/2009-05-01

OMG (2009d) Organization structure metamodel (OSM) 3rd initial submission. OMG document no bmi/09-08-02

OMG (2010) OMG Unified Modeling Language™ (OMG UML), superstructure. Version 2.3, OMG document formal/2010-05-05

OMG (2011) A foundation for the agile creation and enactment of software engineering methods request for proposal, OMG document ad/2011-05-22

OOSPICE (2002) Software process improvement and capability determination for object-oriented/component-based software development. www.oospice.com

Opdahl A, Henderson-Sellers B (2000) Evaluating and improving OO modelling languages using the BWW-model. In: Dampney CNG (ed) Proceedings of the information systems foundations workshop—ontology, semiotics and practice 1999, Lighthouse Press, Macquarie University, Sydney, pp 31–38

Opdahl A, Henderson-Sellers B (2002) Ontological evaluation of the UML using the Bunge-Wand-Weber model. Software Syst Model 1(1):43–67

Opdahl AL, Henderson-Sellers B, Barbier F (2001) Ontological analysis of whole-part relationships in OO models. Inform Software Tech 43(6):387–399

OPF (2005) Open process framework. http://www.opfro.org

Osterwalders A, Pigneur Y (2010) Business model generation: a handbook for visionaries, game changers and challengers. Wiley, Chichester, NY

Pareto L, Staron M, Eriksson P (2008) Strategic software process improvement by technology roadmapping. In: Proceedings of the Nordic workshop on model driven engineering NW-MoDE 2008 Reykjavík, Iceland 20–22 August 2008, Engineering Research Institute, University of Iceland, pp 145–159

Parnas DL (1972) A technique for software module specification with examples. Comm ACM 15 (5):330–336

Parnas DL, Clements PC (1986) A rational design process: how and why to fake it. IEEE Trans Software Eng 12(2):251–257

Partridge C, Gonzalez-Perez C, Henderson-Sellers B (2013) Are conceptual models concept models. In: Ng W, Storey VC, Trujillo, J (eds) Proceedings of ER 2013. Lecture notes in computer science, vol 8217. Springer, Heidelberg, pp 96–105

Patel C, De Cesare S, Iacovelli N, Merico A (2004) A framework for method tailoring: a case study. In: Serour M (ed) Proceedings of the second workshop on method engineering for object-oriented and component-based development. Centre for Object Technology Applications and Research, Sydney, pp 23–37

Paulk MC, Curtis B, Chrissis MB, Weber CV (1993) The capability maturity model: version 1.1. IEEE Software 10(4):18–27

Pedreira O, Piattini M, Luaces MR, Brisaboa NR (2007) A systematic review of software process tailoring. ACM SIGSOFT Software Eng Notes 32(3):1–6

Pereira EB, Bastos RM, da C Mora M, Oliveria TC (2011) Improving the consistency of SPEM-based software processes. In: Zhang R, Cordeiro J, Li X, Zhang Z, Zhang J (eds) Proceedings of the 13th international conference on enterprise information systems (ICEIS 2011), volume 3, Beijing, China, 8–11 June 2011. SciTePress, Beijing, pp 76–86

Perez G, El Amam K, Madhavji NH (1995) Customising software process models. In: Proceedings of the 4th EWSPT, Leiden, Holland, March 1995, pp 70–78

Pfleeger SL (1999) Albert Einstein and empirical software engineering. Computer 32(10):32–38

Plihon V (1996) Un environnement pour l'ingénierie des méthodes. Ph.D. Thesis, University of Paris I, Paris, France

Plihon V, Ralyté J, Benjamen A, Maiden NAM, Sutcliffe A, Dubois E, Heymans P (1998) A reuse-oriented approach for the construction of scenario based methods. In: 5th International conference on software process (ICSP '98), Chicago, Illinois, USA

Polanyi M (1958) Personal knowledge: towards a post-critical philosophy. Routledge & K. Paul, Chicago

Potts C (1989) A generic model for representing design methods. In: ICSE '89, ACM Press, Washington, DC, pp 217–226

Potts C, Bruns G (1988) Recording the reasons for design decisions. In: ICSE '88, IEEE Computer Society, Los Alamitos, CA, pp 418–427

Prakash N, Goyal SB (2007) Towards a life cycle for method engineering. In: Proper HA, Halpin TA, Krogstie J (eds) Proceedings of the 12th workshop on exploring modeling methods for systems analysis and design (EMMSAD '07), held in conjunction with the 19th conference on advanced information systems engineering (CAiSE '07), Trondheim, Norway, pp 27–36. CEUR workshop proceedings

Prat N (1997) Goal formalisation and classification for requirements engineering. In: Proceedings of the 3rd international workshop on requirements engineering: foundations of software quality REFSQ '97, Barcelona, pp 145–156

Prieto-Diaz R, Freeman P (1987) Classifying software for reusability. IEEE Software 4(1):6–16

Punter HT, Lemmen K (1996) The MEMA model: towards a new approach for method engineering. Inform Software Tech 38(4):295–305

Puviani M, Cabri G, Leonardi L (2009) The future of AOSE: exploiting SME for a new conception of methodologies. In: Proceedings of WOA09

Qumer A, Henderson-Sellers B (2006) Measuring agility and adoptability of agile methods: a 4-dimensional analytical tool. In: Guimarães N, Isaias P, Goikoetxea A (eds) Proceedings of IADIS international conference applied computing 2006, IADIS Press, pp 503–507

Qumer A, Henderson-Sellers B (2007) Construction of an agile software product enhancement process by using an agile software solution framework (ASSF) and situational method engineering. In: Proceedings of the 31st annual international computer software and applications conference, Beijing, China, 23–27 July 2007, vol 1, IEEE Computer Society, Los Alamitos, CA, pp 539–542

Qumer A, Henderson-Sellers B (2008) An evaluation of the degree of agility in six agile methods and its applicability for method engineering. Inform Software Tech 50(4):280–295

Qureshi MA (2012) Interoperability of software engineering metamodels. In: Kienzle J (ed) Models in software engineering. Workshops and symposia at MODELS 2011, Wellington, New Zealand, 16–21 October 2011, reports and revised selected papers. Lecture notes in computer science, vol 7167. Springer, Berlin, pp 12–19

Ralyté J (1999) Reusing scenario based approaches in requirements engineering methods: CREWS method base. In: Proceedings of the 10th international workshop on database and expert systems applications (DEXA '99), 1st international REP '99 workshop, Florence, Italy

Ralyté J (2001) Ingénierie des methods par assemblage de composants. Thèse de doctorat en informatique de l'Université Paris 1, Janvier 2001, France

Ralyté J (2002) Requirements definition for the situational method engineering. In: Rolland C, Brinkkemper S, Saeki M (eds) Engineering information systems in the internet context. Kluwer Academic, Boston, MA, pp 127–152

Ralyté J (2004) Towards situational methods for information systems development: engineering reusable method chunks. In: Vasilecas O, Caplinskas A, Wojtkowski W, Wojtkowski WG,

Zupancic J, Wrycza S (eds) Proceedings of the 13th international conference on information systems development. Advances in theory, practice and education. Vilnius Gediminas Technical University, Vilnius, Lithuania, pp 271–282

Ralyté J (2013) Situational method engineering in practice: a case study in a small enterprise. In: Deneckère R, Proper HA (eds) Proceedings of the CAiSE '13 forum at the 25th international conference on advanced information systems engineering, Valencia, Spain, 20 June 2013. CEUR-WS, vol 998, pp 17–24

Ralyté J, Rolland C (2001a) An assembly process model for method engineering. In: Dittrich KR, Geppert A, Norrie MC (eds) Advanced information systems engineering. Lecture notes in computer science, vol 2068. Springer, Berlin, pp 267–283

Ralyté J, Rolland C (2001b) An approach for method engineering. In: Proceedings of the 20th international conference on conceptual modelling (ER2001). Lecture notes in computer science, vol 2224. Springer, Berlin, pp 471–484

Ralyté J, Rolland C, Plihon V (1999) Method enhancement by scenario based techniques. In: Advanced information systems engineering. In: Jarke M, Overweis A (eds) Proceedings of the 11th international conference, CAiSE '99, Heidelberg, Germany, 14–18 June 1999. Lecture notes in computer science, vol 1626. Springer, Berlin, pp 103–118

Ralyté J, Deneckère R, Rolland C (2003) Towards a generic method for situational method engineering. In: Eder J, Missikoff M (eds) Advanced information systems engineering. Proceedings of the 15th international conference, CAiSE 2003, Klagenfurt, Austria, 16–18 June 2003. Lecture notes in computer science, vol 2681. Springer, Berlin, pp 95–110

Ralyté J, Rolland C, Deneckère R (2004) Towards a meta-tool for change-centric method engineering: a typology of generic operators. In: Persson A, Stirna J (eds) Proceedings of CAiSE 2004. Lecture notes in computer science, vol 3084. Springer, Berlin, pp 202–218

Ralyté J, Rolland C, Ben Ayed M (2005) An approach for evolution-driven method engineering. In: Krogstie J, Halpin T, Siau K (eds) 'Information modeling methods and methodologies' (advanced topics in database research). Idea Group, Hershey, PA, pp 80–100

Ralyté J, Backlund P, Kühn H, Jeusfeld MA (2006) Method chunks for interoperability. In: Embley DW, Olivé A, Ram S (eds) Proceedings of ER2006. Lecture notes in computer science, vol 4215. Springer, Heidelberg, pp 339–353

Ralyté J, Brinkkemper S, Henderson-Sellers B (eds) (2007) Situational method engineering: fundamentals and experiences. Springer, New York, NY

Ralyté J, Mirbel I, DeneckèreR (eds) (2011) Engineering methods in the service-oriented context. Proceedings of the 4th IFIP WG8.1 working conference on method engineering, ME 2011, Paris France, April 2011. Springer, Heidelberg

Ramesh B, Dhar V (1992) Supporting systems development by capturing deliberations during requirements engineering. IEEE Trans Software Eng 18(6):498–510

Rausch A, Höhn R, Höppner S (2005) Das V-modell XT. Springer, Berlin

Recker J, Rosemann M, Green P, Indulska M (2007) Exending the scope of representation theory: a review and proposed research model. In: Hart DN, Gregor SD (eds) Information systems foundations: theory, representation and reality. ANU E Press, Canberra, pp 93–114

Reinertsen DG (2009) The principles of product development flow: second generation lean product development. Celeritas Publishing, Redondo Beach

Reinicke B (2012) It's 2012, so why am I driving a 1972 bug? IEEE Comput 45(10):100–103

Rettig M (1994) Prototyping for tiny fingers. Comm ACM 37(4):21–28

Riemenschneider CK, Hardgrave BC, Davis FD (2002) Explaining software developer acceptance of methodologies: a comparison of five theoretical models. IEEE Trans Software Eng 28 (12):1135–1145

Rising L, Janoff NS (2000) The Scrum software development process for small teams. IEEE Software 17(4):26–32

Rogers B, Henderson-Sellers B (2014) Applying a test for atomicity of method fragments. In: Grossmann G, Saeki M (eds) 10th Asia-Pacific conference on conceptual modelling (APCCM

2014), Auckland, New Zealand, 20–23 January 2014. Conferences in research and practice in information technology (CRPIT), vol 154, pp 49–54
Rolland C (1998) A comprehensive view of process engineering. In: Pernici B, Thanos C (eds) Advanced information systems engineering: proceedings of the 10th international conference, CAiSE '98, Pisa, Italy, June 1998. Lecture notes in computer science, vol 1413. Springer, Berlin, pp 1–24
Rolland C (2002) A user centric view of Lyee requirements. In: Fujita H, Johannesson P (eds) New trends in software methodologies, tools and techniques. IOS Press, Tokyo
Rolland R (2005) Modelisation of the O* process with MAP, internal report of the 'Centre de Recherche en Informatique', University Paris 1 Sorbonne
Rolland C (2009) Method engineering: towards methods as services. Software Process Improv Pract 14(3):143–164
Rolland C, Nurcan S (2010) Business process lines to deal with the variability. In: Proceedings of the 43rd HICSS, IEEE Computer Society, Los Alamitos, CA, pp 1–10
Rolland C, Plihon V (1996) Using generic chunks to generate process models fragments. In: Proceedings of the 2nd IEEE international conference on requirements engineering, ICRE '96, Colorado Springs
Rolland C, Prakash N (1996) A proposal for context-specific method engineering. In: Brinkkemper S, Lyytinen K, Welke RJ (eds) Method engineering. Principles of method construction and tool support. Proceedings of IFIP TC8, WG8.1/8.2 working conference on method engineering, 26–28 August 1996, Atlanta, USA. Chapman & Hall, London, pp 191–208
Rolland C, Souveyet C, Moreno M (1995) An approach for defining ways-of-working. Inform Syst 20(4):295–305
Rolland C, Plihon V, Ralyté J (1998) Specifying the reuse context of scenario method chunks. In: Pernici B, Thanos C (eds) Advanced information systems engineering: proceedings of the 10th international conference, CAiSE '98, Pisa, Italy, 8–12 June 1998. Lecture notes in computer science, vol 1413. Springer, Berlin, pp 191–218
Rolland C, Prakash N, Benjamen A (1999) A multi-model view of process modelling. Requir Eng 4(4):169–187
Rolland C, Nurcan S, Grosz G (2000) A decision making pattern for guiding the enterprise knowledge development process. J Inf Software Technol 42:313–331
Rombach D (2005) Integrated software process and product lines. In: Li M, Boehm B, Osterweil LJ (eds) ISPW. Lecture notes in computer science, vol 3840. Springer, Berlin, pp 83–90
Rooksby J, Sommerville I, Pidd M (2006) A hybrid approach to upstream requirements: IBIS and cognitive mapping, chapter 6. In: Dutoit AH, McCall R, Mistrik I, Paech, B (eds) Rationale management in software engineering. Springer, Berlin, pp 137–154
Rossi M (1995) The MetaEdit CAME environment. In: Proceedings of MetaCase 95, University of Sunderland Press, Sunderland
Rossi M (1998) Advanced computer support for method engineering—implementation of CAME environment in MetaEdit+ dissertation, Jyväskylä studies in computer science, economics and statistics, vol 42. University of Jyväskylä, Finland
Rossi M, Brinkkemper S (1996) Complexity metrics for systems development methods and techniques. Inform Syst 21(2):209–227
Rossi M, Tuunanen T (2010) A method and tool for rapid consumer application development. Int J Organ Des Eng 1(1/2):109–125. doi:10.1504/IJODE.2010.035189
Rossi M, Tolvanen J-P, Ramesh B, Lyytinen K, Kaipala J (2000) Method rationale in method engineering. In: Proceedings of the 33rd Hawaii international conference on systems sciences (HICSS-33), IEEE Computer Society, Los Alamitos, CA, p 10
Rossi M, Ramesh B, Lyytinen K, Tolvanen J-P (2004) Managing evolutionary method engineering by method rationale. J Assoc Inform Syst 5(9):356–391

Röstlinger A, Goldkuhl G (1994) Generisk flexibilitet—På väg mot en komponentbaserad metodsyn. In Swedish: "Generic flexibility—towards a component-based view of methods". Department of Computer and Information Science, Linköping University, Linköping

Ruiz F, Hilera JR (2006) Using ontologies in software engineering and technology. In: Calero C, Ruiz F, Piattini M (eds) Ontologies for software engineering and software technology. Springer, Berlin, pp 49–102

Rumbaugh J, Blaha M, Premerlani W, Eddy F, Lorensen W (1991) Object-oriented modelling and design. Prentice Hall, Englewood Cliffs, NJ, p 500

Rupprecht C, Funffinger M, Knublauch H, Rose T (2000) Capture and dissemination of experience about the construction of engineering processes. In: Proceedings of the 12th conference on advanced information systems engineering (CAISE). Lecture notes in computer science, vol 1789. Springer, Berlin, pp 294–308

Russo NL, Stolterman E (2000) Exploring the assumptions underlying information systems methodologies: their impact on past, present and future ISM research. Inform Tech People 13(4):313–327

Saeki M (2002) Role of model transformation in method engineering. In: Banks Pidduck A, Mylopoulos J, Woo CC, Tamer Ozsu M (eds) CAISE 2002. Lecture notes in computer science, vol 2348. Springer, Berlin, pp 626–642

Saeki M (2003a) Embedding metrics into information systems development methods: an application of method engineering technique. In: Eder J, Missikoff M (eds) Proceedings of CAiSE '03. Lecture notes in computer science, vol 2681. Springer, Berlin, pp 374–389

Saeki M (2003b) CAME: the first step to automated method engineering. In: Gonzalez-Perez CA, Henderson-Sellers B, Rawsthorne D (eds) Process engineering for object-oriented and component-based development. Proceedings of the OOPSLA 2003 workshop. Centre for Object Technology and Applications, University of Technology, Sydney, pp 7–18

Saeki M, Kaiya H (2007) On relationships among models, meta models and ontologies. In: Proceedings of the 6th OOPSLA workshop on domain-specific modeling

Saeki M, Iguchi K, Wen-yin K, Shinohara M (1993) A meta-model for representing software specification & design methods. In: Proceedings of IFIP WG8.1 conference on information systems development process, Come, pp 149–166

Scheer AW (2000) ARIS—business process modeling. Springer, Berlin

Schön D (1983) The reflective practitioner. Basic Books Inc., New York, NY

Schwaber K (1997) Scrum development process. In: Sutherland J, Patel D, Casanave C, Miller J, Hollowell G (eds) Business object design and implementation: proceedings of OOPSLA '95 workshop. Springer, London

Schwaber K, Beedle M (2001) Agile software development with SCRUM. Prentice Hall, Upper Saddle River, NJ

Scott L, Carvalho L, Jeffery R, D'Ambra J (2001) An evaluation of the Spearmint approach to software process modelling. In: Ambriola V (ed) Software process technology. Proceedings of the 8th European workshop, EWSPT 2001. Lecture notes in computer science, vol 2077. Springer, Berlin, pp 77–89

Searle JR (1969) Speech acts: an essay in the philosophy of language. Cambridge University Press, Cambridge

SEI (2001) Standard CMMI appraisal method for process improvement (SCAMPI). CMU/SEI-2001-HB-001

SEI (2005) Process maturity profile—CMMI 2005 year-end update

SEI (2006) CMMI® for development, version 1.2. CMU/SEI-2006-TR-008

Seidewitz E (2003) What models mean. IEEE Software 20(5):26–31

Seidita V, Ralyté J, Henderson-Sellers B, Cossentino M, Arni-Bloch N (2007) A comparison of deontic matrices, maps and activity diagrams for the construction of situational methods. In: Proceedings of the CAiSE Forum, CAiSE2007, Trondheim, June 2007

Sen S, Moha N, Baudry B, Jezequel JM (2009) Metamodel pruning. In: ACM/IEEE 12th international conference on model driven engineering languages and systems (MODELS '09), Springer, pp 32–46

Serour MK (2003) The effect of intra-organisational factors on the organisational transition to object technology. Ph.D. Thesis, University Technology, Sydney, Australia

Serour MK, Henderson-Sellers B (2004a) OPEN for agility: an action research study of introducing method engineering into a government sector. In: Vasilecas O, Caplinskas A, Wojtkowski W, Wojtkowski WG, Zupancic J, Wrycza S (eds) Proceedings of the 13th international conference on information systems development. Advances in theory, practice and education. Vilnius Gediminas Technical University, Vilnius, Lithuania, pp 105–116

Serour MK, Henderson-Sellers B (2004b) Introducing agility: a case study of situational method engineering using the OPEN process framework. In: Proceedings of the 28th annual international computer software and applications conference. COMPSAC 2004, IEEE Computer Society, Los Alamitos, CA, pp 50–57

Serour M, Henderson-Sellers B, Hughes J, Winder D, Chow L (2002) Organizational transition to object technology: theory and practice. In: Bellahsène Z, Patel D, Rolland C (eds) Object-oriented information systems. Lecture notes in computer science, vol 2425. Springer, Berlin, pp 229–241

Serour MK, Dagher L, Prior J, Henderson-Sellers B (2004) OPEN for agility: an action research study of introducing method engineering into a government sector. In: Vasilecas O, Caplinskas A, Wojtkowski W, Wojtkowski WG, Zupancic J, Wrycza S (eds) Proceedings of the 13th international conference on information systems development. Advances in theory, practice and education. Vilnius Gediminas Technical University, Vilnius, Lithuania, pp 105–116

Siau K, Rossi M (1998) Information modeling methods and methodologies—evaluation techniques. Proceedings of HICSS, vol 5, pp 312–313

Siau K, Rossi M (2007) Evaluation techniques for systems analysis and design modelling methods—a review and comparative analysis. Inform Syst J 21:249–268

Siau K, Tan X (2005) Improving the quality of conceptual modeling using cognitive mapping techniques. Data Knowl Eng 55:343–365

Silver B (2009) BPMN method & style. Cody-Cassidy Press, Aptos, CA

Simidchieva BJ, Clarke LA, Osterweil LJ (2007) Representing process variation with a process family. In: Wang Q, Pfahl D, Raffo DM (eds) ICSP 2007. Lecture notes in computer science, vol 4470. Springer, Berlin, pp 109–120

Smith B (2004) Beyond concepts: ontology as reality representation. In: Varzi A, Vieu L (eds) Proceedings of FOIS 2004. International conference on formal ontology and information systems, Turin, 4–6 November 2004. IOS Press, Amsterdam, pp 73–84

Smolander K (1990) Metamodels in CASE environments. Licenciate Thesis, computer science reports, University of Jyväskylä, Jyväskylä, Finland

Smolander K (1992) OPRR—a model for modeling systems development methods. In: Lyytinen K, Tahvanainen V-P (eds) Next generation CASE tools. IOS Press, Amsterdam, pp 224–239

Smolander K, Tahvanainen V-P, Lyytinen K (1990) How to combine tools and methods in practice—a field study. In: Steinholtz B, Sølvberg A, Bergman L (eds) Proceedings of the second Nordic conference CAiSE '90. Lecture notes in computer science. Springer, Berlin, pp 195–211

Smolander K, Tahvanainen V-P, Lyytinen K, Marttiin P (1991) MetaEdit—a flexible graphical environment for methodology modeling. In: Andersen R, Bubenko J, S¢lvberg A (eds) Advanced information systems engineering. Springer, Berlin, pp 168–193

Song X (1995) A framework for understanding the integration of design methodologies. ACM SIGSOFT Software Eng Notes 20(1):46–54

Stallinger F, Henderson-Sellers B, Torgersson J (2003) The OOSPICE assessment component: customizing software process assessment to CBD, chapter 7. In: Barbier F (ed) Business component-based software engineering. Kluwer Academic, Dordrecht, pp 119–134

Standards Australia (2004) Standard metamodel for software development methodologies, AS 4651-2004. Standards Australia, Sydney

Stapleton J (1997) DSDM: the method in practice. Addison-Wesley, Reading, MA

Stevens P, Pooley R (2006) Using UML: software engineering with objects and components. Addison Wesley, Essex

Stevens WP, Myers GJ, Constantine LL (1974) Structured design. IBM Syst J 13(2):115–139

Stojanovic Z, Dahanayake A, Sol H (2004) An evaluation framework for component-based and service-oriented system development methodologies. In: Siau K (ed) Advanced topics in database research, vol 3. IGI Global, Hershey, PA, pp 45–68

Stolterman E (1992) How system designers think about design and methods: some reflections based on an interview study. Scand J Inform Syst 4:137–150

Stolterman E, Russo NL (1997) The paradox of information systems methods: public and private rationality. Paper presented at the British Computer Society 5th annual conference on methodologies, Lancaster, UK

Stőrrle H (2001) Describing process patterns with UML (position paper). In: Ambriola V (ed) Software process technology. Proceedings of the 8th European workshop, EWSPT 2001. Lecture notes in computer science, vol 2077. Springer, Berlin, pp 173–181

Sunyaev A, Hansen M, Krcmar H (2008) Method engineering: a formal description. In: Proceedings ISD 2008, 17th international conference on information systems development, Paphos, Cyprus, 25–27 August 2008. Also in: information systems development—towards a service provision society, Springer, pp 645–654

Svahnberg M, van Gurp J, Bosch J (2005) A taxonomy of variability realization techniques. Software Pract Ex 35(8):705–754

Tasharofi S, Ramsin R (2007) Process patterns for agile methodologies. In: Ralyté J, Brinkkemper S, Henderson-Sellers B (eds) Situational method engineering: fundamentals and experiences. Proceedings of the IFIP WG 8.1 working conference, 12–14 September 2007, Geneva, Switzerland. IFIP series, vol 244. Springer, Berlin, pp 222–237

Ter Hofstede AHM, Verhoef TF (1997) On the feasibility of situational method engineering. Inform Syst 22(6/7):401–422

Ter Hofstede AHM, Proper H, van der Weide P (1993) Formal definition of a conceptual language for the description and manipulation of information models. Inform Syst 18(7):489–523

Tolman E (1948) Cognitive maps in rats and men. Psychol Rev 55:189–208

Tolvanen J-P (1998) Incremental method engineering with modeling tools. Dissertation, Jyväskylä studies in computer science, economics and statistics, vol 47, University of Jyväskylä, Finland, p 301

Tolvanen J-P, Lyytinen K (1993) Flexible method adaptation in CASE—the metamodeling approach. Scand J Inform Syst 5:51–77

Tolvanen J-P, Marttiin P, Smolander K (1993) An integrated model for information systems modelling. In: Nunamaker JF, Sprague RH (eds) Proceedings of the 26th annual Hawaii international conference on systems science. IEEE Computer Society, Los Alamitos, CA

Tolvanen J-P, Rossi M, Liu H (1996) Method engineering: current research directions and implications for future research. In: Brinkkemper S, Lyytinen K, Welke RJ (eds) Method engineering. Principles of method construction and too support. Proceedings of IFIP TC8, WG8.1/8.2 working conference on method engineering, Atlanta, USA, 26–28 August 1996. Chapman & Hall, London, pp 296–317

Tran Q-NN, Low G (2005) Comparison of ten agent-oriented methodologies, chapter XII. In: Henderson-Sellers B, Giorgini P (eds) Agent-oriented methodologies. Idea Group Publishing, Hershey, PA, pp 341–367

Tran Q-NN, Low G (2008) MOBMAS: a methodology for ontology-based multi-agent systems development. Inform Software Tech 50(7–8):697–722

Tran HN, Boulette B, Dong BT (2005) A classification of process patterns. In: Proceedings of the international conference on software development, Reykjavik, Iceland, 27 May–1 June 2005
Tran Q-NN, Low G, Beydoun G (2006) A methodological framework for ontology centric oriented software engineering. Int J Comput Sci Eng 21(2):117–132
Tran N, Henderson-Sellers B, Hawryszkiewycz I (2007) Method fragments to support collaborative teamwork for software development projects. In: Proceedings of EMCIS 2007
Tran QNN, Henderson-Sellers B, Hawyrszkiewycz IT (2008a) Some method fragments for agile software development, chapter XVI. In: Syed MR, Syed SN (eds) Handbook of research on modern systems analysis and design technologies. IGI, Hershey, PA, pp 235–255
Tran QNN, Henderson-Sellers B, Hawyrszkiewycz IT (2008b) Agile method fragments and construction validation, chapter XVII. In: Syed MR, Syed SN (eds) Handbook of research on modern systems analysis and design technologies. IGI, Hershey, PA, pp 256–283
Unhelkar B (2005) Verification and validation for quality of UML 2.0 models. Wiley, Chichester
Unhelkar B, Henderson-Sellers B (1995) ODBMS considerations in the granularity of a reusable OO design. In: Mingins C, Meyer B (eds) TOOLS 15. Prentice Hall, Upper Saddle River, NJ, pp 229–234
Unhelkar B, Henderson-Sellers B (2005) Applying syntax, semantics and aesthetic checks to verifying and validating the quality of UML models. In: Proceedings of IRMA 2005. Idea Group, Hershey, PA
van de Hoef R, Harmsen AF, Wijers GM (1995) Situatie, Scenario En Succes, Memoranda Informatica, International research report. University of Twente, Enschede
van de Weerd I, Souer J, Versendaal J, Brinkkemper S (2005) Situational requirements engineering of web content management implementation. In: Ralyté J, Agerfalk PJ, Kraiem N (eds) Proceedings of the first international workshop on situational requirements engineering processes: Methods, techniques and tools to support situation-specific requirements engineering processes (SREP '05), Paris France, August 2005. In conjunction with the Thirteenth IEEE requirements engineering conference (RE '05), pp 13–30
van de Weerd I, Brinkkemper S, Souer J, Versendaal J (2006) A situational implementation method for web-based content management system-applications: method engineering and validation in practice. Software Process Improv Pract 11(5):521–538
van de Weerd I, Brinkkemper S, Versendaal J (2007) Concepts for incremental method evolution: empirical exploration and validation in requirements management. In: Krogstie J, Opdahl AL, Sindre G (eds) CAiSE 2007. Lecture notes in computer science, vol 4495. Springer-Verlag, Berlin, pp 469–484
van Slooten K, Brinkkemper S (1993) A method engineering approach to information systems development. In: Prakash N, Rolland C, Pernici B (eds) Information systems development process. Proceedings of IFIP WG 8.1. Elsevier Science B.V., North-Holland
van Slooten K, Hodes B (1996) Characterizing IS development projects, In: Brinkkemper S, Lyytinen K, Welke R (eds) Proceedings of IFIP TC8 working conference on method engineering: principles of method construction and tool support. Chapman & Hall, London, pp 29–44
Vavpotic D, Bajec M (2009) An approach for concurrent evaluation of technical and social aspects of software development methodologies. Inform Software Tech 51:528–545
Vessey I, Glass RL (1994) Application-based methodologies: development by application domain. Inform Syst Manag 11(pt 4):53–57
Vlaanderen K, van de Weerd I, Brinkkemper S (2011) The online method engine: from process assessment to method execution. In: Ralyté J, Mirbel I, Deneckère R (eds) Engineering methods in the service-oriented context. Proceedings of the 4th IFIP WG8.1 working conference on method engineering, ME 2011, Paris France, April 2011. Springer, Heidelberg, pp 108–122
Waller V, Johnston RB, Milton SK (2006) Development of a situation information systems analysis and design methodology: a health care setting. In: Irani Z, Sarikas OD, Llopis J, Gonzalez, R, Gasco J (eds) Proceedings of the European and Mediterranean conference on information systems 2006 (EMCIS2006), CD, Brunel University, West London, paper C94, p 8

Wand Y (1996) Ontology as a foundation for meta-modelling and method engineering. Inform Software Tech 38:281–287

Wand Y, Weber R (1988) An ontological analysis of some fundamental information systems concepts. In: Proceedings of the ninth international conference on information systems, Minneapolis, 30 November to 3 December 1988

Wand Y, Weber R (1990) An ontological model of an information system. IEEE Trans Software Eng 16(11):1282–1292

Wand Y, Weber R (1993) On the ontological expressiveness of information systems analysis and design grammars. J Inform Syst 3:217–237

Wand Y, Weber R (1995) On the deep structure of information systems. Inform Syst J 5(3):203–223

Weber M (1978) Economy and society. University of California Press, Berkeley, CA (originally published in 1922 in German)

Welke RJ (1988) The CASE repository: more than another database application. MetaSystems Ltd., Ann Arbor, MI

Welke R, Kumar K (1991) Method engineering: a proposal for situation-specific methodology construction. In: Cotterman WW, Senn JA (eds) Systems analysis and design: a research agenda. Wiley, Chichester

Weyuker E (1988) Evaluating software complexity measures. IEEE Trans Software Eng 14 (9):1357–1365

Whitmire SA (1997) Object oriented design measurement. Wiley, New York, p 452

Winter R (2011) Design solution analysis for the construction of situational design methods, In: Ralyté J, Mirbel I, Deneckère R (eds) Engineering methods in the service-oriented context. Proceedings of the 4th IFIP WG8.1 working conference on method engineering, ME 2011, Paris France, April 2011. Springer, Heidelberg, pp 19–33

Wistrand K (2009) Method rationale revealed: communication of knowledge in systems development methods. Doctoral dissertation. Örebro University. Intellecta Infolog, V. Frölunda: Sweden. ISBN 978-91-7668-659-1

Wistrand K, Karlsson F (2004) Method components—rationale revealed. In: Persson A, Stirna J (eds) Advanced information systems engineering: proceedings of the 16th international conference, CAiSE 2004, Riga, Latvia, 7–11 June 2004. Lecture notes in computer science, vol 3084. Springer, Berlin, pp 189–201

Wyssusek B (2006) On ontological foundations of conceptual modelling. Scand J Inform Syst 18 (1):63–80

Wyssusek B, Klaus H (2005) Ontological foundations of information systems analysis and design: extending the scope of the discussion. In: Green P, Rosemann M (eds) Business systems analysis with ontologies. IGI Group, Hershey, PA, pp 322–344

Xu P, Ramesh B (2003) A tool for the capture and use of process knowledge in process tailoring. In: Proceedings of the 36th Hawaii international conference on systems sciences (HICSS '03), IEEE Computer Society, Los Alamitos, CA

Yang J, Unhelkar B (2010) Iterative class diagram construction in consideration of modeling granularity. In: Proceedings of RCIS 2010, IEEE Computer Society, Los Alamitos, CA

Yap L-M, Henderson-Sellers B (1993) A semantic model for inheritance in object-oriented systems. In: Proceedings of ASWEC '93, IREE, Sydney, pp 28–35

Yau SS, An HG (2011) Software engineering meets services and cloud computing. IEEE Comput 44(10):47–53

Yourdon E (1999) Software process for the 21st century. Cutter IT Journal 12(9):12–15

Zdravkovic J, Zikra I, Ilayeruma T (2011) An MDA method for service modelling by fomalizing REA and open-edi business frameworks with SBVR. In: Ralyté J, Mirbel I, Deneckère R (eds) Engineering methods in the service-oriented context. Proceedings of the 4th IFIP WG8.1 working conference on method engineering, ME 2011, Paris France, April 2011. Springer, Heidelberg, pp 219–224

Zhu L, Staples M (2007) Situational method quality. In: Ralyté J, Brinkkemper S, Henderson-Sellers B (eds) Situational method engineering: fundamentals and experiences. Springer, New York, NY, pp 193–206

Zoukar I (2005) MIBE: Méthode d'Ingénierie des Besoins pour l'implantation d'un progiciel de gestion intégré (ERP). Ph.D. Thesis, University of Paris I, Paris, France

Zoukar I, Salinesi C (2004) Using goal/strategy/maps to reduce the language disparity issue in ERP projects. In: Grundspenkis J, Kirikova M (eds) Knowledge and model driven information systems engineering for networked organisations, proceedings. Faculty of Computer Science and Information Technology, Riga, vol 2, pp 325–339

Zowghi D, Firesmith DG, Henderson-Sellers B (2005) Using the OPEN process framework to produce a situation-specific requirements engineering method. In: Ralyté J, Agerfalk PJ, Kraiem N (eds) Proceedings of the first international workshop on situational requirements engineering processes: methods, techniques and tools to support situation-specific requirements engineering processes (SREP '05), Paris France, August 2005. In conjunction with the thirteenth IEEE requirements engineering conference (RE '05), pp 59–74

Zuse H (1994) Software complexity: measures and methods. Walter de Gruyter, Berlin, p 605

Žvanut B, Bajec M (2010) A tool for IT process construction. Inform Software Tech 52:397–410

Index

B. Henderson-Sellers et al., *Situational Method Engineering*,
DOI 10.1007/978-3-642-41467-1, © Springer-Verlag Berlin Heidelberg 2014

Printed in the United States
By Bookmasters